Managing Economies, Trade and International Business

Also by Aidan O'Connor

TRADE, INVESTMENT AND COMPETITION IN INTERNATIONAL BANKING

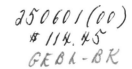
Managing Economies, Trade and International Business

Edited by

Aidan O'Connor
Professor of Strategy and International Business
ESCEM School of Business and Management, France, and
Visiting Professor, University of Osnabrück, Germany

palgrave
macmillan

First published 2010 by
PALGRAVE MACMILLAN

Palgrave Macmillan in the UK is an imprint of Macmillan Publishers Limited,
registered in England, company number 785998, of Houndmills, Basingstoke,
Hampshire RG21 6XS.

Palgrave Macmillan in the US is a division of St Martin's Press LLC,
175 Fifth Avenue, New York, NY 10010.

Palgrave Macmillan is the global academic imprint of the above companies
and has companies and representatives throughout the world.

Palgrave® and Macmillan® are registered trademarks in the United States,
the United Kingdom, Europe and other countries.

ISBN 978–0–230–20256–6

This book is printed on paper suitable for recycling and made from fully
managed and sustained forest sources. Logging, pulping and manufacturing
processes are expected to conform to the environmental regulations of the
country of origin.

A catalogue record for this book is available from the British Library.

A catalog record for this book is available from the Library of Congress.

10   9   8   7   6   5   4   3   2   1
19   18   17   16   15   14   13   12   11   10

Printed and bound in Great Britain by
CPI Antony Rowe, Chippenham and Eastbourne

*To those who have inspired us so that
we may inspire others*

Contents

List of Tables

List of Figures

List of Abbreviations

ACEA	Association des Constructeurs d'Automobiles Européens
ACV	Agreement on Customs Valuation
AD	Anti-Dumping
ADA	Anti-Dumping Agreement
ALOP	appropriate level of protection
AQIRP	Auto-Oil Air Quality Improvement Research Programme (USA)
ARO	Agreement on Rules of Origin
BAT	best-available technology
BCBS	Basel Committee on Banking Supervision
BI	Balassa Index
BMW	*Bayerische Motoren Werke*
BRC	British Retail Consortium
CA	Central America
CACM	Central American Common Market
CAD	cash against documents
CARS-21	Competitive Automotive Regulatory System for the Twenty-First Century
CBIS	computer-based information systems
CCC	Community Customs Code
CDM	clean development mechanism
CEDEFOP	European Centre for the Development of Vocational Training
CER	certified emissions reductions
CES	constant elasticity of substitution
CFCs	chlorofluorocarbons
CFI	Court of First Instance
CFR	cost and freight
CFR	Charter of Fundamental Rights (EU, 2000)
CIF	cost, insurance, freight
CIP	carriage and insurance paid to
CLTV	customer life time value
CO2	carbon dioxide
CODEX	Codex Alimentarius Commission
COP	Conference of the Parties
CPT	carriage paid to
CRM	customer relationship management
CTM	Community Trademark

CVD	countervailing duty
CVM	countervailing measures
D/A	documents against acceptance
D/G	documents against bank guarantee
D/P	documents against payment
DAF	delivered at frontier
DBMS	database management system
DDP	delivered duty paid
DDU	delivered duty unpaid
DEQ	delivered ex-quay
DES	delivered ex-ship
DG	Directorate-General
DOC	Department of Commerce (USA)
DOE	designated operational entity
DSS	decision support system
DSU	Dispute Settlement Understanding
E-Commerce	electronic commerce
EC	European Commission
ECE	Economic Commission for Europe (UN)
ECHR	European Convention on Human Rights
ECHR	European Court of Human Rights
ECJ	European Court of Justice
ECLAC	Economic Commission for Latin America and the Caribbean
ECT	Treaty establishing the European Community 1992
EEA	European Economic Area
EEB	European Environmental Bureau
EGAT	Economic Growth and Agricultural Trade (USAID Bureau)
EP	European Parliament
EPEFE	Europe Programme on Emissions, Fuels, and Engine technologies
EPLA	European Patent Litigation Agreement
EPO	European Patent Office
EPO	European Patent Organization
ES	expert system
ETS	Emissions Trading Scheme (EU, 2003–)
EU	European Union
EUCD	EU Copyright Directive (2001)
EurepGAP	Euro Retailer Produce Good Agricultural Practices
EUROPIA	European Association of the Oil Industry

Eurostat	Statistical Office of the European Communities (European Commission)
EXW	Ex-Works (Incoterms)
FAS	free alongside ship
FCA	free carrier
FMCG	fast-moving consumer goods
FDI	foreign direct investment
FOB	free on board
FTAs	free-trade agreements
G7	Group of Seven
G8	Group of Eight
G10	Group of Ten
GATS	General Agreement on Trade in Services
GATT	General Agreement on Tariffs and Trade
GDP	Gross Domestic Product
GEF	Global Environmental Facility
GHGs	greenhouse gases
GMSS	global management support systems
GRC	Governance, Risk Management, and Compliance (banking)
GSP	Generalized System of Preferences
Hong Kong SAR	Hong Kong Special Administrative Region
HRO	harmonized rules of origin
HS	Harmonized System of Commodity Description and Coding
HSBC	Hongkong and Shanghai Banking Corporation
IATRC	International Agricultural Trade Research Consortium
IBP	Institute of Bankers (Pakistan)
ICC	International Chamber of Commerce
ICT	information and communications technology
ILP	Import Licensing Procedures
IMF	International Monetary Fund
IMP group	Industrial Marketing and Purchasing Group
Incoterms	International Commercial Terms
IP	intellectual property
IP	Internet Protocol
IPCC	Intergovernmental Panel on Climate Change
IPPC	International Plant Protection Convention
IPRs	Intellectual Property Rights
IRWR	Internal Renewable Water Resources
IS	information systems

ISBP	International Standard Banking Practice for Examination of Documents under Documentary Credit
ISCED	International Standard Classification of Education
ISDN	International Standard Dialling Number
IT	information technology
ITC	International Trade Centre
ITC/CS	International Trade Centre and Commonwealth Secretariat
IWRA	International Water Resources Association
IWRM	integrated water resources management
IZA	Institute for the Study of Labour, Universität Bonn, Germany
JI	joint implementation (Kyoto Protocol)
KBS	knowledge-based system
LDCs	least-developed countries
LTV	loan-to-value
M-Commerce	mobile commerce
MCU	multiple connection unit
ME	market economy
MEP	Member of the European Parliament
MERCOSUR	Southern Cone or South American Common Market
MET	market-economy treatment
MFN	most-favoured nation
MIS	management information system
MNEs	multi-nation enterprises
MNF	multi-national firms
MOI	market-oriented industry
MOP	Meeting of the Parties
MRL	maximum residue limit
MVEG	Motor Vehicle Expert Group
NAFTA	North American Free Trade Agreement
NGOs	non-governmental organizations
NME	non-market economy
NOx	nitrogen oxide(s)
OECD	Organisation for Economic Cooperation and Development
OEEC	Organization for European Economic Cooperation
OHIM	Office for the Harmonization of the Internal Market (EU)
OIE	International Office of Epizootics
OJ	Official Journal of the European Union

OM	operations management
PCT	Patent Cooperation Treaty
PCT	Patent Cooperation Treaty
PFCs	perifluorinated compounds
PPS	Purchasing Power Standards
PSI	pre-shipment inspection
RTAs	regional trade agreements
SAA	Stabilization and Association Agreement
SAFE	secure and facilitate global trade
SAR	Special Administrative Region (Hong Kong)
SCM	Subsidies and Countervailing Measures
SIECA	Secretaría de Integración Económica Centroamericana
SIPO	Chinese Patent Office
SMEs	small and medium-sized enterprises
SPS	Sanitary and Phytosanitary (measures)
STOP	Strategy of Targeting Organized Piracy (USA)
SUVs	Sports Utility Vehicles
SWIFT	Society for Worldwide Interbank Financial Telecommunication
TCG	Trade Contact Group
TCM	trade and customs management
TDC	Trade Development and Cooperation Agreement (EU-South Africa, 1999)
TNCs	trans-national corporations
TPRD	Trade Policies Review Division
TPS	transactional processing system
TRADE	Trade-Related Agenda, Development, and Equity
TRIPS	Trade-Related Aspects of Intellectual Property Rights
UCP	Uniform Customs and Practice for Documentary Credits
UK	United Kingdom
UN	United Nations
UNEP	United Nations Environmental Programme
UNESCO	United Nations Educational, Scientific and Cultural Organization
UNESCO-IHE	United Nations Educational, Scientific and Cultural Organization, Institute of Water Education
UNFCCC	UN Framework Convention on Climate Change
URC	Uniform Rules for Collections
USAID	US Agency for International Development
USC	United States Court

USPTO	United States' Patent and Trademark Office
VA	ACEA Voluntary Agreement
VDA	Verband der Automobilindustrie
VOIP	Voice Over Internet Protocol
WBCSD	World Business Council for Sustainable Development
WCO	World Customs Organization
WHO	World Health Organization
WIPO	World Intellectual Property Organization
W-LAN	Wireless Local Area Network
WMO	World Meteorological Organisation
WTO	World Trade Organization

Notes on the Contributors

Isabel Álvarez is Assistant Professor at the Department of Economics at Complutense University, Madrid, Spain and a Research Fellow at the Complutense Institute for International Studies. She obtained her PhD in Economics, and also has a Masters in Science, Society and Technology of the European Interuniversity Network ESST. She has recently been Visiting Scholar at Rutgers University, New Jersey, USA. Her main research topics are focused on the internationalization of technology and the relationship between foreign direct investment, innovation and development. She has been involved in several international research projects and has published in diverse co-edited books and in several international journals.

Laura Carola Beretta is Professor of International Trade and Customs Law at Bocconi University School of Management, Milan, Italy, and is also responsible for the management of postgraduate courses there. Dr Beretta obtained her PhD from Bocconi University. She is an experienced international consultant, specializing in advising firms, governments and non-governmental organizations in the legal implications of international trade and customs management. She has consulted and published widely in Italian, English and Spanish and is the author of numerous national and international publications, many of which focus on rules of origin and origin marking. She is a speaker at many conferences both in Italy and abroad.

Michael Braulke is Professor of Economics and Dean Emeritus of Studies at the University of Osnabrück, Germany. He has taught at the universities of Frankfurt-am-Main and Konstanz in Germany and the Graduate School of Economics, St Gallen, Switzerland He has served for a number of years on two different occasions at the International Monetary Fund, Washington DC, USA and has also been a consultant to the World Bank. His research in microeconomic theory and his applied work has been published in leading academic journals. Dr Braulke obtained his doctorate from the Johann Wolfgang Goethe University, Frankfurt-am-Main and received his post-doctoral habilitation from the University of Konstanz, Germany.

Dora Castañeda is a Legal Officer at the Rules Division of the World Trade Organization (WTO), Geneva, Switzerland. She has practised widely as a trade lawyer in leading international law firms in Brussels, Belgium. Her areas of practice are International Trade Law, particularly the law of the General Agreement on Tariffs and Trade (GATT) and the WTO, and European Union Trade and Customs Law. She also advises leading industries in Central America on the current negotiations on an Association Agreement between the European Union and Central American countries. She graduated in Law from Universidad Rafael Landivar, Guatemala, and obtained an LL.M. in International Legal Studies at Georgetown University Law Center, Washington DC, USA from where she also obtained a WTO Studies Certificate from the Institute of International Economic Law.

Andrew Cornford is a Consultant and Expert in Banking and was previously the Senior Economist responsible for Banking Services and International Financial Markets and Regulation at the United Nations Conference on Trade and Development (UNCTAD) until his retirement in 2003. His recent writing has consisted mainly of consultancy papers for UNCTAD related to the Doha-round negotiations on financial services and for the Intergovernmental Group of Twenty-Four on International Monetary Affairs. He is currently also Associate Commentator at the Observatoire de la Finance, Geneva and a financial commentator for the on-line daily publication of the Third World Network, SUNS-South-North Development Monitor. Dr Cornford completed his undergraduate studies at Cambridge University, UK, and received his PhD from Oxford University, UK.

Antonio Di Meo is a Consultant in International Trade Payments and Settlements and a Visiting Professor at the University of Macerata, Italy. He also teaches at other Italian universities and institutes including Bocconi University School of Management, Milan and at the Italian Banking Association (ABI) and the Italian Institute for Foreign Trade (ICE). His postgraduate studies were conducted at the School of Management, Bocconi University. He has prior business experience in banking, export trade and in country risk and is the author of several books on International Payments and Documentary Credits, as well as publications in leading practitioner journals. He is a regular contributor to the Italian financial newspaper *Il Sole 24 Ore* and is also active in training with the Italian Chambers of Commerce, ICC-Italia.

Claudio Dordi is Associate Professor of International Law at Bocconi University, Milan. He has been visiting Professorial Fellow at the International Economic Law Institute, Georgetown Law School, Washington DC, USA, and he has taught in many universities in Asia, Europe and Latin America. In addition, he has directed international projects aimed at promoting trade-related law reforms in South-East Asia. He is also currently Head of a European Commission sponsored project in Vietnam and was previously a consultant to the Vietnamese government on banking law during its accession negotiations to the WTO. Dr Dordi obtained his PhD from Bocconi University. He has published books and articles on trade and WTO-law related issues, international public and private law and European law.

Andreas Irmen is Professor of Economics at the Ruprecht-Karls-University of Heidelberg, Germany and Director of the Alfred-Weber-Institute. Previously, he was Professor of Economics at the Free University of Bolzano, Italy, and Assistant Professor at the University of Mannheim, Germany. He is affiliated with the Centre for Economic Studies, Munich, Germany. He received his PhD in Economics from the University of Lausanne, Switzerland and his post-doctoral habilitation from the University of Mannheim. He has been a Visiting Professor in New Zealand and France and a visiting scholar at Harvard University, the Massachusetts Institute of Technology, Boston, USA, and the Hebrew University, Jerusalem, Israel. Dr Irmen's areas of research focus on innovation and economic growth and he has published widely in leading academic journals.

Andreas Knaden is Business Manager of the Centre of Information Management and Virtual Teaching (virtUOS) at the University of Osnabrück, Germany. His experience extends to virtual teaching, change management and in managing academic projects in German university networks. He is also a member of the management staff of the E-Learning Academic network of the State of Lower Saxony, Germany. His research focuses on different aspects of E-Learning and in particular on the strategic impact of new media use for the quality of teaching in academic organizations. For several years he was head of a research project on cost controlling, as well as Software Engineering at Ford Europe, Cologne, Germany. Dr Knaden obtained his doctorate from the University of Osnabrück, Germany.

Andrea Lenschow is Professor of European Politics and Integration at the University of Osnabrück, Germany. She is also visiting professor at the College of Europe, Bruges, Belgium. Dr Lenschow obtained her PhD from New York University and she also conducted postgraduate studies at Erasmus University, Rotterdam, the Netherlands and at the European University Institute, Florence, Italy. She was previously Assistant Professor at Paris Lodron University, Salzburg, Austria. Her research focuses on EU governance and environmental policy making. She recently co-edited a book on *Innovation in Environmental Policy – Integrating the Environment for Sustainability* published by Edward Elgar Publishing.

Laurent Manderieux is Senior Intellectual Property Expert for various international organizations and governments, and is a member of the Expert Group of the United Nations Commission on International Trade Law. He is also Adjunct Professor of Intellectual Property Law at Bocconi University, Milan, Italy, and Visiting Professor at many other universities in Europe, the Americas, Asia, and Africa. He was previously Head of Public Affairs and Media Relations at the World Intellectual Property Organization and earlier in his career he was with the Food and Agriculture Organization of the United Nations in Rome, Italy and at the European Union in Brussels, Belgium. In addition to his intellectual property teaching and research activities he is the author of numerous publications and training materials in this area.

Raquel Marín is a Researcher with the Research Group on Innovation Economics and Policy (GRINEI) and a Research Fellow at the Complutense Institute for International Studies (ICEI), Complutense University, Madrid, Spain. She is also a Lecturer at the Department of Business Economics, European University, Madrid. She graduated in Economics from Complutense University, and she is currently developing her doctoral dissertation at the same university. Her research interests are modes of foreign market entry, the internationalization of technology and multinational companies' strategies and innovation.

Robert E. Martin is a Consultant in Sustainable Water Management to international firms and supranational organizations, including United Nations agencies and the European Investment Bank. He has extensive international experience in the water sector and formerly directed the water programme of the World Business Council for Sustainable Development. He was previously in senior management in Suez Environment, a major international firm providing water and environmental services. His current consultancies focus on improving water supply and sanitation for underserved populations in developing economies, and promoting global sustainable water management, particularly with regard to the role of business. He obtained his engineering degree from Yale University, New Haven, USA and his PhD in Environmental Health Sciences from Johns Hopkins University, Baltimore, USA.

Lorenza Mola is Research Fellow in International Law at the University of Turin, Italy and also a professor in European Union Internal Market Law and Globalization at the Faculty of Political Science there. She also has international experience through training and consultancy in supranational organizations, such as the World Trade Organization, Geneva, Switzerland, the Training Centre of the International Labour Office, Turin, Italy, and the European Commission, Brussels, Belgium. Her research focuses on international trade and investment law, and European Union law and she has published articles in Italian in both international academic journals and books. Dr Mola was educated in Italy, France and Belgium and obtained her PhD in International Economic Law from Bocconi University, Milan, Italy.

Aidan O'Connor is Professor of Strategy and International Business at ESCEM School of Business and Management, Tours-Poitiers, France. He has extensive experience in banking and academic experience in several European countries. He was awarded a Fellowship by the Council of Europe for research. He is also Visiting Professor at the University of Osnabrück, Germany. His research focuses on international business and bank strategy and his book *Trade, Investment and Competition in International Banking* was published by Palgrave, and he has also published in international journals. He completed postgraduate studies in statistics and economics at Trinity College, University of Dublin, Ireland. He obtained his doctorate from the University of Lausanne, Switzerland, with a specialization in trade in services. Dr O'Connor is Associate Editor and Book Review Editor of the *International Journal of Strategic Decision Sciences*.

Katja Rottmann is Head of the Liaison Office of the Green Parliamentary Group of the German Bundestag, Brussels, Belgium. Previously, she was a researcher at the University of Osnabrück, Germany, on a European Union funded project on governance and regulation. Her research focuses on European Union policy making and, in particular, on environmental policy. She also has practitioner experience in these policy areas with various organizations, such as, the Wuppertal Institute for Climate, Environment and Energy, Germany, and the Worldwatch Institute, Washington DC, USA. She studied at the University of Osnabrück, Germany and the Institute of Political Studies (IEP), Grenoble, France, and holds an MA in European Studies.

Gianluca Rubagotti is a Diplomat with the Ministry of Foreign Affairs, Rome, Italy. Following his undergraduate studies in law he obtained a Masters in Environmental Law from the State University of Milan, Italy and a PhD in International Law and Economics from Bocconi University, Milan. Before joining the Italian diplomatic service he taught International Trade Law as well as International and European Law at Bocconi University, and also lectured on issues of Public International and European Union Law in various universities in Italy and abroad. Dr Rubagotti was a Marie Curie Fellow at Amsterdam University and a Visiting Scholar at the Indian Society of International Law, in New Delhi. He was also consultant to the Egyptian Ministry of Foreign Trade and Industry on behalf of the European Union.

Francisco Javier Santos-Arteaga is a Researcher in the Grinei Research Group in Economics and Innovation Policy at Complutense University, Madrid, Spain. He completed his PhD in Economic Theory at York University, Toronto, Canada, from where he also graduated with a Masters degree in Economics. Prior to this he completed his undergraduate studies in Economics and a Masters degree in Philosophy of Science at the University of Salamanca, Spain. He is a lecturer in the Economics Faculty of the Free University of Bozen-Bolzano, Italy. Dr Santos-Arteaga was awarded grants from the Spanish Education and Culture Ministry and the European Union and also the Dean's Academic Excellence Award from York University. He has several publications in international academic journals ranging from economics to decision sciences and applied mathematics.

Jörg Schimmelpfennig is Professor of Theoretical and Applied Microeconomics and Dean of Studies at the Ruhr-University, Bochum, Germany. His main research areas are economic regulation, rail transport economics and defence economics. He is a regular contributor at international conferences and has published in leading academic journals. He is a member of, *inter alia*, the Institute for Defence and Government

Advancement, the US Naval Institute and the Army Records Society. He served as an advisor to renowned institutions and companies, as well as, regulatory authorities. He is also a contributor and reviewer on the arts. Dr Schimmelpfennig studied mathematics, physics and economics at the University of Bielefeld, Germany and obtained his Doctorate in Economics from the University of Osnabrück, Germany.

Stefan Schlangen is Research Assistant for Intercultural and International Management at the University of Osnabrück, Germany. His undergraduate studies were conducted at the University of Osnabrück and at Wilfrid Laurier University, Waterloo, Canada and obtained a Masters in Business and Economics from the University of Osnabrück. He commenced his business experience with Tecis, a financial services firm and a subsidiary of AWD, Switzerland, an independent reseller of financial products, and this was followed with Swiss Life, and later with Deutsche Bank, Germany. His research interest include virtual teams, sales and retail banking and he is currently completing his Doctorate at the University of Osnabrück.

Eric Stevens is Professor of Marketing at ESCEM School of Business and Management, Tours-Poitiers, France. He has many years' business experience in the design and development of FMCG products, and has also been a consultant in business and academia. He obtained his Doctorate in Business Administration from the University of Newcastle, UK. Dr Stevens' research interests are customer relationship management, services innovation, and the management of development teams. He is a co-author of the French language edition of the textbook *Customer Relationship Management* published by Pearson and has published in both French and English academic journals.

Kathryn A. Szabat is Assistant Professor of Statistics and Chair of the Management Department at LaSalle University, Philadelphia, USA and is also a Professor at Wharton School of the University of Pennsylvania, Philadelphia. Dr Szabat provides statistical advice to numerous business, non-business, and academic communities. Her most recent involvement has been in the areas of education and medicine. Her most recent collaborative applied research efforts include the investigation of Academic Health Centre strategic ventures, assessment of concept-mapping as an enabling technique for meaningful learning in accounting education, and evaluation of non-profit capacity building. Dr Szabat holds a PhD in

Statistics, with cognate field in Operations Research, from the Wharton School of the University of Pennsylvania.

Madjid Tavana is Professor of Management Information Systems and Decision Sciences and the Lindback Distinguished Chair of Information Systems at La Salle University, Philadelphia, USA. He has been a distinguished faculty fellow at the National Aeronautics and Space Administration (NASA), the US Naval Research Laboratory, and the US Air Force Research Laboratory and was awarded the prestigious Space Act Award by NASA. He holds a PhD in Management Information Systems from the American University, London and received his post-doctoral diploma in Strategic Information Systems from the Wharton School of the University of Pennsylvania. He is the Editor-in-Chief of the *International Journal of Applied Decision Sciences* and the *International Journal of Strategic Decision Sciences*.

Acknowledgements

Many of the contributors to this book have participated as visiting faculty members on a Masters programme in International Business for which I am Academic Director, and it was from this that the initial inspiration for the book emerged. Other contributors are colleagues from several academic institutions.

I would like to thank Andreas Irmen of the University of Heidelberg and Francisco Javier Santos-Arteaga of Complutense University, Madrid, who were instrumental in proposing additional contributors. My thanks also to Laura Carola Beretta and Claudio Dordi of Bocconi University School of Management and Bocconi University, Milan, respectively, for also proposing colleagues and for their support in this endeavour. For similar reasons, I am most grateful to Michael Braulke and Bernd Faulwasser of the University of Osnabrück, and also for their valued support to me as a Visiting Professor there, and for my honorary membership of their Stammtisch.

Of course, I am extremely grateful to all the authors for their chapter contributions and their enthusiasm for the project and for their understanding of the complexities of coordinating, assimilating and aligning many different subjects and styles and enduring my many queries and referrals during the editing process. I very much appreciate their enormous effort which it is a pleasure to have been responsible for instigating. This book is merely providing a tableau to display and diffuse their specific knowledge and ideas.

Besides the direct editorial aspects there are many other essential aspects to the publishing process and I would like to thank Keith Povey and his associates for their efficiency and expert proofing and indexing.

I would also like to thank Paul Milner, Editorial Assistant, for the very efficient and helpful manner in which he conducted and accomplished the editorial administration.

Finally, I must acknowledge the contribution of Virginia Thorp, Senior Commissioning Editor, for her prompt response to my book proposal, and I thank her most sincerely for her advice and patience in managing the process.

France   AIDAN O'CONNOR

Permission for publication is gratefully acknowledged for Figure 7.1, reproduced with permission from Business in the World of Water: *WBCSD Water Scenarios to 2025*, p. 41 © World Business Council for Sustainable Development, for Table 8.1, reproduced with permission from *World Investment Report 2008*, © United Nations, 2009, and for Chapter 9, reproduced with permission from *Basel II and Banking in Emerging and other Developing Economies, Multi-Year Expert Meeting on Services, Development and Trade: The Regulatory and Institutional Dimension*, United Nations Conference on Trade and Development © United Nations, 2009.

Introduction

Aidan O'Connor

The current phase of globalization and the increased interconnect-edness of economies through trade, foreign direct investment and portfolio investment have influenced the management and growth rates of economies and have also been a factor in the emergence of some formerly developing economies as important economic forces in the global economic and trading system.

Globalization is a very broad term and its significance differs between countries, cultures and perspectives. There is the globalization of standards, brands, and communications, among others, and in previous epochs there was the globalization of specific languages, literature, sports and religions, primarily due to colonization and migration. Essentially, globalization is due to the reduction in economic and legal barriers to the flows of goods, services, labour, capital, information and knowledge, as well as cultural and social barriers.

What is indisputable is the increased interconnectedness between economies, coordination between governments in managing economies, a more important role for supranational agencies in regulation, and increased competition between international firms in global markets. Globalization, then, in its current sense may be traced to liberalization in trade and capital movements, the increase in scale and scope of multinational firms, and innovations in information and communications technology.

Managing economies

The focus in this book is on economic globalization. An influencing factor and a catalyst for the interconnectedness between economies has been the increased coordination and cooperation between governments on a regional basis and through trade agreements at a supranational level and at a bilateral level, as well as other associated, though not directly trade related, agreements, such as multilateral environmental agreements.

Managing economies is the domain of governments, and achieving economic growth is a core role and a fundamental aim. In an increasingly globalized trading system countries must cooperate and their indigenous firms must compete while governments must ensure economic growth. However, there has undoubtedly been both economic development and economic growth due to increased globalization. Some countries are engaging in tax competition, which in the long term affects the sustainability of such economic growth models.

There has been an increased awareness of, and focus on, sustainability issues, such that its impact have been incorporated into governments' economic policies. This occurred contemporaneously with the commencement of the Uruguay Round of the General Agreement on Tariffs and Trade, now the World Trade Organization.

The management of economies has an effect on the social and culture fabric of countries, and also on its natural resources and on the legacy of governments for future generations. The increased level of economic growth has also had an impact on social and natural environments. These economic growth models must be sustainable to ensure that there is a more inclusive approach when estimating their effect on economies, communities, cultures, climate and natural resources. Managing sustainable development by governments is accomplished with the cooperation of, and often legal obligations on, firms.

Managing trade

The development of an economy and economic growth are influenced by the traded sectors of an economy. The increasing mobility of firms and a more integrated global economy and also competition from some emerging and developing countries make it more difficult for some developed countries' governments to manage economic growth, and in particular tax revenue. In addition, supranational and bilateral trade agreements, as well as regulations in certain sectors, such as banking, have impacts on developed and developing economies and influence economic policies.

The increased role of supranational agencies means that governments have less regulatory control over their economies, especially the traded economy, and over sectoral economic policies.

International trade consists of cross-border trade, foreign direct investment or portfolio investment. There has been increased trade with and investment in developing countries partly due to firms seeking lower costs of production and also due to the increase in demand from these countries for goods and services from developed countries. Private capital flows to developing economies account for more than official capital flows, primarily though foreign direct investment. However, international trade law, trade agreements and regulations devised and agreed by governments and supranational agencies may divert or distort trade and also shape firms' strategies.

Free trade agreements between countries have proliferated recently. This is partly in response to the outcome of multilateral trade negotiations, with countries circumventing exclusions in the general agreement by negotiating bilateral agreements. These are influenced by politics. Trade in services is increasing as a share of international trade, and this was recognized through the completion of the General Agreement on Trade in Services as part of the Uruguay Round of negotiations of the General Agreement on Tariffs and Trade.

It may be argued that many multinational firms have undue influence on economies, especially in developing economies. While there has been liberalization in trade there are now more onerous regulations on these firms than in the past. There must also be consideration of the influence of these multinational firms, in addition to governments, in the negotiations between countries as governments attempt to protect their own firms in specific sectors and industries that they consider to be of strategic importance.

Managing international business

The liberalization of trade and globalization have also had an impact on international firms, particularly in protecting intellectual property rights, ensuring payments and settlements of imports and exports, and information and communication technology on the management of widely dispersed firms.

With the increased dispersion of production and the wider reach of sales there is increased pressure on firms to protect their intellectual property rights, especially those relating to brands, patents, trademarks and design. The pressures of competition and of managing intellectual property are significant for firms. Similarly, with an increase in trade and an enlargement and extension of markets, there are increased risks in terms of payments and settlements. Firms must also balance costs of managing geographically dispersed international operations and the demands of a wider international customer base.

International competition has increased for firms, partly due to the liberalization of trade and also due to lower transport costs and increased outsourcing and captive offshoring. Innovations in information and communications technologies and the diffusion of information through virtual communications have also increased competition. Furthermore, these innovations have influenced firms' business models and systems and the manner in which they manage their foreign operations and conduct business with information, data and financial flows being transacted through electronic data interchange. Much of the management and coordination of internationally dispersed firms is also conducted through the means of virtual communication. Innovations in communications technologies allow firms to achieve significant reductions in production costs and in the management of flows of information internally and the diffusion of information externally.

Focus and format

The interconnectedness between governments managing economies and the impact on sustainable development, the interconnectedness between governments and supranational agencies negotiating trade and regulatory agreements and their impact on trade diversion and distortion, and also their impact on trading conditions and consequentially on international firms, as well as innovations in technology, are the foci of the book. It is within this milieu of economic, political, legal, regulatory conditions, with cognizance of their effect on the competitiveness and management of international firms, that the concept for the contents of this book was developed and this is the basis for the underlying principal themes.

The themes selected are representative of current issues for governments, regulators and international firms in a globalized trading system. While other themes and issues could be included, it is intended that the selection epitomizes specific aspects of economics, sustainability, trade, regulation, law, politics and management rather than be a complete index of the entire attendant and associated issues.

As such, it may be considered a compendium and the themes incorporated and grouped here provide a thematic reference and a complementary resource for academic programmes. The contents of the book represent a multidisciplinary and multicultural approach and a transversal focus. The contributors have international academic and practitioner experience in their respective areas of competence and represent many disciplines, such as economics, law, politics and management, and there is a balance in terms of diversity of academic profile, business experience, gender, and nationality.

The book is divided into three parts to reflect these themes and to group the various perspectives on these specific issues. The first part is 'Economic Growth and Sustainable Development', the second part is 'Trade, Law and Regulation', and the third part is 'Competitive and Managerial Issues in International Business'. While each of the three parts is discrete the chapters in each part are associated with its thematic title. Furthermore, each part is interrelated and there are many overlapping and interconnected themes such that the division into these three parts could have been quite different depending on perspective and interpretation.

The issue of economic growth is the focus of the first four chapters in Part I. Chapter 1 models the gains from specialization, differentiated activities and population growth on economic growth. Chapter 2 continues the theme of human capital and focuses on investment in education and training and on migration. Chapter 3 extends this theme, and models the effect of technological innovation on economic growth. Another effect on economic growth is tax competition policy between countries, and Chapter 4 models the effect of this and capital mobility. The other three chapters of Part I focus on sustainable development. Chapter 5 focuses on environmental governance and in particular on carbon emissions and the automobile industry and European Union policy. Chapter 7 continues with this theme of emissions by focusing on the production and consumption of energy and the opportunities for firms to reduce these emissions as part of the Kyoto Protocol. Chapter 7 is the final chapter in this part and analyses the effect on the supply of water resources due to increased demand.

The first three chapters in Part II focus on trade and regulation in relation to developing countries. Chapter 8 analyses the diversity between countries and regions as recipients of foreign direct investment strategies and the increasing importance of developing economies on the distribution. Chapter 9 focuses on the implications of capital adequacy regulations, the Basel Accords, on banking, and investigates the effect on emerging and developing economies' banking industries. Chapter 10 focuses on the implications of membership of the World Trade Organization of an emerging market economy and the specific aspects of antidumping and countervailing duties. The other three chapters in this part focus on the legal aspects of trade agreements. Chapter 11 evaluates trade and customs management and, in particular, the increasing importance of rules of origin and the implications for firms' customs compliance role. Chapter 12 focuses on trade in agricultural products between the European Union and Central American countries, the ongoing negotiations between these regions, and the capability of developing countries to comply with stringent technical regulations. Chapter 13 considers the jurisprudence aspects of the right to review customs authorities' decrees and practice and the recent challenges to customs law and administration in the European Union.

Part III focuses on competitive, managerial and technological issues for firms that conduct international business. The first two chapters focus on regulations that specifically impact on firms operating internationally. Chapter 14 discusses intellectual property rights, an issue that is important for firms to maintain competitive advantage and protect their intellectual property, and also analyses the type and territorial aspects of intellectual property rights. Chapter 15 analyses payments and settlements and the importance for firms to ensure that they comply with international regulations and practice and outlines the aims and the various types of instruments utilized. The other chapters in this part focus on marketing, virtual communications and technology in international firms. Chapter 16 considers the principles to guide, structure and organize international firms and marketing departments that are internationally dispersed. Chapter 17 outlines the advances in virtual communications and the requirements to implement this technology in managing groups that are geographically dispersed. Chapter 18 considers the firm in the knowledge age and the evolution and role of integrated global management support systems to assist in the integration of firms in different geographic locations and to manage data, information and knowledge.

Part I
Economic Growth and Sustainable Development

1
Population, Specialized Occupations and Semi-Endogenous Growth

Andreas Irmen

The division of labour may be defined as 'the division of a process or employment into parts, each of which is carried out by a separate person'.[1] Adam Smith[2] put this idea at the forefront of his inquiry into the nature and the causes of the wealth of nations. He thought of the division of labour as an important source of gains from specialization that increase the productivity of labour and, therefore, account for the growth of per-capita income. Smith's central claim is that the division of labour depends upon the extent of the market.[3] The extent of the market is also at the heart of Allyn Young's view of the growth process.[4] Unlike Smith, his emphasis is on specialized inputs and the associated gains from specialization, which he sees to be more likely to occur in larger markets.[5]

A version of the neoclassical growth model is developed with an endogenous savings rate in the spirit of Ramsey,[6] Cass,[7] and Koopmans[8] that incorporates gains from specialization in the sense of Smith and Young.[9] These gains act as a countervailing force to diminishing returns to capital such that the model exhibits endogenous growth. The steady-state growth rate of per-capita magnitudes features the key parameters of the analysis: gains from specialization, differentiated activities in which the labour force specializes, and the population growth rate, which determines the evolution of the size of the market.

To capture the notion of gains from specialization in the spirit of Smith and Young, we extend the neoclassical production sector and introduce an intermediate-good sector and a final-good sector. Labour is the only input in the production of differentiated intermediates. Workers spend a fixed amount of time learning how to manufacture a particular intermediate before production occurs one-to-one. Due to a quasi-fixed cost of learning, the equilibrium has a single producer of each intermediate. As the economy grows, more and more of these producers enter the market,

3

and the division of labour increases. Final-good production requires capital and differentiated intermediates. Gains from specialization derive from the use of these intermediates.

This analytical framework has some similarity to the seminal analysis of Paul Romer,[10] which is often associated with the ideas of Young.[11] For instance, gains from specialization in the production of the final-good stem from a CES-aggregator *à la* Ethier[12] and the continuous introduction of new intermediates. However, unlike Romer, these intermediates are manufactured by labour. This allows us to depict the division of labour as perceived by Groenewegen.[13]

Due to the presence of capital in the production technology of the final-good the dynamical system of the model may be analysed in terms of the capital intensity per unit of efficient labour. The steady state is unique and saddle-path stable. Moreover, the steady state does not exhibit the often criticized scale effect that appears in Romer's analysis.[14] Instead, the steady-state growth rate of per-capita magnitudes depends positively on the population growth rate and not on population size. This growth rate is the one that a social planner would also select. However, generically, there is a static inefficiency since there may be too much or too little variety in equilibrium. An appropriate tax or subsidy on training costs implements the efficient static and, thereby, the efficient dynamic allocation.

A model of growth due to gains from specialization

Consider a closed economy with a production sector comprising a final-good sector and an intermediate-good sector, and a household sector. Time is continuous, i.e., $t \in [0;\infty)$. The 'final good' is a commodity that serves for consumption today and for investment in future capital. In all periods there is a market for the consumption good, for capital, for risk free bonds, for all available varieties of the intermediate good, and for labour. The final good is the *numéraire*.

The production sector: the final-good sector

The final-good sector has many competitive firms producing a homogeneous good under constant returns to scale. We may therefore describe the final-good sector in terms of the actions of a single, aggregate firm. Its production function is[15]

$$Y = \Lambda K^\beta D^{1-\beta}, \quad 0 < \beta < 1 \tag{1.1}$$

where Y is output at t, Λ a constant reflecting the choice of units, K the employed capital stock at t, and D the quantity index

$$D \equiv \left[A^{(\sigma-1)(1-\alpha)} \int_0^A x(j)^\alpha dj \right]^{\frac{1}{\alpha}}, \quad 0 < \alpha < 1 \tag{1.2}$$

where $x(j)$ denotes the amount of intermediate j used at t, and $A \in R_+$ is the measure of varieties of intermediates available at t. The parameter α determines the elasticity of substitution between any pair of intermediates, $\in \equiv 1/(1-\alpha)$. Following Ethier,[16] the term in front of the integral allows us to introduce $\sigma \in [0,\infty)$ as a measure of gains from specialization. If $\sigma = 1$, then D exhibits the same degree of gains from specialization as the CES specification used by, for instance, Paul Romer or Grossman and Helpman.[17] If σ falls below unity these gains decrease. In the limit $\sigma \to 0$, they vanish. To grasp the implications for steady-state growth, let us jump ahead and suppose that the equilibrium is symmetric with $x(j) = x$ and that A is proportionate to the economy's labour endowment, L. Then, the equilibrium value of D satisfies

$$D \propto L^{\frac{(\sigma-1)(1-\alpha+1)}{\alpha}} x \tag{1.3}$$

Accordingly, if x remains constant over time

$$\gamma_D \equiv \frac{\dot{D}}{D} = \frac{(\sigma-1)(1-\alpha)+1}{\alpha} n \tag{1.4}$$

where $n > 0$ is the growth rate of L. Clearly, $\gamma_D(\sigma = 0) = n$ and $\partial\gamma_D/\partial\sigma > 0$. Thus, due to gains from the exploitation of the division of labour, which arise for $\sigma > 0$, D grows faster than the labour endowment. If in addition K also grows at rate $\gamma_D > n$, then per-capita income growth is strictly positive.

Denote R the rental price for a unit of capital services, $p(j)$ the price of intermediate-good j, and

$$P \equiv \left[A^{\sigma-1} \int_0^A p(j')^{1-\varepsilon} dj' \right]^{\frac{1}{1-\varepsilon}} \tag{1.5}$$

the minimum cost of one unit of D. Choose units such that

$$\Lambda \equiv \left[\left(\frac{\beta}{1-\beta} \right)^{1-\beta} + \left(\frac{\beta}{1-\beta} \right)^{-\beta} \right] \tag{1.6}$$

Then, the cost function is

$$R^\beta P^{1-\beta} Y \tag{1.7}$$

We can use (1.5) and (1.7) to obtain the conditional factor demands for capital and each intermediate good from an application of Shephard's lemma. Having in mind that unit cost are equal to unity, this gives

$$K = \beta \frac{Y}{R} \tag{1.8}$$

and

$$x(j) = \frac{(1-\beta)Y}{\int_0^A p(j')^{1-\varepsilon} dj'} p(j)^{-\varepsilon} \quad \text{for all } j \in [0,A] \tag{1.9}$$

The production sector: the intermediate-good sector

The intermediate-goods sector produces each variant according to the production function

$$x(j) = \max\{0, l(j) - \bar{l}\} \tag{1.10}$$

here $l(j)$ is the total amount of labour employed by firm j, and $\bar{l} > 0$ denotes the amount of quasi-fixed labour. The latter can be thought of as time devoted to on-the-job training.

There is free entry into the production of each variety. The quasi-fixed wage cost implies that the equilibrium has only one manufacturer of each variety earning zero profits. With w denoting the real wage, the per-period profit of the manufacturer of variety j is

$$\pi(j) = (p(j) - w)x(j) - w\bar{l} \tag{1.11}$$

In view of (1.9), the profit-maximizing price is

$$p(j) = p = \frac{w}{\alpha} \tag{1.12}$$

and implies that $x(j) = x$. The zero-profit condition

$$(p - w)x = w\bar{l} \tag{1.13}$$

in conjunction with (1.12) determines the equilibrium output of each intermediate $j \in [0; A]$ as

$$x^* = \frac{\alpha}{1-\alpha} \bar{l} \tag{1.14}$$

The household sector

The household sector at t comprises $L(t)$ identical workers/consumers. Each worker has a per-period labour endowment equal to one. Labour is inelastically supplied in exchange for wages. Let $L(0) = 1$ and recall the growth rate of the labour endowment, $n > 0$. Then, the aggregate labour supply at t is

$$L(t) = e^{nt} \tag{1.15}$$

Workers/consumers belong to infinitely lived dynasties with identical intertemporal preferences. The representative dynasty maximizes

$$U = \int_0^\infty \frac{c(t)^{1-\theta} - 1}{1 - \theta} e^{-(\rho-n)t} dt \tag{1.16}$$

where $c(t)$ is per-capita consumption, $\theta > 0$ is the inverse of the intertemporal elasticity of substitution, and $\rho > 0$ is the instantaneous rate of time preference.

The dynasties own the economy's capital stock and rent it to the final-good sector. Moreover, they own the shares of all firms in the economy and receive profit income, if any. Let a denote per-capita net assets and r the real rate of return on assets. Then, the flow budget constraint of the representative dynasty is

$$\dot{a} = w + ra - c - na \tag{1.17}$$

The dynasty's optimization problem is to maximize U of (16), subject to (17), the stock of initial assets $a(0) > 0$, and the appropriate Ponzi condition. Setting up the present-value Hamiltonian and following some routine transformations, the relevant first-order conditions comprise the Euler condition

$$\frac{\dot{c}}{c} = \frac{r - \rho}{\theta}, \tag{1.18}$$

and the transversality condition

$$\lim_{t \to \infty} \left\{ a(t) \exp\left[-\int_0^\infty [r(v) - n] dv \right] \right\} = 0 \tag{1.19}$$

Equilibrium analysis

Given $K_0 > 0$ and the evolution of the labour endowment (1.5), the equilibrium determines a price system, i.e. a sequence

$\{R(t), p(j, t), w(j, t), r(t)\}_{t=0}^{\infty}$, and an allocation, i.e., a sequence $\{Y(t), K(t),$ $A(t), x(j, t), l(j, t), c(t), a(t)\}_{t=0}^{\infty}$ that satisfy for all t conditions (1.8), (1.9), (1.12) and (1.13) for the production sector, conditions (1.17), (1.18) and (1.19) for the household sector, and the respective market clearing conditions of all markets.

First, consider the labour market equilibrium

$$A(x^* + \bar{l}) = L \tag{1.20}$$

With (1.14) this gives the equilibrium measure of varieties

$$A^* = \frac{1 - \alpha}{\bar{l}} L \tag{1.21}$$

Thus, the division of labour is determined by the degree of substitutability of intermediates, α, the quasi-fixed costs, $\bar{l}$, and the extent of the market, L. Intuitively, the right-hand side of (21) is aggregate labour supply divided by employment per firm. Since, a rise in α and/or in $\bar{l}$ requires production at a larger scale, employment per firm rises leaving less scope for the division of labour.

Observe that our interpretation of $\bar{l}$ as time for on-the-job training is most natural under the additional normalization $\bar{l} = 1 - \alpha$. Then, in equilibrium each intermediate-good firm has one worker who spends the fraction $1 - \alpha$ of his time on learning and the fraction α on producing x^*.

Since bonds and capital holdings are perfect substitutes as stores of value, the real rate of return on these assets must coincide, i.e., in equilibrium $R - \delta = r$, where $\delta \geq 0$ is the instantaneous rate of depreciation. In conjunction with (1.18) and (1.8), this implies that along a balanced growth path the productivity of capital, Y/K, must be constant. Using (1.14) and (1.21) in (1.1), aggregate output of the final good is

$$Y^* = \Lambda^* K^\beta L^{\left(1 + \sigma\left(\frac{1}{\alpha} - 1\right)\right)(1 - \beta)} \tag{1.22}$$

where

$$\Lambda^* \equiv \Lambda \left[\left(\frac{1 - \alpha}{\bar{l}}\right)^{\sigma\left(\frac{1}{\alpha} - 1\right)} \alpha \right]^{1 - \beta} > 0 \tag{1.23}$$

is a constant reflecting our choice of units. Since $Y^*/K = \Lambda^* \tilde{k}^{\beta - 1}$, we choose

$$\tilde{k} \equiv \frac{K}{L^{1 + \sigma\left(\frac{1}{\alpha} - 1\right)}} \tag{1.24}$$

as an auxiliary variable for the analysis of the dynamical system. Observe that $\tilde{k}$ has an interpretation as capital per unit of efficient labour. Though, unlike the neoclassical model with exogenous technical change, the efficiency level of labour obtains semi-endogenously and depends on the aggregate labour endowment and the associated gains from specialization.

Let $\tilde{c} \equiv cL^{-\sigma\left(\frac{1}{\alpha}-1\right)}$ denote consumption per unit of efficient labour. Then, the Euler condition (1.18) can be expressed as

$$\frac{\dot{\tilde{c}}}{\tilde{c}} = \frac{1}{\theta}[\beta\Lambda^*\tilde{k}^{\beta-1} - \varphi] \tag{1.25}$$

where $\varphi \equiv \delta + \rho + \sigma\left(\frac{1}{\alpha} - 1\right)n\theta$.

Next, we aim at expressing the flow budget constraint and the transversality condition in terms of $\tilde{k}$ and $\tilde{c}$. With both sectors earning zero profits, per-capita net assets must be equal to capital per worker, that is, $a(t) = k(t)$. Moreover, factor payments add up to final-good output.[18] From this and some straightforward algebra, we obtain (1.17) and (1.19) as

$$\dot{\tilde{k}} = \Lambda^*\tilde{k}^{\beta} - \tilde{c} - \left[\delta + n\left(1 + \sigma\left(\frac{1}{\alpha} - 1\right)\right)\right]\tilde{k} \tag{1.26}$$

and

$$\lim_{t\to\infty}\left\{\tilde{k}(t)\exp\left[-\int_0^\infty\left[\beta\Lambda^*\tilde{k}(v)^{\beta-1} - \delta + n\left(1 + \sigma\left(\frac{1}{\alpha} - 1\right)\right)\right]dv\right]\right\} = 0 \tag{1.27}$$

The dynamical system is then determined by (1.25), (1.26), (1.27), and the initial condition $\tilde{k}(o) = \tilde{k}_0 > 0$.

Proposition 1

Let

$$\rho > n\left[1 + \sigma\left(\frac{1}{\alpha} - 1\right)(1 - \theta)\right] \tag{1.28}$$

Then, the equilibrium gives rise to a unique, strictly positive steady-state with

$$\tilde{k}^* = \left[\frac{\beta\Lambda^*}{\varphi}\right]^{\frac{1}{1-\beta}} \text{ and } \tilde{c}^* = \tilde{k}^*\left[\frac{\varphi}{\beta} - \left[\delta + n\left(1 + \sigma\left(\frac{1}{\alpha} - 1\right)\right)\right]\right] \tag{1.29}$$

This steady state is saddle-path stable.

Proof: the proposition follows from the observation that our dynamical system coincides with the one of the version of the neoclassical growth model associated with Ramsey, Cass, and Koopmans as presented by Barro and Sala-í-Martin.[19] To observe this, replace

$$f(\hat{k}) \text{ by } \Lambda'\tilde{k}^\beta \quad \text{and} \quad \text{x by } \sigma\left(\frac{1}{\alpha-1}\right)n$$

∎

This proposition illustrates the similarities between our model and the neoclassical growth model with exogenous, labour-augmenting technical change. For instance, the steady state of both models has a constant level of capital per unit of efficient labour, which depends in similar ways on the various parameters of the model. Moreover, the transitional dynamics are governed by diminishing returns and give rise to saddle-path stability. Yet, here the steady-state growth rate of the economy is semi-endogenous.

Corollary 1: the steady-state growth rate of all per-capita magnitudes, is

$$\gamma^* = \sigma\left(\frac{1}{\alpha} - 1\right)n > 0 \tag{1.30}$$

Proof: immediate from the growth rates implied by (1.29). ∎

Hence, the steady-state growth rate, γ^*, features the key elements that are necessary and sufficient for our analytical framework to generate endogenous growth through gains from specialization. First, the aggregate production function must exhibit gains from specialization associated with the introduction of new intermediate goods, i.e., $\sigma > 0$. Second, the presence of a quasi-fixed cost requires intermediate-good firms to charge a markup over variable costs. The margin relative to the wage, $1/\alpha - 1$, represents this feature. Recall that $\alpha < 1$ implies differentiated intermediate goods. Thus, the work force specializes in differentiated activities. More differentiation, that is, a lower α, strengthens the gains from specialization. Finally, the extent to which gains from specialization and product differentiation matter for steady-state growth depends on the growth rate of the size of the market.

Interestingly, we can use Corollary 1 to gauge the size of σ. Following Barro and Sala-í-Martin,[20] we use values $\gamma^* = 0,02$ per year, $n = 0,01$ per year. Moreover, we stipulate $\alpha \in \left(\frac{1}{4}, \frac{1}{2}\right)$, which roughly corresponds to the estimated price-cost margins of Hall.[21] Then, a back-of-the-envelope calculation reveals that $\sigma \in \left(\frac{2}{3}, 2\right)$.

Welfare and its implementation

The analysis of whether the market forces provide adequate incentives for the allocation of the resources has to consider the static and the dynamic allocation problem. The static allocation problem takes the capital stock as given and asks whether the allocation of labour to the production of the differentiated inputs and the equilibrium 'number' of intermediates maximizes the quantity index D. The dynamic allocation problem incorporates intertemporal optimization. The efficient static allocation solves

$$\max_{\{x(j), I(j)\}_{j=0,A}^{j=A,A}} D \quad s.t.\ (1.10) \quad and \quad \int_0^A \left[x(j) + \bar{l}\right] dj = L \quad (1.31)$$

Since D treats all intermediates symmetrically and the input requirements (1.10) are the same for all intermediates, the solution is symmetric and involves $x = l - \bar{l} = L/A - \bar{l}$. Then, with (1.2) the efficient number of varieties, A^{**}, satisfies

$$A^{**} = \arg\max_A \ A^{\frac{(\sigma-1)(1-\alpha)+1}{\alpha}} \left(\frac{L}{A} - \bar{l}\right) \quad (1.32)$$

Proposition 2
The efficient number of intermediates and their efficient scale, x**, satisfy

$$A^{**} = \frac{\sigma\left(\frac{1}{\alpha} - 1\right)}{\sigma\left(\frac{1}{\alpha} - 1\right) + 1} \frac{L}{\bar{l}} \quad and \quad x^{**} = \frac{1}{\sigma} \frac{\alpha}{1-\alpha} \bar{l} \quad (1.33)$$

$$A^{**} \underset{<}{\overset{>}{=}} A^* \quad and \quad x^* \underset{<}{\overset{>}{=}} x^{**} \quad for \ \sigma \underset{<}{\overset{>}{=}} \quad (1.34)$$

Proof: the value A^{**} is the only one that satisfies the first-order condition associated with (1.32). The second-order condition reveals a global maximum. The efficient scale satisfies $x^{**} = L/A^{**} - \bar{l}$. The results of (1.34) follow immediately from the fact that $x^{**} = x^*/\sigma$ and $A^{**} = \sigma A^*/(\sigma(1-\alpha) + \alpha)$. ∎

The value A^{**} balances the advantage from having more intermediates and the disadvantage of a smaller scale. The higher the gains from specialization, the more it pays to have many varieties produced at a smaller scale. Interestingly, the equilibrium may provide too much or too little variety depending on the size of the gains from specialization. For instance, as $\sigma \to 0$, the gains from specialization vanish and the optimal allocation approaches $A^{**} \to 0$ and $x^{**} \to \infty$.

This discrepancy is due to the fact that in the equilibrium the marginal entrant neither accounts or the beneficial effect it has on D nor for the adverse effect on the profit of existing firms.[22]

Alternatively, one may interpret Proposition 2 as stating a generic failure of the economy under laissez-faire to provide adequate vocational training for its current workforce. To see this, we measure aggregate human capital at t, H, as proportionate to the total time devoted to training. Then, under laissez-faire we have $H^* = A^*\bar{l}$ whereas the planner chooses $H^{**} = A^{**}\bar{l}$. It follows that

$$H^{**} \underset{<}{\overset{>}{-}} H^* \Leftrightarrow \sigma \underset{<}{\overset{>}{-}}$$

Proposition 3

Suppose the government taxes or subsidizes on-the-job training costs at rate $\tau > (-1)$ and either redistributes in a lump-sum manner its tax revenues or charges a lump-sum tax to cover its subsidy expenses. A tax rate

$$\tau^{**} = \frac{1}{\sigma} - 1 \tag{1.35}$$

implements the efficient static allocation.

Proof: under symmetry, the profit of an intermediate-good firm becomes $\pi = (p - w)x - w(1 + \tau)\bar{l}$. With a profit-maximizing price equal to $p = w/\alpha$, the zero-profit condition delivers the scale

$$x^*(\tau) = (1 + \tau)\frac{\alpha}{1 - \alpha}\bar{l}$$

The tax rate τ^{**} is the unique solution to $x^*(\tau) = x^{**}$. Since $\sigma > 0$, we have $\tau^{**} > (-1)$. The resource constraint (20) delivers $A^{**} = L/(x^{**} + \bar{l})$. ∎

Thus, the efficient static allocation can be brought about through an appropriate choice of a tax or a subsidy on the wage to be paid during the apprenticeship.

Intuitively, this is due to the fact that both a firm's turnover and the quasi-fixed costs are proportionate to the real wage. Accordingly, an appropriate choice of τ determines the scale that is consistent with zero profits. For instance, if $\sigma > 1$, a subsidy rate $\tau^{**} = 1/\sigma - 1 < 0$ on training induces a smaller than the equilibrium scale and allows to have more varieties.

The efficient dynamic allocation requires static efficiency at all t. To characterize the optimal path, we use A^{**}, x^{**}, and the resource constraint (1.20) to determine aggregate output. Then (1.1) gives

$$Y^{**} = \Lambda^{**} K^{\beta} L^{\left(1 + \sigma\left(\frac{1}{\alpha} - 1\right)\right)(1-\beta)} \tag{1.36}$$

where

$$\Lambda^{**} \equiv \Lambda \left[\left(\frac{\sigma(1-\alpha)}{[\sigma(1-\alpha)+\alpha]\bar{l}}\right)^{\sigma\left(\frac{1}{\alpha}-1\right)} \frac{\alpha}{\sigma(1-\alpha)+\alpha}\right]^{1-\beta} \tag{1.37}$$

Consider the social planner who maximizes the utility of the representative household, U of (1.16), subject to the resource constraint

$$\dot{\tilde{k}} = \Lambda^{**} \tilde{k}^{\beta} - \tilde{c} - \left[\delta + n\left(1 + \sigma\left(\frac{1}{\alpha} - 1\right)\right)\right]\tilde{k} \tag{1.38}$$

and the initial condition $\tilde{k}(0) = \tilde{k}_0 > 0$.

Proposition 4

Suppose condition (1.28) holds.

1. There is a unique, strictly positive, and locally saddle-path stable steady state involving

$$\tilde{k}^{**} = \left[\frac{\beta\Lambda^{**}}{\varphi}\right]^{\frac{1}{1-\beta}} \quad \text{and} \quad \tilde{c}^{**} = \tilde{k}^{**}\left[\frac{\varphi}{\beta} - \left[\delta + n\left(1 + \sigma\left(\frac{1}{\alpha} - 1\right)\right)\right]\right] \tag{1.39}$$

2. It holds that

$$\frac{\tilde{c}^{**}}{\tilde{c}^*} - \frac{\tilde{k}^{**}}{\tilde{k}^*} = \left[\frac{\Lambda^{**}}{\Lambda^*}\right]^{\frac{1}{1-\beta}} \geq 1 \quad \text{with equality only if } \sigma = 1 \tag{1.40}$$

3. The steady-state growth rate of per-capita magnitudes is efficient, i.e. $\gamma^{**} = \gamma^*$.

Proof: consider the efficient static allocation as characterized in Proposition 2. Then the present-value Hamiltonian associated with the social planner's problem is

$$H = \frac{c(t)^{1-\theta} - 1}{1 - \theta} e^{-(\rho - n)t} + \lambda \left[\Lambda^{**} \tilde{k}^{\beta} - \tilde{c} - \left[\delta + n \left(1 + \sigma \left(\frac{1}{\alpha} - 1 \right) \right) \right] \tilde{k} \right]$$

(1.41)

As part of the first-order conditions one obtains the Euler condition

$$\frac{\dot{\tilde{c}}}{\tilde{c}} = \frac{1}{\theta} [\beta \Lambda^{**} \tilde{k}^{\beta-1} - \varphi]$$

(1.42)

and the transversality condition

$$\lim_{t \to \infty} \left\{ \tilde{k}(t) \exp \left[-\int_0^\infty \left[\beta \Lambda^{**} \tilde{k}(v)^{\beta-1} - \delta + n \left(1 + \sigma \left(\frac{1}{\alpha} - 1 \right) \right) \right] dv \right] \right\} = 0$$

(1.43)

The dynamical system is then described by the differential equations (1.42) and (1.38) and the boundary conditions (1.28) and $\tilde{k}(0) = \tilde{k}_0 > 0$. This leads to the three statements of the proposition which are subsequently proven:

Statement 1

The steady-state values given in (1.39) obtain as the only solution to (1.42) and (1.38) for $\dot{\tilde{c}} = 0$ and $\dot{\tilde{k}} = 0$, respectively. Condition (1.43) assures $\tilde{c}^{**} > 0$. Moreover, it implies that the steady state satisfies the transversality condition and that the household's utility remains finite.

Take a first-order Taylor expansion of equations (1.42) and (1.38) and use $\Delta \tilde{c} \equiv \tilde{c} - \tilde{c}^{**}$, $\Delta \tilde{k} \equiv \tilde{k} - \tilde{k}^{**}$, and $X \equiv [\delta + n (1 + \sigma (\frac{1}{\alpha} - 1))]$ This gives

$$\begin{pmatrix} \dot{\tilde{c}} \\ \dot{\tilde{k}} \end{pmatrix} = \begin{bmatrix} \frac{\beta \Lambda^{**} \tilde{k}^{\beta-1} - \varphi}{\theta} & \frac{\beta(\beta-1)\Lambda^{**} \tilde{k}^{\beta-2}}{\theta} \tilde{c} \\ (-1) & \Lambda^{**} \beta \tilde{k}^{\beta-1} - \tilde{c} - X \end{bmatrix} \begin{pmatrix} \Delta \tilde{c} \\ \Delta \tilde{k} \end{pmatrix}$$

(1.44)

Evaluation at the steady state delivers

$$\begin{pmatrix} \dot{\tilde{c}} \\ \dot{\tilde{k}} \end{pmatrix} = \begin{bmatrix} 0 & \frac{(\beta-1)\varphi}{\theta}\frac{\tilde{c}^{**}}{\tilde{k}^{**}} \\ (-1) & \varphi - \tilde{c}^{**} - X \end{bmatrix} \begin{pmatrix} \Delta\tilde{c} \\ \Delta\tilde{k} \end{pmatrix} \qquad (1.45)$$

The determinant of the characteristic matrix equals

$$-\frac{1-\beta}{\theta}\frac{\tilde{c}^{**}}{\tilde{k}^{**}} < 0 \qquad (1.46)$$

Hence, the two eigenvalues of the system have opposite signs and the steady state is a saddle-point.[23]

Statement 2

From Proposition 2 we obtain

$$\Lambda^{**} \geq \Lambda^* \text{ and } Y^{**} \geq Y^* \text{ with equality only if } \sigma = 1$$

Using the expression for $\tilde{c}^{**}$ given in (1.39) Statement 2 follows.

Statement 3

Immediate from the definition of $\tilde{c}^{**}$ and $\tilde{k}^{**}$. ∎

This proposition emphasizes the differences between the properties of our semi-endogenous growth model and the neoclassical growth model with exogenous technical change.

Similar to the neoclassical growth model with exogenous technical change, there is a unique, locally saddle-path stable steady state. Unlike the neoclassical growth model with exogenous technical change the path chosen by the planner generically differs from the path under *laissez-faire*. However, unlike in growth models with scale effects of Grossman and Helpman or Romer,[24] gains from specialization do not affect the steady-state growth rate.[25]

The following proposition states that the allocation chosen by the social planner can be supported as a dynamic general equilibrium.

Proposition 5

Suppose that at all t the government taxes or subsidizes on-the-job training costs at rate τ^{**} given by (1.35) and redistributes tax revenues/subsidy expenses in a lump-sum fashion. This policy implements the allocation chosen by the social planner.

Proof: since τ^{**} implies a level of aggregate output in the general equilibrium equal to Y^{**}, it also implies that the Euler equations (1.25) and (1.42) coincide. Similarly, the resource constraints (1.26) and (1.38) as well as the transversality conditions (1.27) and (1.43) coincide.   ∎

Conclusion

In the neoclassical growth model with an endogenous savings rate, growth may be sustained by the increased specialization of labour across an increasing variety of activities. As a result, this model turns into a semi-endogenous growth model.

To obtain this finding, the neoclassical production technology is replaced by a two-sectoral structure that depicts gains from specialization through specialized inputs made possible by an increase in the division of labour. Then, as the economy grows, the larger market makes it worth paying a fixed cost of producing a larger number of intermediate inputs. Since this raises the productivity of labour and capital, growth can be maintained.

In the model developed and unlike the neoclassical growth model with exogenous technical change, the equilibrium allocation is generically not efficient. However, an appropriate subsidy or tax is found to correct for the inherent static inefficiency and to implement the Pareto optimal dynamic allocation.

This analysis prompts further research questions. For instance, it is assumed in this model that the time necessary to learn and master a profession is a constant. In practice, a higher degree of specialization is likely to require more education and/or longer periods of learning. The question is whether this tendency would reduce the economy's growth rate or even eliminate the possibility of steady state growth.

Another set of questions relates to the assumption of a constant mark-up. Intuitively, competition among an increasing number of intermediate-good firms is likely to intensify price competition and to reduce price-cost margins with price competition having implications for steady-state growth.

Notes

1. Groenewegen, P., 1987, 'Division of Labour', in Eatwell, J., Milgate, M. and Newman, P. (eds),*The New Palgrave, A Dictionary of Economics*, Macmillan, London, pp. 901–6.

2. Smith, A., 1776, (1976) *An Inquiry into the Nature and Causes of the Wealth of Nations,* Clarendon Press, Oxford.
3. Becker, G. and Murphy, K., 1992, 'The Division of Labor, Coordination Costs, and Knowledge', *Quarterly Journal of Economics*, 107, pp. 1137–60. They question the role of the extent of the market and argue that the gains from specialization are often limited by substantial coordination cost if a group of complementary workers becomes large. Even though such considerations seem quite plausible, they are beyond the scope of the present paper.
4. Young, A., 1928, 'Increasing Returns and Economic Progress', *Economic Journal*, 38, pp. 527–42.
5. Romer, P., 1989, 'Increasing Returns and New Developments in the Theory of Growth', National Bureau of Economic Research, Working Paper Number 3098, p. 5.
6. Ramsey, F., 1928, 'A Mathematical Theory of Savings', *Economic Journal*, 38, pp. 543–59.
7. Cass, D., 1965, 'Optimum Growth in an Aggregative Model of Capital Accumulation', *Review of Economic Studies*, 32, pp. 233–40.
8. Koopmans, T., 1965, *On the Concept of Optimal Economic Growth, in The Economic Approach to Development Planning*, North Holland, Amsterdam.
9. This extends the analysis in Irmen, A., 2005, 'Growth and Gains from Specialization - Solow Meets Smith and Young', in ElShagi, M. and Rübel, G. (eds), *Aspects of International Economics*, Deutscher Universitäts-Verlag, Wiesbaden, pp. 65–74, which deals with the case of a constant savings rate in the spirit of Solow, R., 1956, 'A Contribution to the Theory of Economic Growth', *Quarterly Journal of Economics*, 70(1), pp. 65–94.
10. Romer, P., 1987, 'Growth Based on Increasing Returns Due to Specialization', *American Economic Review*, Papers and Proceedings, 77, pp. 56–62.
11. Refer, for instance, to, Aghion, P. and Howitt, P., 1998, *Endogenous Growth Theory*, MIT Press, Cambridge, MA., p. 36 and Lavezzi, A., 2003, 'Division of Labor and Economic Growth, Paul Romer's Contribution in a Historical Perspective', in Salvadori, N., (ed.), *The Theory of Economic Growth: A 'Classical' Perspective*, Edward Elgar, Cheltenham, pp. 318–35.
12. Ethier, W., 1982, 'National and International Returns to Scale in the Modern Theory of International Trade', *American Economic Review*, 72, pp. 389–405.
13. Groenewegen, 'Division of Labour', op. cit.
14. Refer, for instance, to Jones, C., 1995, 'R&D-Based Models of Economic Growth', *Journal of Political Economy*, 103(4), pp. 759–84.
15. To simplify this notation the time argument is omitted except where required for clarity.
16. Ethier, 'National and International Returns to Scale', op. cit.
17. Romer, 1987, 'Theory of Growth', op. cit. and Grossman, G. and Helpman, E., 1991, *Innovation and Growth in the Global Economy*, MIT Press, Cambridge, MA.
18. To observe this, note that by Euler's Law $Y = RK + Ap \, x$. Using (1.12), (1.14), and (1.21) reveals that $A^* p^* x^* = w \, L$.
19. Barro, R. and Sala-í-Martin, X., 2004, *Economic Growth*, MIT Press, Cambridge, MA, 2nd edn, Chapter 2.
20. Ibid., p. 109.

21. Hall, R., 1988, 'The Relation between Price and Marginal Cost in U.S. Industry', *Journal of Political Economy*, 96(5), pp. 921–47.
22. Spence, M., 1976, 'Product Selection, Fixed Costs, and Monopolistic Competition', *Review of Economic Studies*, 43.
23. Refer, for instance, to Sydsæter, K., Strøm, A. and Berck. P., 2005, *Economists' Mathematical Manual*, Springer, Heidelberg, 4th edn, 11.67.
24. Grossman and Helpman, 1991, *Innovation and Growth,*, op.cit., Chapter 3, and Romer, P., 1990, 'Endogenous Technological Change', *Journal of Political Economy*, 98(5), S71–S102.
25. For more on this refer, for instance, to Bénassy, J.-P., 1998, 'Is There Always too Little Research in Endogenous Growth with Expanding Product Variety?', *European Economic Review*, 42, 61–9 and Alvarez-Pelaez, M., and Groth, C., 2005, 'Too Little or too Much R&D?', *European Economic Review*, 49, pp. 437–56.

2
Investment in Human Capital, Migration and Economic Growth

Aidan O'Connor

Human capital is an integral part of production and a determinant of the rate of invention and innovation. The stock of and investment in the development of human capital, combined with social capital and institutions, that is, the intangible infrastructure, are contributors to economic growth due to the increasing returns associated with them. Human capital based economic growth depends on an increasing stock of knowledge and competencies and investment in education and training and an increase in the proportion of the population, both male and female, with the required qualifications. An economy that is unable to meet demand for the relevant required qualifications and competencies, in terms of quantity and quality, is likely to limit its capacity for growth. Human capital in the basis for endogenous economic growth and investment in human capital formation increases productivity.

The endowment of human capital in any economy is limited in quantity and unequal in quality and sometimes there may be excess supply relative to demand and at other times the opposite, and sometimes there is a mismatch in the required type of competencies. However, while fungible and substitutable, human capital is not transferable between individuals, although individuals may learn from others and through experience. When the demand in an economy for either general or specific competencies, or both, is not met, due to factors, such as, shifts in the demographic structure or the lack of investment in education and training, the solutions are either to increase investment in education and training, which has a long-term return, or attract the required human capital through migration. Unless these policies are implemented to ensure a supply of labour to meet demand the most efficacious strategy for firms is to export production by investing directly abroad through captive offshoring or through offshore-outsourcing, thereby transferring knowledge and technology.

Furthermore, in many developed economies the demographic structure of populations and the proportion of the population economically active is an issue, as well as, the differential between qualifications and competencies and the requirements of firms and this may be alleviated through retraining and upgrading of competencies and also extending economic activity and increasing female participation rates. An economy that is unable to supply the relevant required competencies where and when they are required is likely to limit its capacity for economic growth, as firms are incapable of assimilating technological evolutions.

Human capital competencies and firms

Competencies specifically comprise educational qualifications and capabilities and may be general, that is, transferable between industries, or they may be industry specific or occupation specific, and these may be considered professional competencies. There are also individual specific personal-social competencies including initiative, adaptability, and planning and analytical capabilities. The relevance of competencies depends on the requirements of specific tasks, occupations, firms or industries.

Some occupations require specific qualifications and registration, thereby entitling access to and overcoming a barrier to entry to a profession, while others are developed over the career of individuals and may or may not require specific qualifications and registration. More than ever, especially due to advances in technology and the increase in the rate of innovation, and their effect on the relevance of some competencies, continuous professional development is a requirement in practically all careers. Both professional and personal competencies are associated with higher productivity and economic growth.

In an age when developed economies have been transformed into service economies people have never been a more important element for firms in order to supply these services. Services are contained in people, technology and capital. They must be rendered and produced in the same place simultaneously so there are temporal and spatial elements associated with the production of services. The service factor consists of managerial and technical competencies and the service product is the type of service rendered. While many services are non-tradable some may be provided at a distance when there is a movement of people, a flow of information or a flow of capital. Sometimes a service may be produced at a distance through the use of technology.

According to the International Labour Office (ILO) the sectoral shares of agriculture, industry and services of total employment in developed economies, including the European Union, were, respectively, 6.1 per cent, 28.3 per cent and 65.6 per cent in 1997 and 3.9 per cent, 24.5 per cent and 71.5 per cent in 2007.[1] In general the structural changes of economies and the shift from agriculture and manufacturing to the knowledge-based industries in developed economies are such that there is a requirement for different types of competencies.

There has been an increase in manufacturing especially in those countries with relatively lower labour costs, as firms have outsourced or invested directly there. However, some developing economies have a policy of also investing in human capital development is creating competition for developed economies especially as these developing economies have relatively lower labour costs and the outcome is that many high value-added activities are being offshored to these economies to reduce production costs in specific industries and occupations, as well as, to source highly qualified labour. The relationship between the endowment of human capital and foreign direct investment is self-sustaining through their complementarities.

The resource-based theory of the firm focuses on resources and capabilities and these combined are the source of a firm's distinctive competencies. A firm's distinctive competencies are composed of its resources and capabilities including its general organizational capabilities. A firm's resources are both tangible and intangible and may be grouped as proprietary, physical, financial, human and organizational. Human and organizational resources essentially comprise individuals, that is, directors, managers and employees, in a firm, as well as, the interdependent outsourced and contracted services that so many firms avail of and depend on to obtain goods and services they are not capable of producing themselves or to reduce costs of production. A firm may have a strategic advantage through better resources and capabilities, through innovations in products and processes and by continuous development that allows it to gain and maintain a competitive advantage. Human and intellectual capital is an important, competitive and strategic advantage for firms.

Innovation in products and processes is one of the primary sources, often considered the most important source, of competitive advantage for firms, as well as better quality products and processes, more efficient production processes and responsiveness to customer requirements, all of which are derived from innovation. Essentially, many of these sources of competitive advantage are based on the distinctive competencies of the firm and the quantity and quality of human resources available to firms. Of course, technology may substitute sometimes for people. However, the introduction of technology while replacing some of the competencies required has simultaneously tended to create demand for different competencies. Therefore, retraining and continuous development is an important element in firms maintaining their strategic and competitive advantage.

Sectoral level employment in the European Union

The European Centre for the Development of Vocational Training (CEDEFOP) published a report in 2008 on employment levels and competency requirements in the European Union.[2] The increase in the level of employment between 1996 and 2006 in all sectors, except in the primary sector and utilities and in the manufacturing sectors, was positive.[3] The highest increase was in business and other services. There was a slight increase in the level of employment of less than one per cent on average per annum with a total aggregate increase of 9.3 per cent during this period. Table 2.1 outlines the broad trends in employment at a sectoral level between 1996 and 2006.

The projections for the level of employment in 2020 assume levels of economic growth based on low, base and high demand, and were, of course, formulated before the current economic and financial crisis that commenced in 2008. Therefore, the most realistic of the three in the current economic conditions is low demand in the short term, especially in expansion demand, and base to high demand in the medium term to long term, mainly due to an increase in expansion demand, assuming there are corrections in the European economies well before 2020.

Table 2.1   Sectoral level employment trend in the European Union* 1996–2006

Sector	Actual 000s		Percentage per annum
	1996	2006	1996–2006
Primary sector and utilities	15,052	11,918	−2.3
Manufacturing	37,802	34,871	−0.8
Construction	13,729	15,141	1.0
Distribution and transport	48,356	54,242	1.2
Business and other services	34,022	45,638	3.0
Non-marketed services	43,753	48,846	1.1
Total	192,714	210,656	0.9

* EU25 plus Switzerland and Norway.
Source: European Centre for the Development of Vocational Training, CEDEFOP, 2008, *Future Skill Needs in Europe*, Medium Term Forecast, Synthesis Report, Table 1, p. 41

The broad sector, primary sector and utilities, which includes agriculture, mining and quarrying and electricity, gas and water utilities, and also the manufacturing sector, which includes food, drink and tobacco, engineering and other types of manufacturing, declined in levels of employment between 1996 and 2006 and are also projected to decline between 2006 and 2020. The other broad sectors outlined have positive projected increases in the level of employment.

The total projected increase in the level of employment in EU25 between 2006 and 2020 due to an increase or decrease in expansion demand and based on conditions of base demand suggest an increase in the level of employment of 21,353,000 an increase of 9.7 per cent. The majority of the increase is in the first period between 2006 and 2015 of 13,280,000, an increase of 6.3 per cent, although this could be 8,054,000 in conditions of low demand, an increase of only 3.8 per cent, or as much as, 17,961,000, an increase of 8.5 per cent, in conditions of high demand. This projected demand must, of course, be met with a similar supply of labour so that economic growth is not constrained. This is outlined in Table 2.2.

Table 2.2   Projected sectoral level of employment projections in the European Union* 2006–2020

Sector	Actual 2006 000s	Level projection base demand 2020 000s	Percentage projection base demand 2006–2020
Primary sector and utilities	11,918	8,871	−25.6
Manufacturing	34,871	34,146	−2.1
Construction	15,141	15,580	2.9
Distribution and transport	54,242	58,843	8.5
Business and other services	45,638	59,820	31.1
Non-marketed services	48,846	53,749	10.0
Total	210,656	231,009	9.7

* EU25 plus Switzerland and Norway.
Source: Compiled from European Centre for the Development of Vocational Training, CEDE-FOP, 2008, *Future Skill Needs in Europe*, Medium Term Forecast, Synthesis Report, Table 1, p. 41 and 2008, *Panorama, Skill Needs in Europe, Focus on 2020*, Table A.1, p. 16.

The projections by type of broad occupation for all sectors are outlined in Table 2.3. High-level occupation groups comprise legislators, senior officials and managers, professionals and technicians and associate professionals. Medium-level occupational groups are defence forces, skilled agriculture and fisheries, plant and machine operators and assemblers, clerks, crafts and related trades and service, shop and market

Table 2.3   Projected level of employment by broad occupation in the European Union* 2006–2020**

Occupation	National accounts actual 2006 000s	Projected base demand 2020 000s	Projected base demand 2006–2020 percentage
Defence forces	1,215	1,130	−7.0
Skilled agriculture and fisheries	7,789	5,549	−28.8
Plant and machine operators and assemblers	17,314	18,260	5.5
Clerks	23,317	21,437	−8.1
Crafts and related trades	28,845	26,385	−8.5
Legislators, senior officials and managers	18,405	22,722	23.5
Professionals	27,349	33,275	21.7
Elementary occupations	22,980	28,047	22.0
Service, shop and market sales	29,490	32,702	10.9
Technicians and associate professionals	33,952	41,502	22.2
Total	210,656	231,009	9.7

* EU25 plus Switzerland and Norway.
** Expansion demand.
Source: Compiled from European Centre for the Development of Vocational Training, CEDE-FOP, 2008, Table 3, p. 48 and 2008, *Panorama, Skill Needs in Europe, Focus on 2020*, Tables A.3, p. 16 and Table A.4, p. 17.

sales. The low-level occupations are in the elementary occupations group.

The base-level projections for 2020 is the net increase or decrease in the level of employment by broad occupation due to expansion demand only. Replacement demand depends on the attrition rate and, assuming there are total replacements, the net effect of this attrition and the projected expansion demand represents the total projected requirement. There is a projected 9.7 per cent increase, 20,353,000, in the total of all broad occupational groups due to expansion demand.

However, there is a projected increase of almost 50 per cent in total requirements, that is, the net effect of an increase in replacement demand and an increase or decrease in expansion demand, for all broad occupation groups by 2020. All occupational groups have positive replacement demand and this is higher than expansion demand in

Table 2.4 Projected replacement demand, expansion demand and total demand by broad occupation in the European Union* 2006–2020

Occupation	Replacement demand 2006–2020 000s	Expansion demand 2006–2020 000s	Total demand 2006-2020 replacement and expansion demand 000s	Total demand 2006-2020 replacement and expansion demand percentage
Defence forces	490	−85	405	33.3
Skilled agriculture and fisheries	3,689	−2,240	1,449	18.6
Plant and machine operators and assemblers	6,714	945	7,659	44.2
Clerks	9,611	−1,880	7,731	33.2
Crafts and related trades	12,519	−2,460	10,059	34.9
Legislators, senior officials and managers	7,276	4,317	11,593	62.9
Professionals	9,497	5,926	15,423	56.4
Elementary occupations	10,357	5,067	15,424	67.1
Service, shop and market sales	13,464	3,212	16,676	56.5
Technicians and associate professionals	11,301	7,550	18,851	55.5
Total	84,919	20,353	105,272	49.9

* EU25 plus Switzerland and Norway.
Source: Compiled from European Centre for the Development of Vocational Training, CEDEFOP, 2008, Table 3, p. 48 and 2008, *Panorama, Skill Needs in Europe, Focus on 2020*, Table A.4, p. 17.

each. Some occupational groups, such as, defence forces, clerks, skilled agriculture and fisheries, and crafts and related trades have negative projected expansion demand. Essentially an increase in expansion demand represents an increase in the levels of employment and a decrease in expansion demand represents a reduction in the levels of employment in any particular occupational group before accounting for replacement demand due to attrition. These projections in order of total requirement are outlined in Table 2.4 and Figure 2.1.

000s

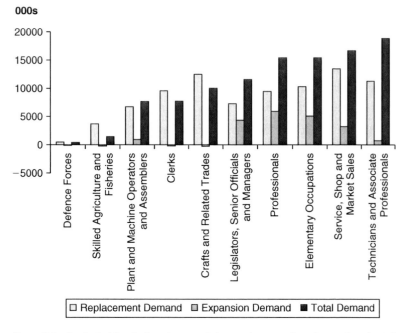

Figure 2.1   Projected level of replacement demand, expansion demand and total requirement by broad occupation in the European Union* 2006–2020
* EU25 plus Switzerland and Norway
Source: Compiled from European Centre for the Development of Vocational Training, CEDE-FOP, 2008, *Future Skill Needs in Europe*, Medium Term Forecast, Synthesis Report, Table 3, p. 48 and 2008, *Panorama, Skill Needs in Europe, Focus on 2020*, Table A.4, p. 17.

The largest increases in projected total requirements under base demand economic conditions by occupational group are in the technicians and associate professionals group, service, shop and market sales group, elementary occupations group, professionals group, and the legislators, senior officials and managers group, in order of size of increase. In terms of expansion demand only, the largest increases are the same five occupational groups and only the rankings differ. Similarly in percentage terms the largest projected increases are in these five occupational groups.

Demand for qualifications in the European Union

There are also shifts in the projected requirements by level of qualifications[4] and these are outlined in Table 2.5. There is a projected

Table 2.5 Employment shares and total demand by level of qualification in the European Union* 2006–2020

Qualifications	Proportion 2006 percentage	Proportion 2020 percentage	Percentage variation in total demand 2006–2020
High Level ISCED 5–6	25.3	31.5	12.8
Medium Level ISCED 3–4	48.5	50.0	36.8
Low Level ISCED 0–2	26.2	18.5	−22.4

* EU25 plus Switzerland and Norway.
Source: Compiled from European Centre for the Development of Vocational Training, CEDE-FOP 2008, *Panorama, Skill Needs in Europe, Focus on 2020*, Table A.6. p. 16, and Tables A.7 and A.8, p. 17.

increase in the requirement for high-level qualifications with a decline in projected demand for low-level qualifications. In terms of the proportion of the labour force the projected proportion of those with medium-level qualifications is much the same. This is consistent with the projections in Table 2.4 for negative expansion demand in occupational groups with relatively lower level qualification requirements, except in the elementary occupations group. As in 2006 the proportion of those with medium-level qualification dominates.

Focusing on expansion demand only, and as outlined in Figure 2.2, there is a projected positive increase in demand for high- and medium-level qualifications and a projected decrease in demand for low-level qualifications. So those broad sectors and occupational groups with positive expansion demand are projected to seek labour with high- or medium-level qualifications.

The projected level of demand for high-level qualifications in terms of numbers is much the same for replacement and expansion demand. However, the level of expansion demand requiring medium-level qualifications is much lower than replacement demand, although medium-level qualifications are the most demanded. While there is a projected significant decline in expansion demand requiring low-level qualifications there is a slight projected increase in total demand for low-level qualifications primarily due to replacement demand. There is almost a 50 per cent projected increase in total for high- and medium-level qualifications with a projected decline in demand of 22 per cent for those with low-level qualifications.

Furthermore, there is almost 50 per cent more projected demand for high-level qualifications than for medium-level qualifications due

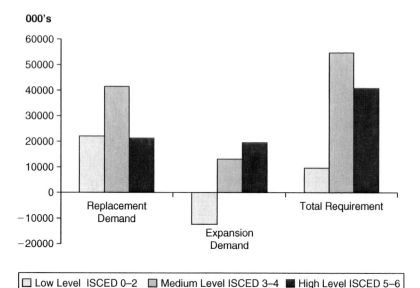

Figure 2.2   Employment shares and total demand by level of qualification in the European Union* 2006–2020

*EU25 plus Switzerland and Norway.

Source: Compiled from European Centre for the Development of Vocational Training, CEDEFOP 2008, *Panorama, Skill Needs in Europe, Focus on 2020*, Table A.6, p. 17.

to expansion demand, 19,574,000 as opposed to 13,132,000, whereas, there is almost double the projected demand for medium-level qualifications, 41,542,000, than for either high-level qualifications, 21,363,000 or low-level qualifications, 22,014,000, due to replacement demand.

Therefore, there is a requirement for more, or an upgrading of qualifications and there are implications for universities and other further education and training authorities, being the competent institutions to meet these requirements.

Investment in education and further training and educational attainment

Human capital formation is partly the result of investment in education and training and is a contributing factor in economic growth although empirical studies on the theoretical link between human capital and economic growth are inconclusive. Notwithstanding the investment in education by governments and further training and development by firms, developing human capital is a long-term investment with a lag between investment, the accumulation of human capital and economic growth. There are different marginal returns to education depending on the type, primary, secondary or tertiary, and the area of studies. The rate of return to an additional year of education also depends on these. Planning for the required level of education investment is important as there may be over-education or under-education and these have effects on labour markets and incomes. Education, along with experience, increases the level of human capital and this increases the productivity of labour. Capital according to Mankiw, includes physical and human capital and they are complimentary in the production process, such that an investment in education and training to attain human capital is an important form of capital accumulation and human capital is the principal determinant in economic growth.[5]

The average years of education of a country's population aged 25–64 may be considered as a broad proxy for its stock of human capital. To meet a demand for human capital there must be an increased investment in education in general and especially in tertiary education in both Type A and Type B programmes. Type A programmes are usually for three years or more and are primarily theory based with progressive access to advanced research programmes, whereas Type B programmes are usually for two years or more and while there is some theoretical base to these they focus more on the development of practical, technical or occupational competencies.

In terms of expenditure on tertiary education as a proportion of GDP in the Group of Seven (G7) countries Canada and the United States have the highest proportions of investment. The level of investment in each of these countries is double that of each of the European countries represented and also that of Japan. These countries are each almost double the OECD average and double the EU19[6] average. They also have the highest proportion of educational attainment in the 25–64 age cohort of their respective populations. Japan has one of the highest proportions of its population in the 25–64 age cohort with tertiary education attainment among these countries. It has achieved this with similar investment levels to France and Germany, whose educational attainment levels are much lower, and also the United Kingdom, although its educational attainment levels are higher than the other selected European countries. Japan's investment in tertiary education is less than half that of the United States in terms of proportion of GDP with similar educational attainment levels. It also has a balance between the proportion of those with Type A and Type B qualifications. This balance is similar to Canada's

Table 2.6 Expenditure on tertiary education* and educational attainment G7 countries and OECD and EU27 averages

Country	Tertiary education 2005 Percentage of GDP	Educational attainment 2006 Percentage of population aged 25–64		
		Type A	*Type B*	*Total*
France	1.3	15	11	26
Germany	1.1	14	9	23
Italy	0.9	12	1	13
United Kingdom	1.3	21	9	30
United States	2.9	33	5	38
Canada	2.6	24	23	47
Japan	1.4	23	18	41
OECD Average	1.5	n.a.	n.a.	27
EU27 Average	1.2	n.a.	n.a.	24

* Tertiary education excluding advanced research programmes.
Sources: Compiled from Organisation for Economic Co-operation and Development, *Education at a Glance, 2008*, Tables B.2.4 and A1.1a; and Eurostat, 2008, *Statistics in Focus, Population and Social Conditions*, Number 117/2008, Luxembourg, Table 1, p. 6.

and in contrast to the United States whose focus is primarily Type A qualifications similar to the United Kingdom. This is outlined in Table 2.6.

The selected European countries have lower percentages of GDP investment in tertiary education than the average for member countries of the Organization for Economic Cooperation and Development (OECD) and none has higher than the European average. The United Kingdom has the highest proportion of its population with tertiary educational attainment among the main European economies and is the only one above the OECD average.

The total expenditure represented by Purchasing Power Standards (PPS) per pupil/student in education from primary to tertiary education in EU27 in 2005 was 5,657 PPS per pupil/student ranging from 1,454 PPS in Romania to 8,293 PPS in Austria.[7] The level of expenditure increases as the level of education increases so that in 2005 the expenditure was 8,303 PPS per student in tertiary education.[8] There were eight member states with an expenditure of more than 10,000 PPS per student in tertiary education.[9] This is similar to the expenditure in Japan where it is slightly more than 10,000 PPS per student, and which has the one of the highest levels of educational attainment among G7 countries as outlined in Table 2.6, although the level of expenditure, in terms of expenditure on tertiary education as a percentage of GDP and in PPS, is much lower than in the United States where the expenditure on tertiary education was 20,876 PPS per student and where the education attainment at tertiary level is one of the highest among developed economies. In total the EU27 expenditure is 40 per cent less than the United States expenditure on tertiary education. When research and development from tertiary education expenditure is excluded the comparative data is 18,500 PPS per student in the United States and 5,700 PPS per student in the EU27.[10] A study by the OECD concludes that the accumulation of human capital significantly influences and affects output per capita growth and an additional year of education has a long run effect on output of approximately 6 per cent.[11]

Participation rates and returns to education

The participation rate of females in the labour force was 4.6 per cent in 1890 in the United States and this increased to 61.4 per cent in 2001. The equivalent male participation rates were 84.3 per cent and 75.1 per cent respectively. Female incomes also narrowed from 30 per cent to 80 per cent of male income levels during this period.[12] During this period investment in education, human capital formation, and participation rates at university for females, human capital acquisition, also increased. Furthermore, the type of competencies required shifted from physical to intellectual in many industries.

In an article by Galor and Weill they state that increases in capital accumulation have a positive effect on females' relative income, as capital is more complementary to females' input than males' input. There is a subsequent reduction in the fertility rate and this leads to an increase in the level of capital per employee followed by higher economic growth. They qualify this by stating that legal and social pressures are also responsible for the increase in female earnings, as well as the increase in the level of capital accumulation, although it may be that economic growth was a catalyst for these economic and social changes. Furthermore, the investment by females in human capital is likely to be determined by the relative return in terms of income and their anticipated labour force participation.[13]

However, the OECD estimated in 1995 that the average earnings of females with a university tertiary education was 60 per cent more, and a non–university tertiary education 24 per cent more, than someone with an upper secondary education. For males the average earnings are similar though slightly less whereas in the United Kingdom they are slightly more at 62 per cent and 15 per cent respectively.[14]

The level of qualification of individuals is generally positively correlated with income. The stock of human capital, gender participation rates and demographic profile of the labour force affect income. Gender differences in rates of return to education may be partly due to gender differences in the type of human capital accumulation. Returns to human capital and to education depend on the cost and the demand for labour. These returns may only be achieved by participating in the labour force and supplying labour, so withdrawal from the labour force is another possible reason for the gender income gap. Furthermore, occupational segregation may result in gender earnings differentials, especially if some relatively higher or lower remunerated occupations tend to have high concentrations of one gender. Occupation segregation by gender may occur due to self-selection preferences by the majority of one gender and to the task characteristics associated with specific occupations. In addition, not all investment in education by individuals is to obtain the highest monetary return.[15]

There were 17,704,100 students in tertiary education, including university and other further education institutions in EU25 in 2006, an increase of 16.4 per cent from 15,208,800 in 2000. The proportion of females in tertiary education is more than half in all EU25 countries, with Germany at 49.7 per cent. The proportion in 2006 was 55.1 per cent an increase from 53.5 per cent since 2000. The equivalent rates in the United States and Japan in 2006 were 57.4 per cent and 45.7 per cent respectively. However, in EU25 in 2006 in the science, mathematics and computing areas the proportion of females was only 36.7 per cent, a decline from 38.7 per cent since 2000. Italy, Portugal, Ireland, and Sweden had female participation rates in 2006 of 49.7 per cent, 49.5 per cent, 42.3 per cent and 42.9 per cent, respectively, in these areas. The equivalent female participation rates in the United States and Japan in 2006 were 38.6 per cent and 25 per cent respectively. Similarly, in the engineering, manufacturing and construction areas the proportion of females was 23.9 per cent, a slight increase from 22.4 per cent since 2000, with Denmark having the highest rate at 32.9 per cent. The equivalent female participation rates in these areas in the United States and Japan in 2006 were 16.2 per cent and 11.7 per cent respectively.[16]

Migration of labour

There are various theories of migration. These include a neoclassical approach focusing on income differentials and convergence whereas the dual labour market approach suggests that income differentials alone are not the reason. According to this theory, economies are composed of primary and secondary labour markets and the specific structure and demography in some countries create a demand for labour. Other approaches also suggest that income differential is not a necessary condition for migration and that migration may not necessarily be permanent and that networks influence the source and destination of migrants and through this migrationary system it becomes self regenerating.[17]

The nineteenth and early twentieth centuries were remarkable for the increase in international trade and financial flows and innovations in transport and communications. Barriers to trade were replaced by free trade policies and it was also a period of migration, especially to North America. It is argued by Hatton and Williamson that the economic convergence that occurred during the last quarter of the nineteenth century and up to World War I, was primarily due to migration and economic integration of the world economies.[18] Following the interwar period, mostly characterized by protectionism, and World War II, there has been an increase in the liberalization of trade in goods and services and flows of capital, especially since the 1970s. During this period there has been a concomitant increase in restrictions in migration and the liberalization of trade and increased foreign direct investment may be considered substitutes for migration.

In another study by Hatton and Williamson, along with Clark, they state that both theoretically and empirically, income relative to education is the main stimulus for migration. They also argue that the reasons for immigration into the United States, besides income and education and source country demographics, are the stock and origin of previous emigrants, contacts through relations and shifts in government policy. One of the policy shifts in 1965 had an impact on the source and type of migrants as it promoted the inmigration of those who already had relatives in the United States. They conclude, based on data for 81 countries accounting for 82.5 per cent of US immigration in the period 1971 to 1998, that a 10 per cent increase in a source country's income per capita reduces immigration by 5 per cent, and an increase in years of education of 10 per cent increases the immigration rate by 13 per cent although these rates vary from country to country.[19]

A report by the Australian Government Productivity Commission on the effects of the economic impact of migration and population growth concluded that migration has affected the economy and society in terms of the composition of the labour force, especially with the shift in policy to an emphasis on highly qualified migrants and an increased diversification of source countries, as well as, an increase in temporary migrants. The increased population and a diverse geographical location of migrants have also had a positive effect. It also concludes that although there is high net positive inmigration in recent years there is less impact on income per capita and productivity due to the annual number of migrants that is low relative to the population and labour force. However, the policy of focusing on highly qualified migrants has been a factor in the integration of immigrants into the labour force and society, especially those with language proficiency.[20]

There are many instances where the migration of lower qualified individuals resolves the unwillingness of indigenous labour to perform certain tasks and many developed countries are dependent on this migration to ensure that their economies operate efficaciously. However, often migrants perform tasks for which they are overqualified. Based on data from 2002–2004 the proportion of highly qualified immigrants in medium or low-level occupations in Australia was 31.9 per cent, Canada 33.3 per cent, France, 21.2 per cent in Germany 33.5 per cent, the United Kingdom, 23.2 per cent and the United States 28 per cent. However, the proportion of overqualified natives in these countries was similar except for some countries, such as, Australia 23.1 per cent, Canada, 18.5 per cent and Germany 22.2 per cent.[21]

In Sweden in 2003 only 60 per cent of immigrants with a tertiary qualification were in high-level employment compared to 97 per cent of those of Swedish origin with a tertiary education and 37 per cent were in medium and low-level employment compared to 3 per cent among those of Swedish origin. The equivalent proportions in Germany for those with a tertiary education was 50 per cent in high-level and 43 per cent in medium-level employment whereas for those of German origin the proportions were 66 per cent and 34 per cent respectively. In the United Kingdom the difference is less pronounced with tertiary educated immigrants in high-level and medium-level employment at 60 per cent and 34 per cent respectively compared to those of British origin at 66 per cent and 32 per cent respectively.[22] In another study by the OECD it is stated that in Portugal 90 per cent of highly qualified immigrants from eastern and southeastern Europe are in occupations for which they are overqualified.[23] However, those who are overqualified often have higher income than those in equivalent positions with the required education levels.[24]

Migration in the European Union

In the European Union one of the four freedoms is the free movement of labour, part of the free movement of persons. With the accession of ten new member states in Eastern Europe, the Baltics and the Mediterranean in 2004, only some member states of EU15,[25] such as, Ireland, Sweden and the United Kingdom, fully opened their labour markets to labour from these new member states and these destination member states have benefited from the migration. The others had transitional regimes in place that restricted migration.[26] The type of employment of EU8[27] nationals in these countries varied significantly. In Ireland most migrants were in the construction, manufacturing and mining, and hotels and restaurants sectors. In Sweden they were primarily in the health, trade, transport and communication, and manufacturing and mining sectors. While in the United Kingdom they were mostly in the public adminis-tration and defence, and the hotels and restaurants sectors.[28] In Sweden and the United Kingdom many highly qualified migrants are in relatively low-level positions in sectors, such as construction and hospitality.

Based on the experience of migration from EU8 to the three open member states of EU15 the reasons were due to labour market disequi-libria in the source member states and the demand for relatively lower cost labour and opportunities and that the migrant labour supplemented rather than replaced indigenous labour, which moved to higher remu-nerated positions. There has also been an economic growth effect from this migration. Some migrants are highly qualified and migrate seeking higher returns and there have been implications for source member states in terms of meeting their own economies' demands in some sectors with inflationary pressure on labour costs in those sectors.[29] Another study on the effect of labour migration and convergence in the new member states of the European Union concludes that it has increased the rate of convergence, and also releases pressure on these economies' labour markets and could increase human capital with returning migrants who have gained knowledge and experience.[30]

A report by the OECD published in 2006 states that almost half of the migrants in EU15 are from other EU15 member states. A third of migrants originate from other European countries, especially those in the Mediter-ranean basin, and also the Asian sub-continent. Among highly educated migrants in EU15 the majority are from Africa, followed by Asia and the rest of Europe. In 2000 it was estimated that there were 20 million highly educated foreign nationals in OECD countries, with two thirds of these opting to reside in North America compared to less than a quarter in EU15. Eight million of these migrated in the 1990s. However, 40 per cent of these tertiary educated migrants are from other OECD countries. The other 60 per cent of these migrants are from outside the OECD. Those from outside the OECD are primarily from East Asia, with 80 per cent opting to reside in North America. This is similar to the 70 per cent of tertiary educated migrants from South Asia, the Caribbean and South America who also have opted to reside there. A higher proportion of highly educated sub-Saharan Africans reside in North America than in EU15, despite the political and economic links that many of the countries have to certain European former colonial countries and also the linguistic similarities with these countries, along with existing networks and connections to relations, not to mention geographic proximity. Furthermore, those migrants in the EU with low levels of qualifications originate mostly from high-income countries.

According to Docquier *et al.* 64.5 per cent of total immigrants in OECD countries in 2000 originated from developing economies and almost 75 per cent of these are in Australia, Canada and the United States and 20 per cent are in one of the member states of EU15. They also state that geographic distance is not an issue for qualified migrants.[31] This means that the EU is at a disadvantage in attracting highly qualified migrants and there are, therefore, implications for taxation.[32]

The percentage shares of total immigration into the United States between 1971 and 1998 were Latin America 33.1 per cent, of which Mexico was 21.7 per cent, Asia 31.5 per cent, Europe 13.3 per cent, and the Caribbean 12.8 per cent. There were 25 million immigrants into the United States between 1950 and 1998 and approximately 20 million of these were admitted since 1970 with the annual rate increasing from a quarter of a million in the 1950s to half a million in the 1970s to almost a million in the 1990s.[33]

However, despite *de jure* freedom of movement of labour within the EU, albeit with some restrictions on the movement of labour from the new member states, for many there are also *de facto* barriers to mobility, such as, cultural differences and linguistic barriers. In a survey in 2005 of the reasons for long distance migration within the EU only 38 per cent of respondents stated that they moved for career reasons while 42 per cent moved for reasons, such as, marital or residential relocation.[34]

Policy on migration from outside the European Union

Net migration in EU25 has been positive in recent years increasing from 727,949 in 2000 to 1,890,680 in 2007 but was projected to decline to 1,466,917 in 2008.[35] Article 63 of the Treaty of Rome 1957 establishes the European Union's competence in migration policy and, while the Maastricht Treaty 1992 recognizes common issues, the Treaty of Amsterdam 1997 provides for a binding common policy. In order to have a common policy on immigration the European Council adopted the Tampere programme from 1999 to 2004 followed by the Hague programme from 2005–2010. The European Commission proposed a Directive on economic migration in 2001. However, due to divergent policies among member states, there was no agreement on this and only a policy plan was agreed in 2005. This plan also considers the effect on the economic development of countries of origin of migrants. Directives 2003/86 and 2003/109 relating to family reunification and long-term residency status respectively were agreed and implemented by 2005 and 2006, respectively. Directives 2004/14 and 2005/71 relating to studies, pupil exchange, unremunerated training and also the entry of researchers, respectively, have been agreed and were implemented by 2007. Member states have agreed in principle on a European Union wide policy on immigration from outside the EU to be considered for discussion.

In the United Kingdom, the Migration Advisory Committee recently established rules and a points-based system, to be reviewed biennially, on inward migration from outside the European Economic Area – the European Union and Iceland, Liechtenstein and Norway – and specified those sectors where specific competencies are required, while placing a prohibition on some sectors so as not to deter firms in the United Kingdom from the training and development of indigenous labour. This limitation, of course, could have the effect of driving labour costs upwards in the prohibited sectors although that may make them more attractive to indigenous labour.

Canada introduced a points-based system for immigration in 2002 with 25 per cent of the points allocated to education at postgraduate level, 24 per cent for proficiency in English or French, and 21 per cent for experience.

Many firms are constrained by the restrictions on migration of highly qualified individuals especially in the technology sector. Since 1990 special conditions apply for specialized and high skilled individuals to migrate to the United States for a period of six years and eventually obtain residency and there have been demands by firms for the limit on the number of migrants to be increased. Much of the migration observed recently from the new member states in the European Union has been temporary.

Migration of students

There are approximately between 400,000 and 500,000 students from EU25 or EEA countries studying in another EU25 or EEA country.[36] However, the inflow of students is dominated by the United Kingdom, with

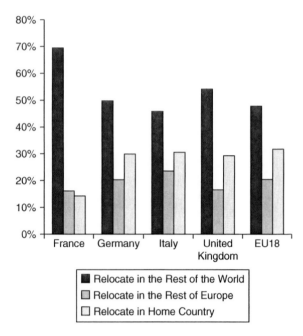

Figure 2.3   Attitudes to migration among European graduates
Source: Trendence Institute, 2007, *The European Student Barometer.*

an inflow of 144,400 and Germany with an inflow of 119,300. France is another country with a high inflow of students at 45,200. These countries' outflows are 10,400, 57,900 and 47,200 respectively. Greece at 36,900 and Poland 33,900 are also member states with large numbers of students in other EU25 and EEA member states.[37]

In a survey by Trendence Institute in 2007 of 39,000 economics, business, management, engineering and information technology graduates in 18 European countries to determine their propensity and attitude to employment mobility, the majority, 47.8 per cent, had a preference to relocate elsewhere in the world, while only 20.4 per cent opted to relocate elsewhere in Europe and 31.8 per cent had a preference to stay in their home country. This is outlined in Figure 2.3.

In France the proportions are 69.5 per cent to relocate elsewhere in the world, 16.1 per cent elsewhere in Europe and 14.3 per cent to remain in their home country, while in Germany the respective responses are 49.8 per cent, 20.3 per cent and 29.9 per cent, in Italy 45.8 per cent, 23.6 per cent and 30.6 per cent, and in the United Kingdom 54.1 per cent, 16.6 per cent and 29.3 per cent.

Interestingly the responses for the Czech Republic, Hungary, Poland and Slovakia have a much higher proportion opting for a preference for relocating elsewhere in Europe at 30.4 per cent, 36 per cent, 23.8 per cent and 32.6 per cent respectively, and also to stay in their home country 42.7 per cent, 26.8 per cent, 47.2 per cent and 27.8 per cent respectively, despite the relatively lower remuneration levels in their own respective countries, than relocating outside Europe. This is illustrated by the variations in expected salary by graduates in business and engineering. The average expected salary for business graduates ranges from the highest of Euro 50,389 in Denmark to the lowest of Euro 10,670 in Poland, with a European average of Euro 28,191. It is similar for engineering graduates with the average expected salary ranging from Euro 53,958 in Denmark to Euro 11,665 in Slovakia with a European average of Euro 29,606.[38] Furthermore, these countries have similar taxation rates although the participation rates in the labour market are quite different.

The effects of migration on countries

The country of destination of highly qualified migrants gains through an increase in human capital and conversely, the sending country has a drain on its human capital and a low or no return on its investment in education. It is also inefficacious in terms of return on investment when immigrants perform tasks that are at a lower level than their qualifications and capabilities. According to Docquier *et al.*, the proportion of qualified and competent migrants of total migrants from developing countries is on average 33 per cent whereas the proportion is only on average 6 per cent of the total labour force of these countries. In an article by Wong and Yip they state that if human capital accumulation is the main source of economic growth a brain drain has a negative impact on the economy and also has adverse effects on the non-migrants of the source country.[39] Furthermore, there may be either a positive or a negative effect on participation rates in education if the perception is that the highly qualified emigrate. That depends on whether emigration is considered positive or negative by individuals, on extended relation networks and on the social and cultural context and existing prior networks among migrants from the same country. It also depends on the perception of the benefits of education if previous migrants are not utilizing their qualifications and competencies. That is not to state that there are only negative effects on the source countries, such as, a low return on investment in education due to migration of the highly educated and repeated migration through family and migrant networks. In many instances, migration relieves pressure on labour markets and remittances also provide income for dependent relatives. In some developing countries remittances account for more than foreign direct investment. For instance, during the period 2000–3 remittances by emigrants from Africa were on average approximately US$17 billion per annum which was more than the average foreign direct investment flows of approximately US$15 billion per annum.[40] Furthermore, outsourcing creates networks between developed and developing economies and this leads to technology and knowledge transfers and may thus lead to further outsourcing and foreign direct and portfolio investment.

Conclusion

The implications of the sectoral, occupational and qualification level projections in the European Union suggest that there must be a major investment by governments in education to increase the proportion of the population with higher qualifications and training for the development. This is a long-term solution, however, to overcome imbalances in supply of and demand for labour with the required competencies. In addition, continuous professional development must be encouraged and supported so that the labour force is capable of adapting to evolutions in technology and preventing obsolescence in competencies for sustainable economic growth. The participation rate of females in engineering and science studies must be addressed. Furthermore, participation rates in the labour force among females must be increased and fiscal and labour policies should be implemented to ameliorate this.

Another solution available to governments is a focused migration policy. Governments in developed economies have realized that due to the demographics of their economies and the demand for labour they must implement policies to attract labour from diverse sources of origin. Europe lags behind North America in attracting highly qualified migrants from other OECD and non-OECD countries for the labour market and for further education. Governments should attempt to overcome the *de facto* barriers to migration, as they have the *de jure* barriers. Furthermore, universities should be more innovative in attracting foreign students and firms must recognize foreign qualifications and overcome another *de facto* barrier. The Bologna Accord in tertiary education of 1999 is a partial response to harmonization and overcoming this. Integration must be broader than merely on an economic or social level and there should be a policy of assimilation with the culture and values of the country of migration. That does not mean that migrants must necessarily forego the culture and values of their country of origin. However, governments in developed countries must also recognize the impact that migration of highly qualified and competent labour has on economically developing countries and the implications for these countries' return on investment in human capital, though the individual return for these migrants may be high.

Other than these policies the options available to firms are the captive offshoring and offshore outsourcing of the production of goods and certain services, with the concomitant necessary transfer of technology and knowledge.

Notes

1. International Labour Office, Global Employment Trends, Geneva, 2008.
2. European Centre for the Development of Vocational Training, CEDEFOP, 2008, *Future Skill Needs in Europe*, Medium Term Forecast, Synthesis Report and 2008, *Panorama, Skill Needs in Europe*, Focus on 2020.
3. There are 27 countries included. The EU25 member states are Austria, Belgium, the Czech Republic, Cyprus, Denmark, Estonia, Finland, France, Germany, Greece, Hungary, Italy, Ireland, Latvia, Lithuania, Luxembourg, Malta, the Netherlands, Poland, Portugal, Slovakia, Slovenia, Spain, Sweden, the United Kingdom plus non-EU members Norway and Switzerland.
4. The highest level of qualifications, tertiary education, equates to International Standard Classification of Education (ISCED) levels 5 and 6, medium-level qualifications to ISCED 3 and 4, and low-level qualifications, ISCED 0–2.
5. Mankiw, N., The Growth Of Nations, Brookings Papers on Economic Activity, Volume 1995, Number 1, pp. 275–326.
6. EU19 comprises the 19 member states of the European Union that are also member countries of the 30-country OECD. These include the EU-15 member states plus four of the new member states: the Czech Republic, Hungary, Poland and Slovakia.
7. Reis, F., Eurostat, 2008, Statistics in Focus, Population and Social Conditions, Number 117/2008, p. 5. PPS refers to Purchasing Power Standards and are used to compare expenditure between countries. They allow for differences in prices, although not for the differences in salaries in education.
8. Tertiary education ISCED levels 5 and 6.
9. The member states with an expenditure of more than 10,000 PPS per student in 2005 were Belgium, Denmark, Germany, Netherlands, Austria, Finland, Sweden and the United Kingdom, with Sweden the highest at 13,490 PPS per student.
10. Reis, Eurostat, 2008, op. cit., p. 5.
11. Bassanini, A. and Scarpetta, S., 2001, 'Does Human Capital Matter for Growth in OECD Countries?' Organisation for Economic Co-operation and Development, ECO/WKP(2001)8, p. 24. Studies on the effects of education on individual incomes are inconclusive. The return to education differs between individuals and also diminishes unless there is continuous development.

Furthermore, when someone withdraws from the labour force the return approaches zero until a return to the labour force. In addition, there is debate as to whether the economic growth rate is due to the stock of high levels of education or an increase in education, although it is agreed that education is a prerequisite for technological development and implementation.

12. Polachek, S., 2004, 'How the Human Capital Model Explains How the Gender Wage Gap Narrowed', Institute for the Study of Labor (IZA), Germany, Discussion Paper Number 1102, p. 1.
13. Galor, O., and Weill, D., 1996, 'The Gender Gap, Fertility and Growth', *The American Economic Review*, 86(3), pp. 374–87.
14. Organisation for Economic Cooperation and Development, Human Capital Development, Paris, 1998.
15. Refer to Yashiv, E., 2007, 'Labor Search and Matching in Macroeconomics', *European Economic Review*, 51, pp.1859–95 for a review of these issues.
16. Eurostat, Statistical Office of the European Communities, European Commission, 2009.
17. For a synopsis of the various theories refer to World Bank, 2006, EU8 Quarterly Economic Report, Part II, Labor Migration from the New EU Member States, Annex 1, pp. 33–5.
18. Hatton, T., and Williamson, J., 1992, 'International Migration and World Development: A Historical Perspective', National Bureau of Economic Research, Working Paper H0041.
19. Clark, X., Hatton, T. and Williamson, J., 2004, 'Explaining U.S. Emigration', World Bank Policy Research Working Paper No. 3252.
20. Australian Government, 2006, Productivity Commission Research Report, Economic Impacts of Migration and Population Growth.
21. Liebig, T., 2006, 'The Labour Market Integration of Immigrants in Australia', Organisation for Economic Cooperation and Development, Table 7, p. 37.
22. Lemaître, G., 2006, 'The Labour market Integration of Immigrants in Sweden', Organisation for Economic Cooperation and Development, Table 9, p. 44.
23. Organisation for Economic Cooperation and Development, 2008, Labour Market Integration in Belgium, France, the Netherlands and Portugal.
24. García Aracil, A. and Van der Velden, R., 2008, 'Competencies for Younger Higher Education graduates: Labour Market Mismatches and their Payoff', *Higher Education*, 55, p. 221.
25. Austria, Belgium, Denmark, Finland, France, Germany, Greece, Italy, Ireland, Luxembourg, the Netherlands, Portugal, Spain, Sweden and the United Kingdom.
26. Finland, Greece, Portugal and Spain fully opened their labour markets in May 2009.
27. The EU8 member states are the Czech Republic, Estonia, Hungary, Latvia, Lithuania, Poland, Slovakia and Slovenia.
28. World Bank, 2006, EU8 Quarterly Economic Report, op. cit., Chart 8, p. 13.
29. Ibid., p. 28.
30. Bems, R. and Schellekens, P., 'Macroeconomics of Migration in New Member States, International Monetary Fund', Working paper Number WP/08/264.
31. Organisation for Economic Co-operation and Development, 2006, *Effects of Migration on Sending Countries*, Paris, and Docquier, F., Lohest, O. and

Marfouk, A., 2007,'Brain Drain in Developing Countries', *The World Bank Economic Review*, 21(2), p. 198 and p. 216.

32. There are implications for taxation in the migration of both qualified and competent migrants, net contributors, and migrants with relatively lower level competencies, net beneficiaries. Qualified and competent migrants are preferred by countries as they contribute to the state in taxes and are net contributors. Countries with relatively better benefits in a regime of free migration, such as in the European Union, exerts a pull on labour with relatively lower level competencies and has an adverse effect on the proportion of migrants with qualifications and competencies. These migrants are also probably net beneficiaries in that they contribute less in taxes than they obtain as state welfare. However, there is a positive effect of higher welfare when combined with a controlled migration policy on the proportion of migrants who have relatively higher qualifications and competencies. For further information refer to Razin, A., Sadka, E. and Suwankiri, B., 2009, *Political Economy Approach to Migration into the Welfare State*.

33. Clark, X., Hatton, T. and Williamson, J., 2004, 'Explaining U.S. Emigration', op. cit. There are 81 countries included in the data accounting for 82.5 per cent of US immigration in the period 1971 to 1998.

34. European Foundation for the Improvement of Living and Working Conditions, 2007, Economic Benefits of Long Distance Mobility.

35. Eurostat, Statistical Office of the European Communities, European Commission, 2009. Net migration is the difference between the number of immigrants and the number of emigrants or in the absence of accurate data or no data net migration may be estimated as the difference between the total change and the natural change of population between the specific dates.

36. Eurostat, Statistical Office of the European Communities, European Commission, 2009.

37. Trendence Institute, 2007, The European Student Barometer.

38. Ibid.

39. Docquier, *et al.*, 2007,'Brain Drain in Developing Countries', op.cit., p. 198 and Wong, K. and Yip, C., 1999, 'Education, Economic Growth, and Brain Drain', *Journal of Economic Dynamics and Control*, 23, pp. 699–726.

40. United Nations, Office of the Special Adviser on Africa, 2005, Resource Flows to Africa: An Update on Statistical Trends.

3
Technological Innovation and Divergence in Economic Growth

Francisco J. Santos-Arteaga

The club convergence phenomenon among countries that occurred during the last half of the twentieth century and persists has been widely documented, and remains a main subject of study nowadays.[1] Despite early growth theories relying on the advantage of backwardness as a catching up mechanism, the expected convergence between different growth clubs of countries did not take place. The emphasis was then moved towards endogenous growth mechanisms,[2] educational systems,[3] as well as, financial development and credit market imperfections.[4] While recognizing the important role played by the financial sector in the technological development of countries,[5] there is a concentration on endogenous growth mechanisms and human capital. In the first instance, the literature has advanced towards the recognition that the assimilation of the most advanced technological capital by less developed countries constitutes a growth mechanism that requires important amounts of both physical and human capital investment.[6] Education, though an important factor for growth, has been displaced by differences in total factor productivity among countries, from which education is only partially responsible.[7]

Contemporaneously, the business cycle literature has highlighted the importance of investment specific technological innovations as the main source of growth in output through the cycle.[8] Such a phenomenon implies the need for specialized capital in production, which builds on already existing knowledge in the innovator country. Thus, imitation requires highly specialized human capital and infrastructures in order to achieve the same factor productivity as the innovator country.

Divergence in factor productivity levels

The empirical regularities described above have been assimilated within the neoclassical growth literature. Divergence in factor productivity levels has been illustrated to be caused by barriers to technology adoption, which prevent the creation and diffusion of knowledge in the world economy.[9] In the same vein, Prescott[10] emphasizes the fact that knowledge is transmitted among countries but, in general, not adopted, that is, technological knowledge is available but purposely not implemented due to the existence of monopoly rights within the less technologically developed countries. While Parente and Prescott[11] emphasize the role of differences in factor productivity levels among countries as the main factor triggering the club convergence phenomenon, it is interesting to understand the causes and effects of such strategic coalitions that block the adoption of new, that is, more productive, technologies among developing countries. That is, considering the current globalization phenomenon in terms of costless technology transmission among countries, the ability of the lesser technologically developed ones to implement the existing leading-edge technology within their production systems and converge is analysed. This acknowledges explicitly the partial role of education in the technological assimilation process of countries as the level of human capital does seem to influence growth.[12] Indeed, the empirical relevance of education combined with technical efficiency as two of the main growth enhancing factors among countries has also been illustrated by de la Fuente and Domenech.[13] Even though the education acquisition process is not formalized human capital differentials are assumed and are incorporated into the tacit knowledge required to generate the most advanced technological good. Besides, the technological infrastructure of a country, which constrains its capacity to innovate and imitate, defines the total factor productivity differentials that lead to divergent levels of technical efficiency among countries.

When analysing technology diffusion, the current endogenous growth literature concentrates mainly on industrial dynamics and technology races leading to equilibrium diffusion rates.[14] However, these models do not illustrate the process governing knowledge acquisition and assimilation, in spite of the fact that the cumulative nature of technology and knowledge are widely recognized,[15] and the costs of learning a new technology are known to be high, as outlined by Jovanovic.[16] In general,[17] knowledge does not immediately flow among agents, but spills following an endogenously determined sigmoid accumulation function. The complex nature of technology and its diffusion dynamics have already been widely studied and even describe the existence of divergent technological gaps among developed countries.[18]

A model of the velocity of technological assimilation among groups of countries

A quality ladder growth model of technology assimilation through a technological cumulative process is constructed. Heterogeneity in the level of technological assimilation among different countries leads not only to temporal divergences in income and productivity levels, due to differences in capacity utilization, but also to multiple diverging growth paths for identical available technologies. The capacity utilization of innovative technology and the sequential arrival rate of innovations are based on the distance from the technological frontier, defined by the new technology relative to the current state of knowledge, determined by a country's level of technological development. Technological cycles are only efficient in terms of convergence if the assimilation process of innovations is simultaneous among countries. Otherwise, convergence is not guaranteed and different divergent clubs of countries would be generated. This occurs despite ignoring most of the complex strategic problems associated with technology diffusion and assimilation.[19]

The technological assimilation capacity of a country defines the dynamic evolution of its factor productivity. That is, the technological base or infrastructure of a given country, which is determined among others by the existence of techno-economic webs of networks and industrial districts, limits its ability to innovate and grow through imitation. In other words, imitation and the assimilation of new technologies, as well as, innovation, require the existence of a skilled labour base and a technological infrastructure that can either be hired or developed within the country. If human capital lacks the technological infrastructure to apply its capabilities, it becomes unexploited and thereby inefficacious. Simultaneously, the technological infrastructure of a country develops cumulatively, constrained by the already existing one and the level of knowledge exhibited by its labour force.

The accumulation of technological knowledge and infrastructures determines the total productivity of newly acquired technology through imitation, as well as the ability to obtain additional knowledge and innovate. The farther away from the technological development frontier required to assimilate the current innovation, that is, the lower the knowledge of the labour base or the technological infrastructure level, the lower the factor productivity obtained from the new technology, and the probability of innovating. It is assumed that all agents are equally skilled in all countries. However, as noted above, basic human capital differentials must be incorporated into the tacit knowledge required to generate the most advanced technological good. In particular, basic differences in human capital skills are implicitly included within the technological assimilation capacity of countries to account for the previously described complementarities between knowledge accumulation and technological infrastructures.

The expected level of output and the stochastic process governing the arrival rate of innovations are defined by the technological assimilation capacity of a country and the proposed model focuses on the dynamic effects of innovation in the assimilation of technology as opposed to the static ones obtained through imitation. Significant differences in the level of technological assimilation among countries would tend to lead to those countries that are technologically less developed to stagnate economically and diverge from those that are technologically developed. This would be such that convergence between these types of countries is only achieved if the rate of technological process ceases in those that are technologically developed, that is, if innovations arrive with zero frequency to the technologically developed countries.[20]

Introducing the world economy

The model is a partial equilibrium model with only the production side of the economy being explicitly modelled. Labour markets are assumed to clear and remain in equilibrium always. Besides, the financial side of the economy is assumed to provide identical amounts of funds to all firms in the economic system. These funds can be used either to innovate or imitate the existing innovations and it is clear that this assumption is far from being neutral. Indeed, funds should be optimally allocated according to the expected returns obtained from other corresponding financial assets. The world distribution of financial assets should, therefore, depend on the expected profits obtained by the firms that imitate within each country and it is assumed that all firms are always supplied with the same amount of funds independently of the expected profits firms obtain. The main purpose of such an assumption is the elimination of all economic effects unrelated to the transmission and assimilation of technology among countries.

Consider, without loss of generality, a world economy composed of two countries and two firms per country. These firms represent a given sector within a continuum of industries. At the same time, each industry is defined by an optimally determined quality level, as in the quality ladder literature.[21] Strategic considerations regarding information spill-overs between countries or within sectors are not included.[22] Indeed, it is assumed that the latest most advanced innovation is immediately available to all firms in both countries. However, firms must assimilate the new technology in order to increase the probability of becoming the next innovator. While diffusion is immediate assimilation depends on the technological infrastructure of a country and the firms within it. This idea is similar to that presented in Mukoyama,[23] where technology diffusion depends on the assimilation characteristics defined by the heterogeneous skills of the labour market. It is also acknowledged that there are complementarities between the supply of skills and the innovation activity of firms at a country development level.[24]

The model may be interpreted as a quality ladder with immediate technology diffusion and production complementarities within countries depending on the development level of their respective technological infrastructure. At each point in time, one of the firms becomes an innovator while the others remain as imitators. Consumers are identical in both countries regarding preferences and endowments. The structure of the labour base is optimally chosen by each country per time period.

Countries differ in their capacity to innovate and the determinants of this have been empirically identified by Furman *et al*.[25] Their general equilibrium model, defined for each country, consists of a given innovation infrastructure, a cluster-specific innovation environment and the quality of the existing linkages between both. The empirical regularities observed by them illustrate that countries satisfy the equilibrium requirements to a certain extent, but no country fits a perfect innovation model. The proposed model does not analyse the causes leading to imbalances in technological development levels between countries but does focus on the ability of countries to converge in factor productivity levels given an already existing imbalance in their innovation capacity. Furthermore, the exchange rate is fixed and identical unitary prices in both countries for the most technologically advanced good are assumed.

Introducing firms, competencies and productivity

There are N agents in each country. The labour force is composed of *skilled* workers who may be used to either innovate or imitate, n_{sn} and n_{sm} respectively, with $n_{sn} + n_{sm} = 1$. If labour is used to imitate, it generates output per period at a rate limited by the technological development level of the country, denoted by ξ. Conversely, if labour is used in innovative activities it increases the probability of achieving a higher productivity level in the following period.

There is a single wage rate, *w*, independently of whether labour is used in innovative activities or to imitate. Since the price of output is the *numeraire*, wages are expressed in real terms. By allowing *all* agents to be skilled we ignore explicitly human capital accumulation as a requirement for growth. The results presented remain unaffected by such simplification. However, education policies could be assumed to be included in ξ, as illustrated by Furman *et al.*[26]

Labour productivity is a function of the level of technological development achieved by a country. This technological level is an index that is used as a proxy variable for the innovation capacity of a country. In other words, the index consists mainly of industrial clusters and scale economies, education levels, research and development incentives, in addition to any other factors favouring the technological enhancement of a country. It is important to note that this level is not equivalent to the productivity of the technology, *per se*, owned by the country, which will be denoted by A. Nevertheless, it affects the innovation probability, as well as, the capacity utilization of the acquired innovations. Therefore, the productivity of the technology used by a given country is separated from its innovation and utilization capacities. The high imitation costs illustrated in the literature,[27] arising from the relative level of technological development of a country, are also translated into the partial ability of imitators to fully exploit the new technology.[28] It follows that owning a leading-edge technology may assist in the development of a better one, thereby increasing the probability of generating an innovation, but only to the extent allowed by national capacity constraints. Due to this restriction the production function available to a firm that has not developed the current leading technology is:

$$Y_{sm} = \xi A^{1-\alpha} K^{\alpha} n_{sm}^{1-\alpha} \tag{3.1}$$

where

$$\xi = \frac{\lambda^c}{\lambda^*} \tag{3.2}$$

denotes the relative level of technological development of the country. This level reflects the distance between countries within a particular technological paradigm. In this regard, λ^* indicates the level of technological development necessary to generate the latest productivity improving innovation, that is, it defines the technological frontier, while λ^c stands for the level achieved by the country. The productivity of the production technology is given by A and is assumed equal to the productivity frontier A^* at each point in time. The other part of equation (3.1) is standard, with K referring to the physical capital used in production and α to its elasticity. However, firms do not differ in the quality of their final product, as they do in the quality ladder literature, but in their factor productivity. Equations (3.1) and (3.2) imply that all firms are capable of producing the highest quality technological good, but their factor productivity differs depending on the value of ξ.

The difference between the technological and productivity frontiers should be intuitively clear from an economic viewpoint. As already noted, all countries have access to the same technology, since no trade barriers have been assumed. However, the implicit knowledge tacit to each technologically advanced product is not freely available, as it is part of the product generating process, directly related to the innovation capacity of a country. The productivity frontier, to which all countries have access by acquiring the latest product, and by definition the most advanced, available differs from the technological frontier, which is reachable only by the most technologically advanced countries.

Time is continuous and measured by discrete innovations, where one unit of time lasts as much as it is required for the next innovation to appear. If two innovations occur simultaneously, this continuity allows for their separation into two different time units.[29] The production function of a firm after it introduces an innovation is given by:

$$Y_{sn} = \Gamma Y_s \tag{3.3}$$

where $\Gamma > 1$, $\xi = 1$ and $Y_s = A^{1-\alpha}K^\alpha n_{sm}^{1-\alpha}$.

It is assumed that the innovator country reaches the technological frontier as soon as one of its firms develops an innovation irrespective of its previous ξ value. That is, any innovation advantage in reaching the technological frontier is perfectly and entirely transmitted between countries independently of their relative positions prior to the innovation. Such an assumption increases the innovation incentives of a laggard country but does not guarantee convergence.

Given that equation (3.1) defines the production function of all the firms that must imitate the newly introduced technology, an innovation by a previously imitator firm incrementally increases the production of the innovator by

$$\Delta Y = Y_{sn} - Y_{sm} = (\Gamma^2 - \xi)Y_s$$

At the same time, the production function of the previous industry leader is given by ΓY_s. Thus, an innovation allows the innovator to increase its production by a factor of Γ over that of the current industry leader. Besides, the innovator firm is able to update its innovation capacity and that of the country where it is established as a direct result of the innovation.

Labour productivity increases with respect to that of the current innovator by

$$\Delta Y_s = \frac{\Delta Y}{\Gamma Y_s} = \frac{Y_{sn} - Y_{sm}}{\Gamma Y_s} = \left(\Gamma - \frac{\xi}{\Gamma}\right) \tag{3.4}$$

if the firm was previously an imitator. If the firm was already an innovator, $Y_{sm} = \Gamma Y_s$, equation (3.4) translates into a labour productivity increase equal to $(\Gamma - 1)$.

The evolution of productivity reflects the so called Arrow effect, implying that no innovator would invest to improve its own technology, as this defines the highest productivity level within each technological cycle. That is, research costs may always be imposed on firms such that no innovator would find it profitable to invest in innovation research while imitators would.[30]

Optimization process of countries and firms

A unique representative sector is considered, whose behaviour reflects that of the remaining industries in the country. There exists a unique innovator per sector and unit of time. However, the latest production technology is available to all the imitator firms within the corresponding sectors in both countries. One can think of a system of *free* licences that become immediately available to all the firms within each industry as a new technology is developed. Demand is perfectly elastic, i.e. horizontal, at the unitary price of the most technologically advanced good. Thus, all produced output is completely absorbed by the markets in both countries for each innovation introduced. Innovations are therefore demand driven, with innovator firms obtaining a higher profit than imitators per time period due to the existing differences in productivity levels. Finally, the main purpose of the paper is to analyse the convergence ability of technologically underdeveloped countries if perfect technology transmission is assumed among countries. Therefore, the analysis is concentrated on the optimal behaviour of imitator firms within the technologically lagged country, and omits the modelization of innovator firms. It follows that firms are equivalent to countries through the rest of the paper.

Consider the problem of a profit maximizing country that must decide how to distribute its labour force between innovative and imitative activities. An imitator country maximizes the expected flow of profits obtained from its firms based on their level of technological development and innovation capacity

$$\Pi(t) = E \int_t^\infty e^{-\rho[\tau-t]} \pi(n_{sm}) d\tau$$

where

$$\pi(n_{sm}) = \xi A^{1-\alpha} K^\alpha n_{sm}^{1-\alpha} - w(n_{sn} + n_{sm})$$

and ρ represents the rate of time preference for a given firm, which is assumed identical between both firms and countries. Firms obtain profits each period from the sale of the most technologically advanced product at a given productivity level. Note that profits decrease for lower levels of technological development, which define ξ. Assume, for simplicity, that profits are always positive independently of the value of ξ.

In order for countries to increase their level of technological development and innovation capacity, they must allocate labour resources to innovative activities. Innovation is governed by a Poisson process, whose arrival rate is given by

$$\theta_\xi = \frac{\lambda^c}{\lambda^*} n_{sn}^{1-\varphi} \tag{3.5}$$

where $(1 - \varphi)$ defines the elasticity of labour used in innovative activities, which is assumed higher than the labour elasticity derived from imitative ones, $\varphi < \alpha$.[31] The arrival rate of an innovation depends both on the amount of skilled labour used in innovation-related activities and the level of technological development reached by the country.

Technological progress is governed by random discoveries that increase the productivity level relative to that of the current innovator according to the following process

$$d\left(\frac{\xi}{\Gamma}\right) = \left(\Gamma - \frac{\xi}{\Gamma}\right) dz_\xi \tag{3.6}$$

The firm generating an innovation increases its productivity by a factor of Γ over its current level relative to the productivity of the previous innovator, ξ/Γ. Clearly, the dynamic structure of the model, described in terms of productivity changes, depends on the technological development level of a country, which defines the stochastic arrival rate of the corresponding Poisson process z_ξ.

Note that, despite the continuous structure of the profit function, the model is discrete in nature, that is, the continuous flow of technology has a direct effect on the profit function of a country, which changes every period. However, after an innovation takes place, each country is subject to the same decision problem regarding their labour allocation between innovative and imitative activities, given their relative level of technological development and the probability that any of their firms develops the next innovation. In this regard, the current setting highlights the lack of intertemporal effects derived from imitative activities, since only innovative ones can increase the innovation capacity of a country. Namely, a country is able to develop the technological structure that allows it to grow through time only by innovating continuously. Imitation leads to lower productivity levels and does not generate convergence *per se*, since it does not affect the arrival rate of innovation.

The Bellman equation defining the intertemporal optimization problem of imitator countries is given by[32]

$$\rho V\left(\frac{\xi}{\Gamma}\right) = \max_{n_{sm}, n_{sn}}\left[\pi(n_{sm}) + \theta_\xi\left[V(\Gamma) - V\left(\frac{\xi}{\Gamma}\right)\right]\right]$$

which allows for a direct comparison between the *immediate* benefits of imitation, $\pi(n_{sm})$, and the *expected* benefits from innovation, $\theta_\xi[V(\Gamma) - V\left(\frac{\xi}{\Gamma}\right)]$. The following first order conditions are obtained from the above optimization problem

$$n_{sm}: \quad (1-\alpha)\xi A^{1-\alpha}K^\alpha n_{sm}^{-\alpha} = w$$

$$n_{sn}: \quad (1-\varphi)\xi n_{sn}^{-\varphi}\left[V(\Gamma) - V\left(\frac{\xi}{\Gamma}\right)\right] = w$$

These conditions can be solved to obtain a break up rule that defines the optimal allocation of skilled labour depending on the value of ξ

$$(1-\alpha)\xi A^{1-\alpha}K^\alpha n_{sm}^{-\alpha} = (1-\varphi)\xi n_{sn}^{-\varphi}\left[V(\Gamma) - V\left(\frac{\xi}{\Gamma}\right)\right] \qquad (3.7)$$

The left hand side of equation (3.7) illustrates the instantaneous gain derived from imitation, given by the marginal production obtained from using an additional unit of skilled labour in imitative activities.

The right hand side represents the marginal *expected* gain from using an additional unit of skilled labour in innovative activities.[33] Equation (3.7) simplifies to

$$\frac{n_{sn}^{\varphi}}{n_{sm}^{\alpha}} = H\left(\frac{1-\varphi}{1-\alpha}\right)\left[V(\Gamma) - V\left(\frac{\xi}{\Gamma}\right)\right] \tag{3.8}$$

with

$$H = \frac{1}{A^{1-\alpha}K^{\alpha}}$$

Equation (3.8) defines the optimal allocation of skilled labour between innovative and imitative activities as a function of the relative productivity gain obtained from a successful innovation. That is, large increases in factor productivity relative to the current level defined by the technological development of a given country will promote the use of skilled labour in innovative activities over imitative ones. In other words, countries with a low degree of technological development would use their human capital resources to innovate rather than to imitate. This result could be considered as an updated version of Gerschenkron's advantage of backwardness.[34] However, the innovation incentives resulting from the relative level of backwardness of a given country do not guarantee convergence.

Divergence among groups of countries with identical availability of technology

The stochastic evolution of the partial equilibrium defined for the world economic system presented in the previous section is given by equation (3.8)

$$\frac{n_{sn}^{\varphi}}{n_{sm}^{\alpha}} = H\left(\frac{1-\varphi}{1-\alpha}\right)\left[V(\Gamma) - V\left(\frac{\xi}{\Gamma}\right)\right]$$

This equation defines the equilibrium in the production side of the economy, such that labour markets clear and human capital is distributed according to the productivity (and asset value) gains to be obtained from a successful innovation. On the other hand, the financial side of the economic system is assumed to remain in equilibrium and allocate the same amount of resources to all the firms within the world economy.

The following proposition emanates directly from equation (3.8) such that

Proposition 1

There exists a technological poverty trap generated by the production side of the economic system.

Proof: as the technological development gap between countries increases, so does the value gain obtained from a successful innovation, $V(\Gamma) - V\left(\frac{\xi}{\Gamma}\right)$, leading countries with a low level of technological development to invest a larger proportion of their skilled labour force in innovative activities. However, the probability that a given country generates the following innovation is an increasing function of ξ, i.e. $\theta_\xi = \xi n_{sn}^{1-\varphi}$. Thus, countries with a relatively low level of technological development will dedicate an increasingly larger proportion of their skilled labour force to innovative activities, even though their innovation probability does not necessarily increase and would eventually converge to zero in the limit as the technological development gap keeps increasing through time. ∎

The importance of technological development and innovation capacity for convergence is better understood in a dynamical context. Consider two groups of countries that differ in their corresponding ξ values. Countries within the low technological development group will tend to converge due to their backwardness advantage, which leads to additional investment in innovative activities despite the fact that their innovation probability does not necessarily increase. If the technological gap does not widen excessively, convergence may eventually occur, even though it does so with increasingly lower probability as the technological gap widens through time. The existing technological gap between the United States and the European Union could be considered as illustrating this. Besides, the empirical evidence presented by Patel and Pavitt[35] regarding divergent technological accumulation processes among technologically advanced countries provides additional support for this conclusion. At the same time, if the technological gap does widen enough, convergence will eventually cease as the innovation probability approaches zero. The existing and increasing technological gap between technologically developed countries and underdeveloped countries illustrates this case.

Conclusion

It has been emphasized that technology *per se* does not generate growth and convergence, even if it is freely available and costlessly transmitted among countries. It should also be noted that it is the level of technological development that determines total factor productivity in the model and accounts for the existing differences observed among countries.[36] Indeed, these existing differences in factor productivity do generate the advantage of backwardness phenomenon in the current framework, as is the case in the standard neoclassical literature. But, at the same time, it is the influence of ξ on the innovation probability what prevents countries from making full use of the existing backwardness advantage. That is, it is the whole technological infrastructure of a country, defining at the same time its innovation capacity, that determines its convergence abilities.

Finally, the complexity implied by any innovation process has been clearly identified by endogenous growth theorists,[37] while often ignored by the standard literature. Globalization, understood here as a phenomenon allowing for perfect technology transmission among countries, does not guarantee convergence, even within the current highly unrealistic environment: there are no patents, all firms are equally financed independently of their innovation success probabilities, there are no strategic transmission costs of innovation, no transportation costs, geography is irrelevant, imitation is costless, as well as the implementation of new technologies by imitators, demand is identical and perfectly elastic in all countries, and a long etcetera of additional factors all acting against convergence.

Notes

1. Refer for instance, to Howitt, P. and Mayer-Foulkes, D., 2005, 'R&D, Implementation and Stagnation: A Schumpeterian Theory of Convergence Clubs', *Journal of Money, Credit and Banking*, 37, pp. 147–77.
2. Aghion, P. and Howitt, P., 1992, 'A Model of Growth through Creative Destruction', *Econometrica*, 60, pp. 323–51.
3. Lucas, R., 1988, 'On the Mechanics of Economic Development', *Journal of Monetary Economics*, 22, pp. 3–42.
4. cf. Bencivenga, V. and Smith, B., 1991, 'Financial Intermediation and Endogenous Growth', *Review of Economic Studies*, 58, pp. 195–209, and Aghion, P., Howitt, P. and Mayer-Foulkes, D., 2005, 'The Effect of Financial Development on Convergence: Theory and Evidence', *Quarterly Journal of Economics*, 120, pp. 173–222.
5. Dosi, G., 1990, 'Finance, Innovation and Industrial Change', *Journal of Economic Behavior and Organization*, 13, pp. 299–319.
6. Aghion, P. and Howitt, P., 2005, 'Growth with Quality-Improving Innovations: An Integrated Framework', in Aghion, P. and Durlauf, S., (eds), *Handbook of Economic Growth*, Chapter 2, pp. 67–110.
7. Howitt and Mayer-Foulkes, 'R&D, Implementation and Stagnation: A Schumpeterian Theory of Convergence Clubs', op.cit.

8. Greenwood, J., Hercowitz, Z. and Krusell, P., 1997, 'Long-run Implications of Investment-Specific Technological Change', *American Economic Review*, 87, pp. 342–62.
9. Parente, S. and Prescott, E., 1994, 'Barriers to Technology Adoption and Development', *Journal of Political Economy*, 102, pp. 298–321.
10. Prescott, E., 1998, 'Needed: A Theory of Total Factor Productivity', *International Economic Review*, 39, pp. 525–51.
11. Parente, S. and Prescott, E., 2000, *Barriers to Riches*. MIT Press, Cambridge.
12. Mankiw, G., Phelps, E. and Romer, P., 1995, 'The Growth of Nations', *Brookings Papers on Economic Activity*, pp. 275–326.
13. de la Fuente, A. and Domenech, R., 2001, 'Schooling Data, Technological Diffusion, and the Neo-classical Model', *American Economic Review*, 91, pp. 323–27.
14. For further information refer to Jovanovic, B. and MacDonald, G., 1994, 'Competitive Diffusion', *Journal of Political Economy*, 102, pp. 24–52; Segerstrom, P., 1994, 'Innovation, Imitation and Economic Growth', *Journal of Political Economy*, 99, pp. 807–27; Grossman, G. and Helpman, E., 1991, 'Trade, Knowledge Spillovers, and Growth', *European Economic Review*, 35, pp. 517–26; and Grossman, G. and Helpman, E., 1991, 'Quality Ladders in the Theory of Growth', *Review of Economic Studies*, 58, pp. 43–61.
15. Refer for instance, to Jovanovic, B. and Nyarko, Y., 1995, 'A Bayesian Learning Model Fitted to a Variety of Empirical Learning Curves', *Brookings Papers on Economic Activity* Microeconomics 1995, pp. 247–305; Mukoyama, T., 2003, 'Innovation, Imitation and Growth with Cumulative Technology', *Journal of Monetary Economics*, 50, pp. 361–80.
16. Jovanovic, B., Learning and Growth, in Kreps, D., and Wallis, K. (eds), 1997, *Advances in Economics and Econometrics: Theory and Applications*, Volume 2, Cambridge University Press.
17. Aghion, P. and Howitt, P., 1999, *Endogenous Growth Theory*, Cambridge: MIT Press.
18. For instance, Silverberg, G., Dosi, G. and Orsenigo, L., 1988, 'Innovation, Diversity and Diffusion: A Self-Organisation Model', *The Economic Journal*, 98, pp. 1032–54; Chiaromonte, F., Dosi, G. and Orsenigo, L., 'Innovative Learning and Institutions in the Process of Development: On the Microfoundations of Growth Regime's, in: Thomson, R. (ed.), 1993, *Learning and Technological Change*, New York; Patel, P. and Pavitt, K., 'Uneven (and Divergent) Technological Accumulation among Advanced Countries: Evidence and a Framework of Explanation', in Archibugi, D. and Michie, J. (eds), 1998, *Trade, Growth and Technical Change*, Cambridge University Press.
19. There is the possibility that countries that are at similar levels of economic development could have similar rates of innovation and therefore could club converge although there would tend to be at a divergence between the respective clusters of countries.
20. The model assumes a cessation of innovation and a zero arrival rate although this could be merely a slowdown in the rate in innovation or a lower frequency of arrival rate.
21. cf. Grossman and Helpman, 1991, 'Trade, Knowledge Spillovers, and Growth', op. cit., Grossman and Helpman, 1991, 'Quality Ladders in the Theory of Growth', op. cit., and Mukoyama, T., 2003, op. cit.

22. Sanna-Randaccio, F. and Veugelers, R., 2007, 'Multinational Knowledge Spillovers with Centralized versus Decentralized R&D: a Game Theoretic Approach', *Journal of International Business Studies*, 38, pp. 47–63.
23. Mukoyama, T., 2004, 'Diffusion and Innovation of New Technologies under Skill Heterogeneity', *Journal of Economic Growth*, 9, pp. 451–79.
24. Lloyd-Ellis, H. and Roberts, J., 2002, 'Twin Engines of Growth: Skills and Technology as Equal Partners in Balanced Growth', *Journal of Economic Growth*, 7, pp. 87–115.
25. Furman, J., Porter, M. and Stern, S., 2002, The Determinants of National Innovative Capacity, *Research Policy*, 31, pp. 899–933.
26. Idem.
27. Refer to Jovanovic, B., 'Learning and Growth', in: Kreps, D. and Wallis, K., (eds), 1997, *Advances in Economics and Econometrics: Theory and Applications, Volume 2*, Cambridge University Press.
28. cf. Mukoyama, T., 2004, 'Diffusion and Innovation of New Technologies under Skill Heterogeneity', Journal of Economic Growth, 9, pp. 451–79.
29. This is similar to Aghion, P. and Howitt, P., 1992, 'A Model of Growth through Creative Destruction', *Econometrica*, 60, pp. 323–51.
30. In this regard refer to Mukoyama, T., 2003, 'Innovation, Imitation and Growth with Cumulative Technology', *Journal of Monetary Economics*, 50, pp. 361–80.
31. Refer to Aghion, P. and Howitt, P., 2004, 'Growth with Quality-Improving Innovations: An Integrated Framework', mimeo.
32. The Bellman Equation

Basic Theory

Wälde's model (cf. Wälde, K., 1999, 'Optimal Saving under Poisson Uncertainty', *Journal of Economic Theory*, 87, pp. 194–217) is the basis for introducing a Poisson process within the stochastic framework of the problem. Wälde's model utilizes the following version of Ito's lemma. Let $z \equiv (z_1, z_2)^T$ be a vector-valued Poisson process consisting of two independent Poisson processes, z_1 and z_2. Let $f(x) \equiv (f_1(x), f_2(x))^T$, $g(x)$, and $\sigma(x) \equiv (\sigma_1(x), \sigma_2(x))^T$ be continuous real functions of $x \equiv (x_1, x_2)^T$.

Let $\mathbf{x}$ follow $d\mathbf{x} = f(\mathbf{x})dt + \sigma(\mathbf{x})dz$, then the differential $dg(\mathbf{x})$ equals

$$dg(\mathbf{x}) = [g_{x_1}(\mathbf{x})f_1(\mathbf{x}) + g_{x_2}(\mathbf{x})f_2(\mathbf{x})]dt$$
$$+ [g(x_1 + \sigma_1(\mathbf{x}), x_2) - g(\mathbf{x})]dz_1 + [g(x_1, x_2 + \sigma_2(\mathbf{x})) - g(\mathbf{x})]dz_2 \quad (3.9)$$

If a unique Poisson process defines the stochastic evolution of $g(x)$, i.e. $dz_1 = dz_2 = dz$, the differential $dg(\mathbf{x})$ becomes

$$dg(\mathbf{x}) = [g_{x_1}(\mathbf{x})f_1(\mathbf{x}) + g_{x_2}(\mathbf{x})f_2(\mathbf{x})]dt + [g(x_1 + \sigma_1(\mathbf{x}), x_2 + \sigma_2(\mathbf{x})) - g(\mathbf{x})]dz \quad (3.10)$$

At the same time, the differential generator D can be applied to $g(x)$

$$Dg(\mathbf{x}) = g_{x_1}(\mathbf{x})f_1(\mathbf{x}) + g_{x_2}(\mathbf{x})f_2(\mathbf{x}) + [g(x_1 + \sigma_1(\mathbf{x}), x_2 + \sigma_2(\mathbf{x})) - g(\mathbf{x})]a \quad (3.11)$$

where adt denotes the probability per unit of time that x jumps with amplitude of $\sigma(x)$, while $Dg(x)$ gives the expected change of $g(x)$ per unit of time.

Countries

Consider the unique Poisson process (per country) triggering the productivity increases of the innovator industry

$$d\left(\frac{\xi}{\Gamma}\right) = \left(\Gamma - \frac{\xi}{\Gamma}\right) dz_\xi$$

Replace the corresponding variables in equation (3.11) according to $x = \left(\frac{\xi}{\Gamma}\right)$, $f_1(x) = f_2(x) = 0$, $g(x) = V(x)$, $\sigma_1(x) = \left(\Gamma - \frac{\xi}{\Gamma}\right)$, $\sigma_2(x) = 0$ and $a = \theta_\xi$ to obtain

$$E\left(\frac{dV\left(\frac{\xi}{\Gamma}\right)}{dt}\right) = \theta_\xi\left[V\left(\frac{\xi}{\Gamma} + \left(\Gamma - \frac{\xi}{\Gamma}\right)\right) - V\left(\frac{\xi}{\Gamma}\right)\right]$$

Include the expected temporal evolution of the value function in the Bellman equation corresponding to this type of dynamic problems, (cf. Kamien, M. and Schwartz, N., 1981, Dynamic Optimization: The Calculus of Variations and Optimal Control in Economics and Management, Section 21, Elsevier North Holland), which is given by

$$\rho V\left(\frac{\xi}{\Gamma}\right) = \max_{n_{sn}, n_{sm}}\left[\pi(n_{sm}) + E\left(\frac{dV\left(\frac{\xi}{\Gamma}\right)}{dt}\right)\right]$$

to obtain the final Bellman equation that must be optimized by each country based on their achieved value of ξ

$$\rho V\left(\frac{\xi}{\Gamma}\right) = \max_{n_{sn}, n_{sm}}\left[\pi(n_{sm}) + \theta_\xi\left[V(\Gamma) - V\left(\frac{\xi}{\Gamma}\right)\right]\right]$$

33. Note that the RHS may be rewritten as $\theta_\xi \frac{(1-\varphi)}{n_{sn}}\left[V(\Gamma) - V\left(\frac{\xi}{\Gamma}\right)\right]$.
34. Gerschenkron, A., 1952, 'Economic Backwardness in Historical Perspective', in: Hoselitz, B. (ed.), *The Progress of Underdeveloped Areas*, Chicago: University of Chicago Press.
35. Patel, P. and Pavitt, K., 1998, 'Uneven (and divergent) technological accumulation among advanced countries: evidence and a framework of explanation', in Archibugi, D. and Michie, J. (eds), *Trade, Growth and Technical Change*, Cambridge: Cambridge University Press.
36. Refer to Parente, S. and Prescott, E., 2000, *Barriers to Riches*, Cambridge: MIT Press.
37. Refer to Fagerberg, J., Mowery, D. and Nelson, R., 2005, *The Oxford Handbook of Innovation*, Oxford: Oxford University Press.

4
Tax Competition

Michael Braulke and Jörg Schimmelpfennig

Fostering capital account convertibility was not among the mandates of the International Monetary Fund when it was founded in late 1945. And it is still not today in spite of a forceful initiative of the Fund's management in 1990 in this direction, calling for an amendment of the Articles of Agreement that would have transformed the IMF's role in capital account liberalization and capital account issues in general. Support for such an amendment was strong throughout the mid-1990s and it was not until the East Asian crisis of 1997 and the contagion spreading through Asia and beyond that the idea was eventually ceased.[1] Interestingly, Article VI of the Fund's Articles of Agreement is still in place stipulating that a 'member may not use the Fund's general resources to meet a large sustained outflow of capital' and that the Fund may even 'request a member to exercise controls to prevent such use'.

Nevertheless, since at least the 1980s and prior to the second half of the 1990s the IMF has actively encouraged member countries to open their borders to foreign investment, technology and trade as a path to economic growth, emphasizing the benefits of an unrestricted access to international capital markets and paying little if any attention to the potential risks related to the volatility of capital flows and the loss of control of the refinancing behaviour of commercial banks. It is only fairly recently that a rethinking has begun and the prudence of at least some restrictions on unfettered capital mobility is being seen.

This is somewhat surprising because the key theoretical rationale for capital account liberalization is primarily the shaky argument that capital mobility promotes an efficient global allocation of savings and a better diversification of risk.[2] This traditional view amounts to hardly more than an inappropriate generalization of Adam Smith's famous *invisible hand* passage. There he argues that a selfish individual handing his savings to the investor offering the highest rate of interest effectively, if unintentionally, maximizes its contribution to output.[3] While this conclusion is obviously correct for the case of a single country, it need not necessarily be so for two or more countries. The reason is simply that international investors also take into account expected exchange rate changes. Equilibrium in an integrated capital market with capital mobility is characterized by the covered interest rate parity which definitely does not imply that capital necessarily ends up where the real rate of return is highest let alone that real rates of return are equalized across countries as long as exchange rates are flexible. There is consequently no need to recur to the usual suspects, that is, market imperfections such as information asymmetries or domestic distortions[4] to nurture doubts as to the efficiency enhancing role of capital mobility.

The race to the bottom

Volatility of investor sentiments, herd behaviour, contagion effects, and the loss or at least impairment of monetary control are all downsides of unrestricted capital mobility. Another one is tax competition. While some emphasize the virtues of a check on the state's monopoly to set tax rates, others deplore the inequality and inefficiency aspects associated with the ability of a mobile factor to avoid taxation. It was Oates who first articulated the idea that governments, in an attempt to prevent mobile capital from migrating, are forced to adopt inefficiently low taxes on capital and a less than optimal level in the provision of public goods.[5] This view was subsequently formalized in more elaborate models by Wilson as well as Zodrow and Mieszkowski that started a broad discussion.[6]

In the late eighties and early nineties when numerous formerly closed countries started to liberalize their capital accounts the fear was voiced that even large countries would be forced to participate in a race to the bottom. Frey put that very clearly: 'Take the example of a factor ... like capital, which is perfectly mobile between countries. It will flow to the state with the lowest tax rate. In equilibrium, the tax rate in each state will be driven to zero because each one will compete for that tax base'.[7] This assertion is nothing but a straight-forward variant of the famous Bertrand paradox for price competition in homogenous markets. Indeed, if capital is perfectly mobile and nothing but the tax rate matters for its choice of location, a zero tax on capital is the only equilibrium solution. However, already minor deviations from the strong assumptions underlying Frey's proposition suffice to make the paradox disappear and to clear away the fears of a race to the bottom.

Perfectly mobile capital

Let us stick for the moment to perfect capital mobility and start first with the less than convincing notion that investors care for nothing but the tax rate. Rather, one would expect that investors put their capital where its net return is highest. Tax rates therefore do matter, but gross returns do as well. In a competitive neoclassical world with more than one factor general equilibrium requires that net returns on capital be equalized across all countries. This merely implies that countries with higher corporate taxes must have correspondingly higher gross returns on capital. It is not at all apparent whether in such a situation forces are at work that provoke a race to the bottom.

To keep things simple consider a world where all countries i work with the same neoclassical technology and charge exactly the same tax $t_i = t$ on resident capital. If country j would now raise its tax marginally to $t_j > t$, this should normally trigger a capital outflow, yet by no means a landslide that would strip it of resident capital altogether. Making capital more scarce domestically, the outflow would just have to be large enough to boost its marginal productivity to the point where again its domestic net return matches that of all other countries. The magnitude of the required outflow of capital may be small or large, depending essentially on the technology or, more precisely, the relevant elasticity of substitution. But what is more important for our purposes is that the tax hike in country j would lead to larger collections from this tax.[8] So, from a fiscal point of view, there may well be an incentive to raise taxes, but there is certainly none to lower them, let alone to start a race to the bottom.

So far, we have focused exclusively on the cost aspect of taxation, disregarding on what the resulting revenues are spent. A government investing heavily, for instance, in education and infrastructure may noticeably enhance the business environment and thus favourably influence the profitability of enterprises. The drive to migrate from countries with higher taxes referred to in the previous paragraph may hence be mitigated if not eliminated altogether through this indirect effect of taxation. Indeed, one may conceive of companies requiring certain minimum levels of infrastructure and skilled labour to succeed that would voluntarily opt for a tax higher than zero because of the resulting more suitable environment.

The nexus between what tax rate exactly an individual firm would prefer and what rate, in turn, the government would set for the entirety of all firms is technically complex and will not be pursued any further. However, it would not appear appropriate to ignore these indirect effects altogether. Furthermore, another indirect effect that should not be ignored is the impact massive migration of capital to a low tax country may have on that country's factor price system and that of the countries of origin. Ireland is a case in point. Once a low wage country,[9] its policy of low taxes has attracted so much capital that Irish wages rank now among the highest worldwide.

Partially mobile capital

As another case where the race to the bottom would come to a halt, let us return to the assumption that nothing but the tax rate matters for capital owners but assume that only a part of a country's capital is perfectly mobile while the remainder is not. More specifically, assume there are two countries, $i = 1,2$, with two types of companies: firms which are perfectly mobile, labelled *PM*, and completely immobile firms, called the domestic industrial base and labelled *DIB*. We will furthermore assume that pre-tax profits are independent of a country's flat[10] corporate tax rate t_i and write Π_i^{PM} and Π_i^{DIB} for that country's total pre-tax profits of its mobile and immobile sectors, respectively. Once all restrictions on the movement of capital are lifted, the mobile companies will move to the country offering the lowest tax rate. Country i's revenue from the corporate tax is then given by

$$T_i = t_i \Pi_i^{DIB} + \begin{pmatrix} t_i(\Pi_1^{PM} + \Pi_2^{PM}) & \text{iff} & t_i < t_j \\ \frac{1}{2} t_i(\Pi_1^{PM} + \Pi_2^{PM}) & \text{iff} & t_i = t_j \\ 0 & \text{iff} & t_i > t_j \end{pmatrix} \quad (4.1)$$

$$i, j \in 1, 2 \quad i \neq j$$

This is where tax competition sets in. But as is known from Edgeworth's model of homogeneous price competition with constrained capacities, there is a downward limit larger than zero.[11] With tax revenue from the domestic industrial base taking the role of Edgeworth's residual revenue, there must be a lower bound for the corporate tax rate, $\underline{t}_i$, that country i would not be prepared to undercut. This lower bound is defined by the downward 'switch point' where the country is indifferent between maintaining its pre-liberalization tax rate, t_i^0, and offering this lower tax rate $\underline{t}_i$ to attract mobile capital, that is where

$$t_i^0 \Pi_i^{DIB} = \underline{t}_i(\Pi_i^{DIB} + \Pi_1^{PM} + \Pi_2^{PM})$$

holds. Rearranging, we have for this lower bound

$$\underline{t}_i = t_i^0 \frac{\Pi_i^{DIB}}{\Pi_i^{DIB} + \Pi_1^{PM} + \Pi_2^{PM}} \quad (4.2)$$

which implies $0 < \underline{t}_i < t_i^0$ since all terms on the RHS are positive. Without loss of generality we may assume country 1 to be 'large' compared to country 2 in the sense that its domestic industrial base is larger, i.e. $\Pi_1^{DIB} > \Pi_2^{DIB}$. If both countries applied originally more or less identical corporate tax rates so that $t_1^0 = t_2^0$ equation (4.2) implies

$$\underline{t}_1 > \underline{t}_2 \qquad (4.3)$$

The outcome of this game depends, of course, on how it is played. If moves were to be made simultaneously, the result would be an equilibrium in mixed strategies along the lines of the original Edgeworth model. However, since legislators are not used to throw dice and, in addition, typically have to follow their own issue-related agenda of parliamentary readings, a sequential game played either as a one-shot game or over several rounds appears to be the more appropriate setup. Of these the former with the small country moving first is the only convincing one, for two reasons: first, in parliamentary democracies, once a tax system is changed, the change will typically be maintained for at least a couple of years; and second and more importantly, the large country cannot gain from moving first.

To see that, suppose the large country 1 moves first by setting its new tax rate at or above $\underline{t}_1$. In view of (4.3), such a rate could and would be undercut by the smaller country 2, leaving country 1 with but a reduced tax revenue from its domestic industrial base and no revenue whatsoever from mobile capital. Consequently, the large country 1 is better off by leaving its original tax rate unchanged and deliberately foregoing any opportunity to move first. In contrast, country 2's optimal first move would be to set t_2^* equal to $\underline{t}_1$ thereby precluding any incentive for country 1 to undercut.

The resulting Nash equilibrium is hence

$$(t_1^*, t_2^*) = (t_1^0, \underline{t}_1) \qquad (4.4)$$

which means that the 'small' country will exercise tax dumping and attract all mobile capital whereas the 'large' country will stick to its old tax regime and be left with nothing but the revenue from its domestic industrial base.[12] This result is easily extended to the case of more than two countries where again just one country – most likely the one with the smallest domestic industrial base – has an incentive to lower taxes while all others stick to their original rates. The model may thus explain why typically large countries call for 'tax harmonization' whereas small countries do not.

Conclusion

Taking Obstfeld and Taylor's stylized view on capital mobility in modern history for granted, capital mobility was very high already before World War I, dropped subsequently to very low levels through the end of World War II, to rise again sharply after the collapse of the Bretton Woods System and, in particular, after 1980.[13] Today, little prevents internationally oriented firms to settle in the country of their choice. Numerous factors play a role in this decision: taxes certainly do, but so do infrastructure, good governance, reliability of the legal system and, not least, wages. A large body of literature has focused on taxes and the fear that competition for the tax base and for jobs would force governments into a race to the bottom. In the two rather different settings discussed above we found little theoretical evidence for such a race to be inevitable. It is therefore not surprising to see that the vast empirical literature addressing this issue remains predominantly indecisive and that some studies even find evidence to the contrary.[14]

Notes

1. Tagaki, Shinji, Jeffrey Allen Chelsky *et al.*, *The IMF's Approach to Capital Account Liberalization,* Evaluation Report, Washington, DC: International Monetary Fund, 2005, p. 19.
2. Cf. Fischer, Stanley, 'Capital Account Liberalization and the Role of the IMF', in: *Should the IMF Pursue Capital Account Liberalization?*, Essays in International Finance No. 207, Department of Economics, Princeton University, 1998.
3. Smith, Adam, *An Enquiry into the Nature and Causes of the Wealth of Nations* (1776), quoted from R. H. Campell and A. S. Skinner (eds), Glasgow Edition of the Works and Correspondence of Adam Smith, Oxford: Clarendon Press, 1976, p. 456.
4. See for example Stiglitz, Joseph, 'Capital Market Liberalization, Economic Growth and Instability,' *World Development,* 28 (2000), 1075–86 and *idem,* 'Capital-Market Liberalization, Globalization, and the IMF,' *Oxford Review of Economic Policy,* 20 (2004), 57–71.
5. Oates, Wallace E., *Fiscal Federalism,* New York: Harcourt-Brace-Jovanovich, 1972.
6. Cf. Wilson, John D., 'A Theory of Interregional Tax Competition,' *Journal of Urban Economics,* 19 (1986), 296–315, and Zodrow, George R., and Peter Mieszkowski, 'Pigou, Tiebout, Property Taxation, and the Underprovision of Local Public Goods', *Journal of Urban Economics,* 19 (1986), 356–70. An authoritative survey of this literature is given in Wilson, John D., 'Theories of Tax Competition,' *National Tax Journal,* 52 (1999), 269–304.
7. Frey, Bruno, 'Intergovernmental Tax Competition', in: Charles E. McLure, Jr., Hans-Werner Sinn *et al.*, *Influence of Tax Differentials on International*

Competitiveness, Proceedings of the VIIIth Munich Symposium on International Taxation, Deventer: Kluwer Law and Taxation Publishers, 1990, 87–96, p. 87.

8. Cf. Braulke, Michael, and Giacomo Corneo, 'Capital Taxation May Survive in Open Economies', *Annals of Economics and Finance,* 5 (2004), 237–44. It is often maintained that in a context like this and if the country considered is small enough, all revenue collected from an increased tax levied on a perfectly mobile factor will have to be borne exclusively by the immobile factors of that country. What is less known, however, is that world income of this mobile factor would eventually decline by exactly what the tax raising country collects additionally. This was first shown by Bradford, David F. 'Factor Prices May Be Constant But Factor Returns Are Not', *Economics Letters,* 1 (1978), 199–203 for the case of countries of equal size and further elaborated by Kotlikoff, Laurence J., and Lawrence H. Summers, 'Tax Incidence', in: Auerbach, Alan J., and Martin Feldstein, (eds), *Handbook of Public Economics, Vol. II,* Amsterdam: North Holland, 1987, 1043–92, who reach similar conclusions for a model with two countries of unequal size.

9. For an early witness see Keynes, John M., 'Rents, Prices, and Wages', *Economic Journal,* 18 (1908), 47–3.

10. This is the typical property of the corporate tax of most industrialized countries.

11. Edgeworth, Y. Francis, 'La teoria pura del monopolio', *Giornali degli Economisti,* 40 (1897), 13–31.

12. It is quite conceivable that country 1, after loosing part of its tax base to country 2, feels the need to adjust its tax rate.

13. Obstfeld, Maurice, and Alan M. Taylor, *Global Capital Markets: Integration, Crisis and Growth,* New York: Cambridge University Press, 2004, Part II.

14. Cf. Lammert, Christian, 'Modern Welfare States under Pressure: Determinants of Tax Policy in a Globalizing World', *IRPP Working Paper Series,* No. 2004–01, Montreal: Institute for Research on Public Policy, 2004, or Mendoza, Enrique G., Linda L. Tesar, 'Why Hasn't Tax Competition Triggered a Race to the Bottom? Some Quantitative Lessons from the EU', *Journal of Monetary Economics,* 52 (2005), 163–204.

5
The Evolving Role of Industry in European Union Environmental Governance

Andrea Lenschow and Katja Rottmann

Large firms have played a crucial role in the process of European integration. The European Round Table of Industrialists, for instance, provided important inputs to the Single Market Programme in the early 1980s.[1] At the level of day-to-day policy making, firms and industrial associations act typically as pressure groups promoting their particular interests. But increasingly, industrial actors perform direct regulatory functions that have been delegated to them by the European Union (EU) authorities, hence shifting the public-private relationship in EU governance.[2] This shift is particularly interesting in the field of environmental policy. In the context of the traditional legislative approach, that is, producing binding environmental directives and regulations, industries stereotypically lobbied against costly standards. In the new governance context, industries are invited as partners in formulating and implementing environmental policy.

The automobile industry, with the Association des Constructeurs d'Automobiles Européens (ACEA) as its European interest association,[3] was one of the first industries to organize lobbying capacities in Brussels and influence most notably the history of EU automobile emission standards. In recent years, conventional lobbying or advocacy has been complemented by pursuing a participatory policy role. Two prominent examples are the so-called Auto-Oil Programme and the ACEA voluntary agreement (VA) and they serve to illustrate this shift. In the Auto-Oil Programme, both the automobile and the oil industries were invited by the European Commission to inform the traditional regulatory process by participating in a technical work programme, which aimed at providing policy makers with well founded information on how to reduce emissions from transport in a cost efficient manner. This institutionalized Industry-Commission dialogue resulted in a European Commission proposal for future emission reductions. The ACEA VA went much further in delegating responsibility to industry. The European Commission agreed to forgo regulatory activity on condition that the automobile industry engaged in self-regulatory action and succeeded in significantly reducing CO_2 emissions by 2008. It is suggested, however, that none of the 'new governance roles' – expert or self-regulatory – adopted by industry has been successful from the perspective of achieving progress for environmental protection so far.

Business roles in European governance

The literature on the system of interest intermediation in the EU is vast and it cannot be adequately summarized in a short chapter like this. We will therefore start from two important and interrelated observations and their analytical implications.

First, we note that the 'new governance' agenda in the EU suggests a change of roles for business actors from 'interested actor' to 'partner'.[4] In announcing the Fifth Environmental Action Programme in 1993, the European Commission succinctly states what it perceived to be a historic reform in the policy-making process: 'Up to the present, environmental protection in the Community has mainly been based on a legislative approach ("top-down"). The new strategy ... implies the involvement of all economic and societal partners ("bottom-up").'[5] Consequently, traditional lobbying activities of firms and business associations are complemented, and possibly replaced, by participatory roles in the regulatory process, that is, they become involved as policy addressees earlier in the process and may be consulted as experts; they may even be requested to adopt self-regulatory roles.

Furthermore, interest intermediation in the EU has always been conducted jointly – with some division of labour – through European business associations, national associations and individual firms.[6] Arguably, the European industry associations are gaining significance in the new governance context where the EU policy makers – and especially the European Commission in the policy preparation phase – require a direct interlocutor in setting up the new partnership arrangements. Rather than merely lobbying on behalf of their members, the European associations have to balance a representative (*vis-à-vis* the members) with a participatory role *vis-à-vis* EU institutions in the policy process. As it is familiar from corporatist associative structures, industry associations must serve the interest of their members, and hence secure the association's survival with financial and organizational resources that can be exerted from the members (logic of membership), and also satisfy the needs of the public authorities – typically by controlling membership behaviour – in order to secure continued access to and influence over public authorities and, hence, to extract from this exchange resources for survival, such as, recognition, toleration, concessions and subsidies (logic of influence).[7] Such service of two very differently constituted and interested principals places industry associations in a likely dilemma and one that needs to be recognized and carefully analysed before organizing new governance arrangements. There are different roles and functions performed by the automobile industry association in EU policy making and that poses difficulties in seeking an intermediate position between firms and public authorities.

Classical context of environmental policy directed at the automobile sector

Pollution from road transport was recognized early on as an important problem in European policy making. Rapid growth in this sector was a consequence of the economic development of the member states of the EU, as well as, the development in the European transport sector. Despite the close relationship with market increase, however, from the 1970s to the 1980s automobile emissions and fuel quality regulations were primarily initiated at the international level. The United Nations Economic Commission for Europe (ECE) in Geneva was the relevant competent authority for Europe. Internationally agreed regulations in this sector were subsequently adopted as EU directives.[8] But, as so many and very heterogeneous countries were members of ECE, decision making was slow and often resulted in standards at the lowest common denominator. These standards compared negatively with standards outside the ECE, most notably in the US. American emission reduction targets not only better served to protect the environment, they also led to a veritable push in the development of new technologies.[9]

With this in mind, some European countries, such as, Germany and the Netherlands, pushed for tighter emission standards within the EU. In Germany, especially, the environmental problem of *Waldsterben* had become a major issue in the public debate. However, effective European-level decision making was hindered by controversies between member states, technical uncertainties and a lack of organized environmental lobby group pressure. Some member states, such as, the United Kingdom, were very much opposed to the idea of emissions standards at the American level.[10] New discussion fora were established at the European level in order to overcome this deadlock in decision making. The Motor Vehicle Expert Group (MVEG), for instance, was set up in 1985 to advance common problem solving at the technical level. It consisted of technical experts from the member states and industry, but environmental organizations, such as the European Environmental Bureau (EEB) only gained access to the meetings of the MVEG three years later.[11] Nevertheless, reflecting the continuing high level of conflict, negotiations about stricter standards lasted from 1983 until 1991 when the Directive 91/441/EC on mandatory emission limits for automobiles, referred to as EURO I, was finally adopted. This Directive, however, may be considered a breakthrough in automobile emission policy. It stipulated mandatory emission limits that could only be met by applying the three-way catalytic converter. As this technology does not work with leaded gasoline, lead-free gasoline was introduced to the European market. Emission limits were subsequently tightened in EURO II in 1994 and the EU rather than ECE now became the central decision-making forum on this issue for member states.

There are several reasons for this unexpected breakthrough in automobile emission policy. The institutional set-up at the European level as well as national priorities had changed. The European Parliament (EP) had gained influence with the introduction of the co-decision procedure and with increased power argued for 'greening' the single European market. Some so-called environmental laggards, such as Greece, had realized the importance of limiting air pollution and Directive 91/441/EC became one of the most intensely lobbied decisions at EU level. The automobile industry, which was initially divided between producers of large and small automobiles, eventually perceived common standards as technically possible and as mutually advantageous,[12] thereby, facilitating final agreement.

Despite this breakthrough decision, the problem of combating air pollution from automobiles has not been controlled. EU officials still saw the need to set even stricter limits for automobile emissions such as carbon monoxide, nitrogen oxide and others. During the 1990s, another substance became critical to environmental policy-making which had not been taken into account by EURO norms: carbon dioxide (CO_2) leading to global climate change. While the total EU15 CO_2 emissions have decreased in most other sectors the transport sector still produces increasing pollution levels of CO_2.[13] This development stands in sharp contrast to the EU's commitments in the Kyoto Protocol, where it agreed to reduce its CO_2 emissions to approximately 8 per cent below 1990 levels by 2008 and called for further action by the EU.

Generally, traditional environmental policy making directed at regulating the automobile industry was characterized by a high level of conflict and contingent on either dividing an otherwise powerful automobile lobby or convincing it of the merits of common environmental standards. EU standard setting therefore tended to merely confirm the technical *status quo* in lengthy decision making procedures. Nevertheless, automobile manufacturers and their interest associations perceived the constant threat of regulatory action, especially once majority voting and parliamentary co-decision making had been accepted in the EU. Furthermore, green states as well as environmental interest groups gained political opportunities. Hence, both industry and the EU authorities had an interest, though for different reasons, in looking for alternatives to traditional regulatory policy making in order to achieve industrial and environmental objectives in a more effective, and controllable, manner. The Auto-Oil Programme and the ACEA Voluntary Agreement were such alternatives that were introduced to deal with the improvements of the EURO norms in the former case and to control CO_2 emissions in the latter.

The Auto-Oil programme

The Auto-Oil I Programme consisted of a close and institutionalized cooperation between the European Commission and the automobile and oil industries during the policy-formulation phase. It aimed at establishing ambitious and cost-efficient emission standards for automobiles and fuel quality. The European Commission hoped with this new approach to advance environmental policy and overcome existing barriers while respecting industry's concerns about rising costs and international competitiveness. It hoped to improve 'rational' policy making by way of addressing industry less as an interest organization but as owners of technical and scientific information that can be channeled into decision making in order to satisfy environmental and industrial objectives. Conceptually, the coordinated approach implied a departure from the BAT (best available technology) principle by putting more emphasis on marginal utilities of technological innovation and placing a new emphasis on environmental quality objectives to be achieved jointly by all relevant industries responsible for environmental pollution.

The Auto-Oil Programme also constituted an attempt, primarily by the Directorate General (DG) responsible for the environment, to improve cross-sectoral policy coordination between the automobile and the oil sector to jointly arrive at cost-effective solutions. One has to keep in mind that in the field of air pollution from the transport sector with regard to several polluting substances progress can be made by improving fuel quality and by advancing motor technologies. Previously, in a sectorally fragmented setting, the oil and automobile industries were inclined to shift responsibility for reducing emissions to the respective other. This was reflected in organizational relations inside the European Commission. Inspired by a US research programme in the 1990s, the Auto-Oil Air Quality Improvement Research Programme (AQIRP), that brought together public authorities and industry associations to develop automobile and fuel standards, DGs Environment and Energy began to push the idea of the Auto-Oil Programme. In 1992, the European Commission organized a conference titled 'Auto Emissions 2000', whose aim it was to discuss future automobile emission standards for the year 2000, which proved to be an important impetus for the development of the Auto-Oil programme. Against the initial opposition of DG Industry, concerned about losing the leadership in the process, and of the EP and environmental NGOs, who aimed at maintaining the BAT principle as well as their political participation rights, the Auto-Oil Programme was set up and a contract on a two-year European Programme on Emissions, Fuels and Engine technologies (EPEFE) was eventually signed in 1993 between the European Commission and the relevant industry associations ACEA and EUROPIA, the European Association of the Oil Industry.

The Auto-Oil Programme aimed to develop the EURO III norms for automobiles and other vehicles for the year 2000 (Auto-Oil I). A second phase of the programme was envisaged to develop EURO IV norms for 2005 (Auto-Oil II). These norms were supposed to be based on joint research uncovering the most cost-effective measures to reduce automobile emissions. It was thought that this joint research would inform decision making in an 'objective' manner.[14] The Auto-Oil I Programme included research on the emission performances of automobiles and the relationship between automobile emissions and fuel quality.[15] This research was carried out by ACEA and EUROPIA in the framework of the mentioned EPEFE program. It also included cost-effectiveness studies for different packages of measures by a consultancy under the supervision of DG Industry in order to identify those measures that would help to meet the air quality targets in the most cost-effective way. Furthermore, modelling to predict the future air quality for a range of pollutants was included. Where future air quality was predicted to fall below an acceptable standard, namely EU and WHO air quality targets, appropriate emission reduction targets were established.

All research efforts were coordinated by a tripartite working group consisting of ACEA, EUROPIA and the DG Environment, which chaired this working group. In 1996, the European Commission tabled two legislative proposals on the basis of Auto-Oil I. These were a proposal on automobile emissions with binding targets for 2000 and indicative targets for 2005[16] and a proposal on fuel quality targets for petrol and diesel with binding targets for 2000.[17] The commission also published an announcement that targets for 2005 shall be developed by the second phase of the Auto-Oil Programme, and a legally non-binding communication on a future strategy to control atmospheric emissions.[18]

Outcome of the Auto-Oil experiment

The Auto-Oil Programme was criticized on substantive, as well as, procedural grounds. Substantively, the programme was argued to lack ambition, to focus too narrowly on human health issues and to fail in taking sufficiently into account social and environmental costs.[19] A reason for this was seen in the European Commission's over-reliance on industry for information which then led to a situation of capture. Friedrich and colleagues[20] argue that the EC overestimated its own expertise and ability to control the process while underestimating the automobile and oil industries' possibilities to influence the proposal. In light of these substantive problems those actors that were sidelined by the European Commission during the policy formulation phase, that is, the EP, some member states and NGOs, pointed to procedural problems in the programme that were considered responsible for substantive deficits, such as, lack of transparency and access for non-industrial actors.

This dissatisfaction with the policy formulation process shaped the decision-making phase, which was conducted following traditional procedures, through 'co-decision' of the European Council and the EP. The Council first was split on the two European Commission's legislative proposals; the reputed 'green states', Germany, the Netherlands, Sweden and Austria, MEPs criticizing the proposals as being too weak, while the UK specifically refused to consider stronger standards. As already indicated, the EP was very critical on both substantive and procedural grounds and a wide majority of MEPs opposed the European Commission proposal during the first reading in April 1997. A change of government in the UK shifted the Council position in the direction of the EP and in the conciliation committee it was decided in June 1998 to significantly go beyond the environmental standards proposed by the European Commission. Emissions standards for automobiles were made mandatory for

2005, that is, implementing EURO III and IV simultaneously and fuel standards were considerably strengthened,[21] hence strengthening both directives.

With the return to traditional procedures during decision making interest intermediation also reverted likewise. The decision-making process was accompanied by intensive lobbying efforts by NGOs and industry.[22] Compensating limited access to the European Commission during the formulation phase, NGOs put much energy into influencing the outcome of the negotiations at all other levels, from members of the EP and members of national parliaments to government representatives.[23] A strong alliance of counter-balancing forces of those considered green member states, the EP and NGOs was formed not only for substantive reasons but also as a principled reaction to having been sidelined by an industry–European Commission coalition.[24] Interestingly, both industry sectors that had had privileged access during policy formulation under condition of cross-sectoral cooperation, now discontinued joint industry action and even undermined the European Commission's proposal in pushing sector-specific interests. Indeed, the automobile industry proposed to increase further fuel standards, although this was the domain of the oil industry. According to a European Commission official the automobile industry had appreciated the process but did not like the outcome of the tripartite initiative.[25] The oil industry reacted similarly to the proposal by threatening to close down old refineries, especially in southern Europe, where it would become difficult to meet the new standards. This campaign was perceived by many parliamentarians as extremely aggressive, not raising much support. Moreover, both the automobile and the oil industries were internally divided. Some northern European oil companies informed the EP that the ambitious fuel standards put forward by the EP were technically feasible and economically viable[26] and single automobile manufacturers, such as, Renault formed a temporary alliance with environmental NGOs.[27] In short, industrial lobbying was intense but not very successful.

As a consequence of having been corrected in the decision making phase of Auto-Oil I, the European Commission subsequently relinquished the exclusive tripartite approach and broadened participation in the Auto Oil II Programme. As the EURO IV norms had already been decided, the second phase of the programme aimed at laying the analytical foundations for future decisions from 2005 onwards and assessing future air quality and appropriate policy measures.

The Auto-Oil programme aimed at shifting the role of industry during the policy formulation phase from that of a lobby to that of technical consultants. The assumption was that the European Commission proposal would improve due to better and, more importantly, more objective information. For the industry associations this implied that they were expected to adapt their mode of influence in the sense of placing the objective of common problem solving before insisting on their membership's interest. Moreover, both industry associations, ACEA and EUROPIA, were even expected to cooperate, that is, each of them adopting a cross-sectoral, and cross-membership, perspective.

Both in terms of the logic of influence and the logic of membership the programme had politically unanticipated effects, although this was not unusual from a theoretical perspective. The industries were biased towards protecting their respective membership and exploiting the opportunities of new access channels, adopting the partnership role with the European Commission comparatively easily. Wurzel states that the 'DG Environment favoured the adoption of relatively ambitious standards, but had overestimated its own capacity to successfully conclude such a resource-intensive and complex programme as the Auto-Oil I Programme while underestimating the knowledge and power resources of the corporate actors involved'.[28] In other words, the European Commission was naïve to assume it could hold industry to a mere expert role given its incapacity to control. Such imbalance invited regulatory capture of the European Commission during the policy formulation phase.

Besides being in the position to exploit an imbalanced situation, industry had no real incentives to become an agent of the European Commission considering that its exclusive access to the policy-making process discontinued following formulation of these policy proposals. Notwithstanding the importance of the formulation phase, for both establishing the lines of discussion and pre-structuring viable majorities among decision makers, the policy proposals prepared in the tripartite setting were in no way binding for Council and the EP and the arena was now once more opened for multiple interests to intervene. In such a situation the industry associations would clearly adopt a stronger members' interest perspective and defend the automobile and oil industries respectively. Furthermore, individual firms may pursue their own interests by opposing other industry association members if the compromise negotiated within the association or in the tripartite arrangements appears unsatisfactory. In other words, the cooperative structure that was built into the Auto-Oil Programme was likely to disintegrate in the pluralist and conflictual context of decision making.

Auto-Oil II was a concession to the EP and non-industrial interests, and to democratic legitimacy. But by returning to pluralist patterns, it is unlikely to produce credible partnerships between the automobile and oil industries. Likewise, it is unlikely to effectively overcome obstruction in decision making. Due to this the Auto-Oil programmes were not the final governance experiment established for combating air pollution by automobiles.

ACEA Voluntary agreement

The voluntary agreement (VA)[29] developed between the ACEA association and the European Commission DGs Environment and Industry was signed in 1998 and aimed at reducing the level of CO_2 emissions from automobiles by 25 per cent to a value of 140g CO_2/km by 2008 compared to 1995.[30] A VA appeared a promising solution to both the European Commission and to industry. Following the Kyoto commitments, pressure mounted on the European Commission to develop policy solutions for reducing the CO_2 emissions from the transport sector. The alternatives to product regulation, namely the introduction of fiscal measures or interventions into the mobility behaviour of European citizens, proved politically infeasible. But, it also turned out that it was technically difficult to develop a clear standard because the CO_2 emissions of an automobile depend on many different features, such as, the size of the vehicle, its weight and the power of its engine. A collective solution developed among the automobile manufacturers would free the European Commission of the tricky business of proposing a complex regulatory scheme, and it was considered both efficacious and fair by the diverse group of automobile builders. The automobile industry, in turn, was confronted with a credible regulatory threat, despite the political difficulty any European Commission proposal would confront in the decision-making process, and feared that a CO_2 standard would limit its flexibility to construct a wide range of automobiles, especially larger automobiles such as Sports Utility Vehicles (SUVs).

ACEA, therefore, put forward to the European Commission the idea of a voluntary agreement. The automobile industry was familiar with this instrument since the German automobile industry association, VDA, had established a VA in 1995. The approach of a VA had the advantage of setting an average target for the whole sector while leaving it open to industry how to achieve it. Especially the manufacturers of larger automobiles such as BMW or Volvo, favoured a voluntary approach. Bernd Pieschetsrieder, the then President of ACEA and also chief executive officer (CEO) of BMW, was able to convince all constructers of the advantages of a VA, including those of relatively smaller automobiles who could potentially have favoured a uniform standard, as well as, some member states with an important automobile industry.[31]

Inside the European Commission, DG Enterprise and Industry supported a voluntary approach as they did not want to endanger the competitiveness of European automobile manufacturers. DG Environment was more sceptical given the legally non-binding character of the agreement. Finally, the Commission agreed on a voluntary approach taking into account that other measures would probably not be accepted by the Council.[32] A Community strategy to reduce CO_2 emissions from automobiles was developed which consisted of three elements: a voluntary agreement with the automobile industry, a framework for fiscal measures and a fuel economy consumer information scheme.[33] This strategy was subsequently approved by the Council.

The targets of the VA reflected a compromise between the European Commission, supported by the EP, who had previously aimed at an average value of 120g CO_2/km for new automobiles by 2008 at the latest, and ACEA proposing a target of 167g CO_2/km by 2005. Due to these divergent positions, the negotiations were delayed until 1998 when the European Commission made it clear that it was going to follow the legislative route unless ACEA would accept a 25 per cent reduction of the CO_2 emissions, which meant a value of 140g CO_2/km. ACEA finally agreed in order to avoid uniform legal standards.

More specifically, the VA agreement of 1998 consisted of a commitment by all members of ACEA on one side and a European Commission recommendation which officially recognized the commitment in February 1999,[34] on the other. The text of the ACEA agreement set specific targets for the commitment to a reduction in the average CO_2 emissions of new automobiles by 25 per cent by 2008 compared to 1995 to a value of 140g CO_2/km, an interim target of 165–170g CO_2/km by 2003 which corresponds to a CO_2 emissions reduction of 9–11 per cent compared to 1995, and the introduction of automobile models emitting 120g CO_2/km or less in the EU market by 2000 by some manufacturers.[35]

Similar to the Auto-Oil exercise the ACEA agreement placed the automobile industry in an exclusive relation with the European Commission. The negotiations were led by the European Commissioners responsible and the president of ACEA. While the Council was regularly informed and consulted by the European Commission, the EP remained on the sidelines and '[p]ublic participation has been almost non-existent, with NGOs only having been consulted once'.[36] For the implementation phase, ACEA agreed to assess compliance with the commitments in a joint monitoring procedure with the European Commission, as well as conducting a joint major review of the agreement in 2003. It was agreed that the emission data provided for the monitoring reports would be aggregated data indicating the average for all automobile constructers rather than revealing the achievements of individual constructers.[37] While environmental NGOs complained about a lack of transparency,[38] this arrangement secured a certain stability of the agreement and facilitated internal compromises between the members of ACEA. Nevertheless, because this arrangement made public control difficult, the EP and the Council passed a monitoring decision in 2000,[39] which obliged each EU member state to provide data on CO_2 emissions from newly registered automobiles from 2003 onwards, so that independent verification of the results of the agreement became possible.

Outcome of the ACEA voluntary agreement

The implementation of the VA consisted of various elements. In the immediate interaction between ACEA and the European Commission, regular monitoring and reporting constituted the main implementation activities. ACEA would have preferred a simple monitoring system, such as an exchange of letters stating the progress of implementation, but, the European Commission, confronted with criticism from the EP and NGOs, insisted on a more detailed monitoring procedure with joint monitoring reports.[40] Hence, the European Commission and ACEA developed a common reporting format and established working procedures: Regular meetings took place between European Commission and ACEA officials in order to discuss the development of automobile emissions and to produce the annual monitoring report, which was then adopted by the two relevant Directors General of the European Commission and by the President of ACEA. The European Commission prepared a communication for the EP and the Council on the basis of the joint monitoring report. Both documents were published on the website of DG Environment.[41] Apart from the joint monitoring and reporting, the European Commission continued to develop legislative measures on CO_2 emissions in order to have a credible threat if ACEA was unable to reach the agreed targets. In accordance with the 'three element strategy' further measures such as consumer information on the fuel economy of new automobiles and fiscal measures were developed.

The regular meetings at the working level established a close contact between the European Commission and ACEA. ACEA had one and the European Commission two officials from DG Environment and DG Enterprise, respectively, collaborating on a part-time basis on the ACEA agreement. Furthermore, ACEA paid an independent research institute to obtain the CO_2 emission data and, following the monitoring decision, member states were required to allocate resources for the creation of the independent monitoring system from 2003. ACEA invested in the VA in order to stay a partner of the European Commission which at the same time kept emphasizing its prime position in the hierarchy, partly to acquiesce to critics in the EP and among environmental NGOs who considered there was favourable treatment of the automobile industry and to ensure the automobile industry's compliance.

Vis-à-vis its members, ACEA had relatively limited authority and it focused its activities on tasks of coordination. The efforts of automobile constructers in reducing CO_2 emission were discussed quarterly at the CEO meetings. Compared to monitoring and reporting, where ACEA was able to reach compromises with the European Commission, ACEA could not command but only persuade its members to comply with the agreed emission reductions. Despite a relatively small membership and a widely shared interest in avoiding EU regulations, that is, a favourable context for avoiding free-rider problems or the exit of individual members,[42] ACEA was limited in what it could offer to its members other than restraining the European Commission's regulatory urge. This relatively weak framework for committing the automobile industry to the agreed emission reductions became apparent in the process of implementation.

At first, ACEA members were able to reduce CO_2 emissions from new automobiles from an average of 185g CO_2/km in 1995 to 161g CO_2/km in 2004 which represents a reduction of 13 per cent.[43] However, to achieve the target of 140g CO_2/km by 2008 more had to be done. This was signalled 'top-down' in a communication to the Council and the EP, where the European Commission emphasized the significance of the automobile industry meeting this target, which it considered feasible.[44] In addition, both European Commissioners responsible underlined that the European Commission would pursue other measures to ensure that the CO_2 reductions are achieved if the automobile industry does not conform to its commitment.[45] However, potentially undermining the European Commission's hierarchical gestures were activities of the high level expert group CARS 21, the Competitive Automotive Regulatory System for the twenty-first century.[46] This group had been set up by the European Commission's DG Enterprise and Industry and ACEA in 2005 to develop ideas for increasing the competitiveness of the European automotive industry. This expert group emphasized that there are other measures to reduce CO_2 emission besides improving motor technology such as the driver's behaviour, termed 'eco-driving' or tyre pressure, effectively shifting some of the responsibility from industry to users. It especially suggested that the European Commission's aim to raise the emission target to 120g CO_2/km by 2012 may have negative implications for the industry's competitiveness.

Hence the commitment of the automobile industry to stick to the VA's targets (or go beyond) vanished and it soon became obvious that the automobile industry would not reach its voluntary target for 2008. Following though on earlier threats the European Commission published a communication outlining its future strategy in February 2007[47] announcing a legislative framework for new automobiles and vans which it planned to publish by the end of 2007.[48] The reduction target would be 120g CO_2/km by 2012, whereby 130g CO_2/km shall be achieved through improvements in vehicle technology and further 10g CO_2/km through additional measures such as efficiency improvements for tyres or air conditioning or the use of biofuels. This combined target reflects some concession to the automobile industry and DG Industry.

In December 2007 the European Commission proposed a legislative proposal under the co-decision procedure. At its publication, this proposal was heavily contested by the automobile constructers as well as some automobile constructing countries, especially those countries that produce automobiles with high CO_2 emissions, such as Germany. Following lengthy and complicated discussions within the Council and the EP, the proposal was finally adopted in December 2008. Due to heavy resistance from some member states as well as the automobile industry, the proposal of the European Commission was weakened. A legally binding target of 130g CO_2/km was only fixed for 2015 instead of 120g CO_2/km by 2012 which had originally been foreseen in the (non-binding) VA.

While the ACEA VA contributed to the debate on the issue of emissions the agreed environmental targets were not reached and despite the hierarchical presence imposed by the European Commission and ACEA's control of its members it was insufficient to maintain the agreement. Compared to the Auto-Oil agreement, the European Commission's role appeared paradoxically strong. Furthermore, despite the voluntary nature of the agreement, the European Commission could hold the automobile industry accountable by relying on independent information of the progress made. Its regulatory threat was somewhat volatile, considering a strong discourse about international competitiveness inside the European Commission and especially in DG Industry and given potential decision-making blockades inside the Council, both undermining strong environmental policy. However, the parallel discourse on climate change and the international commitments made in the context of the Kyoto Protocol worked in favour of imposing regulatory action. Considering this top-down pressure and the exclusive partnership role ACEA had as long as it met its commitments, it weighs heavy that ACEA proved incapable to coordinate and control its members. While the ACEA members could be convinced – possibly due to the personal leadership of Pieschetsrieder or the powerful role of large manufacturers – to sign the VA, during implementation market pressures weighed heavier than organizational ties inside ACEA or the incentive of no regulatory action at EU level.

Conclusion

There are two new forms of industry-Community relations in the field of EU environmental policy as outlined in the Auto-Oil programme and the ACEA VA initiatives. In the Auto-Oil programme, industry at first effectively 'captured' the Commission's initiatives towards improving environmental performance with the consequence that a weak proposal was developed. Then EP and the Council stepped in and raised environmental regulatory standards against the will of industry. Also the ACEA VA had come under severe criticism as it had become clear that the automobile industry did not meet its own regulatory commitments. In late 2007 the Commission presented a proposal for regulatory action, thus returning to the top-down approach of law-making. The well-known concepts 'logic of membership' and 'logic of influence'[49] were used to characterize the governance role of ACEA (and EUROPIA in the Auto-Oil programme) and to illustrate how an organizational dilemma translates into a governance dilemma, where the replacement of hierarchical relations seems to depend on the hierarchy's persistence, at least in a shadowy form, both inside the industry federation and within EU-industry relations.

'New Governance' and the establishment of partnership or network relations between public and private actors has become much *en vogue* in the European Union policy discourse. Both, the Auto-Oil programme, exploring the joint potential for reducing air pollution by the automobile and the oil industry, and the ACEA voluntary agreement to reduce the CO_2 emissions of automobiles place European industrial associations in the position of the exclusive interlocutor or, in new governance-speak, 'partner' of the European Commission. In this role they are expected to act on behalf of its member firms, and secure their compliance. The Auto-Oil programme and the ACEA VA initiatives illustrate that this 'conversion' of participatory rights into rule commitment and compliance is organizationally highly demanding and likely to exceed the capacities of European industrial associations and political structures.

Interestingly, both governance experiments ended with a return to traditional legislative policy making with heavy lobbying activities of individual industrial actors. In the Auto-Oil case this could be considered the consequence of a design failure in the programme – limiting the partnership arrangement to the policy formulation phase and ignoring the conflicting interests of two industries. The ACEA VA seemed more promising at first, displaying several textbook elements of a successful VA, both in terms of creating membership commitment and in securing top-down control. But eventually it faltered as well and neither the shadow of regulatory hierarchy created by EU policy makers nor the organizational strength of ACEA in balancing membership and influence proved sufficient.

Arguably, with regard to both dimensions, the logics of membership and influence, partnership-based policy making suffers structural problems at EU level where we face the absence of a legitimated government that is capable of hierarchy and the presence of highly heterogeneous and competing business actors that resist collective action. Hence, new governance formats relying heavily on the cooperation between European Commission, interest federations and firms risk underestimating the challenge for European industry federations to balance membership and influence logics in a highly competitive and politically only loosely coupled context.

Notes

1. Refer to Green-Cowles, M., 2005, 'Setting the Agenda for a New Europe: The ERT and EC 1992', *Journal of Common Market Studies*, 33 (4), pp.501–26.
2. Egan, M., 2001, *Constructing a European Market. Standards, Regulation, and Governance*, Oxford University Press.
3. All European car manufacturers are represented by ACEA. At the moment, ACEA has 15 members: Bayerische Motoren Werke (BMW), DAF Trucks, Daimler, Fiat, Ford Europe, General Motors Europe, Jaguar and Land Rover, MAN Nutzfahrzeuge, Porsche, Peugeot Citroen, Renault, Scania, Toyota Europe, Volkswagen and Volvo.
4. Commission of the European Communities, 2001, 'European Governance. A White Paper', COM 2001 428 final, Brussels.
5. *Official Journal of the European Communities*, 1993,'Towards Sustainability. A European Community programme of policy and action in relation to the environment and sustainable development', OJ C 138 5, Luxembourg.

6. Refer to Eising, R., 2007, 'Institutional context, organizational resources and strategic choices: Explaining interest group access in the European Union', *European Union Politics* 8 (3).

7. Cf. Schmitter, P. C. and Streeck, W., 1999, 'The Organization of Business Interests. Studying the Associative Action of Business in Advanced Industrial Societies', MPIfG Discussion Paper 99/1, Cologne.

8. Friedrich, A., Tappe, M. and Wurzel, R., 2000, 'A New Approach to EU Environmental Policy-making? The Auto-Oil I Programme', *Journal of European Public Policy*, 7 (4), pp.593–612.

9. Wurzel, R., 2002, *Environmental Policy-Making in Britain, Germany and the European Union. The Europeanisation of air and water pollution control*. Manchester University Press, p.93.

10. In the area of car emission standards, Germany and the United Kingdom had fundamentally different positions. Germany pushed for ambitious regulation similar to the US model whereas the United Kingdom was very much opposed to this. This opposition is described in detail by Wurzel, 2002, *Environmental Policy-making*.

11. Ibid., p.139.

12. Arp, H., 1993, 'Technical Regulation and Politics: The Interplay between Economic Interests and Environmental Policy Goals in the EC Car Emission Legislation', in: Liefferink, J., Lowe, P. and Mol, A.,(eds), *European Integration and Environmental Policy*, John Wiley and Sons Ltd, London and New York, pp.150–71; and Holzinger, K., 1994, 'Politik des kleinsten gemeinsamen Nenners? Umweltpolitische Entscheidungsprozesse in der EG am Beispiel der Einführung des Katalysatorautos', Berlin.

13. European Environmental Agency, 2007, 'Transport and Environment: on the way to a new common transport policy, TERM 2006: indicators tracking transport and environment in the EU', EEA Report No 1/2007, Copenhagen. Other pollutant emissions such as nitrogen oxides, NOx, and carbon monoxide, CO, could be reduced considerably by the measures that have been taken by the EU, although air quality problems persist, especially in urban areas.

14. Commission of the European Communities, 2000, 'A Review of the Auto-Oil II Programme. Communication from the Commission', COM 2000 626 final, Brussels, p.4.

15. Wurzel, 2002, *Environmental Policy-making*, p.158.

16. Proposal for a European Parliament Directive 96/0164 (COD) relating to measures to be taken against air pollution by emissions from motor vehicles and amending Council Directives 70/156/EEC and 70/220/EEC. Refer to the Commission of the European Communities, 1996, A future strategy for the control of atmospheric emissions from road transport taking into account the results from the Auto/Oil Programme, COM 1996 248 final, Brussels.

17. Proposal for a European Parliament and Council Directive 96/0163 (COD) relating to the quality of petrol and diesel fuels and amending Council Directive 93/12/EEC. Cf.: Commission of the European Communities, 1996, 'A future strategy', op.cit.

18. Ibid.

19. Wurzel, 2002, *Environmental Policy-making*, op.cit., p.163.

20. Friedrich *et al.*, 2000, 'A New Approach', op.cit., p.598.

21. Wurzel, 2002, *Environmental Policy-making*, op.cit., p.164ff.

22. Refer to Warleigh, A., 2000, 'The hustle: citizenship practice, NGOs and 'Policy coalitions' in the European Union – the cases of Auto Oil, drinking water and unit pricing', in *Journal of European Public Policy*, 7 (2), pp.229–43.
23. Refer to Friends of the Earth, *The Auto Oil Programme: the need for cleaner cars and fuels*, Briefing from Friends of the Earth.
24. Wettestad, J., 2006, *The Effectiveness of EU Auto-Oil: A Slippery Business?*, Lysaker, p.4.
25. Friedrich *et al.*, 2000, 'A New Approach', op.cit., p.599.
26. Wurzel, 2002, *Environmental Policy-making*, op.cit., p.167.
27. Friedrich, A., Tappe, M. and Wurzel, R., 1998, 'The Auto Oil Programme: An Interim Critical Assessment', *European Environmental Law Review*, 1998, pp.104–11.
28. Wurzel, 2002, *Environmental Policy-making*, op.cit., p.161.
29. The title of the agreement is: 'ACEA commitment on CO_2 emission reductions from new passenger cars in the framework of an environmental agreement between the European Commission and ACEA. ACEA, ACEA's CO_2 Commitment', Brussels, 1998.
30. In 1995, the average CO_2 emission of the total number of cars manufactured was 186g CO_2/km.
31. Rottmann, K., 2005, Neue Formen der Governance in der EU: Die Bedeutung freiwilliger Vereinbarungen in der europäischen Umweltpolitik, Master's Thesis, Osnabrück.
32. Keay-Bright, S., 2000, A critical analysis of the voluntary fuel economy agreement, established between the European automobile manufacturers and the European Commission, Brussels, p.19.
33. Commission of the European Communities, 1995, 'A Community strategy to reduce CO_2 emissions from passenger cars and improve fuel economy', COM 1995 689 final.
34. Official Journal of the European Communities, 1999, 'Commission recommendation of 5 February 1999 on the reduction of CO2 emissions from passenger cars', OJ L 40, Luxembourg, pp. 49–50.
35. ACEA, 2002, 'commitment on CO_2 emission reductions', op.cit., p.11.
36. Volpi, G. and Singer, S., 2002, 'EU-level agreements: a successful tool? Lessons from the Agreement with the automotive industry', in ten Brink, P. (ed.), *Voluntary Environmental Agreements: Process, Practice and Future Use*, Sheffield, p.150.
37. ACEA, 2002, 'commitment on CO_2 emission reductions', op.cit., p.12.
38. World Resources Institute, SAM Group, 2005, 'Transparency issues with the ACEA agreement: Are investors driving blindly?, Washington/Zurich.
39. Official Journal of the European Communities, 2000, Decision No 1753/2000/EC of the European Parliament and the Council of 22 June 2000 establishing a scheme to monitor the average specific emissions of CO_2 from new passenger cars, OJ L 202, Luxembourg, pp.1–13.
40. Rottmann, 2005, Die Bedeutung freiwilliger Vereinbarungen, op.cit., p.63.
41. Refer to http://europa.eu.int/comm/environment/co^2/co^2_monitoring.htm.
42. Cf. Rottmann, K. and Lenschow, A. 2008, 'Privatising' EU Governance: Emergence and Performance of Voluntary Agreements in European Environmental Policy', in: Conzelmann, T. and Smith, R. (eds), *Multi-level Governance in the European Union: Taking Stock and Looking Ahead*, Baden-Baden.

43. Commission of the European Communities, 2006, 'Implementing the Community Strategy to Reduce CO_2 Emissions from Cars: Sixth Annual Communication on the Effectiveness of the Strategy', COM 2006 463 final, Brussels, pp. 3 and 9.
44. Ibid, p. 8
45. Press release IP/06/1134, 2006, 'CO_2 emissions from new cars down by more than 12% since 1995', Brussels, 29 August.
46. For further information, see http://ec.europa.eu/enterprise/automotive/pagesbackground/competitiveness/cars21.htm (20.08.2006).
47. Commission of the European Communities, 2007, 'Results of the review of the Community Strategy to reduce CO_2 emissions from passenger cars and light-commercial vehicles', COM 2006 19 final, Brussels.
48. Other pillars of the strategy corresponded to the recommendations of the CARS 21 expert group. They included measures to promote the purchase of efficient cars such as improved labelling and an EU code of good practice on car marketing and advertising to promote more sustainable consumption patterns.
49. Refer to Schmitter, Streeck 1999, 'The Organization of Business Interests', op.cit.

6
Opportunities for Firms in Reducing Greenhouse Gases through the Kyoto Protocol Flexibility Mechanisms

Gianluca Rubagotti

Climate change has become one of the most frequently debated issues of the multilateral agenda. International organizations such as the United Nations (UN), the European Union (EU), the Group of Eight (G8) deem global warming as a pressing problem, with potential consequences on many concrete aspects of daily life, such as, the way we produce and consume energy and the means of transport we use. Although climate change involves different kinds of expertise, and has been studied by scientists, economists, lawyers, policy-analysts, the first step is to focus our attention on the scientific problem to which the legal texts want to find a solution, that is, global warming of the earth.

The scientific aspect of climate change

Everything revolves around the concept of the greenhouse effect. This is a non-technical expression to indicate the process of absorption and release of solar energy by the terrestrial atmosphere. The energy coming from the sun is in part absorbed by the earth, and in part it flows back towards the original source. Inside the atmosphere though there are several gases, whose characteristic is to be able to trap part of the energy that has not been absorbed by the earth.

This process is of paramount importance, since without this energy being kept in the atmosphere, the average temperature of the earth would be around $-18°$, a level preventing human life. The warming deriving from this function of the atmosphere results in an increase in the temperature of about $33°$. The average level of the temperature of the soil is therefore around $15°$.[1] An important concept to underline is the difference between concentration and emission. By the first we mean a stock, which is the actual presence of the various greenhouse gases (GHG) in the atmosphere, and which is directly influenced by the level of emissions, in terms of the flows of GHGs into the atmosphere. But the general notion of a relationship based on the stock-flow concepts is not enough to give a full idea of the complexity of the problem. GHGs are in fact of various kinds, and each has got its own peculiarities, in terms of the ability to trap the energy, of persistence in the atmosphere and consequently of the time it takes them to fall into decay.[2]

The international community has striven to put in place concrete actions with a view to combating the negative influence that human activities have on the earth's climate, in terms of increase in the emissions and consequently in the concentrations of GHGs. In 1988 a scientific body, the Intergovernmental Panel on Climate Change (IPCC), was established under the auspices of the United Nations Environmental Programme (UNEP)[3] and of the World Meteorological Organisation (WMO).[4] Its mandate is not focused on the effort of making new and original researches, but rather on the tasks of organizing and rearranging all the information on the topic of climate change, of assessing in a comprehensive, objective and transparent manner the most significant impacts and effects on the earth, as well as of putting forward hypotheses to counteract the problem. All the members of the IPCC act in their personal capacities, and are experts of different subjects, since the complexity of the phenomenon requires a wide range of expertise.[5] It is divided into working groups, each with a specific competence either on science, technology or mitigation options and their implications.

The IPCC is a body which tries to combine two different approaches, scientific and technical concerns on the one hand, and more broadly political considerations on the other.[6] It is considered important to inform both public opinion and policy-makers about the actual conditions and the progress regarding the phenomenon, with a view to studying precise international strategies and possibly implementing them domestically. The experts nominated by governments are selected by the bureau of governmental representatives to form writing teams within each of the working groups.[7] All the various drafts are re-examined and further elaborated on by other experts, according to a peer-reviewing process. The IPCC presented its first assessment report in 1990 to the Second World Climate Conference held in Geneva.[8] The experts agreed on the existence of a process of global warming, yet they could not push their conclusions further, and had to admit that the magnitude of global warming could not clearly be attributed to human activity. The Second Assessment Report was accepted in 1995 and published in June 1996.[9]

Its importance results from the more detailed findings, compared to those reached by the First Assessment Report, supported by almost 2,000 pages of analysis. The biggest limit of the First Assessment Report is therefore overstepped, with the acceptance of the idea of a link between the role of human-led activities and the increase of the warming of the earth.

The shift from scientific analysis to economic assessment

The core of the debate thus shifts from the scientific analysis to the economic assessment of the most cost-effective way to face the problem of global warming, partly due to the uncertainties concerning the actual impacts of the phenomenon. If the First Assessment Report called for a response by the international community paving the way to the negotiations of the Framework Convention on Climate Change,[10] the consensus reached in the Second Assessment Report showed that time had come for countries to make a further step in the elaboration of feasible and effective responses. The Kyoto Protocol to the Framework Convention is the direct consequence of this enhanced awareness within the international community.[11]

The Third Assessment Report was published in 2001 and it is the result of almost four years of work, involving some 450 natural scientists, social scientists and technical experts. The final position of the authors is in fact that it is not possible to predict how the future range of emissions shall unfold. This is underlined in academic opinion, for instance by Depledge in 2002, who states that '… this analysis challenged the notion that the future can be predicted and that there might exist an optimum development path.'[12]

Nevertheless, the scientific debate has continued and the most recent results, as contained in the fourth Report (2007), can be summarized as an increase in temperature by the end of twenty-first century, from 1.8°C to 4°C, climatic consequences, such as, extreme heat waves, heavy precipitation events, and tropical cyclones;[13] furthermore, economic costs are strictly linked to the increase in temperature and the alteration of climatic patterns, although each country shall be impacted in a different manner.[14] As a consequence, the policies adopted at both the international and the domestic level can be designed in such a way as to take into consideration the implications for the business sector.

The political choice of mitigation or adaptation

Once the basic elements from the scientific point of view are agreed, questions arise as to how to design a comprehensive solution to the problem of global warming, which could be at the same time effective and not detrimental from the economic point of view. From an abstract point of view, policy makers are faced with the options of mitigation and adaptation, which are not mutually exclusive.

Mitigation means the reduction of the GHG emissions each country produces annually. The current legal regime requires only developed countries to mitigate their emissions in the atmosphere, as a concrete application of the principle of the common but differentiated responsibilities.[15] In other words, developing countries should not be obliged to reduce their emissions in consideration, on the one hand of their significantly smaller contribution to the actual level of concentration, and on the other hand of their limited financial and human resources.

Adaptation means recognizing that a certain degree of climate change is inevitable, and therefore trying to modify domestic policies and development plans in order to be able to face such changes.[16] The consequence is that parties to the protocol are to consider ways also to adapt their situations and conditions to the foreseeable changes due to global warming.[17] For instance, if a country is aware that it is affected by floods it should avoid building houses along the rivers or the shores which are prone to such events. The obligations concerning adaptation are equally applied to all parties, although developed countries are further requested to take the special needs of specific countries into account, in order to minimize the negative impacts of both climate change and response measures.[18] The most debatable aspect of adaptation, of course, is the financial one. Developing countries in fact lack the money which is needed to design effective adaptation plans.

Economically efficient flexibility mechanisms to achieve targets

In consideration of the great difficulties that countries face in their efforts to reduce emissions that are harmful for the climate stability, especially in crucial sectors of economies, such as, energy and transport, the Kyoto negotiators designed some mechanisms to meet the needs of reducing the emissions in a less expensive way. The underpinning idea is to create a free market in which the possibility of emitting GHG is traded by the different actors as any other good.[19] Climate change is the global result of GHG emissions in the atmosphere irrespective of the place where they are released, and consequently any reduction contributes to the curbing of total levels, regardless of the location of the sources. The climate change regime therefore allows parties to achieve their mitigation targets in a flexible way, resorting also to the management of sinks,[20] to cooperation among countries, that is joint implementation,[21] and clean development mechanism, to the exchange of credits for emission reductions through emissions trading, and to time flexibility, such as, carry-over or banking.[22]

The focus of the flexibility of the mechanisms is in geography, and it results from the irrelevance of the place where the abatement measures occur. Therefore, a resolution could be to allow developed countries to perform these measures in developing countries where mitigation costs are lower. Indeed, international cooperation brings about some reduction on expenses and it seems that it should be encouraged. Furthermore, if it is feasible to design a global market of credits of GHG emissions, this possibility should be explored.

The UNFCCC somehow refers to the principle of cooperation between parties,[23] but it was only with the Kyoto Protocol that three innovative mechanisms were introduced. These are (i) joint implementation, Article 6,[24] (ii) clean development mechanism, Article 12,[25] and (iii) emissions trading, Article 17.[26] A fourth way to grant flexibility to the regime is provided for in Article 4, joint fulfilment of commitments. This was designed to meet the needs of regional economic unions like the European Union, but the underlying idea is the same.[27] Besides the specific rules on the clean development mechanisms and on emissions trading, there are some issues of relevance to the flexibility mechanisms in general. The complexity of these mechanisms and the problems they entail have brought about long negotiations, but eventually five main decisions were reached to operationalize them.[28] Some issues have been resolved concerning in general the idea of flexibility within the climate change regime. First of all the concrete modalities, rules and procedures are to be determined by the institution in which the delegations of all member countries take part, that is, the COP/MOP.[29]

To address some equity concerns, the following sentence 'The Kyoto Protocol has not created or bestowed any rights, title or entitlement to emissions of any kind on Parties included in Annex I' was included in the preamble of a decision.[30] The concern was that industrialized countries could seek to crystallize their share of global emissions by resorting to flexibility mechanisms, which was of course opposed by developing countries.

The issue of supplementarity is of paramount importance to fully understand the functioning and scope of the flexibility mechanisms. The Kyoto Protocol, in each article concerning such mechanisms, describes them as 'supplemental'[31] or just 'a part'[32] of the overall commitment. The rationale of the idea of supplementarity is avoiding that developed countries meet their requirements simply by buying credits from other countries or by investing in developing countries, without serious domestic mitigation actions. The point is how to give a quantitative dimension to the concept of supplementarity.

The Marrakesh accords provide that the domestic effort shall constitute a significant element of the total effort. The word 'significant' was preferred to other adjectives, such as, principal and primary, which may entail a more stringent quantitative connotation. But the general principle that flexibility mechanisms must not be the main means of achieving mitigation targets was eventually clearly established.

The fungibility of credits accruing from the different mechanisms is provided for by a COP decision.[33] This makes them interchangeable in almost all respects.[34] The idea of involving stakeholders in the process of the various mechanisms was felt by the negotiators. It is an application of the principle of sustainable development in its procedural aspects, and its purpose is to make the whole process more transparent. The parties are of course not obliged to resort to the flexibility mechanisms, but may do so only if they are parties of the Kyoto Protocol, since the mechanisms may be used to achieve the assigned amounts resulting from Article 3 of the Protocol. These mechanisms have been designed to assist parties that accepted to be bound by a precise target, and therefore should not be available for those countries that have not become party to the international treaty establishing them. This has particular importance in consideration of the refusal by some developed countries to ratify the Kyoto Protocol.

Project-based mechanisms

The first category of flexibility mechanisms entails the possibility, for countries, to invest in specific, climate-friendly projects in another country, and to benefit from the GHG reductions thereby obtained, in terms of GHG reduction units. This scheme is also referred to as baseline and credit: the project, once implemented, should in fact bring about reductions in GHGs as compared to the situation indicated in a baseline.

Both joint implementation (JI) and the clean development mechanism (CDM) fit into this pattern, with the only difference concerning the country in which the investment is made. For instance, if it is a country with an economy in transition, Article 6 on joint implementation will apply, while in case of a developing country, Article 12 on the

CDM will be the applicable rule of law. Focusing on the rules which have been designed for the CDM the most important provision is Article 12 of the Kyoto Protocol, which establishes the basic normative framework for the CDM.[35] The CDM may be deemed as a synthesis of expectations from both developed and developing countries. The leading countries in terms of the size of their respective economies require such a mechanism to curb GHG emissions in a more cost-effective manner,[36] while countries whose economies are emerging or developing may thus be assisted '... in achieving sustainable development and in contributing to the ultimate objective of the Convention.'[37] The principle of sustainable development should therefore underpin the whole mechanism, and this should guide the business sector in the choice of the different projects. For instance, climate-friendly projects, in the field of energy production or forestry management, can have negative impacts on the environment, such as, concerns on the safe disposal of nuclear waste or risks for loss of biodiversity.

The core issue was therefore how to grant effective implementation of the principle of sustainable development, through the creation of an institutional framework, which could grant meaningful participation to all the actors involved. The solution was the establishment of the so-called CDM project cycle,[38] a series of steps necessary to have the project formally approved and thus able to generate credits. In fact the aim of this kind of investment is generating credits, that is, certified emissions reductions or CERs that certify the reduction in GHG emissions.

In Article 12.5 there are three fundamental characteristics of emissions reductions from CDM projects which do not differ significantly from those concerning JI. First, participation is voluntary, as approved by each party involved[39] and in this way concerns regarding national sovereignty, raised by developing countries, are overcome. Second, the environmental outcome should result in real, measurable and long-term benefits related to mitigation of climate change;[40] and third, emissions reductions obtained through CDM projects must be additional to any that would occur in the absence of such activities.[41]

Other principles which should guide the implementation of the CDM are transparency, efficiency and accountability in the verification of the projects. Clearly, they should not be the responsibility of the parties involved and, indeed, they are subject to some sort of independent auditing.[42] The first step of the cycle is the identification of the project and the development of a project design document by project developers, which clearly leaves room for the action of international specialized companies.

Such projects have to be approved by a national authority expressly indicated by each host country. Through this mechanism developing countries' concerns about their national sovereignty were overcome and no country is capable of obliging another country to accept an investment, as a formal act of approval is always required. The project must then be validated by a designated operational entity (DOE), which is an independent certification company acting as an impartial actor. A series of requirements must be met for a private entity to be eligible as a DOE. It must be a legal entity, either a domestic or an international organization, employ a sufficient number of persons, have financial stability, insurance coverage and resources required for its activities, as well as internal procedures for the allocation of responsibility within the organization and for handling complaints.[43]

The following step is registration by the CDM Executive Board, as a guarantee of the respect of the rules. The project is then supposed to commence under the direction of the project developer, who is in charge of both the implementation and monitoring. Eventually, the CDM Executive Board issues the CERs to the project developer, after specific verification and certification by a different designated operational entity, for the possible uses according to the rules of the Kyoto Protocol.

Cap-and-trade mechanisms

The form of emissions trading designed in the Kyoto Protocol is based on the cap-and-trade principle.[44] This means that the regulator establishes an overall limit on emissions, or the emission cap; that is, the total amount of a pollutant that the participants in the programme are allowed to emit in a specific period. A number of allowances equal to all of the emissions permitted under the cap are then distributed,[45] and then they may be traded. The economic benefit for enterprises was made clear by the Commission with a practical example in a paper published online with the aim of clarifying the main issues concerning emissions trading.[46] For example, where there are two firms which both emit 100,000 tonnes of Carbon Dioxide (CO_2) per year, the government permits each of them 95,000 emission allowances. Since one allowance represents the right to emit one tonne of CO_2, it is clear that both firms have to cover 5,000 tonnes of CO_2 and they have two ways of achieving this. Either they reduce their emissions by 5,000 tonnes, or they acquire 5,000 tonnes of allowances in the market. In order to decide which option to pursue, they will compare the costs of reducing their emissions by 5,000 tonnes with the market price for allowances, and then select the less expensive option.

Assuming the market price for an allowance per tonne of CO_2 is higher than a firm's reduction costs per tonne, then it should reduce its emissions because it is less expensive than buying allowances. Furthermore, the firm may even reduce its emissions by more than 5,000 tonnes, for instance 10,000 tonnes. Conversely, a firm whose reduction costs are higher than the market price would likely purchase allowances instead of reducing emissions. To calculate the simultaneous effective gain for these firms, as a consequence of the establishment of a market in which emissions allowances are freely traded, there are several possibilities and outcomes. Assuming the firm with the lower costs compared to the market price reduces 10,000 tonnes of emissions at a cost of €5 per tonne and trades 5,000 tonnes of allowances with another firm at a price of € 10, then it fully offsets its emission reduction costs, and, indeed, may even have a profit. Without the Emissions Trading Scheme there would have been a net cost of € 25,000 to this firm. The firm that acquired the 5,000 tonnes of allowances would have had, in the absence of the flexibility provided by the emissions trading scheme, an expenditure of € 75,000. The economic benefits for the actors involved are therefore clear, at least in theory. It is, nonetheless, fundamental to underline that a regime of emissions trading does not mean there are no costs for firms,[47] but it is probably the best way to achieve a cost-effective allocation of GHG emissions reductions.

The benefits of a system of emissions trading

Primarily, the system of emissions trading allows the possibility of reducing GHGs in a flexible and economically efficient manner, as compared to the usual command-and-control systems of imposing cuts. Furthermore, if properly designed, a system of emissions trading may act as an incentive for research and development in environmentally sound fields. When faced with the opportunity of trading the results of extra reductions as a consequence of better technology, firms have an incentive and are likely to overachieve their reduction commitments. Finally, a cap-and-trade system guarantees the environmental outcome. The more stringent the cap, the more beneficial for the climate. This appears even more evident if we consider an alternative system of taxation, in which higher levels of taxation do not guarantee the environmental outcome, if firms are willing to increase their costs instead of improving production processes and thereby lowering emissions.

Of course there are also reasons against a system of emissions trading. It is sometimes also considered unethical to treat the environment merely like any other good, and the idea of a carbon market in itself raises a moral issue.

There are issues to be resolved with the allocation and how pollution rights may be distributed. A *per-capita* basis is one means of solving the moral dilemma but with possible devastating consequences on the industrial system of developed countries. Another means is to continue as in previous years with the so-called grandfathering system,[48] thus ignoring the claims of developing countries, which are seeking opportunities for development, and not further obstacles. Finally, the so-called problem of hot air occurs if the initial allocations are too generous, as some countries could trade credits which are not the result of precise climate-friendly policies and measures.

According to the Kyoto Protocol 1990 is the baseline year against which all GHG reductions are referenced. All the countries which were the former satellite countries of the Soviet Union, later to become the Commonwealth of Independent States, now emit less GHGs than in 1990. As a consequence, they are meeting their targets without implementing any serious climate-friendly policy, and the amount of GHGs in the atmosphere has decreased only as a result of lower levels of industrial production. The final result is that the exchange of units does not entail a reduction, with no benefits for the climate.

Although this kind of market-based instrument is derived from the experience in the US, following its decision not to ratify the Kyoto Protocol, the most advanced example of emissions trading scheme can be found in Directive 2003/87/EC, in force within the European Union. The Directive is a significant attempt, although there are limitations, commencing with the scope of application, which refers to only four sectors. These are energy activities, production and processing of ferrous metals, the mineral industry and activities relating to the paper industry. It is envisioned to have more sectors and negotiations have already commenced to include, for instance, the transport sector and the chemical industry. The entire European Union system is based on the two fundamental concepts of permits and allowances. The basic idea is that every economic entity within the scope of the Directive shall hold a GHG emissions permit.

An application must be presented to the domestic competent authority,[49] specifying such data as the production unit, its activities, the technologies deployed, the raw and auxiliary materials, the sources of GHG emissions, and the monitoring and reporting measures.[50]

The competent authority then, upon verifying that the firm is capable of monitoring and reporting emissions, issues a GHG emissions permit, which grants authorization to emit such gases from all or part of the installation. A permit contains specific information which clearly identifies the firm and its activities,[51] and specifies the monitoring methodologies and the frequency of monitoring. An allowance authorizes the emission of one tonne of carbon dioxide equivalent during a specified period, which shall be valid only for the purposes of meeting the requirements of the Directive and shall be transferable, thereby creating the possibility of emission allowance trading.[52] In order to prepare the business community, the Directive provided for two different phases. Initially between 2005 and 2007 and then between 2008 and 2012 which coincides with the obligations of the Kyoto Protocol. Therefore, it is not acceptable for firms to claim that there was no transition phase for adapting to utilizing these instruments.[53]

For each of these commitment phases each member state decides in advance upon the total amount of allowances it wants to allocate. By end April each year, at the latest, the relevant firms have to surrender a number of allowances equal to the total verified emissions for the installation during the previous calendar year.[54]

There is additional flexibility through the possibilities of banking and borrowing. Banking means using allowances that have not been deployed for compliance of the year for which they have been issued in order to meet compliance for the subsequent years, at least in the first commitment phase,[55] while borrowing refers to the possibility of using the allowance of a year for compliance of the directly preceding year.[56] There is a penalty for non-compliance,[57] applied to each tonne of surplus CO_2 and the payment of such penalties does not exempt firms from surrendering a compensating amount of allowances in the subsequent year,[58] since the legislation was designed to prevent the penalty acting as a payment to avoid reduction commitments.

The first significant step was the preparation of the so-called national allocation plan. If the aim of the trading regime is to establish a cap on emissions and permit allowances move from one firm to another according to their respective economic advantages the implementation and enforcing of this cap is crucial. There is the risk that it could result in gross quantities of hot air, while setting a limit that is too stringent could make it impossible for firms to comply cost effectively. Each member state, therefore, had to decide on how to allocate among the different economic sectors and firms the total amount of allowances.[59]

For the system to operate efficaciously, a credible legal framework is required, as well as a market established. With the establishment of a clear legal framework, the carbon market could be operational. It is rather intuitive how the project-based mechanisms could interact with a system of free exchange of emissions reduction units. The EU ETS is based on a cap-and-trade mechanism and is centred on an *ex ante* allocation of allowances operated by the domestic authorities, while CDM and JI are project-based and generate credits from an *ex post* verification, that is, a baseline and credit system. The opportunities for firms are therefore clear. A company may invest in specific, climate-friendly technologies, for instance, new production processes with reduced GHGs and a significant part of the investment could be recuperated through allowances trading in the market. The less polluting the technology is the more the company could reduce its emissions in the atmosphere and the more allowances may circulate in the market. Furthermore, firms may specialize in sectors which are of extreme interest to developing countries, such as, waste management and transport and it is possible to design *ad hoc* projects which fit the peculiarities of one or more developing countries, which have the final say on the formal approval. In so doing these firms contribute to reduced emissions and a partial remuneration results from the trading of credits to other firms which overshoot their targets. While nobody doubts that rules have been established, the actual participation of countries in the market is not yet that satisfactory. The absence of countries, such as the US and the generous initial allocation of allowances by countries have resulted in a weak demand for such units reduction, and consequently in a low economic value.

Conclusion

The challenge, therefore, is involving those polluters, such as the US, but also those rapidly emerging economies such as as China and India, which, it is estimated by 2030, could be emitters of more GHGs than the US and the EU.[60] In this sense we have to look positively at the COP/MOP of 2007 in Bali, which paved the way to designing a post-2012 regime in which, it seems, the market-based mechanisms have a crucial role. The CDM in particular may be assessed in favourable terms.[61] Up to recently[62] 1,727 projects have been registered, and various industries are involved. The highest number of projects concerns energy industries, such as, renewable/non-renewable sources[63] and waste handling and disposal,[64] for which technology transfer towards developing countries is already operational. Furthermore, a good number of projects are centred on fugitive emissions from fuels, for instance, methane recovery,[65] agriculture, such as, methane capture and biomass[66] and manufacturing industries.[67] Much more has to be achieved in other industries, such as the chemical,[68] the transport[69] the afforestation and reforestation industries,[70] and the construction sector for which no projects have been registered.

The role of technology and business creativity are, therefore, of paramount importance, and firms have many opportunities to explore new sectors and be at the forefront internationally. The challenge of climate change is destined to be in the public agenda in the future and to affect consumers. For instance, Brazil has become the world leader in the production of ethanol, approximately 42 per cent, which is a supposed climate-friendly alternative to fossil fuels. There have been some adverse effects on consumers, and of course food producers, through an increase in corn price[71] and corn-derived products.[72] If the production of ethanol and other biofuels entails an increased use of primary agricultural food products, such as corn and wheat, these essential foodstuffs may be diverted from their initial purpose, the consumption by people, with either direct or indirect consequences for society and especially consumers.[73]

It is worthwhile to stress the link between international trade and the process of liberalization of multilateral exchanges within the World Trade Organization, the so-called Doha Development Round.[74] One of the points in the agenda in fact relates to the reduction or, as appropriate, elimination of tariff and non-tariff barriers to environmental goods and services.[75] The possibility of climate-friendly goods and services moving from one country to another without trade barriers, whether tariff or non-tariff obstacles, provides a further incentive to concentrate efforts in this area. Environmental services should not be underestimated either. In the CDM project cycle, a fundamental role is played by the designated monitoring and regulating entities, responsible for such processes as validation, verification and certification. The development of this very peculiar kind of service offers another opportunity for firms already operating in similar service sectors.

Developing innovative climate-friendly technologies, enhancing transfers of technology towards developing countries, exploring the advantages of the global carbon market, as well as, of the connected services are the opportunities with which firms are confronted, and seizing them would have a beneficial effect on both the environment and the economies.

Notes

1. The greenhouse effect is therefore a natural phenomenon, essential for the existence of human life on earth and it is not limited to our planet, within the solar system. The first studies and researches date back to the nineteenth century, with the contribution of such scientists as the French Fourier (1827) and the Swedish Arrhenius (1896). For an overview on the problem of global warming see the various documents published in the website of the Pew Center on Global Climate Change (www.pewclimate.org), as well as, Lanza, A., 2000, *Il cambiamento climatico: Perché sale la temperatura del pianeta? Le strategie di intervento per contrastare l'effetto serra*, Bologna, Il Mulino.
2. The most important GHGs are: -CARBON DIOXIDE (CO_2): it is the main anthropogenic GHG, supposed to account for about 70 per cent of the *radiative forcing* (that is the absorbing power of the energy in the atmosphere) of climate over the next century. The main anthropogenic sources are fossil fuel combustion and deforestation; -METHANE (CH_4): it has more than doubled its concentration in the atmosphere, it is the second most important anthropogenic GHG, but has a much shorter atmospheric lifetime than carbon dioxide. The main anthropogenic sources are agriculture, waste disposal, fossil fuel (*in primis* natural gas) production and use, but natural emissions from wetlands account for about one-fifth of its total emissions; -NITROUS OXIDE (N_2O): it has a long persistence in the atmosphere, approximately 120 years, which makes it particularly dangerous especially in the long run. The main anthropogenic sources, although natural sources are considered to be twice as large, are agriculture, especially the use of some kind of fertilizers, and certain industrial processes; HALOCARBONS (CFCs and PFCs): these are mainly industrial chemicals, but some of them, such as CFC-12, are expected to fall due to the control imposed by the Montreal Protocol on the substances depleting the ozone layer.
3. The United Nations Environmental Programme, in Nairobi, Kenya, started to operate in 1972, and it works with the aim of encouraging sustainable development through eco-friendly practices and environmentally sound projects, to be encouraged in every sector and in every place. Its activities range from atmosphere to terrestrial ecosystems, through the promotion and furtherance of information in the field of environmental protection. See the website www.unep.org for a list of current and past projects.
4. The World Meteorological Organisation, in Geneva, was established by the World Meteorological Convention, adopted at the 12th Conference of the Directors of the International Meteorological Organizations, gathered in Washington in 1947. Despite the Convention itself entering into force in 1950, the World Meteorological Organization became fully operational, as a successor to the International Meteorological Organization, in 1951, when it obtained the status of a Specialized Agency of the United Nations as a consequence of an agreement between the United Nations and the World Meteorological Organization. Refer to www.wmo.org.
5. For example, about 2,500 scientists from 100 different countries participated in the IPCC Second Assessment Report; natural scientists, economists, lawyers, all try to contribute to the drafting and elaboration of such complex documents.

6. All countries that are members of the United Nations and of the WMO are therefore members of the IPCC and its three working groups.
7. In this process of selection, concerns on the geographical balance of such teams are very likely to play a major role, besides the obvious requirements of professional and research expertise.
8. The texts of the assessments reports can be found in the IPCC website, www.ipcc.ch, together with other documents and information concerning its work.
9. On the Second Assessment Report refer in general Brack, D. and Grubb, M., 1996, 'Climate Change: A Summary of the Second Assessment Report of the IPCC', The Royal Institute of International Affairs, Briefing Paper 32, July.
10. The UNFCCC was adopted at the end of the World Conference on Environment and Development, held in Rio de Janeiro in 1992. Today it has been ratified by 189 Countries and although its general character of a framework Convention results in vague obligations, it is nonetheless of paramount importance as the instrument establishing a legal regime on climate change, with *ad hoc* institutions, rules and procedures.
11. The Kyoto Protocol was adopted at the end of COP3 in December 1997, entered into force on 16 February 2005, and is now the most important legal text establishing binding commitments for parties to the climate change regime.
12. Refer to Depledge J., 'Climate Change in Focus: the IPCC Third Assessment Report', Briefing Paper New Series 29, The Royal Institute of International Affairs, Sustainable Development Programme, February 2002, p. 2.
13. All these events are considered to be 'very likely', that is, with more than a 90 per cent probability.
14. It has been estimated that an increase in temperature by 3°C will imply economic costs building up to 3 per cent of GDP annually.
15. Refer to Article 4 of the UNFCCC, recognizing that all parties, in carrying out their obligations, take '... into account their common but differentiated responsibilities and their specific national and regional development priorities, objectives and circumstances'.
16. According to the IPCC, 2001, Volume III, Chapter 18, adaptation is any '... adjustment in ecological, social, or economic systems in response to actual or expected climatic stimuli and their effects or impacts' and relates to '... changes in processes, practices, and structures to moderate potential damage or to benefit from opportunities associated with climate change'.
17. On the concept of adaptation refer to Verheyen, R., 2002, 'Adaptation to the Impacts of Anthropogenic Climate Change – The International Legal Framework', in *Review of European Community and International Environmental Law*, 11 (2), pp. 129–43.
18. Refer to UNFCCC, Articles 4.8 and 4.9, as examples of the application of the principle of common but differentiated responsibilities.
19. Refer to Lefevre, J., 2004, 'Greenhouse Gas Emission Allowance Trading in the EU', in *The Yearbook of European Environmental Law, Volume 3*, p. 151, who advises that '... the term emission trading, although most commonly used, does in fact not properly describe the instrument. It is not the emissions that are being traded, but the right to emit a particular quantity of

greenhouse gases, laid down in a permit, credit or allowance.' Therefore the title of the European Directive is welcomed which refers to greenhouse gas emission allowance trading.

20. Since forests can trap and sequester GHGs, they are usually referred to as carbon sinks, and the issue of managing them is part of the general problem of land use, land use change and forestry. On sinks and forests, refer to Fry, I., 2002, 'Twists and Turns in the Jungle: Exploring the Evolution of Land Use, Land-Use Change and Forestry Decisions within the Kyoto Protocol', in *The Review of European Community and International Environmental Law*, 11 (2), pp. 159–68, and Alexander Gillespie, 2003, 'Sinks and the Climate Change Regime: the Country of Play', in *Duke Environmental Law and Policy Forum*, 13 (2), pp. 279–301.

21. On the concept of joint implementation in general refer to Conaty, S., 1998, 'The Potential Utility of Joint Implementation Mechanisms in the Kyoto Protocol', in *Asia Pacific Journal of Environmental Law*, Volume 3, p. 363; Hanafi, A., 1998, 'Joint Implementation: Legal and Institutional Issues for an Effective International Program to Combat Climate Change', in *Harvard Environmental Law Review*, pp. 441–508; Kuik, O., Peters, P. and Schrijver, N., 1994, *Joint Implementation to Curb Climate Change*, Kluwer Academic Publishers; Streck, C., 2005, 'Joint Implementation: History, Requirements, and Challenges,' in Freestone, D., and Streck, C., *Legal Aspects of Implementing the Kyoto Protocol Mechanisms: Making Kyoto Work*, New York; Wiser, G., 1997, 'Joint Implementation: Incentives for Private Sector Mitigation of Global Climate Change', in *Georgetown International Environmental Law Review*, 9, pp. 747-ff; Oberthur, S., and Ott, H., 1999, *The Kyoto Protocol: International Climate Policy for the 21st Century*, pp. 141–207; Grubb, M., Vrolijk, C. and Brack, D., 2001, *The Kyoto Protocol: A Guide and Assessment*, pp. 87–96.

22. Carry-over or banking is the possibility of adding to a subsequent commitment phase the amount of reduction a country has overachieved in the first phase.

23. See UNFCCC, Article 3.3 '[...] Efforts to address climate change may be carried out cooperatively by interested Parties'), and Article 4.2(a) '[...] Parties may implement such policies and measures jointly with other Parties and may assist other Parties in contributing to the achievement of the objective of the Convention [...]'.

24. See Kyoto Protocol, Article 6.

25. See Kyoto Protocol, Article 12.

26. See Kyoto Protocol, Article 17.

27. This is usually referred to as the 'European bubble'.

28. Decision 15/CP.7 covers matters relevant to all three mechanisms, Decision 16/CP.7 covers joint implementation, Decision 17/CP.7 covers the clean development mechanism, Decision 18/CP.7 deals with emissions trading and Decision 19/CP.7 defines accounting modalities. All of these decisions were taken during COP7 in Marrakesh and contained annexes with the draft decisions for COP/MOP 1.

29. Due to the distinct legal authority of the COP and the COP/MOP, the modalities for the mechanisms have been shaped as an annex attached to draft decisions that the COP/MOP has been recommended by the COP to adopt.

30. Refer to Decision 15/CP.7, preamble, paragraph 6.
31. Refer to Kyoto Protocol, Article 6.1(d) 'The acquisition of emission reduction units shall be supplemental to domestic actions for the purposes of meeting commitments under Article 3' and Article 17 '... any such trading shall be supplemental to domestic actions for the purpose of meeting quantified emission limitation and reduction commitments under that Article.'
32. See Kyoto Protocol, Article 12.3(b) 'Parties included in Annex I may use the certified emission reductions accruing from such project activities to contribute to compliance with part of their quantified emission limitation and reduction commitments under Article 3, as determined by the Conference of the Parties serving as the meeting of the Parties to this Protocol'.
33. See Decision 19/CP.7.
34. That's why in academic opinion they are usually referred to as the 'Kyoto units'.
35. Refer to the Kyoto Protocol, Article 12.1, for the definition of a clean development mechanism. According to Oberthur, S., Hermann E. and Ott, H., *International Climate Policy*, p. 168, this language is a compromise and conceals the different positions: developed countries opposed to creating a new financial institution, while developing countries did not trust the Global Environmental Facility (GEF), an independent financial organization, established in 1991, which provides grants to developing countries for projects that benefit the global environment and promote sustainable livelihoods in local communities.
36. Refer to Kyoto Protocol, Article12.2, as well as Article 12.3(b).
37. Refer to Kyoto Protocol, Article 12.2, as well as Article 12.3(a).
38. On the CDM project cycle, as well as, on the different actors involved and the possible conflicts with international rules on investments, refer to Rubagotti, G., 'The Clean Development Mechanism Under the Kyoto Protocol: Designing a Regulatory Framework to Favour Climate-Friendly Investments in Developing Countries', in *Indian Journal of International Law*, 46(2), April–June 2006, pp. 212–39.
39. Refer to Kyoto Protocol, Article 12.5(a).
40. Refer to Kyoto Protocol, Article 12.5(b).
41. Refer to Kyoto Protocol, Article 12.5(c). This is the so-called requirement of additionality.
42. Refer to Kyoto Protocol, Article 12.7.
43. Refer to Decision 17/CP.7, Appendix A, paragraph 1, as well as Appendix E, paragraph 27, establishing requirements to ensure transparency and liability.
44. On emissions trading in the Kyoto Protocol refer to Grubb *et al.*, *A Guide and Assessment*, op. cit. pp. 206–25; Oberthur and Ott, *International Climate Policy* op.cit., pp. 187–206; Yamin, F., and Depledge, J., 2003, *The International Climate Change Regime: A Guide to Rules, Institutions and Procedures*; de Witt Wijnen, R., 'Emissions Trading under Article 17 of the Kyoto Protocol', in Freestone and Streck, 2005, *Making Kyoto Work*, op. cit., pp. 403–16; Driesen, D., 1998, 'Free Lunch or Cheap Fix?: The Emission Trading Idea and the Climate Change Convention', in *Boston College Environmental Affairs Law Review*, 26, p. 1; Ellerman, A., 2005, 'A Note on Tradable Permits', in *Environmental and Resource Economics*, 31, pp. 123–31; Jinnah, S., 2003, 'Emissions Trading under the Kyoto Protocol: Legal and Policy Mechanisms for Domestic Implementation', in *Journal of Energy and Natural Resources Law*, 21(3), pp. 252–76;

Victor, D., 2001, *The Collapse of the Kyoto Protocol and the Struggle to Slow Global Warming*, Princeton, pp. 3–54.

45. The two basic alternatives are free distribution or distribution by auction.
46. Refer to the European Union Questions and Answers on Emissions Trading and National Allocation Plans, available on the webpage http://europa.eu. int/rapid/pressReleasesAction.do?reference=MEMO/04/44&format=HTML& aged=0&language=EN&guiLanguage=en (07.2009)
47. For an analysis on how emissions trading could reduce implementation costs refer to *An Emerging Market for the Environment: a Guide to Emissions Trading*, published by the United Nations Environmental Programme (UNEP) and the United Nations Conference on Trade and Development (UNCTAD) in 2002.
48. By the expression grandfathering we refer to the situation in which the allocation of the emission rights among the different countries is strictly linked to the proportions of the historic emissions, as officially registered in the previous years.
49. According to Article 18 of the European Union Directive 2003/87/EC 'Member states shall make the appropriate administrative arrangements, including the designation of the appropriate competent authority or authorities, for the implementation of the rules of this Directive. When more than one competent authority is designated, the work of these authorities undertaken pursuant to this Directive must be coordinated.'
50. Refer to Article 5 of the European Union Directive 2003/87/EC.
51. Refer to Article 6(a) and (b) of the European Union Directive 2003/87/EC.
52. For a definition of the concept of allowance, see Article 3(a) of the European Union Directive 2003/87/EC.
53. The main differences between the first and second phases concern the method of allocation. While in the first phase the amount of allowances free of charge is at least 95 per cent, during the years 2008–2012 this quantity decreases by 5 per cent, as set out in Article 10 of the European Union Directive 2003/87/EC and the penalties in case of non-compliance are outlined. These are € 40 during the first phase and € 100 during the second phase.
54. Refer to Article 12(4) of the European Union Directive 2003/87/EC.
55. Refer to Article 13.2(2) of the European Union Directive 2003/87/EC.
56. This is possible since, according to Article 11(4) of the European Union Directive 2003/87/EC, allowances for the current year are issued at the latest by end February, whereas the deadline for compliance for the previous year is end April.
57. Refer to Article 16.3 of the European Union Directive 2003/87/EC: 'The excess emissions penalty shall be €100 for each tonne of carbon dioxide equivalent emitted by that installation for which the operator has not surrendered allowances.' During the first phase, the penalty is €40.
58. Refer to Article 16 of the European Union Directive 2003/87/EC.
59. A possibility of loosening the scheme is the so-called 'pooling'. According to Article 27 of the European Union Directive 2003/87/EC, firms may pool their emission allowances both in the first and in the second commitment phases. The installations forming the pool shall nominate a trustee, whose role will be receiving the total allowances of the pool. As far as responsibility is concerned, the trustee is liable to surrender sufficient amounts of allowances for compliance, when there is non-compliance, individual firms forming a pool are responsible for their own firm's emissions.

60. According to Llewellyn, J. and Chaix, C., 2007, in *The Business of Climate Change II: Policy is accelerating, with major implications for companies and investors*, Lehman Brothers (eds), Figure 16, p. 44, the estimate for global emissions contributions in 2030 is as follows: United States, 16.6 per cent; European Union, 10.1 per cent; China, 23.7 per cent; India, 5.7 per cent, Rest of Asia, 13.1 per cent.

61. From the point of view of geographical distribution, it must be underlined that the trend which was originally identified in academic opinion, such as, in Rubagotti, G., 2006, 'The Clean Development Mechanism Under the Kyoto Protocol: Designing a Regulatory Framework to Favour Climate-Friendly Investments in Developing Countries', op. cit., pp. 238–9, is still evident, though 1,727 projects have been registered. There is a geographical imbalance in the distribution, with almost 60 per cent of the projects concentrated in two large developing countries in Asia, India with 444, and which was previously first in number of projects, and China with 588, which is the leading country, with Asia increasing its percentage and obtaining 72.96 per cent of the total and Latin American declining to 24.72 per cent from 34.52 per cent in 2007. Brazil has 160 projects and Mexico 117. Africa does not seem to benefit from the CDM with only 1.8 per cent of the total decline from 3.65 per cent in early 2008.

62. Data as at mid July 2009 which may be obtained in the CDM official website (http://cdm.unfccc.int/index.html).

63. 1,260 projects, that is, 59.41 per cent of the total, with a positive trend.

64. 369 projects, that is, 17.4 per cent of the total, a percentage with a slight decline compared to that of the first 1,000 registered projects.

65. 130 projects, that is, 6.13 per cent of the total.

66. 122 projects, that is, 5.75 per cent of the total.

67. 101 projects, that is, 4.76 per cent of the total.

68. 58 projects, that is, 2.73 per cent of the total, with a slightly positive trend.

69. Only two projects, including the New Delhi underground, which could be considered as a positive instance for the future, although no new projects in this sector have been registered, though the total number has doubled.

70. Only six projects, that is 0.28 per cent of the total but, with very restrictive rules which could be amended in order to enhance economic cooperation in this crucial sector for the post-Kyoto period.

71. According to Llewellyn, J. and Chaix, C., *Business of Climate Change II*, op. cit., p. 69, citing *MIT Technology Review* of February 2007 '… corn prices increased by 50 percent between August 2006 and August 2007, and this increase is directly linked to the increased demand for ethanol.'

72. There was a doubling of corn tortilla prices in Mexico which resulted in protest marches in Mexico City.

73. In this sense we should not ignore the results of the UK House of Commons.

74. During the Ministerial Conference of the World Trade Organization which took place in Doha, September 2001, a new negotiation round was launched, which focused on how to enhance international trade and economic development.

75. Refer to Doha Declaration, paragraph 31(III), available on the official WTO website   http://www.wto.org/english/thewto_e/minist_e/min01_e/mindecl_e.htm

7
Water Resources and Business – Supply, Demand and Security

Robert E. Martin

Political and business leaders in the global economy have been gradually awakening to the increasing role that water plays in shaping decisions in all sectors of society. It is now widely perceived that population growth coupled with economic development means accelerating growth in global demand for freshwater, and that the world is reaching a point where local solutions may no longer be sufficient to meet that demand.

Water management has traditionally been seen as a local matter, which means that water related information has tended to remain in the hands of local, regional or national agencies. As a result, it may be difficult for firms with worldwide operations and markets to effectively integrate water in their strategic planning. Nevertheless it is in the best interest of all firms to give serious consideration to how water could affect their business in the twenty-first century.

Trends in freshwater availability

The trend that has perhaps been the most significant in raising awareness of water as a global issue is the steady and ongoing decline in the amount of water available per person on the planet. This is not because 'the world is running out of water'. It is instead an inevitable consequence of rising population in a world in which the total amount of freshwater is not changing. On a global scale, the term, 'renewable water resources' refers to the amount of precipitation falling on land in the course of a year minus water lost to evaporation. Figure 7.1 illustrates how the average amount of renewable water resources per person has dropped from 140,000 to 6,500 m^3/inhabitant/year from the year 1000 to today, merely as a result of population increase. The world's population is projected to

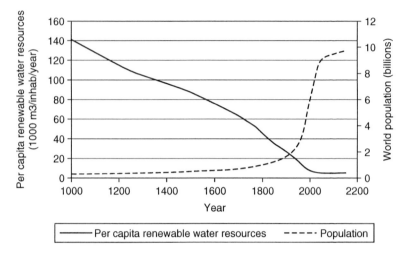

Figure 7.1   Historical and projected world population and per capita renewable water resources

Sources: Population data from United Nations, 1999, *The World at 6 Billion*, Population Division, Department of Economic and Social Affairs, United Nations Secretariat, New York, p. 5; United Nations, 2007, *World Population Prospects, The 2006 Revision*, Population Division, Department of Economic and Social Affairs, United Nations Secretariat, New York; Water resources data from the Food and Agriculture Organization of the United Nations, 2008, Aquastat Database.

continue to increase before stabilizing at just over 10 billion sometime after the year 2200.[1] At that point, the global average of per capita renewable water resources would be 4,500 m^3/inhabitant/year, one-tenth of the level at the start of the industrial revolution.

Various benchmarks have been generally accepted by experts in water resources over the last two decades. First of all, considering that much precipitation runs off directly to the ocean or falls in inaccessible areas, and that ecosystems must also receive adequate flows to sustain them, only about 40 per cent of renewable water resources are considered to be readily available for human use. Indeed, when total water use exceeds 40 per cent of renewable water resources, people are considered to be living under severe water stress.[2] By this standard, when the world population stabilizes, the available per capita renewable water resources would be closer to 1,800 than 4,500 m^3/inhabitant/year.

Another set of commonly used benchmarks is based on the amount of water that is needed to sustain populations. In this approach, it is considered that water shortages start to appear regularly when availability falls below 1,700 m^3/inhabitants/year. Below 1,000 m^3/inhabitant/year water scarcity becomes a limitation to economic development and human health and well-being, and below 500 m^3/inhabitant/year water availability is a main constraint to life.[3] Compared to these thresholds, the projected global average water availability over the next 200 years does not leave a large margin of safety. In fact, the global annual average masks huge variations in water availability between and within countries and from one season to another.

In 1995, the percentage of the population already living in areas with severe water stress ranged from 4 per cent to 95 per cent in 18 regions of the world.[4]

Freshwater availability is usually expressed in terms of natural resources, but it is worthwhile to consider the potential contribution from desalination of seawater. Total installed capacity in the world at the beginning of 2006 was 39.9 million m^3/day and is estimated to be growing at a rate of about 9 per cent per year.[5] The 2006 level corresponds to 2.24 m^3/inhabitant/year or about 0.03 per cent of total natural renewable water resources. If growth in capacity were to continue at the same rate, production capacity in 2050 would still be less than 2 per cent of natural renewable water resources. While desalination is increasingly important as a competitive solution for supplementing local freshwater resources, it is not likely to significantly alter the global availability of freshwater. Furthermore, the long term sustainability of growth in desalination capacity is questionable, since it is inherently an energy and capital intensive solution.

So by generally accepted standards, per capita water availability now and in the foreseeable future is uncomfortably close to the limit for severe water stress. But does that mean that we have a global water crisis on our hands? After all, regions of the world already under water stress according to these benchmarks appear to be managing the situation, including much of the southwestern United States and Israel. To answer this question, it is important to consider how we are using water and how that might evolve in the future.

Trends and issues in demand

A second major trend that has raised questions about whether we face a water constrained future has been economic growth. Everybody knows that water is essential to life, but it is relatively recently that people have started to understand how essential it is to everything in our lives, including food, energy, nature, leisure and virtually all the products we

The Water Ladder

As per capita income increases, demand for water also increases. Similarly, energy demands also increase with income. The water ladder impacts other ladders – for example, the hygiene ladder, the food security ladder, and the dietary preferences ladder.

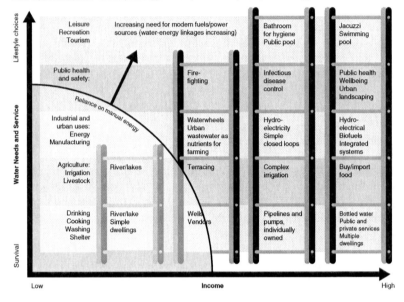

Figure 7.2   The World Business Council for Sustainable Development water ladder relating demand for water to income level
Source: WBCSD Water Scenario Team.

use on a daily basis. This is why water use increased at more than twice the rate of population growth during the twentieth century.

The World Business Council for Sustainable Development (WBCSD) described the effect qualitatively with a 'water ladder', reproduced in Figure 7.2.[6] The vertical axis represents the spectrum of water use from meeting basic survival needs to satisfying lifestyle choices. The horizontal axis represents increasing income and how the various uses take different forms according to the level of income. The higher people climb on the water ladder with increasing per capita income, the greater their per capita demand for water. A second point illustrated in this chart is that using water means expending energy. Lower income groups, who often have difficulties in meeting basic water needs, due to lack of water infrastructure, rely heavily on manual energy to obtain water. As income increases, however, and people move up the water ladder, there is a need for more energy to enable the use of more water in more diverse ways. Since the vast majority of current energy production requires large amounts of water for cooling, climbing the water ladder as a result of economic development also means increasingly significant indirect water use for energy production.

So the issue is whether the combination of growing numbers of people and growing economies lead to a global water crisis requiring radical change in the ways water is used. To better understand the interplay of demographics, economic development and water use on a global scale, it is helpful to introduce a simple model for global water use analogous to one used to describe global energy consumption and its dependence on population and economic growth.[7] In this approach, global water use is measured in terms of the annual rate of freshwater withdrawal from natural resources, primarily rivers, lakes and groundwater. The amount of renewable water resources represents an upper limit to the amount that could be used sustainably. Global water use is expressed in terms of three fundamental factors as follows:

$$W = N \times (GDP/N) \times (W/GDP)$$

in which W is the rate of withdrawal of water, N is the global population, GDP/N is the globally averaged gross domestic product per capita, and W/GDP is the globally averaged water intensity, or the amount of water withdrawn from the environment per unit of GDP. Insofar as per capita GDP may be used as a guide to average living standards,[8] it may also be seen as an indicator of where the world is on the water ladder. The water intensity, which is the inverse of water productivity, reflects water use efficiency. At the global or national level, this includes both the amount of water required for specific processes, such as producing a ton of wheat or meat, or supplying drinking water to a city, and the economic value of different uses, for instance, agricultural versus industrial production.[9] It should be noted that one limitation of this model is that it only considers water withdrawals while the pollution of water resources has a major impact on the availability of water of sufficient quality to meet the needs of people and ecosystems.

This model illustrates to us that the rate of growth in water withdrawal is approximately equal to the sum of the rates of growth in population, per capita GDP and water intensity. Figure 7.3 illustrates projections of per capita water withdrawal compared to per capita availability of renewable water resources. Per capita volumes are used here in order to focus on the effects of economic growth and water intensity. The annual growth

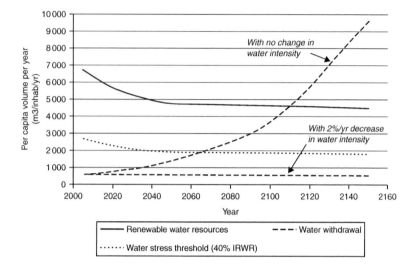

Figure 7.3 Projected per capita water withdrawals according to alternative trends in water intensity compared to per capita renewable water resources and the water stress threshold

Sources: Population data from United Nations, 1999, *The World at 6 Billion*, Population Division, Department of Economic and Social Affairs, United Nations Secretariat, New York, p. 5; United Nations, 2007, *World Population Prospects, The 2006 Revision*, Population Division, Department of Economic and Social Affairs, United Nations Secretariat, New York; Water resources data from the Food and Agriculture Organization of the United Nations, 2008, Aquastat Database.

in per capita GDP has been assumed to be 1.94 per cent, which was the average annual global growth rate from 1961 to 2006.[10]

As the sharply rising dashed line in the graph illustrates, if it is assumed that global water intensity remains constant over the next 150 years, then moving up the water ladder with economic growth would cause the global average rate of per capita withdrawal to cross the threshold of severe water stress by the year 2070, that is, roughly within the next two generations. Given the imperative nature of economic growth, it is difficult to imagine how this powerful driver for increased water use could be diminished.

It might, however, be offset by negative growth in water intensity. Whether this is a reasonable hypothesis may be tested by analysing data for the recent past. The change in the estimated water intensity of 12 countries over a 15 year period from 1985 to 2000 is specified in Table 7.1. The annual change ranged from an increase of 2.13 per cent in the case of Algeria to a 7.14 per cent decrease for China. Nine of the

Table 7.1 Trends in water intensity compared to levels of internal and total renewable water resources and withdrawals: selected countries

Country	Water intensity (m³ per US$ GDP)		Annual change in water intensity	Per capita internal renewable water resources (m³/inhabitant/year)	Per capita total renewable water resources (m³/inhabitant/year)	Withdrawal as % of	
	1983–1987	1998–2002				internal renewable water resources	total renewable water resources
China	1.58	0,52	−7,14%	2,142	2,155	22.4%	22.3%
Israel	0.03	0,02	−4,79%	112	250	244%	110%
Spain	0,13	0,06	−4,74%	2,558	2,569	32.1%	31.9%
India	2,45	1,40	−3,65%	1,112	1,672	51.2%	34.1%
Tunisia	0,22	0,14	−3,21%	416	455	62.9%	57.5%
Switzerland	0,02	0,01	−3,05%	5,442	7,206	6.36%	4.80%
Morocco	0,47	0,33	−2,30%	951	951	43.5%	43.5%
Canada	0,09	0,06	−2,22%	88,315	89 926	1.61%	1.59%
New Zealand	0,05	0,04	−1,41%	79,814	79 814	0.65%	0.65%
Hungary	0,15	0,16	0,63%	595	10,311	127%	7.35%
Brazil	0,08	0,09	1,28%	28,999	44,067	1.1%	0.72%
Algeria	0,08	0,11	2,13%	341	355	54.2%	52.0%
Average	**0,45**	**0,25**	**−2,37%**				52.0%

Sources: Food and Agriculture Organization of the United Nations, 2008; Aquastat Database and the World Resources Institute, 2007; EarthTrends, The Environmental Information Portal: Economics, Business and Environment Searchable Database.

twelve countries exhibited decreases and the average annual change for all twelve countries was −2.37 per cent. In principle, the overall decrease in water intensity is attributable to both shifting patterns of water use, for instance, industrial versus agricultural use, and more efficient water use, but the available data does not allow evaluation of the relative contributions. It is interesting to note that significant decreases in water intensity may be observed even in countries with ample water resources.

Assuming that instead of remaining constant water intensity decreases at a rate of two per cent per year, as in Figure 7.3, then a much different picture of future freshwater withdrawal relative to availability emerges. Indeed, under this assumption, the world would remain well below the threshold of severe water stress at least for another 150 years, as illustrated by the lower dashed line. But it must be argued whether it is realistic to assume that water intensity could continue to decrease at this rate indefinitely.

For several reasons, including regulatory, economic and technological factors, it does seem reasonable to expect overall water intensity to decline over the coming decades. Water abstraction and pollution control regulations have been drivers for more efficient water use in many industrialized countries over the last 30 to 40 years. Effective enforcement of regulations in more and more countries should continue this trend. Furthermore, while the economic value of water has been the subject of much debate, an inescapable fact is that using water generally means moving water, and this requires energy. Water intensity has a direct impact on energy intensity and is therefore subject to the same economic, social and environmental pressures that would limit energy intensity, including reduction of greenhouse gas emissions. In California, it has been estimated that 19 per cent of electricity consumption is water-related; water conservation policies are motivated to a great extent by the need to control energy consumption.[11] Reducing water intensity therefore means reducing the costs of both purchasing it and using it. With regard to technology, advances in water treatment technology such as membrane systems have enabled rapid growth in water reuse and recycling. In agriculture, technological advances have created the potential for substantial gains in the efficiency of irrigation and fertilizer application, thereby mitigating both water quantity and quality impacts. Finally, it is also evident from Table 7.1 that the range of water intensity for this sample of countries spans two orders of magnitude, suggesting that considerable gains remain feasible for many countries.

On the basis of total water withdrawals and world GDP, the water intensity of the global economy in 2006 was on the order of $0.1\,m^3/US\$$

GDP (with GDP in constant 2000 US$).[12] A sustained two per cent annual decrease would bring it down to 0.04 in 2050 and 0.015 in 2100. Decreasing water intensity implies decoupling of water use and economic growth. An analysis of 17 OECD countries illustrated a pronounced decoupling between total freshwater abstractions and economic growth from 1980 to 1998. The water intensity ranged from less than 0.01 to 0.09 in 1998, with a total of 0.05 for all 17 countries.[13] This queries whether this level could be achieved on a global scale, or whether low water intensity in one economy necessarily implies higher water intensity in another. That is whether water use and economic growth could be decoupled at the global level. This is arguably the essence of sustainable water management.

Supply, demand and security

It is not only water intensity that varies enormously between countries. As mentioned previously and outlined in Table 7.1, the amount of water available per person that is renewed by precipitation falling within a country could also vary by two orders of magnitude between countries. This amount is referred to as the per capita internal renewable water resources. It is a measure of whether a country is water rich or water poor. But it does not always reflect the total amount of water that is available to the country. The total renewable water resources include flows coming into a country from beyond its borders. The degree of water stress for a given country may be measured by the ratio of total withdrawals to either internal or total renewable resources.[14,15] As outlined in Table 7.1, the availability of external resources may bring a country below the threshold of 40 per cent, taking it from a state of severe water stress to moderate water stress. This, of course, comes at the price of dependency on neighbouring countries.

Over the last 15 years, another important mechanism compensating for disparities in water resources has become increasingly apparent and understood. This is the flow of so-called 'virtual water' between countries around the globe, not just between neighbouring states as in the case of physical water flows.[16] Virtual water is the water consumed in producing agricultural or industrial products; it is also referred to as 'embedded water'. For instance, between 1,000 and 2,000 kg of water are needed to produce 1 kg of grain. An average of 16,000 kg is required to produce 1 kg of beef. One of the main practical uses of the virtual water concept is in analysing the impact of international trade on water security.[17] Virtual water may be perceived as an alternative source of water with net import of virtual water in a water-scarce nation relieving pressure on the nation's own water resources. Politically, it has been argued that virtual water trade could be an instrument in solving geopolitical problems and preventing wars over water.

The concept of virtual water was first applied to agricultural products, which makes sense since agriculture accounts for such a large share of water use in the world. Freshwater withdrawals for agriculture represent 70 per cent of the global total, and, globally, the vast majority of agriculture is food production. The concept thus helps to link water management to the basic need for food, highlighting the intimate connection between food security and water security.

Water security is also intimately linked to energy security. Some of the energy implications of water use were mentioned above in relation to drivers for reducing water intensity. It is a reciprocal relationship, however. The largest single industrial use of water is for cooling in thermo-electric power generation. The amount of water required varies widely, however, depending on the generating and cooling technologies, as well as ambient meteorological conditions.[18] Water is also essential to fuel production. The water intensity of various fuels spans several orders of magnitude according to the type of fuel and the production process.[19] For petroleum-based fuels, the virtual water content is expected to increase with increasing dependency on less accessible oil resources.

Without water security, food, energy and political security are all at risk. Globally, it seems reasonable to consider that water withdrawals could be kept below the threshold for severe water stress, at least through the twenty-first century. But this fragile global security may only be maintained if mechanisms enabling the flow of physical and virtual water from the water rich to the water poor are allowed to function.

Water usage and resources

One of the main conclusions that may be drawn from reports on climate change is that the recent past is not likely to be a good guide to the future, especially with regard to water resources. The Fourth Assessment Report of the Intergovernmental Panel on Climate Change, released in 2007 and focusing on climate change impacts, stated with a high level of confidence that '... the negative impacts of climate change on freshwater systems outweigh its benefits.'[20] These impacts, some of which may already be observed, include substantial decreases in freshwater reserves stored in mountain glaciers and snow cover in regions where more than one-sixth of the world population currently lives; increased precipitation intensity and variability with increases in the frequency and severity of floods and droughts; large increases in irrigation water demand; and increased salinization of groundwater supplies in coastal areas due to rising sea level.

The relative certainty of significant impacts of climate change on the temporal and spatial distribution of freshwater resources contrasts with the considerable uncertainty in quantitative projections of changes in hydrological characteristics at the level of a drainage basin. Precipitation is not reliably simulated in present climate models.[21]

Inability to accurately assess water use relative to available resources on a global scale is not only an issue for planners estimating the potential impacts of climate change. Consolidated historical data is sparse. Indeed, the twelve countries listed in Table 7.1 were selected because they are the only countries, excluding states that were formerly members of the Soviet Union, for which comparable water withdrawal data is available in the Aquastat data base of the Food and Agriculture Organization of the United Nations (FAO). With the number of reporting countries decreasing from 70 to 12 and their reported withdrawals by a factor of ten between 2000 and 2005, the information gap that this data reveals is striking. The United Nations Statistics Division maintains a separate data base of environmental indicators, which provides data on water withdrawals for 81 countries from 1990 to 2005. Table 7.2 outlines the sum of withdrawals reported for the 81 countries by year, together with the number of countries reporting. It suggests that there is no readily available data to allow accounting for the interdependence of food, energy and water security in shaping international policy, whether regarding international trade in food or measures to mitigate greenhouse gas emissions. That is also why it is difficult to ascertain whether there is actually a global water crisis.

A comparison of *per capita* freshwater withdrawals and *per capita* availability based on information from FAO's Aquastat data base suggests that on the whole, the relationship between the amount of water a country withdraws from the environment and the amount of precipitation in the course of a year is limited. Figure 7.4 is a scatterplot of 167 countries representing over 95 per cent of the world population and illustrates that some of the countries with the lowest level of resources have the highest levels of withdrawals.

The inevitable decline in the amount of water available per person over the next century and the uncertainties of climate change impacts call for more rigorous management of the water budget at all levels, from the household to the planet. Rational and equitable management, however,

Table 7.2   Number of countries reporting data on water withdrawals 1990–2005

Year	Total Reported Withdrawal (million m³)	Countries Reporting* Number	%
1990	1,107,994	55	68
1995	1,235 488	65	80
2000	1,859 968	70	86
2001	1,140 292	44	54
2002	917,230	34	42
2003	836,517	27	33
2004	951,748	29	36
2005	190,647	12	15

* The total number of countries is 81.
Source: United Nations Statistics Division.

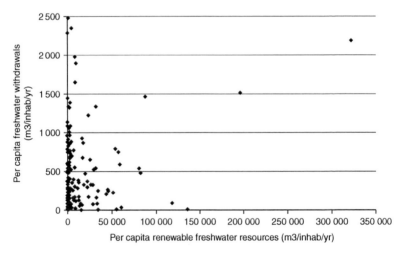

Figure 7.4   Comparison of per capita water withdrawal and per capita internal renewable water resources for 167 countries
Source: Food and Agricultural Organization of the United Nations, 2008, Aquastat Database.

requires adequate information. As described in a UN Water report on global systems and initiatives for water monitoring,[22] global water information management tools are going into place, and it can be hoped that growing concern about the world's water resources will accelerate their effective use.

Global water information management is only possible, however, if the individual countries of the world are effectively managing their water resources. The need for both developed and developing countries to strengthen water management was recognized at the World Summit on Sustainable Development in Johannesburg in 2002 where the target was set to 'Develop integrated water resources management [IWRM] and water efficiency plans by 2005, with support to developing countries, through actions at all levels.'[23] The 2005 deadline has not been met. A 2008 status report acknowledges some progress, but calls for countries to prioritize the development and implementation of IWRM.[24]

Water and business

The primary implication of the world water situation for the business community is that the water intensity of all sectors must diminish. This was already anticipated in the concept of eco-efficiency introduced in 1992, for which the simplest definition is 'creating more goods and services with ever less use of resources, waste and pollution.'[25] In the following years, considerable effort went into understanding how to implement the concept and measure performance, resulting in the emergence of a common framework to guide all companies regardless of their business or geographic base. In this approach, water consumption is one of five generally applicable indicators, all of which meet three criteria: related to a global environmental concern, relevant and meaningful to virtually all businesses, and methods for measurement are established and definitions accepted globally.[26] For leading international firms highly dependent on water and concerned with sustainability, the compelling trend outlined in Figure 7.1 has been sufficient to instigate measures for corporate water management.

Unilever was one of the first to proactively manage its water consumption and has been tracking the amount of water per ton of production since 1995. As illustrated in Figure 7.5, the ratio decreased by 62 per cent from 1995 to 2007, a compound annual rate of −8 per cent. Future targets correspond to an annual rate of −2 per cent until 2012. Figure 7.5 also includes data for The Coca-Cola Company, for which the ratio has declined at a compound annual rate of −5 per cent since 2002, with a 2 per cent decline from 2006 to 2007.

Unilever manufactures food, home and personal care products for consumers throughout the world. With two-thirds of its raw materials coming from farms and plantations, the availability of freshwater is crucial to its success.[27] The Coca-Cola Company is also highly dependent

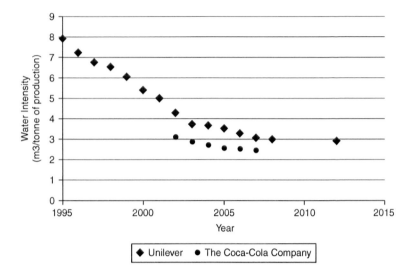

Figure 7.5   Water intensity production for Unilever and The Coca-Cola Company
Sources: Unilever, 2008, Performance Indicators; and The Coca-Cola Company, 2008, 2007/
2008 Sustainability Review, p. 35.

on water availability. Apart from the obvious water content of its main products, it is among the world's largest purchasers of sugar, high fructose corn syrup, citrus and coffee, which all require water for their production.[28] The ratios in Figure 7.5 are based on direct water consumption in plant operations. They are relatively easy to measure and tracking them represents a first step toward responsible water management. But they only reflect a fraction of a company's full water impact.

For Unilever, analysis of the full life cycles of their products revealed that manufacturing operations account for less than 5 per cent of the total amount of water used. For their food products, water used by suppliers of agricultural raw materials represents close to 85 per cent of the total. For home and personal care products, over 85 per cent is associated with consumer use of the products. This insight has led to a four-pronged approach to water sustainability that seeks to reduce water use in manufacturing, work with agricultural suppliers to reduce their usage, design products that require less water during consumer use and participate in cross-sectoral initiatives to better understand the firm's own impacts and to promote better management of water resources.[29] It is an approach that combines mitigating water risks by reducing water dependency with enhancing opportunities and competitiveness in water scarce markets.

Water metrics and eco-efficiency

In the last decade of the twentieth century, firms started to pay attention to their direct water consumption. In the first decade of the twenty-first century, they have begun to assess their water impacts throughout their value chains, from suppliers to end-users of their products. This has given rise to the so-called 'business water footprint' concept, which in 2008 has just begun to be described and refined as a tool for managing water impacts. A first attempt at formalizing the concept defines the business water footprint as 'the total volume of freshwater that is used directly or indirectly to run and support the business'.[30] In this approach, it consists of two components: the operational water footprint, or direct freshwater use of business units within the company, and the amount of freshwater used to produce all the goods and services that form the input of production, or the indirect water use. Whether and how the definition is expanded to consider water associated with the use of products could be influenced by the 'Water Footprint Network', an alliance of businesses, international organizations, academic institutions, government agencies and non-governmental organizations created in 2008.

It is interesting to note a similar process of refining measures of eco-efficiency occurring at the same time with regard to greenhouse gas (GHG) emissions, although the nature of the quantity being measured is entirely different from that of water. The Greenhouse Gas Protocol Initiative was launched in 1998 with the mission to develop internationally accepted GHG accounting and reporting standards for business and to promote their broad adoption.[31] The GHG Protocol Corporate Standard defines three 'scopes' for GHG accounting and reporting purposes. Scope 1 refers to direct GHG emissions from sources owned or controlled by a company. Scope 2 accounts for emissions associated with the generation of electricity purchased and consumed by a company. Scope 3 allows for the treatment of all other indirect emissions; in the 2004 revised protocol, it is an optional reporting category. In September of 2008 the GHG Protocol Initiative launched a two-year collaborative project to develop standards for measuring and managing GHG emissions throughout the product life cycle and across the entire corporate value chain.[32] This is essentially the same challenge that has been taken up by the Water Footprint Network. These parallel efforts are a sign that accounting for water use by business is simply evolving in step with the broader concept of eco-efficiency. Progress should be accelerated by sharing of insights, approaches and methods, which is part of the purpose of the Life Cycle Initiative of the United Nations Environment Programme (UNEP) and the Society for Environmental Toxicology and Chemistry (SETAC).[33]

Conclusion

The fundamental water challenge of the twenty-first century is to make sure that water use does not cross the line of water stress. As discussed above and illustrated in Figure 7.3, this may be achieved by reducing the water intensity of the world's economy at a rate that is equal to or greater than the rate of economic growth. The business community has a key role to play in making this happen. Firms in all sectors could contribute by managing their own direct water consumption; demanding the same standards for water management from their suppliers; providing products and services that enable their customers, including consumers throughout the world, to reduce their water consumption; and encouraging governments to strengthen water management policies and systems.

Notes

1. United Nations, 1999, *The World at 6 Billion*, Population Division, Department of Economic and Social Affairs, United Nations Secretariat, New York, p. 5.
2. Institute of Hydrology and Water Management, 2004, 'Water Management Methodologies for Water Deficient Regions in Southern Europe'. Report, EC 5th Framework Programme Contract No: EVK1-CT-2001-00098, University of Bochum, Germany, p. 81.
3. Ibid., p. 83.
4. Alcamo, J., Henrichs, T. and Rösch, T., 2000, 'World Water in 2025 – Global modeling and scenario analysis for the World Commission on Water for the 21st Century', Report A0002, Center for Environmental Systems Research, University of Kassel, Kurt Wolters Strasse 3, 34109 Kassel, Germany.
5. Global Water Intelligence, 2006, *Desalination Markets 2007: A Global Industry Forecast*, Media Analytics Limited, Oxford.
6. World Business Council for Sustainable Development, 2006, *Business in the world of water: WBCSD Water Scenarios to 2025*, Geneva, p. 41.
7. Lewis, N.S. and Nocera, D.G., 2006, 'Powering the planet: Chemical challenges in solar energy utilization', PNAS 103 (43), pp. 15729-15735.
8. *The Economist*, 2008, 'Economics Focus, Grossly distorted picture', 13 March.
9. United Nations Statistics Division, 2008, 'International Recommendations for Industrial Statistics', pp. 128–9. Additional discussion of water intensity as an indicator of the pressure of an economy on water resources is

at http://www.un.org/esa/sustdev/natlinfo/indicators/methodology_sheets/ freshwater/water_use_intensity.pdf.

10. World Resources Institute, 2007, 'Earth Trends, The Environmental Information Portal: Economics, Business and the Environment Searchable Database', http://earthtrends.wri.org/searchable_db/index.php?theme=5.

11. California Energy Commission, 2005, 'California's Water Energy Relationship', Staff Report Prepared in Support of the 2005 Integrated Energy Policy Report Proceeding, CEC-700-2005-011-SF, November.

12. Total water withdrawal estimated from Food and Agriculture Organization of the United Nations, 2008, Aquastat Database; world GDP from World Resources Institute, 2007, 'Earth Trends', op.cit.

13. Organization for Economic Cooperation and Development, 2002, 'Indicators to Measure Decoupling of Environmental Pressure from Economic Growth', pp. 49-51.

14. Institute of Hydrology and Water Management, 2004, *Water Management Methodologies*, p. 81.

15. The ratio may exceed 100 per cent when a country also withdraws water from non-renewable resources such as aquifers receiving no appreciable recharge.

16. Allan, J.A., 2003, 'Virtual Water – the Water, Food and Trade Nexus, Useful Concept or Misleading Metaphor?', IWRA, *Water International*, 28 (1), pp. 4-11.

17. Hoekstra, A.Y.,(ed.), 2003, 'Virtual Water Trade: Proceedings of the International Expert Meeting on Virtual Water Trade', Value of Water Research Report Series No. 12, IHE Delft, The Netherlands.

18. US Department of Energy, 2006, 'Energy Demands on Water Resources: Report to Congress on the Interdependency of Energy and Water', December, pp. 63-64.

19. Ibid., p. 54.

20. Kundzewicz, Z.W., Mata, L.J., Arnell, N.W., Döll, P., Kabat, P., Jiménez, B., Miller, K.A., Oki, T., Sen, Z. and Shiklomanov, I.A., 2007, 'Freshwater resources and their management, Climate Change 2007: Impacts, Adaptation and Vulnerability'. Contribution of Working Group II to the Fourth Assessment Report of the Intergovernmental Panel on Climate Change, M.L. Parry, O.F. Canziani, J.P. Palutikof, P.J. van der Linden and C.E. Hanson, (eds), Cambridge University Press, Cambridge, UK, 173-210.

21. Ibid., pp. 199-202.

22. UN Water, 2006, Water Monitoring: Mapping Existing Global Systems and Initiatives.

23. UN Water, 2008, Status Report on IWRM and Water Efficiency Plans for CSD16, p. 1.

24. Ibid., pp. 31-32.

25. World Business Council for Sustainable Development, 2000, 'Eco-efficiency: Creating More Value with Less Impact', Geneva, p. 1.

26. World Business Council for Sustainable Development, 2000, 'Measuring Eco-efficiency: A Guide to Reporting Company Performance', Geneva.

27. Unilever, 2000, 'Unilever's Water Care Initiative', p. 3.

28. The Coca-Cola Company, 2008, 2007/2008 Sustainability Review, pp. 34-38

29. Unilever, 2008, 'Sustainable Development Report 2007: Environmental Sustainability', pp. 23–34.

30. Gerbens-Leenes, P.W. and Hoekstra, A.Y., 2008, *Business Water Footprint Accounting: A tool to assess how production of goods and services impacts on freshwater resources worldwide*, UNESCO-IHE Institute for Water Education, Delft, The Netherlands, p. 15.
31. World Business Council for Sustainable Development and World Resources Institute, 2004, *The Greenhouse Gas Protocol, A Corporate Accounting and Reporting Standard*, Revised Edition, p. 2.
32. The Greenhouse Gas Protocol, 2008, GHG Protocol's Product and Supply Chain Initiative Launches in Washington, DC and London.
33. United Nations Environment Programme and the Society for Environmental Toxicology and Chemistry, 2008, 'The Life Cycle Initiative, International Life Cycle Partnership for a sustainable world'.

Part II
Trade, Law and Regulation

8
Foreign Direct Investment and Developing Economies

Isabel Álvarez and Raquel Marín

The evolution of the world economy in the last decades has defined a more integrated framework with a notable resurgence of investment flows; liberalization and innovation trends are the main factors shaping it. The result has been an increasing competition amongst market participants and a higher diversity of attractiveness, leading also to the entrance of new countries into the global game. The evolution of technological innovation in communications and the dynamic behaviour of foreign direct investment (FDI) are contributory factors to globalization.

Large multinational firms (MNF) are traditionally the dominant players in such cross-border transactions. A general assessment of their impacts implies that they may positively affect the competitive position of both, the source – home – and the recipient – host – economy. In particular, it may be thought that one of the missions that firms are increasingly having abroad is levering knowledge from foreign locations. Meanwhile, FDI may contribute to the local upgrading of host economies through technology transfer, taking into account that the type of technological strategies of MNFs may determine the existence and size of spillover effects as well as the increased propensity of MNFs to participate in foreign trade.

One of the crucial issues is that the motives for FDI may differ according to the development level of countries, as is the case with local factors for the attraction of foreign capital flows. In fact, international inequalities persist in the distribution of the flows and both FDI outward and inward are mainly concentrated in the most developed countries. However, there has been a certain shift in the direction of investments, and developing countries are also entering the global scene. On the other hand, it has been noticeable that cross-border mergers and acquisitions have experienced a notable increase during the last decades and, although these operations are also mainly concentrated in developed countries, they being simultaneously home and host economies, it seems that developing countries are also gaining ground in this general trend.[1]

Taking into account the geographical reorientation of FDI flows as well as the different level of interaction with local economies, it is interesting to analyse the conditioning factors of FDI behaviour as well as cross-border mergers and acquisitions. Then, some issues relate to the determinants of FDI, the potential differences for mergers and acquisitions and the introduction of other more qualitative aspects such as the effects of the institutional framework features, these taken as factors of FDI attraction.[2]

Internationalization, foreign direct investment and local factors

According to its general definition, foreign direct investment (FDI) occurs when an investor based in one country, the home country, acquires an asset in another country, the host country, with the intention to manage the asset.[3] Then, FDI provides a means for creating direct, stable and long-lasting links between economies. Nonetheless, regarding FDI entry modes, cross-border mergers and acquisitions show a higher level of interaction with local productive systems and a higher resource commitment than general FDI.

The available empirical evidence, largely based on the Dunning Ownership, Location and Internalization (OLI) paradigm, confirms that some driving forces are common to both greenfield investments and mergers and acquisitions, whereas different effects in host economies may derive from the two modes of entry. Then, it is generally assumed that local conditions in terms of factor costs, market structure, human skills and regulatory frameworks are important factors for attracting foreign investments. However, the explanatory capacity of these local assets as determinants of inward investments could differ between developed and developing economies.

The literature highlights market seeking, efficiency seeking and knowledge seeking among the different motives for FDI.[4] The relative importance of each of them and the evolution of FDI flows interact with the stage of economic development of host countries[5]. According to this perspective, resource-seeking investments prevail in least developed countries (LDCs) while market-seeking investments predominate in catching-up economies. Nonetheless, by introducing the phenomenon of increasing decentralization of production or offshoring and its consequences for developing countries into the focus of the analysis, the factors that determine the location of foreign investments by MNF gain in importance.[6] Considering the effects on host economies, the overall rationale is, then, that MNF may play a fundamental role in the relationship between international generation and diffusion of knowledge, and welfare improvements.

From a macro perspective, the investment development path hypothesis enables us to observe how countries evolve through different stages defining different patterns of FDI behaviour according to their development path.[7] As a result of this approach, there would be a positive relationship between countries catching up and the improvement of their outward position in relation to the inward one. It may be underlined that although the globalization trend has not substantially modified the FDI behaviour, a geographical reorientation of the FDI flows is detected. The main changes may be particularly observed in relation to the greater variety of types of FDI operations, to the benefits that FDI generates and to the way in which there is interaction with local economies. The learning perspective seems to be a good framework from which to analyse the role of the MNF in industrial and technological development of host countries.[8] Previous evidence has settled that among the determinant aspects, one of the key issues is the consideration of absorptive capacities for a better understanding of the evolution followed by FDI in developing economies.

When the international investments are carried out via mergers and acquisitions, firms also consider various local conditions in the host economy, including those related to domestic firms and factors at both industry and country levels. Although there are factors such as capital, labour and natural resource endowment that determine both greenfield and mergers and acquisitions, institutional variables, legal, political and cultural environment, are notably significant in the case of cross-border mergers and acquisitions.[9] Indeed, a major focus of research in this line of the literature is related to market growth in host countries and cultural idiosyncrasies between home and host economies. Empirical findings have confirmed that market growth, cultural proximity and low political and financial uncertainty are factors that increase the likelihood of entry via mergers and acquisitions.[10]

On the other hand, following the effects that FDI may generate in local productive systems, it is generally accepted that a necessary condition for technology transfer is the relative weight that achieves the international generation of knowledge.[11] The expression of technological change in host locations may be manifested by different means: among others, the increase of competition due to the presence of foreign-owned firms, the demonstrative effects as well as the mobility of a highly skilled labour force. Nonetheless, there is no strong support for those positive external effects that foreign subsidiaries generate and, on the contrary, the empirical evidence is mixed and differences among countries are found.[12]

It is plausible to think that positive effects in terms of knowledge spillovers are more likely to occur when considering the types of activities carried out by MNF subsidiaries abroad, whether they are oriented to production or to research and development activities in the host location. Nonetheless, the effects are smaller in LDC due to the existence of a threshold level for the generation of externalities; this would imply that countries need a certain level of education, technology, infrastructures and health to benefit more from investment flows.[13] In particular, the literature has remarked that FDI enhancing growth require a minimum threshold of human capital;[14] although the relevance of both innovation and human capital differs according to industries, it constitutes a basic condition for the upgrading of domestic capabilities from FDI. Besides, the positive effects that MNF may generate in host economies are highly dependent on the size of the gap between domestic and foreign units. Differences arise also when the time dimension is taken into consideration. In fact, the evolution of firms' strategies in foreign countries changes over time: on the one hand, towards being more integrated with local firms and institutions;[15] on the other, due to the cumulative character that the presence of FDI generates in the local economies and how it provides incentives for new inward FDI.[16]

As a consequence, a study of the effects of FDI on host locations requires taking into account aspects related to international business strategies and to local capabilities as well. The choice of location depends on the changing strategies of MNF, that is whether they follow home base augmenting versus home base exploiting strategies, as well as whether subsidiaries are assigned a competence creating or competence exploiting mandate.[17] The original idea is based on findings arising from the international business perspectives along which it is of interest to understand how MNF strategic behaviour affects the development of the global economy.[18] The efficiency searching argument focuses on differences between locations and illustrates the case of both developing and transition economies. The potential interface of national/MNF describes the transitory nature of competitiveness forces – low costs – and the necessary shift toward a higher investment in upgrading knowledge base and human capital. On the other hand, the location characteristics are also relevant, such as those related to adequate infrastructure, public research facilities, the educational system and science bases.[19]

In short, the role of FDI may be seen as a crucial factor for international technology diffusion. It may also be a channel of access to international markets through the dynamics of trade and it may permit the extension of productive systems in which MNF operate. Nonetheless, a greater interaction between domestic and foreign firms in relation to technical change and the greater mobility of MNF do not reduce the likelihood of local capabilities in less developed countries. In fact, a study in a multi-country model of the effects of technological transfer from American MNF confirms the existence of some conditional local factors. Positive and significant effects were detected for developed countries but not for LDC, and human capital levels play a crucial role.[20] Moreover, an analysis of two countries in Latin America by Mortimore and Vergara[21] shows that the nature of FDI and its effect depends on technological capacities, human capital thresholds and supplier capabilities in the host country, defining a minimum level of capability threshold to benefit from technology diffusion from the MNF. These findings provide some plausible arguments to support the idea that for the study of the FDI and its effects, such as the international technology diffusion, it is important to consider both developed and developing countries in differentiated but complementary basis.

Recent trends in foreign direct investment

Since the 1980s, FDI flows have notably contributed to globalization forces, affecting both the behaviour and growth of international production and markets. In fact, FDI inward stock achieved around 25 per cent of world GDP in 2006. Nowadays, the strength of direct investment is greater for cross-border mergers and acquisitions than for greenfield operations since an overwhelming percentage of FDI currently takes place through the former type of investments.[22] As data from UNCTAD reveal there has been a rebound in FDI after three years of declining and, although the evolution of the different entry modes of FDI followed similar trends during the 1990s, there was a spectacular rise in the value of mergers and acquisitions in the second half of the decade, as shown in Figure 8.1.

The geographical distribution of FDI is not uniform but on the contrary, this is a field in which world inequalities still persist. Nonetheless, flows to developing countries and the transition economies attained their highest levels ever and one of the most significant shifts in worldwide trends is the rise of FDI from developing and transition economies and the growth of South-South FDI.[23] The share of developing countries

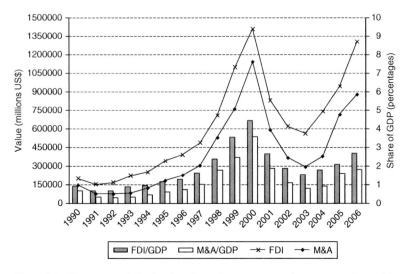

Figure 8.1   Recent trends in foreign direct investment and mergers and acquisitions as flows in the world economy 1990–2006: value and share of GDP
Source: UNCTAD, FDI Statistical Database.

reached 38 per cent of world FDI flows in 2004, which is the highest for this group of countries since 1997. Besides, among the top 100 MNF, four of them are based in developing countries. Some of the most important factors explaining the growth of FDI in developing economies may be summarized as follow: first, the competitive pressures which force firms to look for new ways of improving competitiveness in order to increase their presence and influence in international markets; second, the fast growing of markets which implies increasing economies of scale and a reduction of production costs; and third, an upturn toward cross-border mergers and acquisitions operations.[24]

One aspect to recall is that the significant growth in the level of FDI has gone hand in hand with a higher international pervasiveness. It is notable the diversity of the worldwide direction of the FDI inflows, as illustrated by the combination of the Inward FDI Potential Index[25] and the FDI performance of countries, in Table 8.1. In the first quadrant of the matrix, the group of 'front-runners' that has high FDI potential and high FDI performance is mainly integrated by transition economies and middle-income countries, that is market developing economies, which are gaining weight in the world distribution of FDI. The majority of the richest countries (the US, Japan and most of the European economies) are mainly located in the second quadrant of the matrix, integrating

Table 8.1 Matrix of inward foreign direct investment: performance and potential 2006

	High FDI performance	Low FDI performance
High FDI potential	*Front-runners* Azerbaijan, Bahamas, Bahrain, Belgium, Brunei Darussalam, Bulgaria, Chile, Croatia, Cyprus, Czech Republic, Dominican Republic, Estonia, Hong Kong (China), Hungary, Iceland, Israel, Jordan, Kazakhstan, Latvia, Lithuania, Luxembourg, Malaysia, Malta, Mongolia, Netherlands, New Zealand, Oman, Panama, Poland, Romania, Saudi Arabia, Singapore, Slovakia, Sweden, Thailand, Trinidad and Tobago, Tunisia, Ukraine, Utd Arab Emirates and United Kingdom.	*Below potential* Algeria, Argentina, Australia, Austria, Belarus, Brazil, Canada, China, Denmark, Finland, France, Germany, Greece, Ireland, Islamic Republic of Iran, Italy, Japan, Kuwait, Libyan Arab Jamahiriya, Mexico, Norway, Portugal, Qatar, Republic of Korea, Russian Federation, Slovenia, Spain, Switzerland, Taiwan Province of China, United States and the Bolivarian Rep. of Venezuela.
Low FDI potential	*Above potential* Albania, Armenia, Botswana, Colombia, Congo, Costa Rica, Egypt, Ethiopia, Gambia, Georgia, Guinea, Guyana, Honduras, Jamaica, Kyrgyzstan, Lebanon, Namibia, Nicaragua, Nigeria, Peru, Republic of Moldova, Sierra Leone, Sudan, Tajikistan, the former Yugoslav Rep. of Macedonia, Togo, Uganda, United Republic of Tanzania, Uruguay, Viet Nam and Zambia.	*Under-performers* Angola, Bangladesh, Benin, Bolivia, Burkina Faso, Cameroon, Côte d'Ivoire, Democratic Republic of Congo, Ecuador, El Salvador, Gabon, Ghana, Guatemala, Haiti, India, Indonesia, Kenya, Madagascar, Malawi, Mali, Morocco, Mozambique, Myanmar, Nepal, Niger, Pakistan, Papua New Guinea, Paraguay, Philippines, Rwanda, Senegal, South Africa, Sri Lanka, Suriname, Syrian Arab Republic, Turkey, Uzbekistan, Yemen and Zimbabwe.

Note: Three-year moving average for 2004–2006. Because of unavailability of data on FDI potential for 2007, data corresponding to 2006 have been used.
Source: UNCTAD, *World Investment Report 2008.*

the 'below potential' group where although accounting with a high FDI potential, they show low FDI performance. Moreover, although in both the 'above- potential' and the 'under-performers' groups there is a higher diversity, most of the countries are lower-middle income and low-income

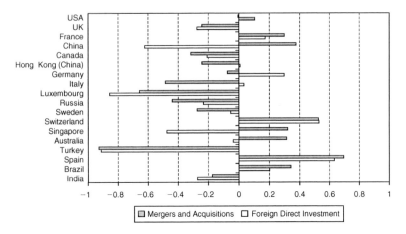

Figure 8.2 Internationalization Index 2006: main recipients and sources of foreign direct investment and mergers and acquisitions
Source: UNCTAD, FDI Statistical Database.

economies; nonetheless, in the last group there is a predominance of low-income and African economies.

Conversely, the main changes in the geographical distribution of FDI may be particularly observed if we analyse the position of countries at an international level according to the Balassa Index.[26] According to this Index, in 2004 China was placed among the predominantly host countries, following the US, UK and France. Analysing more updated data in Figure 8.2, China shows a weaker position as host economy than in previous years but has adopted a more dynamic behaviour in the mergers and acquisitions operations, becoming one of the more active home countries.

Likewise, Russia, Turkey, Brazil and India have occupied a clear position in this group of economies in recent years. Taking into account the most developed countries, Spain and Switzerland are predominantly home countries, in terms of both FDI and mergers and acquisitions flows, while Luxembourg and Italy are featured as predominantly host countries. More interesting is the increasing role played by developing countries which may be observed in the values of the Balassa Index for China and Brazil, these two economies being turned into predominantly home countries in terms of mergers and acquisitions in 2006. Nonetheless, Turkey and Russia are predominantly host countries of these types of investments. Although India does not show yet a prominent rank in either FDI or mergers and acquisitions, this country has already occupied a place in this selected group of economies without predominance of either of the extreme positions. Additionally, the spectacular volume of FDI flows of these economies makes especially noteworthy the position of two middle income countries, China and Turkey.

The process of business internationalization in general, and mergers and acquisitions in particular, finds among the macroeconomic and political factors some additional explanations. The leading players in the rapid growth of cross-border mergers and acquisitions between 1990 and 2002 were developed countries. Developing countries, however, underwent a considerable increase in the volume of assets involved in mergers and acquisitions. According to the regional blocks, Asian and Latin American cases are particularly significant since both contribute over 90 per cent to the total volume of this group of countries, as can be seen in Table 8.2. On the one hand, Latin America is the main recipient region in which the leading players have been Brazil and Argentina. In these countries, privatizations have played a crucial role as a way through which American and European firms, particularly Spanish, may enter these economies. In terms of Central and Eastern European countries, their participation is relatively small although since the mid-1990s they have become predominantly recipient countries. This is mainly due to privatization processes in these economies; Poland, the Czech Republic and Croatia being the main targets of acquisitions and, nowadays, integrated in the EU investment flows. In fact, these European countries are becoming increasingly attractive for FDI on the basis of their technological capabilities, high education levels and research and development potential.[27]

The results in terms of economic growth and the regional integration processes may then be considered as key factors fostering mergers and acquisitions at an international level. Meanwhile, the direction of these deals appears to be also predetermined by industrial and business features of the recipient economy, being sufficiently plausible to think that the existence of local firms worth buying by foreigner investors is a key determinant aspect for cross-border mergers and acquisitions. The sector dynamism of mergers and acquisitions in the last decade is also a prominent feature of cross-border mergers and acquisitions and has achieved greater importance in explaining the strategies of large MNFs. It is clear that services played a leading role in cross-border mergers and acquisitions and, among them, large MNF in financial, business services, transport, storage, communications and utilities – electricity, gas and water.[28] Deregulation and liberalization processes have had a considerable impact on the financial and telecommunications industries, in which the generation of industrial and geographic synergies has brought

Table 8.2   Mergers and acquisitions flows by region 1990–2006: sales US dollars millions

	1990	1995	2000	2003	2004	2005	2006
Developed countries	135,761	169,695	1,074,507	245,841	317,431	604,882	727,955
European Union (25)	62,359	80,638	601,373	126,018	178,772	429,146	432,144
USA	54,697	53,237	324,350	69,670	81,939	105,560	172,174
Japan	148	541	15,541	10,948	8,875	2,512	2,599
Developing countries	14,757	15,792	66,907	38,752	53,120	94,101	127,372
Africa	485	840	3,199	6,427	4,595	10,509	17,569
Latin America and Caribbean	10,199	8,385	41,628	10,671	23,704	24,143	37,562
Asia	4,073	6,500	22,075	21,572	24,768	59,266	71,579
Oceania	0	67	5	83	53	184	661
World	150,576	186,593	1,143,816	296,988	380,598	716,302	880,457

Source: UNCTAD, FDI Statistical Database.

success in the fierce competition of the international market.[29] Likewise, changes in the institutional and regulatory environment, such as the development of capital markets in host economies, are other powerful determinants of the evolution of mergers and acquisitions. Another explanatory factor is technological change and, especially, the development of ICT, which has helped to generate new business opportunities at an international level. In the manufacturing sector, technical change and high cost of innovation are also the main driving forces for the increase in mergers and acquisitions and particularly in the electronics and chemical sector, as well as, in motor vehicles and other transport.[30]

Finally, the level of research and development performed by foreign subsidiaries abroad is an indicator of the degree of internationalization of core technological activities of MNF in recent years and allows us also to observe the existence of some main changes. According to the selection of cases illustrated in Figure 8.3, research and development carried out by foreign firms as the share of total business research and development is higher than 50 per cent in Ireland and the Czech Republic and has increased in the last ten years in most of the economies considered. Nonetheless, it is especially notable the evolution of this indicator in both Czech and Slovak Republic, as well as in Portugal. However,

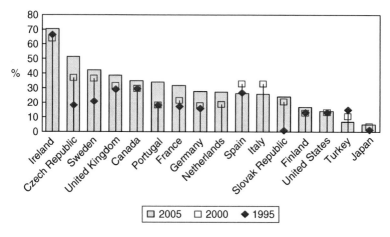

Figure 8.3 Research and development of foreign affiliates 1995–2005
Source: OECD, 2008, *Main Science and Technology Indicators*, Paris.

it has remained invariant for the cases of the US, Finland and Japan, that is, for the most technological advanced countries. Besides, the proportion of foreign research and development has decreased notably in Turkey between 1995 and 2005 while in both the Italian and the Spanish economies this reduction took place in the last year. The relative weight of foreign research and development is conditioned by the changing strategies of large MNF but the changes also found reasonable support in the relative technological advance of the local business sector and in its potential upgrading.[31]

Foreign direct investment and its determinants in the world economy

It is reasonable to think that the determinants of both types of FDI entry modes, greenfield and cross-border mergers and acquisitions, may differ according to the features of host economies. Consequently, one of the interesting issues related to this topic is the assessment of the relationship between inward FDI and national systems of innovation. In this sense, a crucial aspect is to discriminate for how long the foreign capital remains in the host economies and to consider the introduction of more qualitative factors in the explanation of the investment flows. Particularly, it is agreed that the impacts on the host economies may vary with the entry mode and mergers and acquisitions imply a higher degree of interaction in host economies.[32] For these reasons, it is plausible to expect that the impact on the host countries would be higher for mergers and acquisitions since acquired affiliates have a higher local content.

The determinants of FDI compile a set of elements which would reveal the qualification of the type of FDI in host countries. Some of them may be considered as more conventional determinants of FDI, such as productive costs (i.e. wages), the openness level of countries and the size and growth of the internal market. Others are more related to the features of national systems of innovation, such as the human capital level, which provides a plausible argument to explain the evolution of FDI entries in countries and particularly in LDC, as well as absorptive capacities. The latter, adopted from the micro concept formulated by Cohen and Levinthal,[33] is understood as the possibility to benefit from innovation carried out externally to a firm and it would define a second phase of learning; at an aggregated level, absorptive capacities may be measured through national research and development expenditures.[34] On the other hand, we find aspects related to the path of foreign capital presence since the cumulative feature of FDI, this proxy by FDI stock, may become a determinant aspect for new further FDI entries. Finally, institutional and regulatory features of host economies, such as stability or the power of law, may also be considered as extremely important conditional factors of the attractiveness level in locations.

The existence of worldwide differences in the behaviour of FDI may be observed through the level of development across countries. We use World Bank criteria for the classification of countries according to GDP per capita – income variable – in four different groups. We make calculations of some basic statistics for both developed countries – integrated in the high income level group – and developing countries which are divided into three different groups: upper-middle, lower-middle economies and low-income countries. Developing economies are not a homogeneous group but on the contrary, the diversity among them is observable, in Table 8.3; the heterogeneity between groups is even more noticeable in some variables than in others and intra-group differences also arise between the two groups of middle-income countries.

It may be noted that among developing countries, lower-middle and upper-middle income economies present similar mean values in inward FDI flows whereas for the high-income group a notable higher value is found. Nonetheless, middle-income countries show a great distance from the most backward countries or low-income group. The higher dispersion in this indicator corresponds to the group of lower middle-income economies. The heterogeneity of the developing world may also be

Table 8.3 Economic data by type of economy 1998–2004

	High Income		Upper-Middle Income		Lower-Middle Income		Low Income	
	Mean	Std. Dev/Mean	Mean	Std. Dev/Mean	Mean	Std. Dev/Mean	Mean	Std. Dev/Mean
FDI (US $ millions)	17,668.24	2.15	2,561.78	1.65	2,689.10	3.15	271.11	1.58
Mergers and Acquisitions (US$ m)	16,210.32	2.58	1,372.05	2.02	965.75	3.02	101.48	2.81
FDI Stock (US$ m PPP)	137,607.58	1.74	21,889.40	1.44	14,693.69	2.48	3,087.81	2.04
GDP (US$ m constant 2000)	762,398.22	2.29	179,152.19	1.52	330,400.12	2.89	43,620.35	1.54
GDP Growth (%)	3.25	0.82	3.80	1.08	4.16	0.89	4.56	0.92
Openness (%)	96.67	0.65	96.17	0.44	83.12	0.47	71.06	0.45
Income (US$ PPP)	27,320.63	1.90	7,826.94	1.29	7,869.92	1.27	5,182.89	2.26
Human Capital (school enrolment in secondary education, %)	105.80	0.21	83.19	0.17	72.67	0.25	39.27	0.63
Research and Development/GDP (%)	1.92	0.55	0.59	0.51	0.43	0.77	0.29	0.72

Sources: UNCTAD; FDI Statistical Database, UNCTAD; *World Investment Report 2007*; and the World Bank, World Development Indicators Database.

observed in both FDI flows and mergers and acquisitions. Middle-income countries exceed by more than ten times the mean value of low-income countries. Conversely, regarding the profile describing the foreign presence with a higher degree of interaction with host economy, as measured by mergers and acquisitions, it is remarkable that the most developed countries are more homogeneous whereas the highest value of the coefficient of variation in cross-border mergers and acquisitions corresponds to the group of lower-middle income countries, demonstrating the diversity of these operations in the least developed economies considered here. These descriptive come to highlight the relevance of the intragroup heterogeneity in developing countries, aspect that may derive into interesting consequences for the definition of specific policies on the international community, enhancing the development processes in laggard countries.

Moreover, there are large differences in the accumulation of foreign capital, measured by the FDI stock in host economies, and the level of salaries in developed economies compared to the developing world – the dispersion of these two variables is higher in the least income economies. However, in aspects such as the openness level, the averages are very similar. With regard to the dynamism of the market measured through the GDP growth, largest mean values for the countries with least level of development and lower-middle income are revealed, although the dispersion of variable distribution is larger for upper-middle income economies.

The differences between developed and developing countries are even more marked according to the qualitative local factors of FDI attraction, such as educational level and research and development intensity. Two important factors that contribute to defining the existing gap between high-income countries and developing economies are the indicators of human capital and absorptive capacities. It may be observed also that there are significant differences in the mean values of middle-income and low-income countries. These results may reveal the existence of a double gap in local conditions of the most backward countries what weakens their relative position for catching-up in the economic globalization process.[35] In the global economy, the structural heterogeneity is a determinant factor for a better understanding of FDI behaviour in developing economies, this heterogeneity being manifested in the large potential and the weaknesses of the countries belonging to this group.

Figure 8.4 shows the distribution of FDI and cross-border mergers and acquisitions by groups of countries, taking normalized values of the two variables. This would reinforce previous arguments and illustrates

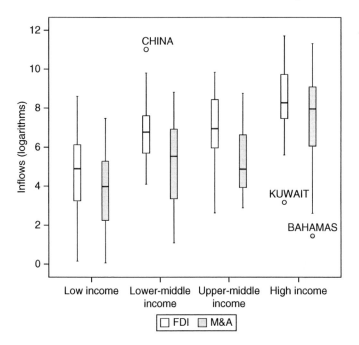

Figure 8.4 Distribution of foreign direct investment and mergers and acquisitions by economic type 2004
Source: UNCTAD, FDI Statistical Database.

first, the positive relationship existing between the two kinds of capital internationalization and the income levels of countries; we may see that there is still a notable gap on the volume of FDI and mergers and acquisitions inflows between the more advanced countries and developing economies. High-income economies present the highest levels of FDI and cross-border mergers and acquisitions, a more homogenous distribution of the two kinds of flows and only a few differences between them. For the middle- and low-income economies, it is noticeable the differences between both kinds of international investments.

However, the heterogeneity of cross-border mergers and acquisitions is more pronounced for lower-middle income countries, emerging countries such as China integrating this group, what underlines the dynamics of the investment flows and then, the non-deterministic behaviour of the relationship between FDI and development.

Considering now some of the more active developing countries entering the global scene, it may be observed whether according to the

Table 8.4   Main recipients and sources of foreign direct investment and mergers and acquisitions 2004: developing economies*

	Research and Development (%GDP)	Human capital	GDP growth	Openness	FDI Stock
Upper-middle income					
Russia	1.46	1.08	1.07	0.91	0.11
Turkey	0.99	0.92	1.34	0.76	0.04
Lower-middle income					
Brazil	0.87	1.35	0.64	0.56	0.18
China	1.17	0.96	1.32	1.05	0.30
Low income					
India**	1.15	1.20	1.14	0.78	0.24

* Data on research and development refers to the year 2000 in the case of low income countries, to the year 2002 in the case of upper-middle income countries, and to the year 2003 in the case of lower-middle income countries.
** Although India is at present integrating the lower-middle income group (UNDP), data correspond to previous years and at the year of reference it was still classified as a low-income economy.
Sources: UNCTAD, FDI Statistical Database; and the World Bank, *World Development Indicators* Database.

determinants of FDI they perform better than the average of their income groups. The analysis for a set of middle-income countries shall allow us also to explain the heterogeneity that was previously underlined. The dynamism of the internal market seems to be a common factor in these emerging economies, with the exception of Brazil with a value under one, in Table 8.4. In fact, for the set of indicators considered, only Turkey shows a value above the mean in the growth of the internal market, a result that could be associated with the role that its geographic position, close to the European market, has in the attraction of FDI. Nonetheless, Turkey shows a very low value in the FDI stock indicator, being far from the average of its group regarding the past presence of foreign capital and similar values to upper-middle income countries in the educational level and research and development intensity.

It is of special interest to note that the value of Russia in the indicator of absorptive capacities is near 50 per cent above the average of its group and, although to a lesser extent, the values for both China and India are also over the average of their groups, respectively. The human capital seems to be remarkable for Brazil, India and Russia, all of them adopting values higher than their groups. Nonetheless, the South American

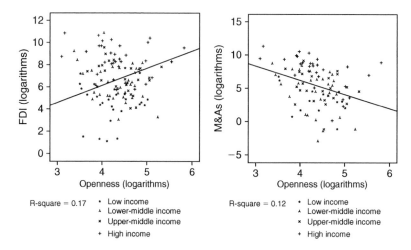

Figure 8.5 Entry modes and openness level 2003
Sources: UNCTAD, FDI Statistics Database; and the World Bank, *World Development Indicators* Database.

economy only exceeds the mean values in this variable while it under-performs in the research and development, the growth in GDP and the openness level. Conversely, only China shows a value above the average in the openness indicator and neither of the countries stands out in the path of foreign capital accumulation, what makes more noticeable the recent changes in FDI entry modes.

Finally, the description of some basic relations between the level of the FDI flows and their determinants allow us to observe, for a broad sample of countries, the existence of differences for the two modes of entry. For instance, the stock of foreign capital in host economies show a positive and stronger relationship for greenfield than for cross-border mergers and acquisitions (lineal R square = 0.84 for the former and 0.63 for the later) while the relationship with the dynamic of the host markets, meas-ured by the growth of the GDP is clearer for mergers and acquisitions. It is less obvious the relationship existing between the level of human capital and merger and acquisition flows (R square = 0.26 versus 0.08). As for the openness level of countries the two entry modes show a very dis-similar behaviour as outlined in Figure 8.5.[36] The internationalization of firms by the creation of new assets seems to have a positive relationship with regard to the openness of the economies while mergers and acquisi-tions are showing a notable tariff jumping component, described by the

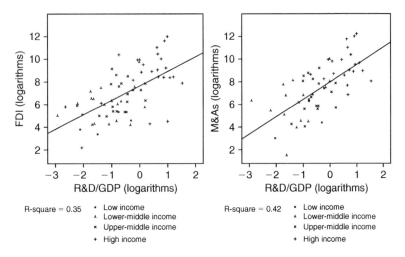

Figure 8.6   Entry modes and research and development 2003
Sources: UNCTAD, FDI Statistics Database; and the World Bank, *World Development Indicators* Database.

negative relationship of the two variables scattered in. Besides, it may be also observe that there is no a clear pattern in the relationship between FDI entry modes and openness in terms of the development level of countries; that is, there are some upper-middle and lower-middle income countries that present similar values in FDI, mergers and acquisitions and openness with regard to the high income economies.

Conversely, although the two entry modes show a positive relationship with the research and development efforts of countries, this proxy for absorptive capacities, it seems to be more related with cross-border mergers and acquisitions, see Figure 8.6. This would justify that this entry mode seems to be more linked to the features of the national system of innovation in host economies. In such a case, there is a clear relationship between FDI entry modes and research and development effort in terms of level of development: the more advanced economies that show higher research and development effort levels, are those that receive higher volumes of FDI and mergers and acquisitions. Nonetheless, it is noticeable the close position shown by some upper-middle and lower-middle income economies with regard to high income countries. In fact, it should be noted that among these developing economies are China, Brazil and India, an aspect that would confirm some of the arguments underlined in previous sections.

Conclusion

It is broadly agreed that FDI entry modes may be affected by international business strategies, as set out in the OLI theory, in which ownership and internalization advantages combine with the features of host locations, altogether defining the determinants of FDI. This chapter highlights the existence of world inequalities in the behaviour of FDI, the emergence of developing economies entering the global scene and the increasing role of mergers and acquisitions as a way of firms' internationalization. Some of the main issues which still deserve further consideration in economic research about the behaviour of FDI are, first, the division of labour in the global value chain and the effects on the competitiveness of developing economies; second, the changing technological strategies of MNCs and the possibilities for reverse knowledge flows; and third, the global consequences of the emergence of alternative countries as the main recipients and sources of investment flows.

Although international investments are still highly concentrated in most developed countries, developing economies are gaining some ground for FDI flows and their path may differ from developed countries. This shift is at least suggestive for broadening the scope of the research on the analysis of the effects of FDI in both home and host economies. Besides, the different entry modes of FDI and the relative importance of the determinants of FDI flows open up new questions about the characteristics of the national systems of innovation, the role of absorptive capacities and the understanding of global learning processes.

The statistical information on FDI flows and cross-border mergers and acquisitions allow an observation of the international differences that persists when both developed and developing economies are analysed and also the noticeable heterogeneity that characterizes the developing economies in which laggard economies co-exist but with different profiles.

Notes

1. UNCTAD, 2007, World Investment Report, *Transnational Corporations, Extractive Industries and Development*, United Nations, New York and Geneva.
2. This aspect is thoroughly analysed in Álvarez, I. Marín, R., 2008, 'FDI and World Heteregoneity', ICEI Working Paper WP06-08, Instituto Complutense de Estudios Internacionales, Madrid, the presence of a co-evolutionary path defined by FDI flows, entry modes and the level of economic development being found. Particularly, the main hypothesis related the fact that the impact of FDI may differ depending on the countries' level of development and on

the characteristics of the national systems which are determinant factors of the catching-up process.

3. It may be found in the *Balance of Payments Manual*, edited by the International Monetary Fund. Moreover, the revision and methodological issues related to the definition and its implications for statistics recompilation may be found in OECD, *2008a, OECD Benchmark Definition of Foreign Direct Investment*, 4th Edition, OECD, Paris.

4. Dunning, J., 2006, 'Towards a paradigm of development: implications for the determinants of international business activity', *Transnational Corporations*, 15 (1), pp. 173–227.

5. Narula, R. and Dunning, J., 2000, 'Industrial development, globalization and multinational enterprises: new realities for developing countries', *Oxford Development Studies*, 28 (2), pp. 141–67; Narula, R., 1996, *Multinational Investments and Economic Structure*, Routledge, London, and Narula, R., 2004, 'Research and development collaboration by SMEs: new opportunities and limitations in the face of globalization', *Technovation*, 24, pp. 153–61.

6. Hatzichronoglou, T., 2008, *The Location of Investment of Multinationals Linked To Innovation, VII Global Forum on International Investment*, OECD, Paris.

7. Dunning, J. and Narula, R., 1994, 'The research and development activities of foreign firms in the US', Discussion Papers in International Investment & Business Studies 189, University of Reading, Reading; Dunning, J. and Narula, R. (eds), 1996, *Foreign Direct Investment and Governments: Catalysts for Economic Restructuring*, Routledge, London, and Lall S., 2002, 'Implications of Cross-Border Mergers and Acquisitions by TNCs in Developing Countries: A Beginners' Guide', QEH Working Paper 88, Oxford.

8. Narula, R. and Lall, S., 2004, 'FDI and its role in economic development: Do we need a new agenda?', *European Journal of Development Research*, 16(3), pp. 447–64.

9. Shimizu, K., Hitt, M.A., Vaidyanath, D. and Pisano, V., 2004, 'Theoretical foundations of cross-border mergers and acquisitions: A review of current research and recommendations for the future', *Journal of International Management*, 10, pp. 307–55, and Globerman, S. and Shapiro, D., 2002, 'Global foreign direct investment flows: the role of governance infrastructure', *World Development*, 30 (11), pp. 1899–919.

10. Kogut, B. and Singh, H., 1988, 'The effect of national culture on the choice of entry mode', *Journal of International Business Studies*, 19 (3), pp. 411–32, and Brouthers, K.D. and Brouthers, L.E., 2000, 'Acquisition or greenfield start-up? Institutional, cultural and transaction cost influences', *Strategic Management Journal*, 21, pp. 89–97.

11. Archibugi, D. and Michie, J., 1995, 'The globalization of technology: A new taxonomy', *Cambridge Journal of Economics*, 19, pp. 121–40.

12. Kokko, A., 1992, 'FDI, host country characteristics and spillovers', The Economic Research Institute, Stockholm School of Economics, Stockholm; Blomström, M. and Kokko, A., 1998, 'Multinational corporations and spillovers', *Journal of Economics Surveys*, 12 (2), pp. 1-31; Perez, T., 1998, *Multinational enterprises and technological spillovers*, Harwood Pub., Amsterdam; Aitken, B.J. and Harrisson, A.E., 1999, 'Do domestic firms benefit from FDI? Evidence from Venezuela', *American Economic Review* 89 (3), pp. 605–618,

and Álvarez, I. and Molero, J., 2005, 'Technology and the generation of international spillovers: an application to Spanish manufacturing firms', *Research Policy*, 34, pp. 1440–52.

13. OECD, 2001, *New Patterns of Industrial Globalization. Cross-border Mergers and Acquisitions and Strategic Alliances*, OECD, Paris; OECD, 2002, *Foreign Direct Investment for Development*, OECD, Paris.

14. Borensztein, E., De Gregrio, J. and Lee, J., 1998, 'How does FDI affect economic growth?', *Journal of International Economics*, 4 (1), pp. 115–35

15. Pearce, R., 1999, 'Decentralised Research and Development and strategic competitiveness: globalised approaches to generation and use of technology in multinational enterprises (MNEs)', *Research Policy*, 28, pp. 157–78.

16. Mudambi, R., 1995, 'The MNE investment location decision: some empirical evidence', *Managerial and Decision Economics*, 16, pp. 249–57.

17. Maytwell, J. and Santangelo, G., 2002, 'Mergers and acquisitions and the global strategies of TNCs', *The Developing Economies*, XL (4), pp. 400–34; Maytwell, J. and Mudambi, R. 2005, 'MNE competence-creating subsidiary mandates', *Strategic Management Journal*, 26 (12), pp. 1109–28.

18. Pearce, R., 2006, 'Globalization and development: an international business strategy approach', *Transnational Corporations*, 15 (1), pp. 39–74.

19. Maytwell, J. and Piscitello, L., 2002, 'The location of technological activities of MNCs in European Regions: The role of spillovers and local competencies', *Journal of International Management*, 8 (1), pp. 69–96.

20. Xu, B., 2000, 'Multinational enterprises, technology diffusion, and host country productivity growth', *Journal of Development Economics*, 62, pp. 477–93.

21. Mortimore, M. and Vergara, S., 2004, 'Targeting winners: can foreign direct investment policy help developing countries industrialise?', *The European Journal of Development Research*, 16 (3), pp. 499–530.

22. UNCTAD, 2003, *FDI Policies for Development: National and International Perspectives*, UNCTAD, Geneva.

23. UNCTAD, 2007, *World Investment Report Transnational Corporations, Extractive Industries and Development*, United Nations, New York and Geneva.

24. UNCTAD, 2005, *World Investment Report Transnational Corporations and the Internationalization of Research and Development*, United Nations, New York and Geneva.

25. The UNCTAD Inward FDI Potential Index is based on 12 economic and structural variables measured by their respective scores on a range of 0–1. It is the un-weighted average of scores on the following variables: GDP per capita, rate of growth of real GDP, share of exports in GDP, telecoms infrastructure (average number of telephone lines per 100 inhabitants, and mobile phones per 100 inhabitants), commercial energy use per capita, share of Research and Development expenditures in gross national income, share of tertiary level students in the population, country risk, exports of natural resources as a percentage of the world total, imports of parts and components of electronics and automobiles as a percentage of the world total, exports of services as a percentage of the world total, and inward FDI stock as a percentage of the world total. For the methodology details for building the index, see UNCTAD, 2002, World Development Indicator 2002, Geneva, pp. 34–36.

26. The Balassa Index (BI) for FDI and Mergers and Acquisitions respectively, is calculated as follows:

$$BI = \frac{FDI_{xw} - FDI_{wx}}{FDI_{xw} + FDI_{wx}} \quad BI = \frac{M\,\&\,A_{xw} - M\,\&\,A_{wx}}{M\,\&\,A_{xw} + M\,\&\,A_{wx}}$$

Where FDI_{xw} or Merger and Acquisition$_{xw}$ is the proportion of outward FDI or Mergers and Acquisitions from country x to the World, and FDI_{wx} or Mergers and Acquisitions$_{wx}$ is the inward FDI or Mergers and Acquisitions from the world in country x. Values of the BI Index between -1 and -0.33 denote predominantly a host country; higher than -0.33 and less than 0.33 means a host and home country; values between 0.33 and 1 correspond predominantly to a home country.

27. Yang, Q., Mudambi, R., and Meyer, K.E., 2008, 'Conventional and Reverse Knowledge Flows in Multinational Corporations', *Journal of Management*, 34 (5), pp. 882–902

28. UNCTAD, 2003, *FDI Policies for Development: National and International Perspectives*, UNCTAD, Geneva.

29. OECD, 2001, *New Patterns of Industrial Globalization. Cross-border Mergers and Acquisitions and Strategic Alliances*, OECD, Paris.

30. Blonigen, B. and Taylor, C., 2000, 'Research and Development activity and acquisitions in High Technology Industries: evidence from the US Electronics Industry', *Journal of Industrial Economics*, 47 (1), pp. 47-71; Danzon, P., Epstein, A. and Nicholson, S., 2004, 'Mergers and Acquisitions in the Pharmaceutical and Biotech Industries', NBER Working Papers 10536, National Bureau of Economic Research, Cambridge MA; Kang, N., Johansson, S., 2000, 'Cross-border Mergers and Acquisitions: Their Role in Industrial Globalization', Working Paper STI DST1/DOC, OECD, Paris, and Maytwell, J. and Santangelo, G., 2002, 'Mergers and acquisitions and the global strategies of TNCs', *The Developing Economies*, XL (4), pp. 400–434.

31. Molero, J. and Álvarez, I., 2003, 'The impact of multinational enterprises technological strategies on national systems of innovation: regularities and national differences' in *Multinational Enterprises, Innovative Strategies and Systems of Innovation*, Maytwell, J. and Molero, J. (eds), Edward Elgar, Cheltenham.

32. Xu, B., 2000, 'Multinational enterprises, technology diffusion, and host country productivity growth', *Journal of Development Economics*, 62, pp. 477–93.

33. Cohen, W.M. and Levinthal, D.A., 1990, 'Absorptive capacity: a new perspective on learning and innovation', *Administrative Science Quarterly*, 35, pp. 128–52.

34. Narula, R., Criscuolo, P. and Verspagen, B., 2002, 'The relative importance of home and host innovation systems in the internationalization of MNE Research and Development: a patent citation analysis', Merit Memorandum MERIT RM 2002-26, Maastricht.

35. Álvarez, I., Magaña, G., 2007, 'Technological development in middle-income countries', in *Cooperation with Middle-income Countries*, J.A. Alonso (ed.), Editorial Complutense, Madrid, pp. 339–69.

36. The analyses in Figures 8.5 and 8.6 refer to 2003 due to data availability reasons.

9
Basel II and Banking in Emerging and Other Developing Economies

Andrew Cornford

In the words of two former senior British financial regulators '... the objective of the new arrangements (Basel II) is to strengthen the soundness and stability of the international banking system while maintaining sufficient consistency so that capital regulation will not be a significant source of competitive inequality among internationally active banks'.[1] Basel II sets levels of minimum regulatory capital for three categories of banking risk – credit, market and operational – according to rules which include a multiplicity of different approaches. This multiplicity reflects the objective of the Basel Committee on Banking Supervision (BCBS) to accommodate within these rules banks of very different levels of sophistication as well as points raised by critics during the long process of drafting Basel II. The effects of the rules of Basel II on different dimensions of banking risk have been extensively debated during the long drafting process and during the current financial crisis. However, this debate was primarily concerned with regulation and risk management in general and devoted only limited attention to the likely impact of the introduction of Basel II in emerging and other developing economies.

The Basel I and II agreements on capital adequacy

Basel I and Basel II are agreements on frameworks for assessing the capital adequacy of banks. The framework sets rules for the allocation of capital to banks' exposures to risks through its lending and other operations. The agreements have two objectives. One is prudential, namely to help to ensure the strength and soundness of banking systems. The other is to help to equalize cross-border competition between banks (provide 'a level playing field') by eliminating competitive advantages due to differences among countries in their regimes for capital adequacy (a special concern of United States and European banks *vis-à-vis* competitors from Japan in the 1980s).

As a measure of the difference between the value of a bank's assets and liabilities capital serves as a buffer against future, unidentified losses. The capital of banks consists of equity and other financial instruments which have the properties of being available to support an institution in times of crisis.

Financial instruments classified as capital are usually associated with higher rates of return, and are thus a more costly way of financing banks' assets than other liabilities such as deposits. The rate of return on capital is a determinant of banks' pricing of loans and of other transactions involving exposure to risk and as such is a factor in their competitiveness *vis-à-vis* other banks.

Capital under the initial version of Basel I agreed in 1988 was to serve as a buffer against credit risk, i.e. that of the failure of borrowers or parties to the other banking transactions to meet their obligations. Under the accord capital was to constitute 8 per cent of banks' risk-weighted assets.

Measurement of these risk-weighted assets was based on the attribution of weights reflecting the credit risk of different classes of counterparty (sovereign, OECD or non-OECD, other public sector, corporate, etc.). Off-balance-sheet exposures (such as guarantees, various contingent liabilities, and interest-rate and exchange-rate derivatives) were converted to their on-balance-sheet equivalents by multiplying them by factors specified for this purpose. The resulting figures were then weighted according to the class of counterparty as for on-balance-sheet exposures. For instance, collateralized documentary credits received a credit conversion factor of 20 per cent and the resulting on-balance-sheet equivalent would be multiplied by the risk weight of the counterparty to which the documentary credit was made available.

The attribution of credit risk weights (0, 10, 20, 50 and 100 per cent) followed a scheme which favoured governments and certain other entities from OECD countries over those from non-OECD countries, and banks over other commercial borrowers. Thus a weight of 0 per cent was attributed to claims on OECD governments and central banks, and one of 20 per cent to claims on banks incorporated in OECD countries and to banks incorporated in non-OECD countries with a residual maturity of up to one year. A weight of 100 per cent was attributed to claims on private sector entities not otherwise specified such as non-financial corporations and non-OECD governments.

Through an amendment in 1996 Basel I was extended to cover market risks, i.e. those due to the impact on a bank's portfolio of tradable assets of adverse changes in interest and exchange rates and in the prices of stocks and other financial instruments. The amendment accommodated two alternative ways of setting minimum capital levels for market risk. One involved the use by banks of their own internal risk-management models, and the other a standardized methodology under which capital requirements are estimated separately for different categories of market risk and then summed to give an overall capital charge (as for credit risks).

Basel I was originally designed for internationally active banks. However, by the second half of the 1990s it had become a global standard and had been incorporated into the prudential regimes of more than 100 countries. Basel I was also the subject of increasingly widespread dissatisfaction so that a decision was taken to initiate what proved to be the lengthy process of drafting a successor agreement. The definitive version of the new accord, Basel II, became available in mid-2006.

Basel II consists of three Pillars. Under Pillar 1 minimum regulatory capital requirements for credit risk are calculated according to two alternative approaches, the Standardized and the Internal Ratings-Based. Under the simpler of the two, the Standardized Approach, the measurement of credit risk is based on ratings provided by external credit assessment institutions. According to the text of the agreement export credit agencies as well as credit rating agencies are indicated for this purpose. However, the expectation of both the BCBS and of national authorities is clearly that the role will most frequently be assumed by credit rating agencies. Owing to perceived shortcomings in the performance of the major credit rating agencies, which are discussed below, this choice has proved controversial.

Under the Standardized Approach of Basel II entities from OECD countries are no longer favoured over those from non-OECD countries. Both banks and non-financial corporations are now differentiated according to their credit ratings (of which the BCBS uses those of Standard & Poor's for illustrative purposes). Thus non-financial corporate borrowers rated between AAA and AA− are attributed a weight of 20 per cent, those rated between A+ and A− one of 50 per cent, those rated between BBB+ and BB− one of 100 per cent, and those rated below BB− one of 150 per cent. Unrated non-financial corporate borrowers are attributed a weight of 100 per cent.

Under the Internal Ratings-Based approach, subject to supervisory approval as to the satisfaction of certain conditions, banks use their own rating systems to measure some or all of the determinants of credit risk, i.e. the probability of default, loss given default, exposure at default and the remaining maturity of the exposure. Under the Foundation version of the Internal Ratings-Based Approach, banks calculate the probability of default on the basis of their own ratings but rely on their supervisors for measures of the other determinants of credit risk. Under the Advanced version of the Internal Ratings-Based Approach, banks also estimate their own measures of all the determinants of credit risk, i.e. the loss to a loan or other exposure given default and the exposure at default as well as the probability of default. Pillar 1 also contains rules for regulatory capital requirements for market risk which follow those of Basel I.

Unlike Basel I, Basel II contains regulatory capital requirements for operational risk which covers losses due to events such as human errors or fraudulent behaviour, computer failures, or disruptions from external events such as earthquakes. Under the Basic Indicator Approach, the simplest of the three options in Basel II, the capital charge for operational risk is a percentage of banks' gross income. Under the Standardized Approach to operational risk the capital charge is the sum of specified percentages of banks' gross income or loans for eight business lines. Under the Advanced Measurement Approach to operational risk, the most sophisticated option of Basel II, subject to the satisfaction of more stringent supervisory criteria, banks estimate the required capital with their own internal measurement systems.

Also unlike Basel I, Basel II contains detailed rules concerning securitization exposures, i.e. the exposures for a bank after the transfer of the risks of assets on its balance sheet to outside investors, a category of risk which was omitted from Basel I. The rules of Basel II are intended to establish stringent conditions for the recognition of the transfer of risk from banks' balance sheets and to set regulatory capital charges for the risks remaining with banks.

Under Basel II the minimum regulatory capital ratio remains at the 8-per-cent figure of Basel I. The denominator of this ratio consists of estimated exposures for credit, market and operational risk. The numerator consists of capital as in Basel I but after adjustment in certain ways. Conceptually the most important of these adjustments is the exclusion of risks corresponding to several categories of expected losses from the denominator of the ratio and of banks' corresponding loss provisions from capital in the numerator. This exclusion brings Basel II more into line with traditional banking practice according to which expected losses are covered by loss provisions, while capital is intended to cover unexpected losses.

Pillars 2 and 3 of Basel II are concerned with supervisory review of capital adequacy and the achievement of discipline in banks' risk management through disclosure to investors. Under the guidelines of Pillar 2 supervisors are to prescribe additional regulatory capital not only for the credit, market and operational risks of Pillar 1 if they judge this to be necessary for supervisory reasons but also for risks not covered under these three headings, such as liquidity risk (which covers banks' ability to obtain funding and the prices at which it could sell assets in financial markets) and interest-rate risks due to changes in the margins between the rates at which banks lend and borrow.

Pillar 3 specifies rules for the disclosure of information concerning banks' capital and risk management. These rules are intended to enable financial market participants as well as supervisors to subject these to scrutiny which will reinforce the effectiveness of Pillars 1 and 2.

The current status of the implementation of Basel II and the difficulties confronting developing countries

Much of the information on implementation concerns the number of countries planning to introduce Basel II. Beyond the raw statistics, however, people are usually also interested in having some kind of assessment of the realism of the plans for introduction and, especially for developing countries, of the pressures on national supervisors which the introduction of Basel II could be expected to generate. Moreover it is also possible to characterize in a preliminary way major features of the pattern of introduction worldwide.

Two surveys of the Basel-based Financial Stability institute in 2004 and 2006 covered the plans of regulators in non-Basel-Committee countries for the introduction of Basel II. If a country announces its intention to introduce the approaches, options, and other rules of Basel II, this means that its regulators will make them available to financial firms in their jurisdictions.

Major findings of the 2006 survey were that 82 of the 98 responding countries planned to introduce Basel II. This figure rises to 95 when the 13 member countries of the Basel Committee on Banking Supervision are added. In comparison with the 2004 survey, the planned schedule for introduction in the 2006 survey was less ambitious in many countries. For most of the regions there were marked increases in the 2006 survey in comparison with the 2004 survey in the proportions of respondents planning to meet the obligations of Pillar 2 (supervisory review) and Pillar 3 (transparency) by 2009. Indeed, the data on meeting the obligations of Pillars 2 and 3 suggest a widespread and understandable tendency among responding countries to give first priority in plans for the introduction of

Basel II to strengthening supervisory capacity – Pillar 2 – and disclosure standards – Pillar 3.

During the drafting process for Basel II there was widespread concern over the difficulties likely to be posed to introduction by limitations on the technical capacity of banks and supervisors. So it is natural to ask the question whether the plans in the replies to the Financial Stability Institute's survey are realistic. Available information does not permit a definite answer to this question but a number of pertinent points may be raised.

The technical capacity of banks and supervisors in many developing countries in comparison with their counterparts in industrialized countries should not be underestimated. Indeed, events during the last decade – and more especially during the last few months – have drawn attention to the sometimes egregious shortcomings of both banks and supervisors in industrial countries. In comparing the risk management capabilities of the large international banks of industrial countries and of banks of developing countries it is important to remember that the activities of the latter are generally more focused on traditional commercial banking and less on the new products and services which are proving more difficult to manage, control, and supervise.

Nevertheless, the strains on national supervisory capacity of introducing Basel II in developing countries should not be underestimated. The scale of these strains is illustrated based on information from the Financial Stability Institute's 2004 survey, which found that non-Basel-Committee countries expected training on Basel II-related topics would be necessary for about 9,400 supervisors or almost 25 per cent of the countries' supervisory staff.

The tasks in developing countries entailed by the introduction of the Standardized Approach for credit risk in Basel II are considerable but manageable. The requirements for introducing the Foundation and Advanced versions of the Internal Ratings-Based Approach, as well as the more advanced approaches for operational risk, are a potential source of greater difficulties. These more advanced approaches of Basel II require data covering substantial periods and the meeting of standards for validation. In the absence of internal sources for the data and models required for validation, banks may have recourse to external providers subject to carefully defined conditions.

In developing countries where key inputs to the Foundation version of the Internal Ratings-Based Approach for credit risk (loss given default and exposure at default) are to be provided not by banks but by supervisors, lack of required data and models may mean that supervisors as well as banks need to have recourse to outside vendors. The danger here is that pressures associated with implementation of the more advanced options of Basel II, according to a timetable determined by political rather than supervisory consideration, may lead to failures to meet proper validation standards for external data and models.

The global pattern of implementation of Basel II will reflect divergences due not only to choices regarding the multiple options under Pillar 1 for minimum regulatory capital requirements for credit, market and operational risk but also to variation in different countries' timetables for adoption and in other rules for introduction at a national level. For instance, under Pillar 2 (supervisory review) of Basel II minimum regulatory capital requirements may vary as a result of the prescription of additional capital by supervisors for risks considered as not covered, or not adequately covered, under Pillar 1 at levels which need not be uniform for different countries.

As a result of these features of Basel II global regulation of banks' capital after Basel II's introduction will remain something of a patchwork. This compromises the second of Basel II's major objectives, namely the achievement of a reasonable measure of competitive equality – the so-called 'level playing field' – by contributing to cross-border consistency in the regulation of banks' capital. However, the patchwork has advantages for developing countries since it entails recognition of countries' need for space in which to adopt policies toward the regulation of banks' capital which are adapted to national needs.

The development dimension and implications of Basel II for investment and growth in developing countries

The 1988 Basel Capital Accord (Basel I), was not designed with economic development in mind. Its objectives, which Basel II has left unchanged, concerned the stability of the international banking system and competitive equality between banks engaged in international lending. The institutions originally targeted by Basel I were the internationally active banks of the Basel Committee's member countries. However, by 1999 Basel I had become a global standard as part of the prudential regimes for strictly domestic as well as international banks in more than 100 countries. Basel II likewise will be a global standard and the plans for the introduction of Basel II in a large number of developing countries raise the question of whether Basel II will have a developmental impact.

One question sometimes raised in this connection is whether the rules of Basel II concerning banks' capital requirements and internal controls will not have the effect of throttling categories of developmental financing which require a long-term perspective and willingness to incur considerable risks. Data bearing on this question include historical statistics for banks' capital in different countries. These statistics refer to simple leverage, i.e. the ratio of equity to a bank's on-balance-sheet assets (or its inverse) and not to the ratio of capital defined by Basel I and Basel II rules to risk-adjusted assets and off-balance-sheet exposures.

For instance, in the US, the average equity-to-total-assets ratio was about 50 per cent in 1840; about 12 per cent in the late 1920s; and (for the 25 largest banks) 5 per cent in 1989. Richard Dale, a scholar of financial regulation, comments as follows: 'These high ratios – as they now seem to us – were the consequence not of any regulatory action but of market forces. That is to say, visibly high equity ratios were necessary to maintain depositors' confidence'.[2] It should also be noted here that under practices common before the American Civil War state banks' capital was often of highly doubtful quality, including, as it might, stock subscriptions which the organizers had borrowed from the very bank being established.[3] Data for Asian banks for the first half of the 1990s, discussed in more detail in below, shows that half of the national groupings probably had leverage levels no higher than would have been compatible with the rules of Basel I.

Thus, partial as they are, the information concerning the US and Asian countries do not point to a strong connection between banks' capital-to-assets ratios and the pace of economic development. Assessment of banks' contribution to development should indeed include the structure and evolution of their balance sheets. But assessment should not place too much emphasis on leverage or capital ratios at the expense of other indicators such as the scale and sectoral distribution of lending, loans-to-deposits ratios, liquidity, and net interest margins.

Leverage ratios for selected Asian countries and the pricing of a bank's transactions

The data for 1994 (see Table 9.1) from Thomson BankWatch on the relation of banks' capital to their assets for selected Asian countries refer to simple leverage calculated as the ratio of a bank's on-balance-sheet assets to equity, and not to the ratio of capital (including non-equity instruments designated as capital under Basel rules) to risk-adjusted assets and off-balance-sheet exposures, that is, the ratio which is the target of Basel I and Basel II.[4] The 8-per-cent minimum capital ratio of Basel I corresponds to a leverage (Assets/Capital) ratio of approximately 12 only if

Table 9.1 Leverage ratios of banks 1994: selected Asian countries

Country	Leverage Ratio
Bangladesh	31.11
China – banks incorporated in Hong Kong SAR	17.29
China – mainland banks	25.33
Hong Kong SAR – excluding HSBC	8.71
India – commercial banks	16.82
India – state banks	28.44
Indonesia – private banks	11.26
Indonesia – state banks	16.17
Macau	12.59
Malaysia	15.08
Pakistan – established banks	31.46
Pakistan – new banks	11.16
Philippines	6.87
Republic of Korea – country banks	14.2
Republic of Korea – nationwide banks	22.25
Republic of Korea – old merchant banks	11.01
Republic of Korea – specialized banks	23.78
Singapore	7.74
Taiwan Province – established banks	18.93
Taiwan Province – new banks	5.32
Thailand	11.69
Vietnam	12.41

Source: Thomson BankWatch Data for 1994.

the banks' loans and other exposures are attributed risk weightings of 100 per cent. In the numerators of the leverage ratios for the Asian countries no allowance is made for the less than 100-per-cent credit weighting attributed under the rules of Basel I to low-risk exposures on banks' balance sheets and, generally, off-balance-sheet exposures are not included in the ratio. Moreover, the denominator generally excludes non-equity capital.[5] These differences should be borne in mind in comparing historical figures for banks' leverage with a Basel-based benchmark.

Thus at least half of the groupings of banks specified in the Thomson BankWatch data for 1994 probably had leverage ratios no higher than would have been compatible with the rules of Basel I, which many of the countries had adopted or were about to adopt, though implementation of this measure probably would have been at most at a highly preliminary stage.

Explicit references to development financing in the text of Basel II are difficult to find. Nonetheless important techniques of development finance could be accommodated under the rules of Basel II for credit risk mitigation, a term which covers loan collateralization, guarantees, and credit derivatives. Guarantees are a standard technique whereby a public entity may substitute exposure to its credit risk for that of another borrower. The lower credit risk of lending backed by state guarantees is recognized in Basel II.

Other provisions of Basel II, which may be useful in the context of lending for development are its preferential credit weightings for lending to small and medium-sized enterprises (SMEs). Some of the relevant rules for such weightings are to be found under those for retail exposures. Nevertheless, there are legitimate concerns as to the developmental implications of Basel II's underlying premises about the nature of a good banking model. Pushed too far, these could prove harmful.

The premises of Basel II about the relationship between a bank and its counterparties are part of the now generally accepted business model for banking in the member countries of the Basel Committee and the rest of developed world. But they diverge to varying degrees from the premises of banking models in several emerging-market countries. In Basel II the assumed relationship is arm's length. This implies that decisions about lending, investment and the provision of other banking services are based on reasoned analysis of the counterparty's capacity to meet interest obligations as well as of other dimensions of creditworthiness as measured by objective rating or scoring systems.

A different model of borrower–lender relations has often prevailed in emerging-market countries. This model involves practices which go by names such as policy or directed lending, relationship or name lending, and collateral-based lending. As part of such practices, loans are made on the basis of criteria different from those of the underlying premises of Basel II. The assumptions about risk sharing between a bank and its borrowers involve a relationship that is less arm's length and in some cases more like an equity investment.

It is often stated by commentators in developed countries that relationship lending could degenerate into 'crony capitalism'. This is true but alternative banking models also have their downside. Relationship lending's opposite, arm's length banking, with its reliance on quantitative criteria derived from supposedly scientific approaches to finance and with its de-emphasis on long-term relations between banks and their customers, pushed to its extreme, led to the financial turbulence engulfing major developed countries since mid-2007.

Where borrower–lender relations, different from those assumed by Basel II, are deeply rooted in national practices the risks to economic activity and development from too an abrupt transition to Basel II could be substantial. Especially in Asia, but also to varying degrees in many other developing countries, a major source of economic growth has been firms, often family-owned or -controlled, which would not necessarily achieve high credit ratings – and thus low weightings for credit risk under Basel II – according to objective, quantitative criteria.

Two PricewaterhouseCoopers authorities on the capital regulation and risk management of banks have posed an important question concerning Basel II and such firms, in that the introduction of Basel II might lead to a credit crunch, with banks less willing to lend to these companies. And as they provide the core financial support of the emerging economies, and would find it difficult to turn to the capital markets for alternative sources of funds, there may be an impact on the economic development of these countries. These issues must be carefully evaluated before implementing Basel II in many of the countries in the Asia-Pacific region.[6]

As to the question of whether there are discernible implications of Basel II for investment and growth in developing countries these are still early days. But there is some anecdotal evidence that in some countries banks are treating Basel II as a justification for tightening lending standards in the way warned against above. Changes in banks' lending practices in response to the introduction of Basel II are a subject which authorities in developing countries need to keep under close scrutiny, using policy space available to them to forestall banks' adoption of potentially damaging lending practices.

Issues in introducing Basel II in developing countries with special emphasis on those related to cyclical effects

Most of the problems of introducing Basel II are common to all countries but some may be more severe in developing countries owing to less adequate supervisory capacity, less developed internal controls within banks themselves, and the shortage of infrastructure such as data on credit risks and credit rating agencies.

The danger that Basel II will aggravate procyclicality has been a major feature of debate on its likely effects. The rules of Basel II are intended to align regulatory capital requirements more closely with economic capital, that is, the level considered by banks to be appropriate as a buffer against unidentified future losses in abstraction from regulatory rules except to the extent that these rules constitute a floor. Traditional features of banking practice mitigate procyclicality. Relationship banking, for instance, could be the basis for assured access to financing for borrowers during difficult times.

Regulatory approaches to smoothing bank lending over the cycle have included counter-cyclical variations in the ceiling on the permissible loan-to-value (LTV) ratios for mortgage lending, a measure successfully deployed in Hong Kong SAR during the property boom of the 1990s, and dynamic provisioning. The latter has attracted special attention during debates on offsetting the procyclicality of Basel II. The Spanish version, 'statistical provisioning', follows a simple principle: when specific loan loss provisions are small, as in economic booms, statistical provisions are high, thus creating a reserve to be drawn on when credit losses increase.

A 2002 report of a G10 Contact Group on assets prices found that relatively few developed countries applied the idea of dynamic provisioning largely owing to the unwillingness of the tax authorities to recognize such provisions as a tax-deductible expense.[7] Available information on the introduction of Basel II indicates that this option is at least under consideration in a number of developing countries. Features of the way in which particular developing countries are approaching some of the problems of introducing Basel II may be illustrated with reference to India, Pakistan, and Sri Lanka.

India[8]

Basel II, like its predecessor, Basel I, has been introduced in a context of continuous upgrading of India's system of financial regulation. Some the measures in this upgrading are directed at reducing the cyclicality of bank lending. In 2002 banks were advised to build up within five years an Investment Fluctuation Reserve amounting to a specified proportion of their financial assets as a counter-cyclical prudential requirement which would facilitate their absorption of increases in interest rates. Credit risk weights for minimum regulatory capital requirements have been varied (mostly in an upward direction) for lending to sectors such as real estate, capital markets, and consumer credit which are particularly sensitive to the business cycle. Prudential norms for loan loss provisioning have been tightened in response to high credit growth. A number of other features of the Indian upgrading of regulation related to capital standards and risk management are also worth mentioning here. The minimum regulatory capital requirement is 9 per cent of risk-weighted assets – i.e. higher than the Basel II minimum of 8 per cent - and banks are expected to operate at levels well above this. Conservative guidelines have been issued for minimum regulatory capital requirements for securitization exposures. Guidelines have also been issued to limit banks' vulnerability to changes in conditions in interbank lending and conditions in the money markets: These take the form of ceilings on banks' interbank liabilities as a proportion of their net worth as well as on banks' access to call money. In the context of introducing Basel II India must also confront problems due to the small number (four) of credit rating agencies and to the limitation of the agencies' ratings to financial instruments as opposed to issuing entities.

Pakistan[9]

As in many other developing countries, the introduction of Basel II should be viewed in the context of broader reforms of the financial sector. In her addresses concerning these reforms the Governor of the State Bank of Pakistan has spoken at length about the upgrading of corporate governance of banks. Some of the subjects under this heading such as limits on banks' exposures to single borrowers and to groups of related borrowers are an integral component of the prudential regime for banks of which Basel II is also a part. Recurring subjects of the addresses of the Governor are the small number of credit rating agencies (two) in Pakistan, the danger that Basel II will contribute to procyclicality in banks' lending, and the possibility that Basel II will further restrict access to finance to sectors, firms and individuals already under-served. On procyclicality the emphasis of the Governor is on the use of supervisors' discretionary powers under Pillar 2 (supervisory review) in such a way as to offset its effects on lending. Restrictions on access to financing that are in contradiction with the thrust of the country's development policy are to be countered by a review of the rating process and scoring mechanisms as they apply to small businesses and those individuals under-served.

Sri Lanka[10]

Here too the introduction of Basel II should be viewed as part of a programme of upgrading the corporate governance and risk management of banks, a programme which the Deputy Governor of the Central Bank denotes with the acronym GRC – Governance, Risk Management and Compliance. The minimum regulatory capital requirement under both Basel I and Basel II is 10 per cent of risk-weighted assets. To counter cyclicality of bank lending the authorities favour a variant of the dynamic provisioning approach under which banks would be encouraged to build up capital buffers in good times to help stabilize lending during downturns in economic activity. The authorities are also concerned at the danger that Basel II will lead to restrictions on firms with low credit ratings under the Standardized Approach to credit risk. Since they do not want firms weightings to move from rated to unrated status in order to improve their Basel II credit, the authorities are considering flexible application of these weightings.

Basel II and financial turmoil in the US

Basel II could not play a significant role in preventing or containing the outbreak of financial turmoil in the US. Only in July 2007 did the four US banking regulators, the Federal Reserve System, the Office of the Comptroller of the Currency, the Office of Thrift Supervision, and the Federal Deposit Insurance Corporation, announce agreement on the implementation of Basel II.

A more serious charge against Basel capital rules is that the absence of a capital charge specifically for securitization exposures under Basel I acted as an incentive to practices which contributed to the credit crisis.

Large-scale securitization of mortgage loans in the US antedated Basel I. Only in the 1990s did securitization spread to higher-risk assets such as subprime mortgages. The involvement of European banks in securitization also began to increase rapidly in the second half of the 1990s. There is evidence that as part of regulatory capital arbitrage banks securitized loans requiring relatively high capital charges for given levels of risk in order to economize on regulatory capital. This evidence is discussed by a working group of the Basel Committee itself in a 1999 report on the effects of Basel I which attributed a major part of the expansion of the securitization of non-mortgage debt to regulatory capital arbitrage.[11]

The lack of internationally agreed rules concerning securitization exposures was regarded by banking regulators as a major weakness of Basel I, and its remedy was a major objective of Basel II. However, the drawn-out character of the Basel II process meant that the Basel Committee's concerns were not reflected during the new millennium in reservations in financial markets about the increasingly unsound structures associated with the 'originate-to-distribute' model.

While the omission of rules for securitization exposures from Basel I thus contributed to the practices responsible for recent financial turbulence, its role should not be exaggerated. The expansion of 'originate-to-distribute' took place in a period when opinion favoured non-interference in financial markets.[12] As the Governor of the Reserve Bank of India put it in a recent speech, '... the balance [between markets and regulation] is right or wrong only ex-post ... when there is all round prosperity, everyone wants everything to be left to the markets; when things go wrong and there is pain, monetary and regulatory policies are invoked to save the situation'.[13]

The expansion of 'originate-to-distribute' was also an integral feature of the movement towards conglomeration in the financial sector which followed the Gramm-Leach-Bliley Act in the US in 1999. In normal times the involvement of the financial holding companies after this reform in a broad range of different financial services might have served the purpose of risk diversification and lower volatility of earnings. But in conditions such as those witnessed since 2007 the involvement has simply multiplied financial enterprises' exposures to different sources of financial turbulence.

Basel II and the future regulatory agenda

The most important official document on the future of regulation drafted in response to the financial turbulence is the Report of the Financial Stability Forum on Enhancing Market and Institutional Resilience, which was issued in April 2007.

The recommendations of this Report come under five headings: 1) strengthened prudential oversight of capital, liquidity and risk management; 2) enhancing transparency and valuation; 3) changes in the role and uses of credit ratings; 4) strengthening the authorities' responsiveness to risk; and 5) robust arrangements for dealing with stress in the financial system.

The Financial Stability Forum accords a central role in its proposals to introduction of Basel II. But it also draws attention to the importance of further work by the Basel Committee on revised rules for banks' securitization exposures and for countering opportunities for regulatory arbitrage through shifts of items between different parts of banks' portfolios.

In discussion outside the regulatory community special attention has been given to the issue of the protection afforded by Basel II to the banks and the economy more broadly against systemic financial risk. Here the question is raised whether this important objective of prudential regulation may be satisfactorily addressed through micro-level measures which address primarily financial firms' internal controls and risk management. Some commentators are advocating a shift away from emphasis on micro-level measures in favour of linking banks' capital to macroprudential indicators such overall levels of bank lending, fluctuations in which portend financial booms and busts.[14]

Towards a more developmental Basel III

The formal initiation of a process for Basel III seems unlikely in the near future. Plans for the introduction of Basel II in the 2006 survey of the

Financial Stability Institute already cover a period extending to 2015. And I doubt whether regulators have the appetite any time soon for another drawn-out process along the lines of Basel II. But this should not be taken to imply that the current rules and guidelines of Basel II will remain carved in stone. The credit crisis is already leading to revisions and elaboration. Future experience with Basel II, once it is in place, will almost certainly lead to further piecemeal development.

As discussed above, Basel II was not intended to be developmental. It is not self-evident that an international agreement on prudential rules for banks should target developmental objectives. Such targeting would presuppose an international consensus on the relationship between banking models as well as on prudential rules, on the one hand, and development, on the other, which is lacking. What is important, however, is that rules such as those of Basel II should accommodate different national developmental policies. Basel II is not binding on national governments which enjoy flexibility as to significant parts of the form in which it is introduced. Governments could and certainly will make use of this flexibility.

Perhaps the most natural part of the agreement for the future inclusion of guidelines designed to accommodate experience of Basel II's interactions with development policies is the supervisory review of Pillar 2. One may envisage the eventual inclusion under Pillar 2 of references to and explanation of regulatory and supervisory options designed to accommodate certain types of involvement of banks in development policies.

Conclusion

Increasingly insistent questions are now being raised as to how developing countries may gain a more enhanced role in the development of policy and in agreements of the Basel Committee now that its publication titled *Core Principles for Effective Banking Supervision* and Basel II has clearly established its status of global standard setter and not just standard setter for banks in G10 countries – even though a standard setter lacking any supranational authority.

This question may be addressed from two arguments often put forward as part of discussion of the Basel Committee's membership which is currently restricted to a group of mainly European developed countries: 1) the need to avoid expansion of the Committee to a size which would be unwieldy and compromise the Committee's efficiency; and 2) the need to maintain the Committee's credibility with the financial sector.

In favour of extension of the Committee's membership to the larger emerging-market countries and other countries which might represent important constituencies such as offshore centres and Islamic banking is the argument that such an extension would align the Committee's membership more closely with the newly emergent structure of world banking and financial markets. Arguably such an extension would enhance rather than diminish the Committee's credibility. Moreover within an enlarged Committee it should be possible to agree ways of avoiding unwieldy methods of working.

Nevertheless, extension of the Basel Committee would probably require agreement on a new institutional basis for it. The Committee was originally established by the G10, and it still formally reports to the central bankers and supervisory authorities of the G10. A new basis would involve a measure of formal recognition of the wider role as the sort of overseer and of universal policy formulator of banking regulation for all member countries of the Bank for International Settlements which, in fact, the Basel Committee now plays.

Notes

1. Davies, H. and Green, D., 2008, *Global Financial Regulation: The Essential Guide*, Polity Press, Cambridge, p.43.
2. Dale, R. 1992, *International Banking Deregulation The Great Banking Experiment*, Blackwell Publishers, Oxford, p.170.
3. Symons, E. and.White, J., 1991, *Banking Law Teaching Materials*, 3rd edition, West Publishing, St Paul, Minnesota, p.25.
4. The data are reproduced from Delhaise, P., 1998, *Asia in Crisis: The Implosion of the Banking and Finance Systems*, John Wiley and Sons (Asia), Singapore, Appendix 4.
5. Rules of thumb sometimes applied here are that a leverage of 12 corresponds to a Basel I capital-to-assets ratio of 11 per cent rather than 8 per cent, and leverage of 20 to a Basel I capital-to-assets ratio of 6.5 per cent.
6. Matten C. and Trout P., 2006, 'Application and Implementation in Asia-Pacific', in Tattersall, J. and Smith, R. (eds), *A Practitioner's Guide to the Basel Accord*, City and Financial Publishing, Old Woking, pp. 268–9.
7. Contact Group on Asset Prices, 2002, 'Turbulence in Asset Market Markets: the Role of Micro Policies', September, pp. 20–1.
8. Information is from senior officials' addresses with extensive use being made of Leeladhar, V., 2007, 'Basel II and Credit Risk Management', inaugural address at the programme on Basel II and Credit Risk Management organized by the Centre for Advanced Financial Learning for the whole-time directors of commercial banks, Goa, September; and Reddy, Y., 2008, 'Global Financial Turbulence and the Financial Sector in India – a Practitioner's Perspective', address at the Meeting of the Task Force on Financial Markets Regulation, organized by the Initiative for Policy Dialogue, Manchester, United Kingdom, July.

9. S. Akhtar, 2006, 'Basel II implementation issues, challenges and implications', speech at the 56th Annual General Meeting of the Institute of Bankers Pakistan, Karachi, 12 September (4/2007 twice and 33/2008); id., 2006, 'Demystifying Basel II', keynote address at the Federation of Indian Chambers of Commerce-Indian Banks' Association (FICCI-IBA) Conference on Global Banking: 'Paradigm Shift' Mumbai, 26 September; and id., 2008, 'Corporate governance for banks', speech at the IBP Convocation, Lahore, 13 March.

10. Jayamaha, R., 2006, 'Glimpse of Current Financial Regulations', Inaugural speech at the Client Seminar on International Trade, organized by Hatton National Bank, Colombo, November'; idem., 2006, 'Basel II – a Roadmap for the Sri Lankan Banking System with International Comparisons', opening remarks at an event of lecture series, organized by the Association of Professional Bankers, Colombo, December'; and idem., 2008, 'Governance, Risk Management and Compliance', keynote address at the Seminar on Governance, Risk Management and Compliance and the Roadmap for the Financial Services Industry, Colombo, February.

11. Refer to Bank for International Settlements, Basle Committee on Banking Supervision, 1999, 'Capital Requirements and Bank Behaviour: the Impact of the Basle Accord', Working Paper Number 1, Basel, pp. 3–4.

12. In the 'originate-to-distribute' model debts generated or originated by one institution are pooled and transferred to a special purpose vehicle. The assets in this vehicle serve as the backing for securities sold to investors, often in tranches carrying returns that vary according to their different degrees of risk.

13. Reddy, Y., 2008, 'Monetary and Regulatory Policies – How to Get the Balance with Markets Right', remarks at the Annual General Meeting Panel of the Bank for International Settlements, Basel, June.

14. For further information refer to Goodhart, C. and Persaud, A., 2008, 'A Party Pooper's Guide to Financial Stability', *Financial Times*, London, 5 June.

10
Antidumping, Countervailing Duties and Non-Market Economies

Claudio Dordi

In the context of international trade in goods, antidumping duties and countervailing measures are the so-called defensive measures that every World Trade Organization (WTO) member state may apply against imported products under certain conditions. They are qualified as defensive measures because they normally consist of additional customs duties which are applicable when, in the case of dumping, the foreign products are imported at a price less than a reference price, that is, normal value, and, in the case of countervailing measures, when the products benefited, in the country of origin or exportation, from a subsidy granted by the government, by local governmental entities, or in other forms. Antidumping duties and countervailing measures may be applied only after the authorities of the importing states have investigated the existence of the margin of dumping or the value of the subsidy, the existence of a risk or of an effective injury to a domestic industry, and the causal link between these. The duties that may be applied must not exceed the level of the margin of dumping, which is the difference between the export price and the normal value, or subsidy. WTO rules provide special procedures that national authorities must follow in deciding whether to impose such measures. The rules are provided in The General Agreement on Tariffs and Trade (GATT)[1] Article VI and, in much greater detail, in the agreement on implementation of Article VI of the GATT, the so-called Antidumping Agreement, and in the Agreement on subsidies and countervailing measures, the Subsidy Agreement. As specified in the WTO case-law, Article VI and the two agreements form an integrated set of rules governing the use of antidumping and countervailing measures, and neither instrument may be applied in isolation.[2] Moreover, the analysis must take into account Vietnam's specific commitments contained in its WTO protocol of accession.

Antidumping measures have been adopted with increasing frequency, and by an ever increasing number of countries. Before the Uruguay Round only the US, the European Union, Canada and Japan made use of these instruments while since the 1990s many developing countries have adopted a national legislation and implemented it. Currently, the four major users of antidumping and countervailing measures are the US, India, the European Union and China. Antidumping and countervailing measures may be considered the only instruments of restricting imports available to WTO member states.

Except what is provided for certain category of subsidies, the prohibited subsidies are outlined in Article 3 of the subsidy agreement, the practice of dumping and of subsidizing goods is not prohibited by the WTO agreements.

However, as stated in Paragraph 1 of GATT Article VI, members 'Recognize that dumping, by which products of one country are introduced into the commerce of another country at less than the normal value of the products, is to be condemned if it causes or threatens material injury to an established industry in the territory of a contracting party or materially retards the establishment of a domestic industry.'

The imposition of antidumping or countervailing measures is completely within the discretion of the importing member authorities and there is no obligation on the country from which the dumped or subsidized products are exported to take restraining action, except for prohibited subsidies. WTO agreements on antidumping and on subsidies provide a general framework aimed at limiting the discretion of WTO member states in applying antidumping and countervailing measures. However, the huge complexity and the lack of precision of both the antidumping and the subsidy agreement rules made it possible for the government authorities of the importing states to use the mechanism both to protect domestic producers from the alleged dumping, or subsidization, by the exporters and as an instrument to over-protect the national industries. Antidumping and countervailing measures are based on a number of costs evaluation and comparisons. Of particular relevance is the fact that many WTO member states have been applying the so-called non-market economy approach towards goods originating or exported from Vietnam, as well as, from some other WTO member states, such as, China. The consequence of qualifying a WTO member state as a non-market economy is particularly relevant in the calculation of the dumping margin, that is, the difference between the export price and the normal value, in antidumping proceedings.

The market economy methodology in antidumping investigations

When a product is imported from, or originates in, a country qualified as market-economy, the normal value is established on the basis of the domestic price in the exporting country of the like product in the ordinary course of trade, as provided by Article 2.1 of the antidumping (AD) agreement. Where there are no or insufficient sales in the ordinary course of trade in the exporting country, or when a particular market situation does not allow a proper comparison – Article 2.2 of AD agreement – the normal value may be determined either by reference to the export price of the like product to an appropriate third country or to the production costs in the country of origin plus a reasonable amount of administrative, selling and general costs and profit. All these costs are calculated according to the information submitted by the exporting producer concerned, with the only exception provided by Article 2.2.2 of the AD agreement, applicable when the administrative, selling and general costs and profit cannot be determined on the basis of 'actual data pertaining to production and sales in the ordinary course of trade of the like product by the exporter or producer under investigation'. Then the amounts may be determined, among the others, on 'any reasonable method', which 'appears to include the possibility of using data from third countries'.[3]

The normal value, then, is compared with the export price of the product, which is, normally, the price at which a product is first sold in the importing country; Article 2.3 of the AD agreement deals with cases where there is no export price or where the export price is unreliable because of association or a compensatory arrangement between the exporter and the importer or a third party; in these cases a constructed export price may be used. The comparison between the normal value and the export price of the like product occurs, normally, on an individual basis: as a consequence, the normal value established for individual exporters is compared with the export price of individual exporters (calculations of individual dumping margins and individual anti-dumping duties).

The non-market economy methodology in antidumping investigations

For non-market economy (NME) countries, the normal value is established on the basis of the information submitted by a producer in a market economy third country, the so-called analogue country, and, as a general rule, that normal value is compared with the average export price of all the product under investigation imported from the non-market economy country: as a consequence, this is finalized with a calculation of a country-wide anti-dumping duty. This normally results in a higher dumping margin and in a higher antidumping duty.[4]

From a legal point of view, the possibility of a WTO member state to qualify another member, for antidumping purposes, as a non-market economy, is regulated by Article 2.7 of the AD Agreement, which refers to the second Supplementary Provision to Paragraph 1 of Article VI in Annex I of GATT 1994 (Note AD Article VI), stating that 'It is recognized that, in the case of imports from a country which has a complete or substantially complete monopoly of its trade and where all domestic prices are fixed by the State, special difficulties may exist in determining price comparability ... and in such cases importing contracting parties may find it necessary to take into account the possibility that a strict comparison with domestic prices in such a country may not always be appropriate.'

The rationale of this approach has to be found in the contrast between the founding principles of the GATT 1947 and the characteristic of a non-market economy country and in the exigency since World War II up to the end of the Cold War era, to have common rules aimed at permitting the development of international trade relations between countries belonging to the two blocks. The GATT was designed by market economies and for market economies while the activities of a non-market economy country during the Cold War era were governed under the non-market system, namely, a centralized state controlled economy, where price did not function as a market signal governing the economic decision-making.

During the Cold War era, when the status of one country as either a market economy or a non-market economy was more poignant, such a differential treatment for the purpose of anti-dumping investigation was not problematic. After all, a hybrid of market and non-market economy was rare amongst countries. The situation changed after the end of the Cold War. Many countries in transition from a non-market to a market regime made their appearances in the international trade arena, with China at the forefront. And with it, what was once a side-lined NME issue in the antidumping institution surfaced. It is apparent that the definition provided in paragraph 1 of Article VI in Annex I of GATT 1994 became outdated if compared with the feature of the so-called transition-economy countries, especially the provision requiring the 'complete or substantially complete monopoly of its trade' and that 'all domestic prices are fixed by the State'. There are very few countries which have a complete or a substantially complete monopoly of their trade and where all domestic prices are fixed by the state. However, other elements may distort the domestic price in a country, such as the absence of currency convertibility for international transactions, the massive presence of state-owned enterprises benefiting from legal privilege, the presence of mechanisms for controlling prices and the attitude of government of granting subsidies to specific enterprises. Therefore, since the accession of China to the WTO in 2001, the WTO members negotiated with the acceding country an *ad hoc* non-market economy definition to be included in the Working Party report annexed to the Protocol of accession. This provision aims at giving a legal justification to the discriminatory treatment applied in antidumping proceedings to the new acceding transition economies where domestic prices are still influenced by the activity of the central government.

However, these provisions are formulated in general terms and do not provide stringent boundaries limiting the discretion of the importing member states. As a consequence, as importing members have wide discretion in formulating the criteria aimed at qualifying a country as a non-market economy, only an analysis of each national legislation, on a case-by-case basis, is functional in evaluating the implications for the exporting members' enterprises and authorities.

Before analysing with more detail the consequences for Vietnamese exporters involved in antidumping or countervailing measures procedures, it is worthwhile to illustrate what are the jurisdictional guarantees available to them after the imposition of an antidumping or a countervailing measure. As most of the WTO member states enacted specific internal laws reproducing the content of the WTO agreements and providing other WTO-consistent rules applicable, aimed at guiding the activities of the competent antidumping and countervailing measure authorities, it should be pointed out that Vietnamese exporters may resort to the following defensive instruments. Where there is a founded doubt that the importing authorities acted inconsistently with their domestic legislation, they could start a procedure before the national court of the importing state; where there is a founded doubt that the implementing legislation of the importing country is not consistent with the WTO agreements, there are two possibilities, to resort to the importing state competent court[5] or to request the Government of Vietnam the activation of bilateral consultations with the importing country to settle the dispute at a diplomatic level. Where the consultation is inconclusive the Government may resort to the WTO Dispute Settlement System.

Antidumping

The antidumping agreement contains provisions regulating both the substance and the procedure to be followed by the competent authorities of importing member states. Antidumping duties and countervailing measures are trade defence measures aimed at protecting national industries from the import of goods at a price which is considered unfair;[6] and while WTO does not prohibit dumping, it provides a framework of substantive and procedural rules to govern how a member may counteract dumping through the imposition of antidumping measures. Even if it is not mandatory for WTO members to enact antidumping legislation, most of the WTO member states make use of antidumping aimed at protecting national industries.

For producers which sell the goods both in the internal market and in third countries, antidumping is an instrument with a twofold attribute. Firstly, they must be aware of the fact that the state where they exported their goods may begin a procedure aimed at imposing an antidumping duty, that is the defensive approach. However, each producer may complain to his national competent authorities aimed at provoking the initiation of an antidumping procedure against products imported from third countries, the so-called offensive approach. The commitments contained in the Protocol of Accession of Vietnam reflect this twofold characteristic.

Antidumping from a defensive approach and the commitment of Vietnam in the Protocol of Accession to the World Trade Organization

After the accession of Vietnam to the WTO, all the antidumping measures applied by a WTO member against products exported or originating in Vietnam must comply with the antidumping agreement as completed with the commitments contained in the Protocol of Accession of Vietnam.

It is relevant to highlight that the substantial and procedural rules provided by the WTO agreement, as well as, by the Protocol of Accession, represent a burden for the importing authorities and confer some rights to the exporters involved in an antidumping proceeding. For Vietnam the rules outlined in antidumping, subsidies and countervailing measures agreements are complemented by some provisions contained in Paragraphs 254 and 255 of the Report of the Working Party on the Accession of Vietnam. Paragraph 254 states that 'Several Members noted that Vietnam was continuing the process of transition towards a full market economy. Those Members noted that under those circumstances, in the case of imports of Vietnamese origin into a WTO Member, special difficulties could exist in determining cost and price comparability in the context of antidumping investigations and countervailing duty investigations. Those Members stated that in such cases, the importing WTO Member might find it necessary to take into account the possibility that a strict comparison with domestic costs and prices in Vietnam might not always be appropriate'.

As it is apparent from the comparison with the above mentioned AD Article VI, Paragraph 254 makes it possible for other WTO member states to apply the so-called non-market economy treatment in antidumping and countervailing measure investigations involving goods exported or originating in Vietnam. Paragraph 254 has been added as Vietnam cannot be qualified, as required by AD Article VI as a country having a 'complete or substantially complete monopoly of its trade and where all domestic prices are fixed by the State'. However, paragraph 254 does not provide any positive criteria to be followed by the other WTO member states for qualifying Vietnam as a non-market economy: and as a consequence, each WTO member state has a wide discretion in this field. Paragraph 255 seems to provide some boundaries in that Vietnam confirmed that, upon accession, Article VI of the GATT 1994, the Agreement on Implementation of Article VI of the GATT 1994, the Anti-Dumping Agreement, and the 'Subsidies and countervailing Measure' Agreement shall apply in proceedings involving exports from Vietnam into a WTO Member and that these would be consistent with the following conditions.

In determining price comparability under Article VI of the GATT 1994 and the Antidumping Agreement, the importing WTO member shall use either Vietnamese prices or costs for the industry under investigation or a methodology that is not based on a strict comparison with domestic prices or costs in Vietnam based on the following rules. If the producers under investigation clearly show that market economy conditions prevail in the industry producing a similar product with regard to the manufacture, production and sale of that product, the importing WTO member shall use Vietnamese prices or costs for the industry under investigation in determining price comparability. In addition, the importing WTO ember may use a methodology that is not based on a strict comparison with domestic prices or costs in Vietnam if the producers under investigation cannot clearly show that market economy conditions prevail in the industry producing the like product with regard to manufacture, production and sale of that product. These conditions seem to limit the discretion of the importing member state to disregard Vietnamese domestic prices or costs in antidumping procedures; indeed, only in case the Vietnamese producers are unable to 'clearly show that market economy conditions prevail' the importing member state 'may use a methodology that is not based on a strict comparison with domestic prices or costs in Vietnam'. However, once more, the provision does not mention any precise criteria either for defining the market economy conditions or for determining the prices and costs that could be adopted as an alternative.

There are the consequences in antidumping proceedings following from the qualification of the exporting country as a non-market economy. Article 9.3 of the Antidumping Agreement states that '...the amount of the antidumping duty shall not exceed the margin of dumping as established under Article 2'. The margin of dumping corresponds to the difference between the export price of the product exported from one country to another and the comparable price, in the ordinary course of trade, for the like product when destined for consumption in the exporting country. When the sales in the domestic price, for various reasons listed in article 2.2.2 of the AD Agreement, do not permit a proper comparison, the agreement lists other methodologies available. These are the export price to a third country and the constructed value using the cost of production in the country of origin. However, non-market economy countries would typically be subject to surrogate constructed value method, which uses the cost of production in a third country market economy, the so-called analogous country.[7]

As WTO agreements do not provide any rule for choosing the analogous country, it is up to the authorities of the importing state to decide, where the only limitation is that represented by footnote 2 of Article 2.2.2 of the AD Agreement, stating that 'Sales of the like product destined for consumption in the domestic market of the exporting country shall normally be considered a sufficient quantity for the determination of the normal value if such sales constitute 5 per cent or more of the sales of the product under consideration to the importing member the domestic prices of the analogue country will normally be considered representative if their volume is at least 5 per cent of the quantities exported to the EU by the non-market economy country.' For instance, this provision has been applied by analogy as an element to verify the suitability of a third country to be identified as the analogous country in some antidumping procedures against products exported from Vietnam. The Commission of the European Union stated that: 'The domestic prices of the analogue country will normally be considered representative if their volume is at least 5 per cent of the quantities exported to the EU by the non-market economy country'.[8]

The absence of any criteria limiting the possibility of choosing the 'analogous country' may lead to high dumping margins, among others, because the analogous country chosen may be at a different stage of economic development, for instance, for bicycles and footwear imported into the European Union from Vietnam the analogous countries chosen were Mexico and Brazil respectively. Once the analogous country has been identified, it is up to the antidumping authority of the importing state to seek the cooperation of the analogous country local producers for the collection of the data necessary for the calculation of the normal value. This situation may lead to a further overestimation of the dumping margin. In fact, as clearly stated by Vermulst, an antidumping lawyer, 'the only reason that producers in the surrogate country (read: analogous) have typically cooperated is to ensure that their non-market economy competitors receive a high antidumping duty'.[9]

The non-market-economy issue is completed by other statements in Paragraph 255. There is a stand still provision, that is, once the importing country has established, under its national law, that Vietnam is a market economy, it cannot, in following cases, restore the non-market-economy treatment in antidumping procedures, except where it has modified the criteria adopted for qualifying a country as a market economy *rebus sic stantibus*. This is applicable both to Vietnam as a country as well as to an industry or sector. There is also a specific date whereby the non-market-economy treatment shall expire at end 2018.

The stand still provision does not really represent a serious limitation to the importing country discretion in applying the non-market-economy treatment to Vietnam. To restore a non-market-economy treatment to Vietnam, after having granted it once would require the modification of the criteria adopted for qualifying Vietnam as a non-market economy as of the date of accession.

As specified above, WTO rules regarding the non-market-economy status in antidumping procedures are quite generic, leaving a high level of discretion to member states in defining the relevant criteria for denying the status of market economy country to another WTO member state.

Antidumping legislation and non-market-economy treatment

The main issues that the administration of the importing countries has to settle in an antidumping procedure involving products originating or exported from a non-market economy are; when a country may be defined as a non-market economy; what the criteria are as agreed by the main WTO member states when has a country been targeted as a non-market economy; the possibility for an enterprise or for an industry to demonstrate that it is market-oriented; and the consequences in the calculation of the normal value for products exported or originating from a non-market-economy country.

The European Community outlines those countries that are considered non-market-economy countries without formally providing any description of the criteria adopted for such decision. According to the EC regulation 384/96,[10] there are 15 non-market-economy countries which are divided into three groups and these are outlined in Table 10.1.

When a country is qualified as non-market economy, the dumping margin is the result of the difference between the export price calculated on the basis of the average of the industry's exporting prices and the normal value calculated in the market of an analogue country. The normal value is based either on the price or on the constructed value, which is the sum of production costs plus general, selling, administrative costs and profit margin, in a market-economy third country, or the price from such a third country to other countries, including the EU, or, where those are not possible, on any other reasonable basis, including the price actually paid or payable in the EU for the like product, duly adjusted if necessary to include a reasonable profit margin.

However, according to the EC antidumping regulation, even if Vietnam is qualified as a non-market economy, the individual enterprises exporting from the countries in the first two groups may obtain either a market economy treatment or an individual treatment if they satisfy certain requirements as described in Table 10.2.

When a company is granted the market economy treatment, the calculation of the normal value is based on the data provided by the exporting companies. As a consequence, the dumping margin is the difference between the export price and the normal value taking into consideration the exporters own data. However, it has been pointed out that, after a liberal approach adopted in the early years of the application of this provision,[11] in the recent Leather and Safety Shoes cases imported from Vietnam and China, the EC rejected all but one the 176 Market Economy claims made by Chinese exporters.[12]

If a firm does not meet the requirements of the market economy test there is another opportunity to avoid the calculation of the margin of dumping based on a comparison between the normal value, calculated according the non-market-economy methodology, and the average

Table 10.1 Countries considered non-market economies by the European Union

Country	Characteristics	Consequences on the normal value
China, Vietnam and Kazakhstan	For these countries the process of reform has fundamentally altered their economies and has led to the emergence of firms for which market economy conditions may prevail.	The normal value shall be determined on the basis of the price or constructed value in a market economy third country, or the price from such a third country to other countries, including the European Union, or where those are not possible, on any other reasonable basis, including the price actually paid or payable in the European Union for the like product, duly adjusted if necessary to include a reasonable profit margin. However, individual companies may apply for market economy treatment and the normal values will be calculated on the basis on their own home market prices or costs, or individual companies may ask for an individual treatment: they may be assigned an individual dumping margin based on the company's own export prices, rather than the country wide margin.
Albania, Armenia, Azerbaijan, Georgia, Kyrgyzstan, Moldova and Mongolia	Non-market-economy countries which are members of the WTO at the date of the initiation of an antidumping proceeding.	
Belarus, North Korea, Tajikistan, Turkmenistan and Uzbekistan	Non-market-economy countries which are not members of the WTO.	The normal value shall be determined on the basis of the price or constructed value in a market economy third country, or the price from such a third country to other countries, including the Community, or where those are not possible, on any other reasonable basis, including the price actually paid or payable in the Community for the like product, duly adjusted if necessary to include a reasonable profit margin.

Table 10.2   Conditions to be satisfied for market economy treatment

Conditions to be Satisfied for Market Economy Treatment	Some Conditions where Market Economy Treatment is Inapplicable
Decisions of firms regarding prices, costs and inputs, including raw materials, cost of technology and labour, output, sales and investment, are made in response to market signals reflecting supply and demand, and without significant state interference in this regard, and costs of major inputs substantially reflect market values.	Firms under the obligation to export all or significant part of the production and firms entirely state owned with direct management link with the state.
Firms have one clear set of basic accounting records which are independently audited in line with international accounting standards and are applied for all purposes.	Firms which have not audited accounts nor published financial statements and firms whose accounting records are not in line with International Accounting Standards and those firms where the verification performed by the auditors was found to be highly insufficient to guarantee the reliability of the accounts.
The production costs and financial situation of firms are not subject to significant distortions carried over from the former non-market-economy system, in particular in relation to depreciation of assets, other write-offs, barter trade and payment via compensation of debts.	Land use rights which do not correspond to market economy conditions but are still centrally determined by the authorities, in particular regarding price setting and price revision and the valuation of the assets of the companies are not transparent or not justified according to a market-economy criterion.
The firms under investigation have to be subject to bankruptcy and property laws which guarantee legal certainty and stability for the operation of firms.	No bankruptcy law enacted in the country.
Exchange rate conversions are at market rate.	

export price of all exporters. Individual non-market-economy exporters to the EU may claim individual treatment provided that they satisfy the following requirements.[13] For wholly or partly foreign owned firms or joint ventures, exporters are free to repatriate capital and profits; export prices and quantities, and conditions and terms of sale are freely determined; the majority of the shares belong to private persons. In addition, state officials on the Board of Directors or holding important management positions shall either be in minority or it must be demonstrated that the company is nonetheless sufficiently independent from state interference; and exchange rate conversions are at the market rate. Finally, state interference is not such as to permit circumvention of measures if individual exporters are given different rates of duty.

Exporters whose normal value is established according to the surrogate country methodology will be assigned an individual rate of duty calculated by comparing the normal value with the exporter's individual export prices instead of the weighted average of prices of all export transactions to the EU. However, when the number of exporters is particularly high the investigating authorities have to resort to sampling. This means that the duty for the exporters excluded from the sample, and meeting the above mentioned conditions for individual treatment, is based on the weighted average duties of the sampled exporters that qualify for individual treatment. The treatment, calculation of the normal price, the export price and the dumping margin are outlined in Table 10.3.

Selection of the 'surrogate country' for the calculation of 'normal value'

Importing countries have a high margin of discretion in choosing the 'analogue country' in investigations against products imported from a non-market-economy country. The European Commission uses a country in which the general capacity and type of production closely approximates that of the investigated country. The intention is to allow investigators to model the costs of production in the investigated country as if that country operated in market economy conditions. It is important to highlight that the intention is not to choose a country that recreates the conditions of production in the investigated country because by definition those conditions are not known, or have been distorted by the fact that market economy conditions do not operate. The analogue country allows investigators to model what those costs might be if market economy conditions prevailed. The two key criteria in the selection of an appropriate analogue country are open and competitive markets and representative domestic sales volume of comparable like products. According to research by the Sweden National Board of Trade[14] the US is the most commonly referenced analogue country in EU cases.

Table 10.3 Consequences following the granting of market economy or individual treatment to a firm

Treatment	Calculation of the normal value	Calculation of the export price	Dumping margin
Firms in countries qualified as market economy. Firms in NME country that obtained market economy status.	The value is calculated by considering the data in the market of export, normally, the data provided by the enterprise subject to investigation.	The price reflects the effective price of export of each company.	Based on genuine data.
Firms in NME country that obtained individual treatment.		The price reflects the effective price of exports of each company.	The margin dumping could be overestimated depending on the analogue country cost.
Firms in NME country which did not obtain neither the MET nor the individual treatment.	The value is calculated according to data collected in an analogue country.	The export price reflects the average of the industry export prices.	The dumping margin could be overestimated depending both on the analogue country cost and that the exporting price reflects the average of the industry exporting prices.

The definition of a non-market-economy country in the United States

Under US antidumping law, countries are entitled to market-economy treatment unless they have been formally designated as a non-market economy country.[15] Therefore, each country not formally designated as NME is treated as a market-economy country for purposes of calculating normal value under section 773(c)(1) of the Antidumping Act 1916.[16] The inquiry proceeds on that basis unless an interested party is able to rebut the presumption of market-economy status within the meaning of section 771(18) (A). However, a mere allegation is not sufficient. It must be adequately and properly supported and documented with respect to each of the six factors listed in section 771(18)(B) of the Act. If the allegation meets these requirements, the Department will initiate a formal inquiry into the status of the country's economy, to determine whether it should be treated as a NME for purposes of section 773(c)(1) of the Act. Even if a country is labelled as a NME, the Department of Commerce (DOC) may use the market economy methodology to determine the normal value if the targeted industry is able to demonstrate that it is a 'market-oriented industry' according to the market oriented industry (MOI) test developed by the DOC. Under this test, an affirmative finding of a market-oriented industry requires, no involvement of the Government in setting prices or amount to be produced for the merchandise under investigation or review, the industry should be characterized by private or collective ownership and all significant inputs must be paid at market prices.

Furthermore, if there is any state-required input in the producing industry the share must be insignificant. So far, in antidumping cases against Chinese exports, not a single industry has met these criteria.

Exporters from non-market-economy countries are assigned one of three types of antidumping duty rates. These are Individual, Section A or Countrywide.[17] To qualify for both Individual and Section A treatment there are the same criteria. The exporters have to demonstrate the absence of *de jure* and *de facto* government control over export activities. *De jure* absence of government control includes the absence of restrictive stipulations associated with an individual exporter's business and export licences; the absence on any legislative enactments decentralizing control of companies, or the absence of any other formal measures by the Government decentralizing control of companies. *De facto* absence of government control stipulates that export prices have not to be set by or subject to the approval of a governmental authority; the respondent must have authority to negotiate and sign contracts and other agreements; the respondent must have autonomy from the government in making decisions regarding the selection of management; and the respondent must retain the proceeds of its export sales and must be free to make independent decisions regarding disposition of profits or financing of losses.

If the criteria to obtain Individual or Section A treatment are identical, there are substantial differences between them for a firm to be classified either one or the other. Individual duties are reserved exclusively for firms selected by the DOC to be mandatory respondents, that is, they are are selected for the collection of the data during the investigation. Mandatory respondents that are capable of satisfying the criteria specified above are entitled to an individual antidumping rate based on the information provided in their own questionnaire responses. Even exporters not selected as mandatory respondents are entitled to demonstrate that they satisfy the criteria and may submit a request for separate rate treatment and must submit responses to Section A of the questionnaire the DOC utilizes for collecting data. When they satisfy the criteria they may be assigned a Section A rate, which is equal to the weighted-average of the rates calculated for the mandatory respondents, excluding those rates that are zero, *de minimis*, or based entirely on facts available. Firms that do not satisfy the criteria and those that do not respond fully to the DOC's information requests are assigned the Countrywide rate, which is usually the highest rate calculated for the mandatory respondents or the dumping margin alleged in the petition.

Selection of the surrogate country

In Title VII of the Tariff Act of 1930, Section 773 (c)(4)(A) there are provisions for the use of prices or costs of factors of production in one or more market economy (ME) countries that are either at a level of economic development comparable to that of the non-market economy country with primary emphasis on per capita GDP in determining economic comparability, or significant producers of comparable merchandise. Further details regarding the selection of the surrogate country are provided in the Policy Bulletin no. 04.1 of the DOC.

Countervailing measures and non-market economy countries

The application of countervailing duties to NMEs is an issue that is widely debated in developed economies, particularly in the US. Countervailing duty (CVD) laws are designed to provide relief to domestic industries that have been, or threatened with, the adverse impact from imported goods sold in the national market that have been subsidized by a foreign government or other public entity. According to the SCM agreement of the WTO, members may impose CVDs when they identify subsidized imports, determine that a domestic industry is suffering injury, or establish a causal link between the subsidized import and the injury suffered. These duties are intended to offset the price advantages that the subsidy confers on the imported product. The SCM agreement requires that the investigating authorities of the importing country quantify the value of the subsidies provided and limit the level of duty imposed to that value. To facilitate identification of subsidies and the evaluation of their trade effects, the agreement requires WTO members to provide the organization with annual notifications on all the specific subsidies they maintain and to provide additional information on any of these programmes when requested. The agreement specifies that member states should provide sufficient information 'to enable other members to evaluate the trade effects and to understand the operation of notified subsidy programmes'.[18]

Vietnam made additional commitments regarding industrial subsidies as part of its agreement to join the WTO upon WTO accession, to terminate all subsidies on exports. The current programmes will be phased out in the period 2007–2012.

With regard to countervailing duties, it has to be stated that the EU and US have not applied any countervailing duties to imports from NMEs so far. However, while in the EU the non-application of CVDs to NMEs has been relatively uncontroversial. Even if there are no explicit legal provisions or judicial decisions that exempt NMEs from countervailing duty law, no countervailing duty investigation have so far been initiated against NMEs. In the US it has been widely debated, especially since the accession of China to the WTO.

The non-application of countervailing duties and laws pertaining to non-market economy countries in the US

Until April 2007, US CVD laws have not been traditionally applied to NMEs. The question of applicability of CVDs to NMEs arose in 1984 when countervailing duty petitions were filed against carbon steel products originating in, then, Czechoslovakia and Poland. The Tariff Act of 1930, Paragraph 303 dealing with CVM, was applicable as 'whenever any country, dependency ... shall pay or bestow, directly or indirectly, any bounty or grant upon the manufacture or production or export of any article or merchandise manufactured or produced in such country'.[19]

The DOC found the above mentioned legislation not applicable to NMEs, as it was impossible, in these cases, to determine 'whether government activities in a NME confer a 'bounty or grant' within the meaning of Section 30.' The DOC determined that countervailable subsidies are not conceptually within a NME and, therefore, may not be included within the scope of 'bounty or grant'.[20] The main reasons for justifying the final determination of the DOC relied on the rationale that a subsidy is an action taken by a government or other public entity that distorts or subverts the operation in the free market. It was clear to the DOC that since all costs, prices and profits in a NME are centrally controlled, the concept of subsidization is meaningless as there are no market forces to subvert or distort. Furthermore, while resources in NMEs may be allocated inefficiently it is impossible to state with any degree of certainty whether this results from subsidization or from central planning. There is also an issue with the calculation of the amount of subsidization from a NME. As all economic activities in NMEs are centrally controlled, there is no way to 'disaggregate government action in such a way to identify the exceptional action that is a subsidy'.[21]

These findings were challenged before the Court of International Trade, which held in the famous Continental Steel case[22] that the CVD law does apply to NMEs. However, upon appeal by the US government, the Court of Appeals for the Federal Circuit reversed this judgment in *Georgetown Steel Corp. v. United States*,[23] holding that the CDM does not apply to NMEs because subsidies in NMEs 'do not create the kind of unfair competitive advantage over American firms against which the countervailing duty act was directed'.

As a result of the above mentioned decision in Georgetown Steel, there were no other CVD investigations of allegedly subsidized imports from NME until 1991, when the DOC examined a petition alleging the subsidization of oscillating fans imported from China.[24] Although China was a NME, the petition was based on the theory that the Chinese industry under investigation was sufficiently market-oriented such that the DOC could reliably use the economic data provided by the country itself consistent with the standards utilized by the CVD investigations in market economies. After an analysis based on the above mentioned MOI (market oriented industry) criteria the DOC concluded that, while some of the inputs of the product under investigation were in fact obtained from market sources, there remained a significant portion of the inputs that were not and, therefore, the industry as a whole did not qualify as a MOI. Although the DOC's negative determination in the above mentioned case appeared to have opened the door to the potential application of

CVD law to non-market economies, the DOC did not accept another CVD petition against a non-market economy until 2006.

Recent application of countervailing duty laws in US to products imported from China

In 2007 the DOC announced that it made an affirmative preliminary determination for subsidy in a CVD investigation against China with respect to coated free-sheet paper. The DOC calculated preliminary estimated countervailable subsidy rates ranging from 10.9 per cent to 20.35 per cent.[25] The case is still ongoing; however, it is interesting to highlight that in publishing its preliminary findings, the DOC also issued a memorandum that directly confronts the Georgetown Steel precedent. The memorandum provides a justification as to why China's economy in 2005, the period for which the investigation is concerned with, and the so-called 'Soviet-style economies' are distinguishable, such that it is now possible to apply CVD law to some NME.[26] It is interesting to point out that the analysis conducted in the memorandum is based on the criteria adopted by the US for granting ME status to third countries. Even though it is still ongoing it is also worthwhile to quote part of the memorandum, thereby permitting a better understanding of the treatment of NMEs in CVD proceedings, which states that:

> private industry now dominates many sectors of the Chinese economy, and entrepreneurship is flourishing. Foreign trading rights have been given to over 200,000 firms. Many business entities in present-day China are generally free to direct most aspects of their operations, and to respond to (albeit limited) market forces. The role of central planners is vastly smaller... Given these developments, we believe that it is possible to determine whether the PRC Government has bestowed a benefit upon a Chinese producer (i.e., the subsidy can be identified and measured) and whether any such benefit is specific. Because we are capable of applying the necessary criteria in the CVD law, the Department's policy that gave rise to the Georgetown Steel litigation does not prevent us from concluding that the PRC Government has bestowed a countervailable subsidy upon a Chinese producer.

Vietnam as a NME in countervailing duty proceedings

The issue of the applicability of CVD law to NMEs is very important for Vietnam, particularly when addressing subsidies as 'the relevant provisions of the SCM Agreement shall apply; however, if there are special difficulties in that application, the importing WTO Member may then

Table 10.4 Comparison of the applicability of CVD law to NMEs in the EU and the US

EU legislation	US legislation
Article 6 d) of Regulation 2026/97 provides that the adequacy of remuneration is to be determined in relation to prevailing market conditions in the country of provision or purchase.	19 USCS §1677(5)(E)(iv): determines whether a benefit has been conferred because goods or services are provided for less than adequate remuneration or sold for more than adequate remuneration.
In case there are not prevailing market terms and conditions for the product or service in question in the country of provision or purchase which may be used as appropriate benchmarks: – the terms and conditions prevailing in the country concerned shall be adjusted on the basis of actual costs, prices, and other factors available in that country, by an appropriate amount which reflects normal market terms and conditions, or when appropriate, the terms and conditions prevailing in the market of another country or on the world market which are available to the recipient shall be used. Article 28.5 of Regulation 2026/97 provides that, where appropriate, information pertaining to the world market or other relevant markets can be used to support best information available.	The adequacy of remuneration needs to be determined in relation to prevailing market conditions for the good or service under investigation: According Section 19 CFR 351.511(a)(2)(ii) and (iii): – if there is no useable market-determined price with which to make the comparison, the adequacy of the remuneration is measured by comparing the government price to a world market price where it is reasonable to conclude that such price would be available to purchasers in the country in question (in case of more than one world price, an average will be calculated) – in case of no world market price available to purchasers in the country in question, the adequacy of remuneration will be evaluated by assessing whether the government price is consistent with market principles

use alternative methodologies for identifying and measuring the subsidy benefits which take into account the possibility that prevailing terms and conditions in Vietnam may not be available as appropriate benchmarks'.[27] This provision gives other WTO members the possibility to use data from other countries as the benchmark to determine whether a benefit has been conferred.

There are differences between EU and US legislation applying to this issue and these are compared in Table 10.4.

Conclusion

The granting of market-economy treatment to Vietnamese firms in the EU suggests that the main criteria for the European Commission considerations were the obligation of Vietnamese firms to export all or part of their production. Other considerations were the accounting methodology to be utilized by firms, which does not conform with international standards and the asset valuations of Vietnamese firm, as well as the land use rights that are an advantage for Vietnamese firms .

There are clearly some sectors that could be the object of future reform. However, with the implementation of the protocol of accession, the issue of an obligation to export all or part of production, which is an export subsidy, has been reformed and, as a consequence, it is not considered relevant by the European Commission. It is important that the Vietnamese government focuses its attention to the accounting methodology of Vietnamese firms and their land use rights.

Before there is an anti-dumping investigation against, Vietnamese firms the Government should cooperate with EU authorities and assist Vietnamese firms in providing more detailed information available on the first three criteria for obtaining market economy treatment by individual firms.

In the EU, before the application of an anti-dumping duty, the European Commission has to verify whether the measures are in its interest. The evaluation of this entails an analysis of the effects following from the application of an anti-dumping duty on some interested groups, such as consumers, distributors and users of the imported products. Adequate support of these groups, through the disclosure of information on the real cost of products, could demonstrate that the application of anti-dumping measures may not be in line with the its interests. Furthermore, according to the decision-making process of the EU the application of an anti-dumping has to be approved by the Council with a simple majority. Where there is division between member states on the anti-dumping measure, the member states that have a particular interest pressurize those conflicting member states and those that have not a specific interest in the issue before there is a decision. The methodology used by the EC for the adoption of the status of 'analogous country' could be important in relationships with other developing countries with the aim of convincing EU decisions in the selection of the 'analogous country'.

In many instances decisions by the EU are not a 'first best' choice due to non-cooperation with the European Commission by the producers of the country selected. The creation of an office comprising representatives of both government and the business sector with the aim of promoting cooperation between countries affected by anti-dumping duties could assist in minimizing the effect of anti-dumping duties for both ME and NME countries.

Notes

1. The General Agreement on Tariffs and Trade is the predecessor of the World Trade Organization.
2. Cf. Report of the Panel on Brazil – measures affecting desiccated coconut, doc. WT/DS22/R, 1996, par. 232 and ff; Report of the Appellate Body, Document WT/DS22/AB/R, sec. IV.B and D.
3. Cf. Cornelis, J., 'China's Quest for Market Economy Status and its Impact on the Use of Trade Remedies by the European Communities and the United States', cited in *Global Trade and Customs Journal*, 2 (2), p. 106.
4. See Sohn, C., 2005, 'Treatment of Non-market Economy Countries under the World Trade Organization Anti-Dumping Regime,' *Journal of World Trade*, 4, p. 763ff.; Polouektov, A., 2002, 'Non-Market Economy Issues in the WTO Anti-Dumping Law and Accession Negotiations: Revival of a Two-Tier Membership?', *Journal of World Trade*, 1, p. 15ff.
5. In the European Union, for antidumping measures, individuals have been attributed the right of asking the European Court of Justice the verification of the consistency of EC legislation with WTO agreements.
6. Subsidization and dumping in exporting countries are not illegal practices according to the WTO agreements. However, they are considered unfair as the lower export price is the result of situations which do not depend on the natural competitive advantage of the enterprises exporting the goods. Where there are subsidies, enterprises may quote a lower price at export because they have been subsidized by the local government; and for dumping the WTO agreement does not identify the causes of this behaviour, simply stating that the importing state can react against products imported at a dumped price. Nevertheless, the economic literature identified that dumping can only occur if two conditions are fulfilled. First, the industry must be imperfectly competitive, so that firms have market power. That is, firms must be able to set prices in the domestic or foreign market rather than take prices as given in both markets. Second, markets must be segmented, so that domestic customers cannot easily purchase products sold at a lower price in foreign market. As to the first condition, it is well known that it is easier to dump products in third markets when the exporting company in the home market is a monopolist or an oligopolist and this is considered unfair where there is a monopoly or oligopoly and when the national government does not provide proper competition rules for controlling monopolists or oligopolists abuse of their dominant position. The second condition is considered unfair when it is the result of a protectionist policy carried out by the government.

7. For a legal analysis of the consistency of this practice with the WTO antidumping rules, refer, for instance, to Czako, J., Human, J. and Miranda, J., 2003, *A Handbook on Anti-Dumping Investigation*, Cambridge University Press, Cambridge and Sohn, C., 2005, 'Treatment of Non-market Economy Countries under the World Trade Organization Antidumping Regime', *Journal of World Trade*, 4, pp. 763–85.

8. The European Commission explicitly recognized this limitation in at least two antidumping cases against Vietnam. For further information refer to the Council Regulation (EC) No 1095/2005 of 12 July 2005 imposing a definitive anti-dumping duty on imports of bicycles originating in Vietnam, and amending Regulation (EC) No 1524/2000 imposing a definitive anti-dumping duty on imports of bicycles originating in the People's Republic of China, in *Official Journal of the European Union*, L 183/1, and Council Regulation (EC) No 1472/2006 of 5 October 2006 imposing a definitive anti-dumping duty and collecting definitely the provisional duty imposed on imports of certain footwear with uppers of leather originating in the People's Republic of China and Vietnam, in *Official Journal of the European Union*, L 275/1.

9. Cf. Vermulst, E., 2005, *The WTO Anti-Dumping Agreement a Commentary*, Oxford University Press, Oxford, p. 45.

10. Cf. Regulation 384/96 and amendments in the *Official Journal of the European Union*, L 56/1, 1996.

11. See J. Cornelis, 'China's Quest', op. cit., p. 107.

12. See EC Reg. No 553/2006 of 23 March 2006 imposing a provisional anti-dumping duty on imports of certain footwear with uppers of leather originating in the People's Republic of China and Vietnam, OJ, L 98/3.

13. This is a reproduction of Article 9.5 of EC Regulation 384/96.

14. Cf. Detlof, H. and Fridh, H., 2007, 'The EU Treatment of Non-Market Economy Countries in Antidumping Proceedings', *Global Trade and Customs Journal*, p. 265.

15. http://ia.ita.doc.gov/policy/bull03-1.html – N_1_#N_1

16. http://ia.ita.doc.gov/policy/bull03-1.html – N_2_#N_2

17. Cf. Ikenson, D., 2005, 'Nonmarket Nonsense, U.S. Antidumping Policy towards China', Trade Briefing Paper, Cato Institute, p. 6.

18. Art. 25 of the WTO agreement on Subsidies and Countervailing Measures.

19. Cf. Tariff Act of 1930, Chapter 479, § 303 (1930).

20. Cf. The Department of Commerce, 1984, Carbon Steel Wire Rod from Czechoslovakia; Final Negative Countervailing Duty Determination, 49 Fed. Reg. 19.370 and 19.371.

21. Ibid., Fed. Reg. 19.372.

22. Court of International Trade, 1985, Continental Steel Corp. v. United States, 614 F. Supp. 548.

23. Federal Circuit Court, 1986, Georgetown Steel Corp. v. United States, 801 F.2d 1308.

24. The Department of Commerce, 1992, Final Negative Countervaling Duty Determinations: Oscillating and Ceiling Fans From the People's Republic of China, 57 Fed. Reg. 24.018.

25. Cf. Coated Free Paper From the People's Republic of China, 72 Fed. Reg. 17.484 (Apr. 9, 2007).

26. Refer to memorandum titled 'Countervailing Duty Investigation of Coated Free Sheet Paper from the People's Republic of China – Whether the Analytical Elements of the Georgetown Steel Opinion are Applicable to China's Present-Day Economy', in Lee-Alaia, S. and Norton, L., 2007, Office of Policy, Import Administration to David M. Spooner, Assistant Secretary for Import Administration.
27. Working Party Report, 2007, Accession of Vietnam to the WTO, Paragraph 255 b, January.

11
Trade and Customs Management: the Increasing Importance of Rules of Origin

Laura Carola Beretta

Approaching imports, exports and outsourcing with a managerial approach is a growing necessity, primarily due to trade liberalization and the opening of markets that exposes national economies to the growing competitive pressure from emerging market economies. In fact, many countries enforce a variety of trade barriers, like antidumping duties, technical standards and origin marking requirements,[1] among others, in order to defend their national production. The second reason is strictly connected to the current lack of harmonization of the rules applying to trade relations and customs procedures. In order to avoid both the competitiveness of exported products being affected and financial and legal consequences being applied for not being compliant, firms must understand and correctly apply trade and customs rules and procedures in force in each importing country. The first step in performing a managerial attitude towards international trade operations is becoming aware of the variety of conditions and costs that may affect traded goods each time they cross borders.[2] Relying upon a specific and qualified knowledge of the complex trade legal framework is important in that it allows firms to take full advantage from the instruments with which they are provided by the international legal framework in order to enhance the competitiveness of their products.

Obstacles to trade – an overview

The success of firms' trade performance strictly depends upon the effective market access of traded goods. In general terms, market access is defined as the openness of a country's markets to foreign goods. From an entrepreneurial point of view, market access may be defined as a firm's capability to export its goods identifying the relevant trade barriers and complying with the customs procedures. Obstacles to trade may be divided into two broad categories: these are, tariff and non-tariff barriers. Customs duties and other charges levied by the customs authorities at the borders are tariff barriers. Tariff levels' reduction and quotas' elimination under the auspices of the General Agreements on Tariffs and Trade (GATT) before, and of the World Trade Organization (WTO) since 1995, have been widely agreed and applied. Nevertheless, the nature of barriers to trade in the global economy has changed in such a way that now, due to the difficulties in detecting, analysing and overcoming them, non-tariff barriers represent the major obstacle to trade in goods. The implementation of new non-tariff protective measures escaping the multilateral regulatory framework as a reaction to trade liberalization has been frequently commented on.[3] The WTO provides for a multilateral regulation for various non-tariff barriers, and the focus here, though to varying degrees, is on customs valuation, technical regulations and standards, sanitary and phytosanitary measures, antidumping, subsidies and countervailing measures, safeguards, import licensing, pre-shipment inspection and rules of origin.

A tariff discriminates between domestically and foreign produced goods and is a cost to the importer that must be recovered when the good is sold in the importing country. Provided the cost of production in both countries is similar this increases the relative price of the foreign produced good relative to the domestically produced good, before allowing for transportation costs. Since domestically produced goods are not subject to the tariff, the domestic producer may often increase the price of its goods to the price level of the imported goods, so as to have a wider profit margin than it could in the absence of a tariff on foreign goods, or charge a lower price with a reduced margin and be more competitive. In this sense, tariffs protect domestic industries from foreign competition.[4] However, where a foreign producer has a significantly lower cost of production then the tariff is limited in effect.

The simplest and most frequently used customs duties are the *ad valorem* duties, expressed as a percentage of the value of goods, such as, a percentage duty-rate levied on an imported good. Specific duties are fixed as a monetary value per unit of measurement of a physical unit. Specific duties lack transparency since it is difficult to know their percentage or *ad valorem* equivalent. The *ad valorem* equivalent of specific rates may be computed directly from the import price, but this is usually known to customs officers and the concerned enterprises only. Since their *ad valorem* incidence is inversely related to the price of the imported product, specific rates tend to fall more heavily on developing countries and low-cost suppliers.[5] Specific duties are still allowed, and are very common in agriculture in all countries.[6] Switzerland uses specific duties for all products.[7] Combined or mixed duties containing both *ad valorem* and specific rates are, though less frequently, levied on some products, such as a percentage of the value plus a monetary value per unit of measurement.

According to one of the main WTO principles, member countries may protect their domestic industries through tariffs only. As a matter of fact, even though the WTO stands for liberal trade, it recognizes that its members may have to protect domestic production against foreign competition. However, countries are required to maintain such protection at low levels and to provide it through tariffs. The principle of protection by tariffs is reinforced by provisions prohibiting member countries from using quotas, otherwise defined as quantitative restrictions, on imports. A quota specifies the quantity of a particular good that a country allows to be imported during a specific time period.[8] Quotas are non-tariff barriers *par excellence*. Exporting firms prefer tariffs to quantitative restrictions. Tariffs are transparent and their incidence is predictable.[9] On the contrary, quantitative restrictions entail a certain uncertainty on trade, as administering authorities have the power to adjust the sizes of quotas from time to time.[10] Moreover, the operation of quota restrictions requires licensing, meaning that firms may export only to the extent they have buyers able to obtain a licence.

According to the WTO rules, customs duties should be reduced and, where possible, eliminated through multilateral negotiations. The rates of tariffs agreed in the negotiations should be bound against further increases. To assure the other WTO member countries that the tariffs imposed do not exceed those agreed during the negotiations, each member country lists its tariff concessions in a schedule of tariff concessions. The rates of tariffs listed in the schedules are known as bound rates of tariffs. They are also called most-favoured nation (MFN) tariffs, since, according to the core WTO non discrimination principle they must be applied on an equal basis to all other WTO member countries, irrespective of the origin of imported goods.[11] MFN-bound tariffs imply the commitment not to apply higher duties except in particular circumstances allowed by the WTO rules, such as antidumping duties, duties imposed to countervail subsidized goods and duties applied to enact safeguard measures. However, these duties may only be imposed upon evidence that the conditions established by the relevant WTO Agreements have been met. Before imposing an antidumping or countervailing duty, or a safeguard measure, an assessment and investigation procedure must be carried out in accordance with the WTO rules. On the contrary, lower duties or no duties apply on goods originating from countries having a preferential agreement with the importing country.

Member states are, on the contrary, free to apply rates of tariffs lower than the bound ones. In fact, a country may bind its tariffs at a ceiling rate which is higher than the rate resulting from the tariff reductions agreed in the negotiations. Thus, a country which agrees to reduce a tariff from 10 per cent to 5 per cent may indicate that, while it applies the reduced rate to imports, the bound rate of the tariff is 8 per cent. In such an instance, the country is free to raise its tariffs to 8 per cent at any time without infringing any of its WTO obligations. It generally follows that bound tariffs are generally higher than applied tariffs, and such a circumstance impairs the predictability of the actual duty rate to be applied by the customs authority upon importation.

Many countries, especially low- and middle-income countries apply a variety of customs fees and charges[12] upon importation. They have been defined as other measures that increase the cost of imports in a manner similar to tariff measures.[13] Recent studies demonstrate that Article VIII of the GATT requires such para-tariff measures to be limited in amount to the cost of the customs services rendered and not to represent an additional protection to domestic products. Even though WTO member countries recognize both the need for reducing the number and diversity of fees and charges, and the importance of minimizing the incidence and complexity of import and export formalities, there is no provision, unlike for customs duties, of binding the use of para-tariff measures. This circumstance, together with the lack of a provision regarding the notification to the WTO explains why complex schemes of fees and charges still exist. This lack of information affects exporters, especially when they are small and medium-sized enterprises (SME) not having the means and the infrastructure for keeping themselves updated.[14] Customs and administrative procedures, when inefficient or more burdensome than necessary, affect the costs of trade operations.[15]

The WTO agreements on technical barriers to trade, sanitary and phytosanitary measures, import-licensing procedures, customs valuation, pre-shipment inspection and rules of origin seek to ensure transparency of laws, regulations and practices regarding these rules of trade and, ultimately, to harmonize them to facilitate international trade. The WTO agreements on antidumping, subsidies and countervailing measures, safeguards and trade-related investment measures are viewed as related to trade competition policies.[16]

Specific requirements are adopted by countries either for the protection of the health and safety of their people or for the preservation of their environment. To reach these goals countries' regulations specify the characteristics that products should comply with, such as, their size, shape, design, functions, performance and the way they are labelled before they are offered for sale. The 1995 WTO Agreement on Technical Barriers to Trade (TBT) approaches this issue distinguishing between standards and technical regulations.[17] The difference between a standard and a technical regulation lies in compliance. While conformity to standards is voluntary, technical regulations are mandatory and these have different implications for international trade. If an imported product does not fulfil the criteria of a technical regulation, it may not be allowed to be offered for sale. Referring to standards, non-complying imported products are allowed on the market. Nevertheless, exporting firms may find that some standards have the mandatory effect of technical regulations. This happens when large industries refuse to buy goods that do not conform to the standards they impose. Governments often lay down health and safety standards for various products. Standards are also established to protect the environment and the natural resources. When product standards adopted at national level vary from country to country, manufacturers have to adjust their production processes to meet the differing technical specifications of their target markets. The TBT Agreement requires mandatory product requirements not to be applied as to cause unnecessary obstacles to international trade. This may be avoided to the extent they are based on internationally agreed standards. Furthermore, they should be built upon scientific information and evidence. The need to comply with different foreign technical regulations and standards involves costs for producers and exporters, arising from the translation of foreign regulations, the assistance of technical experts and the adjustment of production facilities to comply wth the requirements.

A number of imported agricultural products, particularly plants, fresh fruits and vegetables, meat, meat products and other food products, may be required to satisfy sanitary and phytosanitary regulations. Many countries restrict the import of these products if they do not satisfy the quality requirements specified by their regulations. The scope of the WTO Sanitary and Phytosanitary (SPS) Agreement differs from the purpose of the TBT Agreement in that it covers all measures whose purpose is to protect human or animal health from food-borne risks; human health from animal-or plant-carried diseases and animal and plants from pests or diseases, whether or not these are technical requirements.[18]

The 1995 WTO Agreement on Import Licensing Procedures (ILP) defines import licensing as those administrative procedures 'requiring the submission of an application or other documentation (other than those required for customs purposes) to the relevant administrative body as a prior condition for importation'.[19] The main objectives of this agreement are to simplify and bring transparency to import licensing procedures, to ensure their fair and equitable application and administration, and to prevent procedures applied for granting import licences from having in themselves restrictive or distortive effects on imports.[20] By obliging national licensing authorities to follow its principles and rules, the ILP Agreement seeks to protect the interests of both foreign suppliers wanting to export products subject to licensing and of producing industries interested in importing such products.[21]

Pre-shipment inspection (PSI) is the practice of employing specialized private companies to check shipment details, such as quality, quantity, price, currency exchange rates, financial terms and customs classification of goods to be exported to the territory of the user member. Used by governments of developing countries, the purpose is both to safeguard national financial interests, such as, preventing capital flight and customs duty evasion, and to compensate for inadequacies of administrative infrastructures. The 1994 WTO Agreement on PSI attempts to strike a balance between the concerns expressed by developed countries' exporting firms and the need to safeguard the essential interest of developing countries that consider PSI services useful. In fact, countries' governments using PSI benefit from the increased customs revenue resulting from the detection of undervaluation and from the decline in the flight of capital through overvaluation.

As a reaction to 'unfair' trade practices, countries may react by imposing, according to the circumstances, either an antidumping or a countervailing duty. Dumping occurs when a company exports at a price lower than the price it normally charges on its own home market. Whenever the product being dumped is not sold on the domestic market, the price charged by the exporter in another country is taken as a first alternative reference. To the extent the latter method for the determination of the price is not possible, a calculation taken based on the exporter's production costs plus other expenses and normal profit margins is carried out. A product is also considered to be dumped if it is sold for less than its cost of production. Being focused on how governments may or may not react to dumping, the WTO Antidumping Agreement (ADA) does not judge whether dumping practices are unfair or not. Governments are allowed to act against dumping when they are able to prove the occurrence of three circumstances. These are, the extent of dumping, or, in other terms, how much lower the export price is compared to the exporter's home market price, the injury or the threat of injury to the importing country's industry, and the causal link existing between dumped products and the injury. In order to reach the conclusion that an antidumping duty may be imposed, a detailed investigation must be conducted according to specific rules. In this respect, the ADA sets out procedural rules on how antidumping cases are to be initiated, how the investigations are to be conducted, and the conditions to ensure that all the interested parties are given an opportunity to present evidence.[22] Antidumping measures must expire five years after the date of imposition, unless the investigation shows that ending the measures would lead to injury.

Countervailing duties may be applied to react to imports that benefited from a specific subsidy. The 1995 WTO Agreement on Subsidies and Countervailing Measures (SCM Agreement) defines the term subsidy and explains the concept of specificity. The SCM Agreement defines a subsidy as a financial contribution granted by a government, or any public body within the territory of a country, which confers a benefit. Grants, loans, fiscal incentives, provision of goods or services are among the types of measures representing a financial contribution listed by the SCM Agreement. Furthermore, the SCM Agreement applies not only to measures of national governments, but also to measures of sub-national governments and such public bodies, such as, state-owned enterprises. In addition, a financial contribution by a government is not a subsidy unless it confers a benefit.[23] The two elements must occur in order for a subsidy to exist. A subsidy is not subject to the SCM Agreement unless it has been specifically provided to an enterprise or industry or a group of enterprises or industries. The basic principle is that a subsidy that distorts the allocation of resources within an economy may be countervailed. On the contrary, where a subsidy is widely available within an economy, such a distortion in the allocation of the resources is presumed not to occur. Similar to the antidumping WTO provisions, countervailing duties may only be charged after a detailed investigation procedure shows that a product has been subsidized, that subsidized products has caused an injury to the domestic industry and that there is a causal link between the subsidy and the injury caused. Also countervailing duties may be imposed for 5 years. While the target of antidumping duties are exporting firms, countervailing duties are imposed on countries.

Countries may restrict imports on a temporary basis by taking 'safeguard' actions if their industry is either injured or threatened with injury by a surge in imports. Affected firms may request a safeguard action to their governments that may start safeguard investigations according to the procedural rules set out by the WTO Agreement on Safeguards.

Where quotas are the necessary measures taken to perform the safeguard action, they should not normally reduce the quantities of imports below the annual average for the last three representative years for which statistics are available, unless clear justification is given that a different level is necessary to prevent or remedy serious injury. In principle, safeguard measures may not be targeted at imports from a particular country and should not last more than four years although they may be extended if they are proved to be necessary and the competent authority may provide evidence that the industry is adjusting. When a country restricts imports to safeguard its domestic producers, it must, in principle, give something in return. Exporting countries may seek consultations to agree compensations.[24] In a safeguard action, similarly to that required in an antidumping or countervailing procedure, the causal link between increased imports and serious injury or threat of serious injury is a condition to be satisfied.

Determination of the applicable duties

MFN and preferential customs duties, antidumping and countervailing duties, and safeguard measures are levied by the authorities of each importing country according to three elements which the customs declaration contains: customs value, tariff classification code and origin of imported goods. The incidence of *ad valorem* duties depends to a large extent on the methods used to determine the dutiable value. The benefits to the trade arising from tariff bindings could be considerably diminished according to the rules and practice applied to determine the customs value of imported goods. According to the main principle of the 1995 WTO Agreement on Customs Valuation (ACV), the value for customs purposes should be based on the price actually paid or payable when sold for export to the country of importation.[25] Such value, also called transaction value, is the invoice price, and may be adjusted, where appropriate, to include certain payments made by the buyers.[26] The ACV requires all members to harmonize their national legislation on the basis of its rules, with the purpose of ensuring uniformity in the application of the customs valuation procedures, so that importers may assess in advance of imports the amounts of duties to be paid. When customs authorities have reasons to doubt that the value declared in the invoice is lower than the actual transaction price, the burden of the proof falls upon the importer. In order to ensure that the transaction value declared is rejected by customs authorities on an objective basis, the ACV stipulates that national legislation should provide certain rights to importers.[27] However, in practical terms, there are several reasons why the benefits potentially arising from the ACV are diminished. The elements that should be included in the invoice price are not clear to all exporting firms and not all importers are acquainted with the elements that may be excluded from the determination of such price for customs valuation purposes. In addition, the lack of harmonization requires the knowledge of the national rules and customs practice, thus complicating a correct preliminary assessment of the value of imported goods. Such an assessment is quite important especially for firms exporting towards emerging markets like China, India and Brazil, where the concern for under-invoiced imported goods is so high as to lead to thorough controls of the declared customs value.

Each importing country determines the applicable duty according to its national customs tariff. All customs tariffs are based on the Harmonized Commodity Description and Coding System (HS Convention), the multilateral convention establishing a code and a description for all traded goods.[28] The HS Convention is administered by the World Customs Organization (WCO) which is based in Brussels. The HS Convention is structured in twenty-one sections subdivided into ninety-nine chapters, categorized by productive sector, with goods grouped either according to the material of which are made or to the use, or function, they are destined to. The first two digits identify the HS chapter, the first four digits the HS heading, and the first six digits the HS subheading. For example, Chapter 90 identifies optical, measuring and medical instruments or apparatus; heading 9004 spectacles; and subheading 9004.10 sunglasses. Signatory countries are obliged to use the same six digits in implementing their national classification system, but are free to add more digits to classify goods.[29] Irrespective of the number of digits of which the classification system of each importing country is composed, one same good is often differently classified according to the country where is being imported. Keeping in mind this circumstance is quite relevant, since the tariff classification code is one of the three elements determining the duty rate applicable upon importation. It follows, then, that the practice of exporting goods identified with the same classification code used upon importation is incorrect, in that it entails the risk that the customs authorities of the country from where the goods are being exported would apply a customs duty which is not necessarily the most appropriate. That is why it is highly recommended to determine in advance the correct classification and duty rates which are to be applied to exports according to the customs classification system of each importing country.

The General Rules of Interpretation of the HS Convention, as well as, the introductory notes to the sections and to the chapters are the first legal instrument applying to the classification of goods.[30] They are helpful in the complicated, and quite frequent, situation in which one good may be included in two or more HS codes.[31] Classifying goods means finding the correct and most appropriate correspondence between the HS code and the description provided by the customs classification system of each importing country.[32] All the countries party to the HS Convention enjoy the right of been represented in the HS Committee, in charge for the administration and revision of the HS. Firms exporting either technologically innovative commodities or goods not being produced in the importing country may represent the interests of their producers of such goods in order to make them have a new and appropriate HS tariff code.[33] Not to have recourse to such an opportunity may be very costly in competitive terms, since the goods would then be classified according to the available code, and this could imply the undue payment of higher customs duties.

The increasing importance of rules of origin

Rules of origin are the legal and administrative criteria applied to determine the nationality of imported goods. Generally speaking, goods originate from the country where they have been wholly obtained. Nevertheless, since firms are outsourcing different stages of the production in countries where labour costs are relatively lower, goods are, in the majority of the cases, processed in two or more countries. In the latter situation, products originate from the country where they have undergone the last substantial transformation. The 1995 WTO Agreement on Rules of Origin (ARO) is based upon this principle,[34] which the US Court decisions,[35] at first, and the Customs Code of the European Community (EC),[36] later, had already affirmed.

There are two types of rules of origin, preferential and non-preferential. Preferential origin rules apply to determine the origin of imported goods for the only purpose of granting the preferential duties agreed in the context of free trade agreements (FTAs). Their main function is to prevent the trade diversion, which may arise when goods originating from third countries would be applied different tariffs in the members to an FTA, thus creating an incentive to bring merchandise into the FTA through the member country with the lowest tariffs and then ship it duty-free to the members with higher tariffs. In the context of FTAs concluded on a reciprocal basis, the advantage of trading goods at a reduced duty, or with the duty exemption, is mutual and for this reason may be obtained in both imports and exports. Nevertheless, most developed countries grant preferential, but not reciprocal, treatment to goods originating from developing countries. The instruments utilized for this objective are unilateral schemes of tariff preferences set out by the industrialized countries, and called Generalized System of Preferences (GSPs). GSPs, being unilaterally granted, it is up to the preference-giving countries to draft the rules of origin to be applied to developing countries' exports.[37] In this instance, and whenever the importing country is an industrialized economy, only imports benefit from the advantages arising from GSPs. Non-preferential rules of origin apply to determine the origin of imported goods to implement trade policy instruments such as antidumping and countervailing duties, safeguard measures and origin marking requirements.[38]

Protocols of origin attached to the text of each free trade agreement are the source where preferential rules of origin are to be found. Nevertheless, preferential rules of origin applying to determine whether imported goods are originating from a developing country, and thus eligible for unilateral preferences, are contained in the national legislation of the importing country.[39] Non-preferential rules of origin are provided for by national regulations as well. The WTO ARO aims at harmonizing non-preferential rules of origin. Once the harmonization process has been completed, common multilateral non-preferential origin rules, instead of national rules, should, in principle, be applied. Both preferential and non-preferential rules of origin are based on three methods. These are, a change in tariff classification, value added and a technical criterion. According to the first method, products originate from the country where, as a result of manufacturing production that was in that country, the final product is classified under an HS code that differs from the code for the non-originating materials. The value added method may occur either as an import content percentage or as a local value-added percentage. In the first instance, it imposes a ceiling on the use of imported parts and materials through a maximum allowable percentage of such parts and materials. In its second form, it requires a minimum percentage of local value added. Finally, the technical method prescribes certain production or sourcing operations that may or may not confer the originating status.[40]

The increasing relevance and importance of rules of origin is the direct consequence of both the proliferation of regional trade agreements[41] (RTAs) and the increased use of antidumping and countervailing duties. The exposure to the growing competitive pressure due, *inter alia*, to the lowering of applicable customs duties drives countries to defend their national producers having recourse to other trade policy instruments.

In this context, rules of origin have been shifting from simple technical regulations, mainly used for statistical purposes, towards instruments of trade policy themselves.[42] Moreover, the fact that many countries are adopting national origin marking regulations based upon the concept of non-preferential origin is a further element accounting for the protectionist nature of rules of origin.

The ARO provides that, while the harmonization process is ongoing, rules of origin should not be used to pursue trade policy objectives, should not be restrictive, should be administered in a consistent, uniform and impartial way, and should be coherent.[43] The harmonization process was supposed to last only for three years, until July 1998, but at the time of writing the transitional period still applies. The negotiation issues of the harmonization work are managed by the Committee on Rules of Origin established by Article 4.1 of the ARO, while the technical work of the harmonization programme has been carried out by the Technical Committee on Rules of Origin under the auspices of the WCO.[44] Both the political nature and the strategic impact performed by rules of origin in countries' trade policy is the major reason why the harmonization process of non-preferential origin rules carried out in the WTO has not come to an end yet.[45] Very divisive issues about which it is still difficult to reach consensus in the negotiation of harmonized rules of origin (HRO), in terms of their suitability in being origin-conferring are, among others, the processing, mixing and blending of agricultural goods,[46] the printing or dyeing of yarns and fibres,[47] assembly operations in the machinery, transport equipment and photocopying apparatus sectors,[48] and the implementation issue.[49]

At the moment only 35 WTO members have notified their non-preferential rules of origin, 42 WTO members have notified that they do not have non-preferential rules of origin, and 47 WTO members have not yet notified their non-preferential rules of origin.[50] Brazil, India and Israel are among the countries having notified that they do not have non-preferential rules of origin.

The relationship between rules of origin and origin marking

Origin marking indicates the origin of a product on the product itself or on its packaging, typically in the form of 'Made in', followed by the name of the country of origin.

The first purpose of this is to inform consumers about the origin of a product, allowing them the opportunity to select their purchases according to the perceived quality that a specific origin is meant to imply.[51] Moreover, many manufacturers do believe the origin of a product to have an impact on the buyer's decisions, so, whenever specific placename origin is perceived by consumers as important, origin marking is an instrument to promote the image of the products.[52]

Article IX of the GATT 1994 and article 1.2 of the ARO provide the relevant WTO rules as regards marks of origin. Article IX of the GATT, though recognizing the necessity of protecting consumers against fraudulent or misleading indications, aims at reducing to the minimum difficulties and inconveniences that may be caused by laws, regulations and administrative practices during the customs clearance of imported products.[53] Whenever it is possible, the authorities of the importing country should permit affixation of the required marks of origin at the time of importation.[54]

Being applicable to all rules of origin used in non-preferential commercial policy instruments, the ARO refers to those countries' legislation in which the country to be indicated on imported products by the origin marking is the country where the goods, whenever processed in two or more countries, have undergone their last substantial transformation. WTO rules are relevant whenever the legislation or practice of one member country may be restrictive, therefore representing an obstacle to trade.

Origin marking is also dealt with by the international conventions aimed at the protection of intellectual property rights. An interesting debate is whether origin marking should be considered either as an obstacle to trade or as an intellectual property right. There are at least three concepts aimed at indicating the linkage between a good and its place of origin. These are indication of source, appellation of origin and geographical indication. The differences and the overlap among these three concepts have been analysed and debated in the literature on intellectual property rights as related to the multilateral trade rules.[55] Each concept takes into account the relationship between good and place considered in a twofold perspective: the required linkage between product's characteristics and place of origin, and the modalities allowed to express such linkage.

An indication of source is any geographical sign, including names, used to indicate that a product originates in a given country or place. It may either be a placename, such as, a country, region or city, or a sign or a representation of a place or landmark, like a picture representing some geographical physical feature. An appellation of origin is the geographical name used to indicate that the quality and the characteristics of a product originating in a given country or place are exclusively or essentially due to natural climate and soil, and to human just as methods of production,[56] and the denomination must correspond to the geographical name which serves to designate a product and may not be given by a symbol or other kinds of expression. This means that the product and the geographical place name should be the same. The Paris Convention for the Protection of Industrial Property of 1883[57] defines both indications of sources and appellations of origin as objects for protection of intellectual property.[58] This might suggest that both expressions should be considered as synonymous. As a matter of fact, there is a significant difference between them. An appellation of origin requires a quality linkage between the product and its geographical origin. Quite differently, the use of an indication of source is merely subject to the condition that a given product originates in the place designated by the indication of source.[59] As for legal protection, the Paris Convention provides for the seizure of goods bearing a false indication of source either on importation or in the country of affixation.[60] The seizure of goods only applies to false indications of source and not to the deceptive ones, and it is not always mandatory.[61] In this respect the Madrid Agreement for the Repression of False or Deceptive Indications of Source on Goods of 1891[62] goes further than the Paris Convention by providing for the seizure on importation of goods bearing not only false but also deceptive indications of source. Nevertheless, it must be noted that as the Madrid Agreement is in force in only 34 countries, its legal effectiveness in guaranteeing an appropriate origin practice at multilateral level is quite limited. The World Intellectual Property Organization (WIPO) assimilates origin marking to the indication of source. Although the Paris Convention and the Madrid Agreement do not provide a definition of 'indication of source', Article 1(1) of the Madrid Agreement is interpreted as follows:

> an indication of source may be defined as an indication referring to a country, or to a place in that country, as being the country or place of origin of a product. It is important that the indication of source relates to the geographical origin of a product and not to another kind of origin, for example, an enterprise that manufactures the product. This definition does not imply any special quality or characteristics of the product on which an indication of source is used. Instances of indications of source are the mention, on a product, of the name of a country, or indications such as 'made in'.[63]

This interpretation does not seem to impede an indication of source being used even when materials or inputs originating in different countries have been used to produce the good that bears the indication.

Article 22.1 of the WTO Agreement on Trade-Related Aspects of Intellectual Property Rights (TRIPS) provides for the more recent multilateral concept of geographical indications defined as 'indications which identify a good as originating in the territory of a Member, or a region or locality in that territory, where a given quality, reputation or other characteristic of the good is essentially attributable to its geographical origin'.[64] Unlike an appellation of origin, a geographical indication could be any expression that could serve the purpose of identifying a given geographical place, and not necessarily the name of the place where the product originates. For instance, a country's flag could be used to identify wines of a certain quality or reputation. This means that geographical indications could also be expressed by a symbol; moreover, they also refer to the reputation of the product which must be essentially, but not exclusively, attributable to a given geographical origin. The concept of geographical indication is then more general than the one of appellation of origin.[65]

Each importing country is free to rule on the compulsoriness of origin marking and to set out rules and procedures applied to assess its correctness. This means that exporting firms wishing their products to accede to foreign markets must ensure themselves that exported products comply with the origin marking requirements of each country they are exporting to. In general, while some countries, like Russia and Israel, regulate origin marking in the context of their labelling provisions, others, like Canada and the US provide for an *ad hoc* legislation for origin marking. Furthermore, whenever countries require some substantial rules to be satisfied in order to consider imported products appropriately marked, the substantial rules to be satisfied are the non-preferential rules of origin, as applies in Canada, China, Russia and the US. In countries like Turkey and China, origin marking for imported products is a voluntary practice but, whenever the country of origin is indicated, the non-preferential rules of origin of Turkey and China, respectively, must be satisfied. For exports destined to the European Union, origin marking is not obligatory, but if the exporter wants its products to be identified with the country of origin, compliance with the EC non-preferential origin rule may be required.[66]

As for lacking, false, misleading or inaccurate country of origin marking, seizure of the imported merchandise is the first consequence provided for in many countries.[67] This inconvenience is likely to cause delays in the delivery of goods. According to each importing country's legislation stricter penalties may be applied.[68] From the point of view of export-oriented firms, complying with different origin marking requirements according to the country targeted for their exports, implies financial and organizational costs deriving from the need for arranging the production accordingly. In this respect, origin marking affects international trade acting as a non-tariff barrier.

Trade and customs management

The complexity of the legal framework applying to the international trade relations implies both costs and risks whenever imports and exports are carried out and outsourcing decisions taken. Despite the multilateral efforts aiming at harmonization, different sets of rules, ranging from the bilateral and regional preferential trade agreements to the national legislation, apply. Furthermore, ease and cost of access to the sources of the applicable trade rules are different from country to country, depending upon both the publicly available resources and the transparency of the country concerned. For these reasons, trade and customs management, meant as a managerial approach for imports, exports and outsourcing is the only way for a firm to achieve a twofold purpose: minimizing costs and optimizing customs compliance of international trade operations. Customs compliance is ensured when import and export operations are carried out complying with the rules, procedure and customs practice of each importing country.[69] As a matter of fact, whenever one good arrives at the borders ready to be imported, the concerns of the importing country in terms of financial revenue, defence of the national businesses from foreign competition, protection of the environment and consumers' security become relevant. Verifying costs and conditions for the access in each country should be part of the project of a new product. The country where the inputs should be bought and the extent to which manufacture is outsourced should be decided in relation to the type of product and countries targeted for its exportation.

Against this background, the under-estimation of the customs function as a consequence of the generally considered-to-be-low duty rates is one of the most common attitudes.[70] In fact, the customs department is generally attached to one of the following departments: the procurement department, in charge of the imports, the marketing department, in charge of the exports, the logistics department, the financial accounting department or the tax department. Lack of coordination among these departments could hardly result in a successful trade and customs performance, thus paving the way to disruption of deliveries, post-clearance recovery of large amounts or customs penalties. Furthermore, these occurrences imply damage both in the relationship with clients, due to delaying deliveries, and with the customs authority, which tend to target their checks to the same non-complying company.[71]

Against customs charges and customs procedures there are few options, except being aware of their incidence on the competitiveness of the goods being exported. The same is to be said as regards technical standards, origin marking requirements and sanitary and phytosanitary measures, which if not complied with and if verified, may result in either during the import clearance process or once the import procedure has been completed, in impediments to market access. An evaluation in terms of incidence of these non-tariff barriers should definitely be part of the assessment of the attractiveness of new markets. It is different for either new products or outsourcing decisions. In fact, the tariff classification and origin issues, being fundamentals of the customs identity determining the duties to which the new product is subjected, should be raised and treated as elements influencing the success of the commercial performance.

Considering the preceding, trade and customs management (TCM) should be implemented according to three levels of activity. These are assessment of the conditions required by each importing country in order to act as a compliant trader, strategic planning to minimize market access costs, and periodical monitoring of how trade rules and customs procedures evolve. There is not a one-size-fits-all method to set out this threefold action. On the contrary, one product may be considered, and consequently treated as particularly sensitive by a given importing country; or considered and treated as such in a particular period of time, for instance when the importing country legislation is enforcing an antidumping duty. For these reasons, an individual approach, to be modulated according to a both country-specific and product-specific perspective is the best method. As for strategic planning, the proliferation of free-trade agreements is a big opportunity in terms of preferential market access. Nevertheless, the overlapping of preferential arrangements is a burden in the real evaluation of the best way to benefit from preferential trade conditions. Not to mention the different sets of preferential origin rules whose knowledge is indispensable to benefit from the preferential trade regimes. This level of complexity suggests at first that the responsibility of the customs function may not be completely delegated outside the firm. The use of customs agents is useful and its cost-effectiveness may be optimized by developing the strategic management of the trade and customs function inside the firm with an appropriate coordination of the different functions. According to the complexity implied, which is different in each firm, this fundamental process may be carried out in conjunction with experienced consultants. Once the strategy has been established, it is important to provide customs agents with all the relevant information to enable them to implement the decided strategy and perform the best day-by-day operational activity.

Conclusion

A globalized context implies either suffering from the risks and costs that the lack of knowledge of the rules entails or benefiting from the opportunities of such an interdependent scenario. Customs duties have been generally lowered but are still high for sensitive products and when exporting to developing countries. As a reaction against increasing competitive pressures countries enforce a range of non-tariff barriers making access to their markets more difficult and costly. Furthermore, the lack of harmonization implies that the trade rules and customs procedures of each importing country must be complied with. This, together with the different attitude to transparency performed by countries, requires the adoption of a managerial approach to trade and customs operations. TCM is then the only successful method to be applied to imports, exports and outsourcing operations. The purpose of TCM is twofold in that it aims at optimizing customs compliance and cutting costs of international trade operations. At the level of each firm TCM is efficient if developed according to its main three lines of actions. These are, assessment of the conditions required by each importing country in order to act as a compliant trader, strategic planning to minimize market access costs, and periodical monitoring of how trade rules and customs procedures evolve.

Firms should become more aware of the role of the value of the customs function and how it could foster competitiveness. The size, type and number of products and the complexity implied by the legislation of each country targeted for exports are the parameters to be taken into consideration to build up the team in charge to perform the best TCM. A balance of internal and external resources could be the solution. Information and services that may be obtained from chambers of commerce, customs brokers and customs authorities may be very useful as practical support. Nevertheless, for strategic advice and planning, more information and more advanced professional skills, like those that specialized experts may guarantee, are the most appropriate solution.

Notes

1. Many countries require specific information to be written in a label and affixed to a product destined for consumption, for the purpose of protecting, or simply informing, the consumer. Environmental protection is another aim generally pursued by labelling requirements. Marking is the term used both by the WTO disciplines and the US trade legislation, specifically referring to the indication of the country of origin of the product. Such an indication is normally to be found either directly on the product and/or its label or container.

2. Trade operations involving the role of customs are within the scope of this chapter, whose first aim is to describe the elements that should be considered in order to perform a managerial approach to imports, exports and outsourcing operations. In fact, whenever tangible goods cross the custom's territory of the exporting and importing country, the twofold issue of paying customs duties, whenever due, and complying with the customs' legislation requirements arises. It is not the same for international trade in services, characterized by regulatory barriers. Due to their intangible nature, applying border measures to services is often impossible or too costly. For these reasons international trade in services is outside the scope of this chapter.

3. As stated by Jackson, Davey and Sykes: 'The discovery of new protective devices appears to be an endless process. As soon as the international system establishes restraints or regulations on a particular protective device, government officials and human ingenuity seem able to turn up some other measures to accomplish at least part of their protective purposes. Consequently, any international regulatory system must be designed so as to cope with the constant change in protectionist techniques'. Refer to Jackson J., Davey W. and Sykes A., 2002, *Legal Problems of International Trade Relations*, West Group, St. Paul, Minnesota, p. 410.

4. Ibid., p. 376.

5. Laird, S., 1998, 'Multilateral Approaches to Market Access Negotiations', Staff Working Paper TPRD-98-02, World Trade Organization, p. 6.

6. With a few exceptions, most countries levy *ad valorem* duties. Governments prefer to levy such duties for two reasons. First, it is easier for the authorities to estimate collectable revenue from *ad valorem* duties, which are assessed on the basis of value, rather than estimating revenue from specific duties, which are levied on the basis of units. Second, in international negotiations for reductions in tariffs it is easier to compare the level of tariffs and negotiate reductions if duties are *ad valorem*. International Trade Centre, UNCTAD/WTO, Business Guide to the Uruguay Round, 1995, ITC/CS, Geneva, p.85.

7. Cf. WTO Doc. WT/TPR/S/141, 2004, Trade Policy Review Body, Trade Policy Review, Switzerland and Liechtenstein, report by the Secretariat, p. 45.

8. Article XII of GATT 1994 provides an important exception permitting countries that are in balance-of-payments difficulties to restrict imports in order to safeguard their external financial position. Article XVIII of GATT 1994 allows greater flexibility to developing countries. cf. World Trade Organization, 1994, The Results of the Uruguay Round of Multilateral Trade Negotiations,

the Legal Texts, Geneva, p. 27. The passage from the General Agreement on Tariffs and Trade (GATT) to the WTO has brought about a change in the use of quantitative restrictions and other non tariff-measures affecting agricultural imports. In the agricultural sector, in fact, in accordance with the WTO Agreement on Agriculture, WTO member countries committed to abolish quantitative restrictions replacing these with tariffs. The new tariff rates have been determined by 'tariffication', that is calculating the incidence of quantitative restrictions and other measures on the price of the imported products and adding it to the then-prevailing tariffs; International Trade Centre, UNCTAD/WTO, 1995, Business Guide to the Uruguay Round op. cit., p. 68. As regards, the textile and clothing sectors, and from the expiry of the WTO Agreement on Textiles and Clothing on 1 January 2005, WTO member countries are compelled to have phased out quotas on the imports of textile and clothing goods.

9. The EU Market Access Database is a useful instrument to be consulted in order to quickly assess the customs duties applied to imports. The Applied Tariffs Database is a direct link to the National customs tariffs of selected non-EU countries. Refer to http://mkaccdb.eu.int/mkaccdb2/indexPubli.htm. Customs duties applied upon importation into the EU are available on the EU customs tariffs database at http://ec.europa.eu/taxation_customs/dds/tarhome_en.htm.

10. See, OECD Working Party of the Trade Committee, 2004, 'Analysis of Non-Tariff Measures: the case of Prohibition and Quotas', OECD Trade Policy Working Paper, No. 6, pp. 1–49

11. For an extensive analysis of the non-discrimination principle in international law refer to Dordi C., 2002, *La Discriminazione Commerciale nel Diritto Internazionale*, Giuffrè, Milano.

12. According to recent studies dedicated to the customs fees and charges applicable upon importation at the border, taxes on transport facilities, like airport taxes and port taxes, taxes for sensitive product categories and environmental taxes, as well as customs surcharges are the most commonly applied. Customs surcharges are special surcharges or additional duties that are levied for different purposes, like financing infrastructure projects, development funds or other special causes or institutions. On the contrary, import licence fees, consular invoice fees and statistical taxes are less frequently applied. OECD, Working Party of the Trade Committee (a), 2005, Analysis of Non-Tariff Measures: Customs Fees and Charges on Imports, OECD Trade Policy Working Paper Number 14, p. 11 ff.

13. Definition of the United Conference for Trade and Development (UNCTAD) Trade Analysis and Information System (TRAINS).

14. OECD, Working Party of the Trade Committee (a), Analysis of Non-Tariff Measures, op. cit., p. 26.

15. Recent economic studies have analysed the impact of customs and administrative procedures according to three parameters drawn from surveys conducted by the World Bank: the number of documents, the number of signatures and the days at the border required for the import/export operations. cf. OECD, Working Party of the Trade Committee (b), 2007, 'Examining the trade affect of certain customs and administrative procedures', OECD Trade Policy Working Paper No. 42.

16. Gürler O., 2002, WTO 'Agreements on Non-tariff Barriers and Implications for the OIC Member States: Customs Valuation, Pre-Shipment Inspection, Rules of Origin and Import Licensing', *Journal of Economic Cooperation* 23 (1), pp. 61–88.
17. Cf. Article 2, Article 4 and Annex I to the TBT Agreement, in World Trade Organization, 1994, Results of the Uruguay Round, op. cit., p. 138 ff.
18. The TBT Agreement covers all technical regulations, voluntary standards and the procedures to ensure that these are met, except when these are sanitary or phytosanitary measures as defined by the SPS Agreement. It is thus the type of measure which determines whether it is covered by the TBT Agreement, but the purpose of the measure which is relevant in determining whether a measure is subject to the SPS Agreement. cf. World Trade Organization, 2007, Understanding the WTO, Geneva, p. 30. Furthermore, the SPS Agreement allows member countries to introduce or maintain an SPS measure resulting in a higher level of protection than that achieved by an international stand-ard if there is scientific justification or when the country determines that a higher level of protection would be appropriate and the SPS Agreement states that the appropriate level of protection should be based on an assessment of risk appropriate to the circumstances, available scientific evidence, relevant process and production methods, and the prevalence of specific diseases or pests. cf. World Trade Organization, 1994, Results of the Uruguay Round, op. cit., p. 69 ff.
19. Article 1 of the ILP Agreement, ibid., p. 255
20. The ILP Agreement divides licences into two categories: automatic and non-automatic. Import licensing maintained to collect statistical and other factual information on imports is automatic, meaning that the approval of the application is granted always. Automatic import licensing may be necessary whenever other appropriate procedures are not available. It is to be removed as soon as the circumstances which have given rise to its introduction no longer prevail. Non-automatic import licensing is defined, *a contrario*, as licensing not falling within the definition of automatic import licensing. Non-automatic licensing is used to administer trade restrictions such as quan-titative restrictions which are justified within the WTO legal framework. Refer to Articles 2.1, 2.2b and 3.1 of the ILP Agreement ibid., p. 257 ff.
21. International Trade Centre, UNCTAD/WTO, 1995. Business Guide to the Uruguay Round, op. cit., p. 135. See also OECD Working Party Trade Com-mittee, 2002, Analysis of Non-Tariff Measures: the case of Non-Automatic Import Licensing, Unclassified, pp. 1–36.
22. Antidumping investigations must be completed immediately when either the margin of dumping is less than 2 per cent of the export price of the products or the volume from one country is less than 3 per cent of total imports of that product. Nevertheless, investigations may proceed if several countries, each supplying less than 3 per cent of the imports, together account for 7 per cent or more of total imports. Refer to Article 5.8 of the ADA in World Trade Organisation, 1994, Results of the Uruguay Round, op. cit., p. 117.
23. The issue of the meaning of 'benefit' is not fully resolved. For a cash grant, the existence of a benefit and its valuation is clear. On the contrary, extent to which a loan by the government confers a benefit is contestable. Although the SCM Agreement does not provide guidance in this respect, the WTO

Appellate Body has ruled that the existence of a benefit is to be determined by comparison with the market, that is on the basis of what the recipient could have received on the market.

24. If no agreement is reached, the exporting country can retaliate by taking equivalent action, for instance raising customs duties on exports from the country that is enforcing the safeguard measure. If the measure conforms with the provisions of the WTO Agreement on Safeguards, and if it is taken as a result of an increase in the quantity of imports, the exporting country has to wait for three years to retaliate. Article 8 of the WTO Agreement on 'Safeguard's, ibid., p. 319.

25. Where there is no transaction value, or where customs authorities do not accept the transaction value because they consider the price have been distorted, five other methods can be use to determine the customs valuation. The ACV limits the discretion of customs authorities in using such alternative methods by requiring that they should be used in the sequential order in which they appear in its text. This implies that whenever customs officers find that the first method based on the transaction value cannot be used, they cannot choose one of the other five available methods without respecting the following sequential order: the transaction value of identical goods, the transaction value of similar goods, the deductive value, the computed value and the fall-back method. Articles 2, 3, 5, 6 and 7 of the ACV, ibid., p. 200 ff.

26. Among the elements that can be added to the invoice price by the importer for imported goods are: i) commissions and brokerage, except buying commissions; ii) costs of, and charges for, packing and containers; iii) assists, that is goods (materials, components, tools, dies, etc.) or services, such as, designs and plans supplied free or at reduced cost to the buyer for use in the production of imported goods; iv) royalties and licence fees; v) the cost of transport, insurance and related charges to the place of importation, if the country bases its valuation on CIF prices. On the other hand, freight after importation into the customs territory of the importing country, cost of construction, erection, assembly, maintenance or technical assistance occurring after importation, and duties and taxes of the importing country, to the extent they can be distinguished from the price actually paid or payable, should not be added to the customs value. The rule that transaction values declared by importers should be used for valuation of goods applies as well to transactions between related parties. In these kind of transactions, generally taking place among transnational corporations and their subsidiaries or affiliates, prices are charged on the basis of transfer pricing which may not always reflect the correct or true value of the imported goods and the ACV requires customs authorities to enter into consultations with the importer, in order to ascertain the type of relationship, the circumstances surrounding the transaction and whether the relationship has not influenced the price. Article 8 of the ACV, ibid., p. 203.

27. In general terms, importers should be given the right to be consulted throughout all stages of the determination of value. When customs authorities express doubts as to the truth or accuracy of a declared value, importers should have a right to provide an explanation, including documents or other evidence to prove that the value declared by them reflects the correct value of the imported goods. If customs authorities are not satisfied with the explanation

given, importers should have a right to ask customs to communicate to them in writing their reasons for doubting the truth or accuracy of the declared value. This provision intends to safeguard the interests of importers, by giving them the right to appeal against the decision to higher authorities and, if necessary, to a tribunal or other independent administration. Moreover, whenever a delay in the determination of customs value is likely to take place, importers should be given the right to withdraw imported goods from customs offices by providing a deposit, or other form of surety, covering the payment of customs duties for which goods may be liable. Finally, importers have the right to expect that any information of a confidential nature that is made available to customs officers shall be treated as confidential in a decision where customs administrations have reasons to doubt the truth or accuracy of the declared value, ibid., p. 454.

28. As of August 2009, the HS convention has 137 signatories and at least 73 other countries use it on a *de facto* basis.

29. Each national classification systems may be developed using a different number of digits. For instance, Cuba, Chile, Mexico and Australia, among others, apply an eight-digit classification system. The US, Japan, Canada, the EC and Russia apply, among others, a ten-digit classification system. Thailand applies seven digits; Philippines nine, while Angola applies the six HS digits. For further information refer to Weerth, C., 2008, 'Structure of Customs Tariffs Worldwide and in the European Community', *Global Trade and Customs Journal* 3 (6), p. 222.

30. In some instances, introductory notes to the chapters are specific and others require to be interpreted. Goods may be classified in chapters other than similar goods due, for instance, to their purpose, or due to their transformation or treatment.

31. For further information refer to Weerth C., 2008, 'Basic Principles of Customs Classification under the Harmonized System', *Global Trade and Customs Journal*, 3 (2), pp. 61–7.

32. According to the first General Rule of Interpretation the four digit level is the relevant level in which goods are to be at first classified. It has been noted that '...tariff classification might be regarded as an operation putting millions of different kinds of goods into a limited number of pigeon holes', cf. Asakura H., 1993, *Journal of World Trade*, 27 (4), p. 13.

33. The HS System has been last revised in 2007. See, Wind I., 2007, HS 2007: 'What's it All About?', *Global Trade and Customs Journal*, 2 (2), pp. 79–86.

34. Article 3 b of the ARO.

35. Refer to Annheuser Busch Brewing Association v. United States, 207 U. S. 556 (1907).

36. Article 36.2 of the Modernised Community Customs Code provides that 'Goods the production of which involved more than one country or shall be deemed to originate in the country or territory where they underwent their last substantial transformation', cf. Regulation of the European Parliament and of the Council of 23 April 2008 laying down the Community Customs Code (Modernized Customs Code), in *Official Journal* L 145/2008.

37. UNCTAD has made numerous efforts aimed at reforming GSPs rules of origin, not to make the tariff preferences granted by GSPs vain. In fact, provided that GSPs grant preferential market access to developing countries products, the

provision for stringent rules of origin empties the value of such concession. Consider the preferential duty granted by the EC GSP to clothing originating in developing countries. The relevant EC GSP rule of origin requires the transformation to be started from yarn. This means that a developing country can use non-originating yarn, that is yarn produced by another developing country, to the extent that, starting from the imported yarn, all the transformation necessary to obtain the finished garment are carried out in its territory. This requirement can be too stringent and developing countries, whose economy relies upon exports of garments, but lacks the industrial capacity of carrying out all the stages of production required to comply with the origin rules. Refer to UNCTAD, 2007, Erosion of Trade Preferences in the Post – Hong Kong Framework: from 'Trade is Better than Aid' to 'Aid for Trade', p. 35. A proposal made within the WTO Committee on Trade and Development Developing illustrates how least-developed countries have finally become aware about the necessity of having simpler and more transparent rules of origin. WTO Doc. TN/CTD/W/30, 2006, Least Developed Countries' Proposal on Rules of Origin, p. 1.

38. The ARO applies to all rules of origin used in non-preferential commercial policy instruments, such as MFN, anti-dumping and countervailing duties under Article VI of GATT 1994, safeguard measures under Article XIX of GATT 1994, origin marking requirements under Article IX of GATT 1994 and any discriminatory quantitative restriction or tariff quotas. Rules of origin used for governmental procurement and trade statistics are also covered by the ARO. Refer to Article 1.2 of the ARO.

39. The EC GSP is provided by Official Journal of the European Union, 211/2009, Regulation 732/2008 of 22 July 2008 applying a scheme of generalized tariff preferences, while the EC GSP rules of origin are provided by Articles 66 to 97 and annexes 14 to 18 and 21 of the consolidated version of the Commission Regulation 2454/93 laying down the implementing provisions of the Community Customs Code.

40. For an exhaustive analysis of the three criteria in a comparative perspective, see Beretta L. and Dordi C., 2000, 'Rules of Origin in International Trade Agreements: a Comparative Analysis between NAFTA, MERCOSUR an the European Union', in Valladao, A. Giordano, P. and Durand, M. F., (eds), *EU-MERCOSUR Free Trade Area*, Editions des Presses, Science Po, pp. 1–27.

41. According to the WTO, some 380 RTAs have been notified to the GATT – WTO up to July 2007. Accounting for RTAs that are in force but have not been notified, those signed but not yet in force, those currently being negotiated, and those in the proposal stage, we arrive at a figure of close to 400 RTAs which are scheduled to be implemented by 2010.

42. See Vermulst E. and Waer P., 2005, 'Anti-Diversion Rules in Anti-Dumping Proceedings: Interface or Short-Circuit for the Management of Interdependence?', in *Customs and Trade Laws as Tools of Protection: Selected Essays*, Cameron May, pp. 429–516.

43. Article 9 of the ARO. For an exhaustive technical description of the harmonization programme, cf. Himagawa H., 2005, *The Agreement on Rules of Origin, in The World Trade Organization: Legal, Economic and Political Analysis*, Oxford University Press, pp. 601–78.

44. This Committee was created by Article 4.2 of the ARO.

45. For the last updated status of the negotiations, refer to WTO Doc. G/RO/W/111, 2007, Committee on Rules of Origin, Draft, Consolidated Text of Non-Preferential Rules of Origin, Harmonization Work Programme, Note by the Secretariat, pp. 1–542.

46. Some countries support the position that the origin of agricultural products should always be carried forward from the original product having been wholly obtained in the country and cannot be changed by subsequent processing. Under this scenario there exists no substantial transformation for agricultural goods. For those countries having made a considerable investment in promoting the image of a particular commodity linked with the country of origin as a brand name, retaining the origin of the source material is the only suitable option. On the other hand, countries importing source materials and processing them support the position that the processing of agricultural raw materials is a substantial transformation, and origin should conferred on the processed goods in the country where these processes are carried out. Ibid., p. 654.

47. 'An important agreement has been reached in that the production of: (i) yarn from fibre, (ii) fabric from yarn, and (iii) apparel, parts or accessories of garments knitted or crocheted to shape are, by themselves, origin-conferring. The principle, common to many preferential origin rules currently in force in the majority of countries, of a "two stage-double jump", that is, fabrics from fibres or garments from yarns has not been adopted in the harmonization work. Nevertheless, there is still a sharp division between the negotiating delegations around the role of printing and dyeing'. idem.

48. 'Regardless of the size or value of the goods, that is from semiconductors or portable radios to gas turbines, oil tankers or spacecrafts, the predominant production process for goods of Chapters 84 to 90 is an assembly operation.... for this generic issue, two generic views were first presented. One position was to recognize a change from parts (suitable for use solely or principally with a particular kind of machine) to articles expressed by a change-of-classification rule to be origin conferring. The proponents of this view were confident that the inherent HS structure was suitable for the purpose of origin determination; thus, a tariff-shift rule alone should be used. As the HS forms the basic foundation, the term 'parts' is subject to the definition under the HS. Another position put forward was not to recognize a change from parts (suitable for use solely or principally with a particular kind of machine) to articles as origin conferring. This view begins with the premise that the HS is not created for purposes of origin determination; consequently, even the so-called screwdriver assembly meets a change-of-tariff-classification criterion. Paradoxically, when the quality of a good is improve significantly, the classification remains unchanged. The proponents argued that such assembly operations could be considered as substantial transformation when a specified *ad valorem* percentage of added value prescribed for a particular good was achieved'. Ibid., p. 656.

49. The relationship between the harmonized rules of origin and other WTO agreements, especially the WTO Antidumping agreement, has been debated since the beginning of the harmonization process, and with very different positions. The lack of consensus among those countries actively participating in the negotiations and the manner in which such a relationship should be

considered, has led to the 'implementation issue'. Himagawa describes the positions of the major trading partners as follows 'The United States argued, from the very early stages of the negotiations, that the use or application of rules of origin for a particular administrative purpose may be a separate matter from the development and implementation of a particular trade measures or commercial policy instruments (such as application of antidumping measures) that fall under the jurisdiction of other Agreements. Consequently, the issue is most certainly not a sector or product-specific matter, but broadly extends to all sectors of industry, from agriculture to a wide range of consumer products. Considering the fact that many of the then 38 (currently 41) Members that had notified that they do not have non-preferential rules of origin were known to utilize anti-dumping measures, rules of origin were not being used for such measures. Consequently the United States raised a question as to whether the existence of HRO would require changes in those practices by those Members. ... The European Union made it clear that the HRO should be applied equally for all purposes as set out in Article 1 of the Agreement (Article 3(a) of the ARO) and suggested an explicit common understanding: "if other WTO Agreements require that origin be determined for specific purposes of those Agreements, HRO would then have to be used".... as far as the applicability of the ARO to other WTO Agreements was concerned, Canada opined that it was the other WTO Agreements that had to determine whether or not rules of origin would be applied to them and that, if Members had to use rules of origin, they then had to apply the HRO. On the contrary, Argentina understood that since the provisions of the ARO were more specific than those of other WTO Agreements, the ARO had precedence over other WTO Agreements.' Ibid, pp. 658–659.

50. Cf. WTO Doc. G/RO/65, 2007, Thirteenth Annual Review of the Implementation and Operation of the Agreement on Rules of Origin, pp. 1–7.

51. The effect of a product's country of origin on purchasers is one of the most widely studied consumer behaviours. It has generated numerous marketing studies detailing the strong impact origin labelling has on consumers throughout the world. Refer to Guerini C., 2004, 'Made in Italy e mercati internazionali', Egea; Corbellini E. and Saviolo S., 2004, 'La scommessa del Made in Italy e il futuro della moda italiana', Etas; Liefeld J., 2004, 'Consumer Knowledge and Use of Country of Origin Information at the Point of Purchase', *Journal of Consumer Behaviour*, 4 (2); Peterson R. and Jolibert J., 1995, A Meta Analysis of Country of Origin Effects, *Journal of International Business Studies*, 26 (4), p. 883; Maheswaran, D., 1994, 'Country of Origin as a Stereotype: effects of consumer expertise and attribute strength on product evaluations', *Journal of Consumer Research: an Interdisciplinary Quarterly*, 21 (2), p. 354; Wall M., Liefeld J. and Heslop, L. A.,1991, 'Impact of Country of Origin Cues on Consumer Judgements in Multi-cue Situations: A Covariance Analysis', *Journal of the Academy of Marketing Science*,19 (2), p. 105–13; Han, C., 1989, 'Country Image – Halo or Summary Construct', *Journal of Marketing Research*, 26 (2), pp. 222–229; Han, C. and Terpstra V., 1988, 'Country of Origin Effects on Uni-National and Bi-National Products', *Journal of International Business Studies*, 19, pp. 235–55. These and other studies suggest that while origin marking on imported product may not be the sole or

even primary determinative factor, they do have an influence on consumer purchasing.

52. For an analysis of the origin marking issue, refer to Beretta L., 'The Legal Protection of 'Made in': a Comparative Analysis', *Global Trade and Customs Journal*, pp. 1–19, forthcoming; Beretta L., 2008, 'Oltre le Violazioni della Proprietà Intellettuale: la Violazione del Marchio di Origine 'Made in Italy'. Le risposte Italiane ed Europee, pp. 36–57, in Jullion M. and Manderieux L. (eds), *Mediare e Rimediare: la contraffazione nella Prospettiva Franco-Italiana ed Internazionale*, Aracne Editrice, Roma, pp. 1–241.

53. Article IX.2 of GATT

54. In the same trade facilitating perspective, Article IX.5 requires that '...no special duty or penalty should be imposed [...] for failure to comply with marking requirements prior to importation unless corrective marking it's unreasonably delayed or deceptive marks have been affixed or the required marking has been intentionally omitted.'

55. Refer to Escudero S., 2001, International Protection of Geographical Indications and Developing Countries, in Trade-Related Agenda, Development and Equity (TRADE), Working Papers no. 10, South Centre, 1–57; O'Connor B., 2004, *The Law of Geographical Indications*, Cameron May, pp. 1–500.

56. For further information refer to Article 2 of the Lisbon Agreement for the Protection of Appellations of Origin and their International Registration of 1958. The Agreement was revised in 1967 and 1979. It currently has 25 contracting parties, status April 15, 2006, see http://www.wipo.int/treaties/en/documents/pdf/lisbon.pdf

57. Hereinafter referred to as the Paris Convention. This Convention has been revised in 1925, 1934, 1958 and amended in 1979. Originally signed by 11 countries it now has 169 signatory countries, status as at April 15, 2006.

58. Article 1.2 of the Paris Convention

59. Escudero, International Protection, op. cit., p. 3

60. Articles 9–10 of the Paris Convention

61. In fact, Article 9.4 of the Paris Convention provides that 'the authorities shall not be bound to the seizure of goods in transit'; according to Article 9.5 'If the legislation of a country does not permit seizure on importation, seizure shall be replaced by prohibition of importation or by seizure inside the country'; finally, Article 9.6 states that: 'If the legislation of a country permits neither seizure on importation nor prohibition of importation nor seizure inside the country, then, until such time as the legislation is modified accordingly, these measures shall be replaced by the actions and remedies available in such cases to nationals under the law of such country.'

62. Hereinafter referred to as the Madrid Agreement. The Agreement was revised in 1911, 1925, 1934, 1958 and supplemented by the Additional Act of Stockholm in 1967. It currently has 34 countries, status as at April 15, 2006.

63. For further information refer to the World Intellectual Property Organization document WIPO/GEO/SFO/03/1, 2003, Worldwide Symposium on Geographical Indications organized by the WIPO and the United States Patent and Trademark Office (USPTO), San Francisco, California, July, 2003, Introduction to Geographical Indications and Recent Developments in the World Intellectual Property Organization, p. 2.

64. A clear EU definition of geographical indications and designations of origin had been given less recently by the European Court of Justice as follows: 'Whatever the factors which may distinguish them, the registered designations of origin and indirect indications of origin [...] always describe at the least a product coming from a specific geographical area. To the extent to which these appellations are protected by law they must satisfy the objectives of such protection, in particular the need to ensure not only that the interests of the producers concerned are safeguarded against unfair competition, but also that consumers are protected against information which may mislead them. These appellations only fulfil their specific purpose if the product which they describe does in fact possess qualities and characteristics which are due to the fact that it originated in a specific geographical area. As regards indications of origin in particular, the geographical area of origin of a product must confer on it a specific quality and specific characteristics of such a nature as to distinguish it from all other products.' *EC Commission v. Germany, 1975, ECR* point 7.

65. Escudero, International Protection, op. cit. p. 5.

66. The lack of a harmonized legislation on origin marking at EU level is due to the fact that the importance of regulating the 'made in' indication is felt differently throughout the EU member states. According to the contacts with some customs authorities, it seems that controls on origin marking labels are quite frequent in Italy. For a comment on the Italian customs practice in checking the 'made in' indication see Beretta L., 2008. On the contrary, according to the opinions given by the Dutch Chambers of Commerce and Customs Authorities, checking origin marking is nearly a non-issue. The proposal of a harmonized origin marking system at EU level aims at making origin indication compulsory for some categories of imported products. These are: textile goods, footwear, ceramic products and furniture. Refer to the Commission of the European Community, 2005, 'Proposal for a Council Regulation on the Indication on the Country of Origin on Certain Products Imported from Third Countries', COM (2005) 661 Final, pp. 1–52. Nevertheless, due to fierce opposition and lobbying by the European productive sectors that have outsourced their production, it is quite unlikely to enter into force.

67. For instance, when articles or containers are found upon examination not to be legally marked, the US legislation provides the importer the possibility to arrange with the port director's office to properly mark the articles or containers, or to return all released articles to Customs custody for marking, exporting, or destruction. 19 C.F.R. Subpart F 134.51. Similar rules are applied by the Japanese customs administration providing for the possibility to correct the improper origin marking in order to obtain import permission.

68. According to the US legislation, if a false certificate of marking is filed indicating that goods have been properly marked when in fact they have not been so marked, a seizure or a claim for monetary penalty, that can amount to a 10 percent of additional *ad valorem* duty, may be made. Israeli's Consumer Protection Law of 1981 provides for compulsory origin marking for some goods. Lacking origin marking results in a fine of three times the amount stated in Article 61 of the Penal Code.

69. In a trade and customs perspective the term 'country' can also be referred to separate customs territories possessing full autonomy in the conduct of their external commercial relations and various matters covered by the WTO Agreements, such as, currently Hong Kong, Macau and Chinese Taipei. The three of these countries are independently members of the WTO. As regards the issues being part to the common commercial policy, the European Communities are also to be considered as one importing country. Those issues are listed in Article 133 of the EC Treaty, cf. Eeckhout P., 2007, *External Relations of the European Union*, Oxford University Press, pp. 86 ff.
70. Lux. M., 2002, *Guide to Community Customs Legislation*, p. 528.
71. Idem.

12
Technical Regulations in Agricultural Trade Agreements between the European Union and Central American Countries

Dora Castañeda

Agricultural export market growth is a key factor for rural income generation and rural development in all developing countries. In this respect, international trade in agricultural products, specifically, the exports of agricultural products and commodities to developed countries, with the United States (US) and the European Union (EU) foremost, and the increasing spread of different technical regulations, termed Sanitary and Phytosanitary (SPS) measures, adopted in this sector by developed countries in the last decade have acquired a significant importance for developing countries trade.[1]

Indeed, since the tariff elimination or reduction resulting from the Uruguay Round of the General Agreement on Tariffs and Trade (GATT) and the proliferation of Free Trade Agreements (FTA), SPS measures requirements have been largely implemented or strengthened by countries, sometimes with protectionist ends, that is, as a *de facto* protectionist measures to protect the domestic industry.[2]

The competitive advantage that developing countries have in the production of agricultural products might be seriously decreased by their lack of understanding and their inefficient manner of handling SPS matters. Such deficiencies result from a lack of human, technical and budgetary resources. Indeed, this inefficiency in managing SPS matters might prevent developing countries from taking advantage of globalization, that is, export market growth, access to foreign capital and technology, opportunities for specialization, and increased profits for the private sector in the various agriculture-based supply chains. It is widely recognized that 'standards' management and technical capacity is of vital importance for agricultural and food exports from developing countries.[3]

In the view of the ongoing negotiations of an Association Agreement, including a FTA, between the European Union (EU) and five Central American countries, Guatemala, El Salvador, Nicaragua, Honduras and Costa Rica,[4] it is suggested that FTAs represent an important mechanism of trade development for these developing countries since the basic principles of the World Trade Organization (WTO) Agreement on the Application of Sanitary and Phytosanitary Measures at the bilateral and/or plurilateral level could be strengthened therein.

Indeed, the effective regulation of SPS measures in the resulting FTA between the EU and the Central American countries will help these developing countries to overcome, or at least to improve, the compliance obstacles that such countries encounter, and facilitate their real market access possibilities to the EU.

The main features of the sanitary and phytosanitary agreement

Since the signing of the Protocol known as the General Agreement on Tariffs and Trade (GATT) in 1947, governments, although purporting to establish a system to gradually reduce the barriers to international trade, have always advocated themselves the sovereign right to unconditionally restrict international trade when necessary 'to protect human, animal or plant life or health', provided that the 'measures are not applied in a manner which would constitute a means of arbitrary or unjustifiable discrimination between countries where the same conditions prevail, or a disguised restriction on international trade'.[5]

The substitution of non-tariff measures for tariffs (tariffication) in the agricultural sector and the tariff elimination or reduction resulting from the GATT-Uruguay Round, alerted governments that alternative forms of protection and the use of alternative non-tariffs barriers to imports, including arbitrary SPS measures, could have been utilized instead, in order to grant protection to their own internal agricultural products. Therefore, during the 1986–1994 GATT Uruguay Round of governmental multilateral trade negotiations that brought forth to the establishment of the WTO, governments negotiated and adopted a separate Agreement on the Application of SPS measures, the so called SPS Agreement.

To achieve its objectives, the SPS Agreement (1995) – built on the previous GATT 1947 provisions applying to sanitary and phytosanitary measures – contains a set of substantive and procedural principles that regulate the implementation and maintenance of SPS measures by WTO Members. The substantive principles are aimed at protecting human, animal, and plant health and life while preventing unjustifiable barriers to trade.[6] The procedural principles create a framework to improve communication between members regarding proposed changes to SPS national regulation, and provide a forum for dispute settlement.

The basic rights and obligations of WTO Members are covered by Article 2 of the SPS Agreement. Accordingly, members have the right to set out their own SPS measures in pursuit of their objectives relating to ensure food safety, to protect human health from plant- or animal-spread diseases, to protect animal and plant life or health from pests and diseases, or to prevent other damage from pests. However, such SPS measures must be based on science, that is, based on principles generally accepted by the international scientific community and, as far as possible, on the analysis and assessment of objective and accurate scientific data).[7]

In addition, members must ensure that the SPS measures are applied only to the extent necessary to protect human, animal or plant life or health and that the measures adopted do not arbitrarily or unjustifiably discriminate between members where identical or similar conditions prevail, including between their own territory and that of other members. Basically, SPS measures should not be applied in a manner which would constitute a disguised restriction on international trade.

In order to comply with the SPS Agreement obligations, members are required to respect the substantive principles set forth in such agreement and particularly to comply with the following principles:

Harmonization: Member countries are encouraged to harmonize their adopted SPS measures to the international standards, guidelines and recommendations where they exist.[8] However, this conformity requirement is not absolute. Members may establish SPS measures which implement some (not necessarily all) of the elements of an international standard.[9] On the other hand, members may introduce or maintain SPS measures that result in a higher level of protection than is achieved by measures based on relevant international standards.[10] In such circumstances, members must provide a scientific justification,[11] or ensure that the measures are based on an assessment of the risk to human, animal or plant life or health (as the case might be), taking into account risk assessment techniques developed by relevant international organizations so long as the approach is consistent with the other provisions of the SPS Agreement and is not arbitrary.[12]

Equivalence: The SPS Agreement requires members to recognize the equivalence of specified sanitary or phytosanitary measures. Members are expected to accept the SPS measures of other members as equivalent to theirs, if exporting members demonstrate that their measures achieve the importing members' appropriate level of sanitary or phytosanitary protection.[13] To that effect, members are encouraged to achieve bilateral and multilateral agreements on recognition of the equivalence of specified SPS measures.[14]

Appropriate level of protection: According to the SPS Agreement[15] the appropriate level of protection (ALOP) is the level of protection deemed appropriate by members to protect human, animal or plant life or health within their territory. It is important to clearly distinguish between the ALOP established by a member and a SPS measure. While the ALOP is a broad objective, the SPS measures are established to attain that objective. The determination of the ALOP logically precedes the establishment of an SPS measure. Each member has the right to determine its own ALOP. However, in determining their ALOP, members should take into account the objective of minimizing negative trade effects.[16] In addition, members are required to apply the concept of ALOP consistently, that is, they must 'avoid arbitrary or unjustifiable distinctions' that 'result in discrimination or a disguised restriction on international trade'.[17]

Risk assessment: The SPS Agreement requires members to adopt their SPS measures on the basis of an appropriate assessment of the actual risks to which human, animal or plant life or health are and/or may be exposed. In conducting such risk assessment, members are required to take into consideration risk assessment techniques developed by relevant international organizations. Additionally, available scientific evidence, and the existence of pest- or disease-free areas, *inter alia*, must be taken into consideration.[18]

Not more trade restrictive than required: When establishing or maintaining SPS measures, members must ensure that such measures are not more trade-restrictive than required to achieve their ALOP.[19] A measure is considered to be so if there is not another measure, which is reasonably available taking into account technical and economic feasibility, which achieves the ALOP and is significantly less restrictive to trade.[20]

Regionalization: Members are required to ensure that their SPS measures are adapted to the characteristics of the geographic region – whether all of a country, part of a country, or all or parts of several countries. The SPS Agreement, in general terms, ascribes the sanitary and phytosanitary characteristics of a geographic region to the expression regional conditions, from which the product originates and to which the product is destined.[21] Furthermore, the SPS Agreement requires members to recognize that an exporting region, that is, part of a country or a border-straddling zone, is disease-free or pest-free or an area of low pest or disease prevalence. To that effect, reasonable access must be given to importing members to inspect and to establish the pest or disease status of a particular area.[22]

Transparency: Members must promptly publish all their adopted SPS regulations as to enable other members to become informed about such regulations.[23] Governments must also designate one enquiry point responsible for replying to information requests related to the notified regulations, and a national authority responsible for the notifications procedures.[24] Members are obliged to notify the WTO Secretariat of new measures or amended measures where content is not the same as the content of an international standard, and that may have a significant impact on other members' trade. Such notifications must be made in a timely manner, when amendments can still be introduced and comments of other WTO members can be taken into account.[25]

As for the standing of developing countries' needs within the SPS Agreement, some provisions have been set thereof to help such developing countries to overcome, in particular, their difficulties and challenges in implementing and complying with the SPS Agreement. Accordingly, when preparing and enforcing SPS measures members are required to take into account the needs of developing country Members.[26]

Conversely, the SPS Agreement sets members' commitment to facilitate technical assistance to developing country members, either bilaterally or through the appropriate international organizations.[27] Members are required to facilitate the active participation of developing countries in the relevant international organizations such as the Alimentarius Commission (CODEX), the International Office of Epizootics (OIE) and the International Plant Protection Convention (IPPC).[28] In order to allow such countries to adjust to, and comply with, SPS measures in exporting markets, technical assistance, such as, advice, credits, donations, grants, training and equipment, may be provided, *inter alia*, in the areas of processing technologies, research and infrastructure, including the establishment of national regulatory bodies.[29]

In addition, where substantial investments are required in order for an exporting developing country member to comply with the SPS requirements of an importing member, the importing member should consider the provision of technical assistance to such trading partner country as to allow it to maintain and expand its market access opportunities.[30]

Finally, if the appropriate level of sanitary or phytosanitary protection so allows, longer time-frames for compliance should be accorded on products of interest to developing country Members so as to maintain opportunities for their exports.[31] Similarly, time-limited exceptions to comply with the SPS Agreement might be also granted.[32]

The main implications of the sanitary and phytosanitary agreement for Central American countries

All Central American countries except El Salvador are net agricultural exporters.[33] The EU's market is of great importance for the Central American countries, as the EU is Central America's third largest trading partner.[34] In 2005, exports to the EU accounted for 13.2 per cent of the total exports of Central America and 9.4 per cent of the imports.[35] Exports from Central America consist mainly of agricultural goods, namely, coffee, bananas and pineapples, which together account for 65 per cent of exports to the EU, followed by sugar.[36] Imports from the EU are predominantly industrialized goods, such as transport equipment, machinery, chemical products, ships, boats, and fuels.[37]

It should be noted that few assessments on the socio-economic impact of the implementation of the SPS Agreement have been carried out for the Central American region. However, there is vast evidence that, as a group of small countries, Central America's SPS compliance obstacles are common to developing countries.[38]

As it is widely recognized, the burden of complying with the SPS Agreement and SPS measures is higher for developing countries than for developed countries.[39] In particular, the scarcity or lack of resources, which include lack of information on SPS matters, scientific and technical expertise, appropriate technologies, skilled labour, economic recourses, is the main ground that frustrates developing countries' compliance with the SPS measures applied by exporting countries. The same reasons place developing countries into a disadvantage position as for benefiting from the discipline of the SPS Agreement when, for example, implementing SPS measures.[40]

In particular, for most of the developing countries such compliance with SPS measures is not only onerous and burdensome, in terms of technical implementation of the SPS measures, but it is also highly costly. The World Bank has estimated that to be fully acquainted and have a complete understanding of some WTO Agreements – among which is the SPS agreement[41] – would cost a developing country more than a full year's development budget of many least developed countries.[42]

In a broad sense, the cost of compliance is the sum of all expenses that the public as well as the private sector (for example, farmers and enterprises involved in the supply chain) incur in complying with SPS related matters. It includes not only the cost of adjusting various components of the supply chain in order to conform to the SPS Agreement and SPS measures imposed by importing governments and private enterprises, but also the administrative cost of control, inspection, testing and certification. The cost of delays in exportation, for instance, interest charges, and the loss of export earnings due to the procedures necessary for compliance should also be taken into consideration when determining the exporter's costs of compliance.[43]

Although, governments should ensure that SPS measures are based on sufficient scientific evidence, it has been argued[44] that some of the SPS measures adopted by many of the WTO members developed countries have not been implemented on the basis of scientific evidence in order to protect human, animal, and plant life or health, but enacted with a protectionist aim. Such unjustifiable SPS measures may constitute a 'disguised restriction on international trade' and alter the real capacity of an exporting developing country to penetrate the global and, specifically, the developed countries' internal market.[45]

However, to bring a complaint against unjustified SPS measures, an exporting country must have recourse to the WTO Dispute Settlement System. Such mechanism puts developing countries in a disadvantageous position. In fact, effective application to the WTO dispute settlement system is quite expensive and requires extensive investments of financial, legal and technical resources not always available to developing countries. As it has been notably pointed out 'for the developing countries, effective use of the WTO agreement depends on extensive investments – it is not a matter of applying existing systems of standards to international trade, it is a much broader matter of installing world-class systems'.[46] In fact, as the burden of proof is on the exporting (complainant) country, most of the developing countries have been hesitant to use the WTO dispute settlement system because of the lack of the scientific and financial resources necessary to challenge the inconsistency of these trade-restricting measures with the SPS Agreement, even when they might have a strong case.[47]

Conversely, another onerous obstacle that developing countries normally face in their exporting activity *vis-à-vis* developed countries is that the latter often establishes stricter standards than those developed by international organizations.[48] In Central American trade with the US, it took Costa Rica five years and cost at least US$1 million to be declared as a Newcastle-free country.[49]

Such stricter SPS measures result in having a significant negative effect on developing countries exports as the majority of the agricultural exports from these countries are directed to developed country markets.[50] Indeed, compliance with such standards has reported export losses for developing countries. For instance, African countries are estimated to have lost US$ 670 million in agricultural exports of cereals, fruits, vegetables and nuts due to the higher EU standard for aflatoxin compared to the standard set by CODEX.[51] The impact on the Latin American exports of nuts destined for Europe could surpass the US$ 100 million.[52]

Before the WTO SPS Committee, members have drawn attention to the problem that importing members establish national maximum residue limits (MRLs) for pesticides without scientific justification and which are stricter than those developed by the CODEX.[53] In this regard, it must be noted that while CODEX has set up over 2,500 MRLs, the EU has over 22,000, the US has over 8,600, and Japan has over 9,000 MRLs.[54] Furthermore, fruits and vegetables imported into the EU must comply with the relevant MRLs, yet MRLs have not been harmonized at the EU level and each EU member state has set its own MRLs for imported fruits and vegetables.[55]

In fact, the export scenario for developing countries is aggravated when exporting particularly to the EU market, where besides the application of international standards, there is a growth in private standards by European retailers and supermarkets, such as, Euro Retailer Produce Good Agricultural Practices (EurepGAP), British Retail Consortium (BRC) and Tesco.[56] Consequently, exporting countries to the EU have at least three levels of requirements to tackle. These are public (communitarian) requirements at the EU level, public (national) requirements at the member states level and, various private certification schemes required by European retailers and supermarkets. It is estimated that approximately

400 quality assurance and certification schemes have been introduced in the last few years by local or regional authorities, retailers or agro-food industries.[57]

The most important private standards are the BRC, which lays down specific requirements for food safety management systems where the product is packed for the final consumer, and the EurepGAP, which mainly relates to certification. It has been estimated that EurepGAP standard controls 85 per cent of the western European fresh produce market and that its certification has become a market access condition for 30 European retailers as of 2005.[58] However, individual supermarket chains have developed their own systems of product-safety-quality requirements and labels, which are more detailed and costly than other private standards (for example, EurepGAP).[59]

In some instances, these private standards exceed the EU standards and/or SPS Agreement requirements. It has been stated that while the EU's food legislation only requires food companies to know their immediate suppliers and consumers in the food chain, the BRC also requires that food companies trace production internally down to the batch level. Furthermore, although the SPS Agreement requires equivalence of risk outcome, the EurepGAP requires demonstration of equivalence of systems. Thus, even if developing countries demonstrate that their systems satisfy the importing members' appropriate level of sanitary or phytosanitary protection, equivalence of systems is required within EurepGAP.[60]

Indeed, private standards weaken the export ability of developing countries even more. As has been noticed, cost of compliance with private standards is higher than with public and/or international standards since the former are more complex and are often reliant on process rather than on performance, and many developing countries' suppliers cannot afford the luxury of private certification.[61]

However, being developing countries highly dependent on their ability to boost exports, and being such exports' increase related to the capacity to penetrate or be 'allowed' to enter developed countries' markets, any lack of compliance with the SPS measures adopted and enacted by developed countries would result in restriction or prohibition to exports. On the other hand, when compared with the cost of compliance, the short- and long-run cost of the lack of compliance is enormous, in terms of the loss of foreign exchange, income, employment, and household consumption, particularly in rural areas. Therefore it should not be surprising that most of the developing countries end up with a forced compliance with any type of SPS measures.

Indeed, the fact that on the one side most developing countries cannot effectively implement the SPS Agreement and on the other they have a minor impact on the establishment of the SPS standards determined by international organizations renders their situation even worse and prevents them from taking advantage of the SPS Agreement's potential benefits. The structural conditions of developing countries, such as, small or non-existent representation, or the lack of or weak scientific expertise, do not allow them to provide significant contributions on the risk assessment basis of measures addressing new health dangers. Likewise, developing countries are unable to demonstrate the equivalence of their domestic measures with those implemented by the developed countries. This technical deficiency is probably one of the main factors influencing the ability of developing countries to participate in the SPS Agreement.[62] In the end, developing countries must adjust themselves to standards which have been, in significant part, generalizations of industrial countries' practices and standards.[63]

Participation in the main international organizations dealing with SPS issues is sporadic in Central America, with Costa Rica more active than others. None of the five countries has the financial capability to participate in those meetings. Some countries delegate attendance at these meetings to their diplomatic representatives in Geneva, who sometimes do not have the technical background necessary to active participation. Similarly, Central American attendance to the CODEX meetings is minimal. Two factors make it economically and technically unfeasible to attend all the meetings: the quantity of meetings organized and the specificity of each meeting.[64]

It is worth noting that notwithstanding the insertion of specific provisions in the SPS Agreement providing for differential treatment in favour of developing countries, such as, facilitation of their participation in international organizations, these provisions do not impose any binding obligation upon developed countries to provide technical assistance in respect of SPS matters to developing countries. Indeed, as it has been recognized, we do assist to a somehow paradoxical situation in which technical assistance to developing countries is provided by developed countries only when compliance issues in respect of SPS measures arise or there is the actual need by such developed countries for new suppliers, instead of being – the developed countries – part of a strategy leading to improve a country's existing capacity.[65]

Sanitary and phytosanitary trade related matters in European Union trade agreements

As previously noted, there are important barriers for developing countries, such as those forming the Central American region, to both implementing the SPS Agreement and to complying with SPS measures imposed mainly in the export markets of developed countries. Since lack of compliance could result in a *de facto* restriction or prohibition of exports, developing countries seeking export expansion try to comply with such regulations usually using their own resources.

From a developing country's point of view, bilateral or plurilateral agreements should be used as mechanisms to assist developing countries to overcome the various problems associated with SPS compliance. Actually, it is highly unlikely that the importing developed countries are persuaded to reduce their increasingly rigorous safety-quality requirements through this mechanism. More realistically, the regulation of SPS matters in bilateral and/or plurilateral agreements could help improve trade relations between developing countries and developed countries and better regulate a number of key SPS trade related issues, that is, transparency, harmonization, equivalence, risk assessment, determination of sufficient levels of sanitary and phytosanitary protection, regionalization, mechanisms for the provision of greater legal and technical cooperation, and longer periods in which to achieve compliance.

However, going through the bilateral agreements entered into by the European Union a sort of common EU practice may be noticed in respect to the negotiations concerning SPS matters, which is characterized by the tendency to stipulate provisions that do not go beyond the standard provisions of the SPS Agreement.

With the exception of the Association Agreement with Israel,[66] the Association Agreements concluded by the EU with the Mediterranean region do not provide any more than that provided at the multilateral level in the SPS Agreement. The Association Agreements concluded with Algeria,[67] Egypt,[68] Jordan,[69] Lebanon,[70] Morocco,[71] the Palestinian Authority[72] and Tunisia[73] contain similar unmindful provisions on SPS. There is only an overall emphasis on cooperation while no specific provisions are stipulated in respect of the possible EU assistance towards such countries to overcome the various problems associated with compliance with the stringent SPS requirements set by the EU itself.

With some minor variations, all these agreements emphasize the necessity of economic cooperation on SPS matters. Some agreements go a step further and explicitly mention the aim of harmonizing SPS standards, such as, Algeria, Israel, Jordan, Lebanon, and the Palestinian Authority. For Tunisia and Morocco, it is explicitly provided for the execution of further agreements for the mutual recognition of certifications but at the same time such execution is deferred to a moment when circumstances will favour it. In some agreements, technical assistance is generally recognized under the provisions on agriculture-related assistance, such as, Algeria, Israel, Jordan, and Lebanon.

The Association Agreement with Israel, however, goes a step further although in the form of product-specific exceptions. Phytosanitary certification is required only for certain types of cut flowers and in respect of certain fruits.[74] In addition, the requirement for a phytosanitary permit for the importation of plants or plant products only apply to make it possible to introduce those plants or plant products which would otherwise be prohibited based on a pest risk analysis. Finally, consultations are provided prior to the introduction of new SPS measures which could adversely affect existing trade between the parties, in order to examine the new measures and their effect.

As for the Trade Development and Cooperation Agreement (TDCA) concluded with South Africa,[75] it does not diverge significantly from the agreements concluded by the EU with the Mediterranean countries. The TDCA emphasizes the development of cooperation in animal health, plant health and agricultural production techniques; the examination of measures to harmonize SPS standards, and capacity building programmes.

With the countries of the Balkan region, the Stabilization and Association Agreements (SAA) with Croatia[76] and Macedonia[77] barely contain a provision on cooperation for the gradual harmonization of SPS standards. An exception to the above-referred EU practice in stipulating SPS issues in bilateral trade agreements is represented by the agreements concluded with Mexico and Chile. The Economic Partnership, Political Coordination and Cooperation Agreement, known as the Global Agreement, between the EU and Mexico[78] reaffirms the rights and obligations set out in the SPS Agreement and also establishes a Special Committee on SPS measures. The creation and functions of this Committee play an important role in strengthening the principle of transparency and bilateral cooperation.

Accordingly, the Special Committee, which gathers representatives of both parties, has the main functions of providing a forum to identify and address problems that may arise from the application of specific SPS measures, with a view to reaching mutually acceptable solutions; considering the development of specific provisions for the application of regionalization, or for the assessment of equivalence; considering the development of specific arrangements for information exchange; monitoring the application of the relevant provisions; and establishing contact points for information exchange.[79]

The Association Agreement between the EU and Chile[80] contains an agreement on Sanitary and Phytosanitary Measures applicable to trade in animals and animal products, plants, plant products and other goods and animal welfare which forms part of the main agreement. This agreement reaffirms the rights and obligations governing the parties' relations under the WTO SPS Agreement and goes beyond such rights and obligations by strengthening the principles of transparency, equivalence, and regionalization. Detailed procedural rules are provided for the application and maintenance of such principles.[81]

As for the principle of equivalence, it is recognized on a gradual and progressive basis and to priority sectors. To that effect, a mechanism for the recognition of equivalence of such measures maintained by a party consistent with the protection of public, animal and plant health is established. Accordingly, any determination or recognition of equivalence must be carried out on the basis of an interactive consultation process, which includes the objective demonstration of equivalence by the exporting party and the objective assessment of this demonstration by the importing party. The suspension or withdrawal of equivalence on the basis of any amendment by one of the parties of measures affecting equivalence must be also approved on the basis of a consultation process. In the context of recognition or withdrawal or suspension of equivalence, it is further recognized that when necessary, the importing party may provide technical assistance to the exporting party.[82] These provisions are further developed with procedural rules for the consultation process, the priority sectors concerned, and conditions for provisional approval of establishments, such as, poultry meat establishments, without prior inspection by the importing party.[83]

Moreover, as for transparency, the Chile-EU SPS Agreement aims at ensuring full transparency as regards SPS measures. Therefore, detailed provisions defining specific and strict deadlines for the submission of information between the parties are provided. For instance, upon entry into force of the Agreement, the importing party had to inform the exporting party of its SPS import requirements for the products covered by Chile-EU SPS Agreement and include the models for the official certificates or attestations, as prescribed by the importing party. For the notification of amendments of such import requirements the parties agreed to apply the provisions of the SPS Agreement. However, it was further agreed that not complying with these notification requirements obliges a party to continue to accept the certificate guaranteeing the previously applicable conditions until 30 days after entering into force of the amended import conditions.[84]

As for information exchange, the agreement further mandates that the parties exchange information which is relevant for the implementation of the Chile-EU SPS Agreement on a systematic basis, in order to develop standards, provide assurance, engender mutual confidence and demonstrate the efficacy of the programmes controlled. This information exchange also provides for exchanges of officials. Additionally, in order to maintain confidence in the effective implementation of the provisions of the Agreement, each party has the right, such as, to verify all or part of the other party's control programmes and participate in laboratory tests.[85]

Finally, as in the Agreement with Mexico, a special committee, known as the Joint Management Committee, was established and whose main functions include the monitoring of the implementation of the Chile-EU SPS Agreement, the consideration of any matter relating to the Agreement as well as the making of recommendations for modifications to the Agreement.[86] Indeed, the Association Agreement between the EU and Chile establishes strong mechanisms and procedures for trade facilitation and improves communication and cooperation between the parties on SPS measures.

The possible application of provisions on sanitary and phytosanitary matters to the European Union–Central American Association Agreement

Most EU bilateral agreements with third party developing countries do not add any more than the respective WTO provisions concerning the SPS Agreement. General provisions on technical assistance are provided in the form of rather vague recommendations or recognitions. Only a few agreements contain rules that go beyond the WTO SPS commitments, such as, the limited product-specific provisions in the agreement with Israel. Moreover, only the agreements concluded with Mexico and Chile contain specific procedural and operational provisions with the real potential of strengthening mutual cooperation.

For the time being, pending the outcome of the negotiations for the conclusion of an Association Agreement with the EU, the trade relations between the two regions are governed by the Generalized System of Preferences (GSP) of the EU. In addition to the benefits of the GSP general arrangement, Central American countries are beneficiaries of special arrangements to combat drug production and trafficking – the special arrangement for sustainable development and good governance, known as GSP+.[87] All Central American countries are currently beneficiaries of such a scheme, and most of the region's exports to the EU are duty-free. However, products of great interest for the region, such as coffee and fresh bananas, are not included in the EU GSP. Conversely, the GSP scheme only refers to import duty elimination or reduction, and therefore, products are still subject to the EU's non-tariff regulations or measures, including SPS measures.

Any absence of or weak provisions on SPS measures in the envisaged FTA would affect market access for agricultural products. As previously mentioned, agriculture in Central America is one of the most important sectors of the economy and, being a labour intensive activity, is also crucial to the level of employment in such region. The agricultural exports of the Central American countries represent between 35 per cent in El Salvador and 70 per cent in Nicaragua of their respective Gross Domestic Product (GDP).[88] And exports to the EU mainly consist on agricultural products.

Given the discrepancy in the quality of SPS services that these countries are able to provide for importation and exportation, competitiveness and bargaining power of the Central American countries are limited.[89] However, it should be pointed out that from the negotiation and conclusion of an Association Agreement with the EU, any concession on market access is not meaningful and may lead to benefits in terms of export market growth, and therefore of potentiality to increase penetration in the EU domestic market of agricultural products, if, and to the extent that, the commitments to be undertaken in respect of SPS matters, particularly, on mutual cooperation between the two parties are not binding and thorough.

In general terms, all Central American countries have the basic laws and regulations for animal and plant health as well as food safety in place. All Central American countries inspect agricultural goods coming in and going out on a sampling basis, and also have quarantine, emergency response and internal surveillance procedures in place. The degree of implementation and effectiveness, however, varies across Central American countries. Costa Rica and Guatemala both have stronger SPS systems in general than the other three countries. They are all members of IPPC, OIE, CODEX and WTO, and their inspection and certification systems are aligned with international standards. They have strong private sector participation in SPS activities since past SPS issues have motivated producer and exporter associations to work together with local government officials and the SPS authorities of importing countries.[90]

Significant parts of the Central American countries' existing SPS limitations are mainly related to lack of budgetary resources, which in turn has led to a deficiency of supporting infrastructure, including specialized facilities, laboratory capacity, qualified personnel, technology problems, and last but not least, pertinent literature.[91] For instance, it has been observed that the main problems in the area of infrastructure and equipment are the absence of isolation facilities with air filters and temperature controls and the lack of access to equipment, especially in the area of virology.[92] Indeed, El Salvador, Guatemala and Honduras have a deficiency in the number of diagnostic laboratories and El Salvador and Honduras lack facilities for insects at their entry points.[93] As to the lack of technology, the main issues presented are especially in the identification of pests and diseases, and also in food safety-related analysis such as pesticide residues.[94] In this respect, one of the major deficiencies is the lack of national laboratories that carry out the certification of products.[95]

It follows from the above that capacity building efforts and mindfully regional cooperation are vital for Central American countries, their relevance overcoming even that of technical assistance. Of course, Central America's economic, legislative and technical framework is not as well equipped as the Chilean one, with the result that it is unlikely that the EU–CA FTA contains the same substantial provisions on more sensitive aspects such as harmonization, regionalization, and equivalence as the Chile–EU FTA. However, the position of the Central American countries requires that such an FTA does not limit itself to the very loose and vague provisions set by the Agreements with the Mediterranean countries. It seems very important that the bi-regional relations on agricultural trade and SPS matters are covered by enhanced cooperation with the aim at strengthening transparency, technical cooperation, harmonization, equivalence, and regionalization.[96] Such cooperation would be a vehicle for capacity building and new investments, and would likely result in economic and trade development on the side of CA.[97]

First of all, strengthening the principle of transparency is fundamental to enable Central American countries to gain more rapid access to the EU market and to facilitate the process of convergence with sanitary rules. Therefore, the Agreement should provide for detailed provisions defining specific and strict deadlines for the submission of information between the parties, including commitments on publication of any SPS measures created or amended; on notification of any epidemiologically significant disease or pest found; on notification of significant changes in relation to disease- and pest-status; and on information on the reasons for any rejection of the products from the exporting party.

Conversely, technical cooperation improves the integration on sanitary matters and helps developing countries to improve SPS compliance obstacles. Therefore, commitments on developing joint programmes of technical cooperation, operational coordination, exchange of technical information and specialized professionals, specific phytosanitary programmes and treatments, definition of quarantine methods to expedite trade, or providing that the parties may request technical consultations, *inter alia*, should be agreed.[98]

Moreover, the establishment of task forces to transfer know-how and experience can help build up institutional, technological and productive capabilities. Indeed, the creation of a permanent or periodical committee responsible for the technical and operational side of sanitary initiatives taken by the parties may contribute to reducing SPS obstacles that arise between parties, by serving as an effective forum for expert meetings. In addition, they represent a real channel for assistance and technical cooperation.

Although harmonization, equivalence, and regionalization are the most sensitive aspects of regional integration processes,[99] some rules and specific deadlines for sanitary procedures should be agreed. For instance, steps and schedules for procedures for recognition of disease-free areas or low prevalence should be established. Similarly, standardization of the methodology chosen for risk assessment and specification of deadlines for the stages of risk assessment are fundamental.

In general, harmonization could be sought on gradual and progressive basis and to priority sectors, for example, harmonization systems for sampling, and/or diagnosis, inspection and certification of animals, and/or vegetables, their products and by-products and/or for food safety on some or all of the conformity verification points. Most importantly, the recognition of equivalency is one of the main mechanisms by which agricultural goods gain market access. For this reason, the Central American countries should explore the advantages of further specifying the technical and operational aspects required, such as by facilitating access of technicians to national certification institutions and encouraging laboratories to engage in exchanges of professionals. The parties could also agree on validating the respective countries' process of accreditation of professionals and institutions in order to extend mutual recognition of the service-provision capacity of responsible institutions. Otherwise, it could be provided that the parties will make their respective SPS measures equivalent by means of future bilateral protocols.

Finally, the significant importance that the standards regulating international trade and commerce have for the private sector in developing countries must be reiterated and it is important and necessary that both the private and the public sector cooperate profitably together in order to achieve and realize functioning system of SPS standards.[100]

Conclusion

Although the WTO Agreement on Sanitary and Phytosanitary Measures provides for a multilateral framework to ensure that plant health and food safety requirements are not more restrictive to trade than necessary to protect human and plant health, a growing body of studies and literature highlights the difficulties of developing countries in participating in the instruments developed by the Agreement. As a result, developing countries on the one hand risk losing the significant benefit they can get from a full implementation of the provisions set out therein, but, on the other tend to be more and more on the sidelines of the international debates over the implementation and the settings of the SPS standards.

The proliferation and increasing stringency of SPS measures adopted by developed countries, particularly by the EU, have led many developing countries to be strongly concerned about their administrative, technical and financial capacities to comply with these requirements and consequently to sustain an export market growth especially in respect of the EU domestic market.

Compliance with the SPS measures and implementation of the SPS Agreement demands that countries acquire the technology; infrastructure investments, and qualification of personnel. Capacity, particularly lack of technology and funding, has become the main obstacle for the development of developing countries' agricultural exports.

However, the WTO Agreement does not oblige members to provide help and assistance to developing countries on the matter; it only considers it in terms of auspices, preserving the faculty for them to do so. Also, developing countries should increase their participation in the Committee on Sanitary and Phytosanitary Measures, as well as in international organizations; once again, however, the problem of lack of resources prevents the implementation of such strategy.

The regulation of sanitary and phytosanitary matters in bilateral trade agreements may reduce the gap between multilateral and national standards. Such provisions tend to reinforce the basic principles of the SPS Agreement at the bilateral level. However, the conclusion of a trade agreement would not increase trade flows between the parties to it if, and to the extent that, the commitments to be undertaken in respect of SPS matters, particularly, on mutual cooperation between the two parties, are not binding and thoroughgoing between the parties.

As has been stated throughout, EU bilateral agreements mainly focus on procedural issues. A common characteristic of all EU FTAs reviewed here is their emphasis on facilitating the application of the SPS Agreement. However, from the revision carried out some differences arise: the extent to which they reaffirm WTO SPS principles; the emphasis on cooperation to developing countries on SPS measures; and the level of specification for providing technical assistance in SPS issues. Rarely do the agreements contain specific provisions that go beyond the general principles that instill the SPS Agreement, sometimes reference is made to product-specific provisions, equivalence provisions, and detailed procedural provisions.

Thus, Central American countries, in order to achieve a better articulation of SPS measures and thus facilitate their access to export markets, in the negotiating process of the FTA with the EU, should draw special attention and consideration to the sections specifically dedicated to sanitary and phytosanitary matters or, if these sections are not provided or inserted, set up complementary rules that clearly and precisely indicate the procedure to be followed to make the SPS Agreement's principles more effective. In general, both the EU and Central American countries should aim for the development of proactive initiatives for implementing and creating common SPS rules which may finally bring a common benefit and facilitation to international trade in agricultural products.

Notes

1. The Economic Commission for Latin America and the Caribbean (ECLAC) has stated that tariffs do not constitute an important barrier to Latin American and Caribbean trade since most of the region's exports to the United States (US) entered already duty-free, but that SPS standards in the US, such as, health standards have become a barrier to exports. For further information refer to the United Nations Economic Commission for Latin America and the Caribbean (ECLAC), 1999, 'Barriers to Latin American and Caribbean Exports in the U.S. Market (1998–1999)', LC/WAS/L.55, Washington.

2. A survey made by the United States Department of Agriculture (USDA) Foreign Agricultural Service found that 62 countries reported having questionable technical barriers on US agricultural exports. Over 300 market restrictions were identified that threatened, constrained, or blocked an estimated $5 billion of US agricultural, forestry, and fishery exports. cf. Roberts, D., Josling, T. and Orden, D., 1999, 'A Framework for Analyzing Technical Trade Barriers in Agricultural Markets', US Department of Agriculture, Economic Research Service, Technical Bulletin No. 1876, Washington, DC.

3. Bernardo, T., Aguilar, C., Flores, L., Lamb, J., Karpati, J. and Velez, J., 2003, 'Benchmarking of SPS Management Capacity in Five Central American Countries (Costa Rica, El Salvador, Guatemala, Honduras, Nicaragua)', RAISE SPS Regional Report Number 1.

4. On December 13, 1960 the five Central American countries established The Central American Common Market (CACM) with the aim at facilitating regional economic development through free trade and economic integration. At the European Union-Latin America and the Caribbean Vienna Summit in May 2006, the EU and the Central American countries decided to commence negotiations of an Association Agreement, including a free trade area. On that occasion, Central American countries reaffirmed their commitment to enhance their economic regional integration, including the establishment of a customs union. The first round of negotiations took place in San José, Costa Rica, in October 2007.

5. Article XX (b) of the GATT 1994 and its 'chapeau'.

6. Article 1 of the SPS Agreement: 'This Agreement applies to all sanitary and phytosanitary measures which may, directly or indirectly, affect international trade.'

7. The obligation to base SPS measures on scientific evidence covers all SPS measures except for what is prescribed in Article 5 (7) of the SPS Agreement. This Article allows members to adopt provisional SPS measures where there is insufficient scientific evidence to complete a risk assessment. However, in such circumstances members are required to seek to obtain the additional information necessary for a more objective risk assessment within a reasonable period of time.

8. Article 3 (1) of the SPS Agreement. The Agreement specifically refers to the work developed by the Codex Alimentarius Commission (CODEX) on food safety, the International Office of Epizootics (OIE) on animal health, and the International Plant Protection Convention (IPPC) on plant heath. Article 3(4) of the SPS Agreement. Measures which are based upon international standards are presumed to be consistent with the obligation to be scientifically justified.

9. In the WTO EC-Hormones case, the Appellate Body held that 'a Member may choose to establish an SPS measure that is based on the existing relevant international standard, guideline or recommendation. Such a measure may adopt some, not necessarily all, of the elements of the international standard. The Member imposing this measure does not benefit from the presumption of consistency ... but ... the Member is not penalized by exemption of a complaining Member from the normal burden of showing a *prima facie* case of inconsistency with Article 3.1 or any other relevant article of the SPS Agreement or of the GATT 1994.' Appellate Body Report, EC Measures Concerning Meat and Meat Products (Hormones), WT/DS26/AB/R, WT/DS48/AB/R, adopted 13 February 1998, paragraph 171.

10. Article 3 (3) of the SPS Agreement.

11. According to the SPS Agreement, 'there is a scientific justification if, on the basis of an examination and evaluation of available scientific information in conformity with the relevant provisions of this Agreement, a Member determines that the relevant international standards, guidelines or recommendations are not sufficient to achieve its appropriate level of

sanitary or phytosanitary protection.' Footnote 2 to Article 3 of the SPS Agreement.

12. Articles 3 (3) and 5 (1) of the SPS Agreement.
13. Article 4 (1) of the SPS Agreement.
14. Article 4 (2) of the SPS Agreement.
15. Article 5 of the SPS Agreement.
16. Article 5 (4) of the SPS Agreement.
17. Article 5 (5) of the SPS Agreement accordingly reads '[w]ith the objective of achieving consistency in the application of the concept of appropriate level of sanitary or phytosanitary protection against risks to human life or health, or to animal and plant life or health, each Member shall avoid arbitrary or unjustifiable distinctions in the levels it considers to be appropriate in different situations, if such distinctions result in discrimination or a disguised restriction on international trade.'
18. Article 5 (2) of the SPS Agreement. Furthermore, in assessing the risk and determining the measure to be applied for achieving the appropriate level of sanitary or phytosanitary protection, members should take into account the relevant economic factors which are connected or otherwise related to 'the potential damage in terms of loss of production or sales in the event of the entry, establishment or spread of a pest or disease; the costs of control or eradication in the territory of the importing Member; and the relative cost-effectiveness of alternative approaches to limiting risks.' Article 5 (3) of the SPS Agreement.
19. Article 5 (6) of the SPS Agreement.
20. Footnote 3 of Article 5 (6) of the SPS Agreement.
21. Article 6.1 of the SPS Agreement. In assessing the sanitary or phytosanitary characteristics of a region, members must take into consideration, *inter alia*, the level of prevalence of specific diseases or pests, the existence of eradication or control programmes, and appropriate criteria or guidelines which may be developed by the relevant international organizations.
22. Article 6.3 of the SPS Agreement. According to this Article, a pest- or disease-free area determination must be based on factors such as geography, ecosystems, epidemiological surveillance, and the effectiveness of sanitary or phytosanitary controls.
23. Article 7 and Annex B of the SPS Agreement.
24. Annex B of the SPS Agreement. To date, however, not all members have provided information regarding their national authorities responsible for the notification of changes in SPS measures and their SPS enquiry points. According to the *WTO Annual Report* 2007, as of 31 December 2006, one-hundred thirty-eight members (92 per cent.) had notified an enquiry point and one-hundred thirty-one (87 per cent.) had identified their national notification authority. WTO, *Annual Report 2007*, Geneva, 2007.
25. To that effect, the notification must indicate the products covered, a brief indication of the objective and rationale of the proposed regulation, an identification of the parts which deviate from the international standards (whenever possible), and allow a reasonable period of time for other members to make comments. Paragraphs 5 and 6 of Annex B to the SPS Agreement.
26. Article 10 (1) of the SPS Agreement.

27. Article 9 (1) of the SPS Agreement.
28. Article 10 (4) of the SPS Agreement.
29. Article 9 (1) of the SPS Agreement.
30. Article 9 (2) of the SPS Agreement.
31. Article 10 (2) of the SPS Agreement.
32. Article 10 (3) of the SPS Agreement. Similarly, the Doha Ministerial Declaration calls for a phase-period between the enactment of a measure and its entry into force so that developing countries can adjust to the new regulatory scheme. cf. WTO Document WT/MIN(01)/17, 20 November 2001. More precisely, at least 60 days-period for receiving comments on proposed SPS measures should be allowed. cf. WTO Document G/SPS/33, 2 November 2004.
33. In 2007, the Central American exports to the world amounted to US$ 19,273 millions out of which the main exported goods were originating in the agricultural and agribusiness sector. Secretaría de Integración Económica Centroamericana (SIECA), Situation of State of the Central American Economy, Guatemala City, February 2008.
34. The United States is the main trading partner of the Central American region. In 2005, exports to the United States represented 35.4 per cent of the total exports and 35.7 per cent of the imports. The second trade partner consists of the countries of the region itself, whose trade represents 27.1 per cent of the total exports and 12.3 per cent of the imports. Secretaría de Integración Económica Centroamericana (SIECA), Trade Relations between Central American and the European Union, February, 2007.
35. Idem.
36. Idem. It has been noted that at the global level, the following products have been the most important products affected by border obstacles based on technical standards during the 2000–2001: fish and fishery products, meat and diary products, other processed products, fruits and vegetables, animal feed and grain, tropical beverages, oil seeds, textile fibbers, drinks, tobacco and sugar. Shafaeddin, M., *Who Does Bear the Cost of Compliance with Sanitary and Phytosanitary Measures in Poor Countries?*, Institute of Economic Research, University of Neuchâtel, Switzerland, 2007.
37. Cf. European Commission, Directorate General External Trade http://ec.europa.eu/trade/index_en.htm
38. Takayoshi, J., 2005, 'An Assessment of Technical Barriers in Central American Agricultural and Food Trade', Dissertation submitted to the Faculty of Virginia Polytechnic Institute and State University, Blacksburg, Virginia, April 21. Refer also to Bernardo *et al.*, Benchmarking of SPS Management Capacity, op. cit., and Velez, J.,2007, *Síntesis de los estudios de evaluación de capacidades y estudios de caso relacionados con las normas sanitarias y fitosanitarias realizadas para Centroamérica y Panamá (2000–2006)*, Inter-American Development Bank, Washington.
39. Refer, for instance, to Shafaeddin, M., *Cost of Compliance?*, op. cit.; Henson, S., Loader, R., Swinbank, A., Bredahl, M. and Lux, M. 2000, *Impact of Sanitary and Phytosanitary Measures on Developing Countries*, Department of Agricultural and Food Economics, University of Reading, United Kingdom.
40. Henson *et al.*, *Impact of Sanitary and Phytosanitary Measures*, op. cit.

41. The other mentioned WTO Agreements concern customs valuation, and intellectual property rights.
42. Finger, J. M. and P. Schuler, 2000, 'Implementation of Uruguay Round Commitments: The Development Challenge' World Bank's Policy Research Working Paper No. 2215, seen at http://www.worldbank.org/research/trade (6 May 2008).
43. Shafaeddin, M., 2007, *Cost of Compliance?*, op. cit. According to this author, if exports are reduced, there will be secondary costs in terms of the loss of income at the country, farm and firm levels, as well as the loss of employment and household consumption.
44. For example, before the SPS Committee, it has been argued that members removed active substances from their national registries of permitted products for purely commercial reasons, without scientific justification. WTO Committee on Sanitary and Phytosanitary Measures, Summary of the Meeting of 27–28 June 2007, G/SPS/R/45, 12 September 2007.
45. Indeed, unjustifiable SPS measures have the potential to discriminate among suppliers by redirecting trade from one exporting country to another, and to reduce global trade by increasing costs or raising non-tariff barriers for all potential exporting countries.
46. Finger and Schuler, 2000, 'Implementation of Uruguay Round Commitments', op. cit.
47. Shafaeddin, *Cost of Compliance?* op. cit, and Jayasuriya S., Maclaren, D. and Mehta R., 2006, 'Meeting Food Safety Standards in Export Markets: Issues and Challenges facing Firms from developing Countries', A paper presented at the IATRC summer Symposium: Food Regulation and Trade, Institutional Framework, Concepts of Analysis and Empirical Evidence, Bonn, 28–30 May. As of 2002, 18 complaints had been made under the SPS Agreement, of which developing countries were involved only in four cases. In two of these cases developing countries were defending SPS measures against a complaint filed by a developed country (DS 96: EU – Indian import quotas; DS 203: US – Mexican import restrictions on live swine); in a third case, both the defendant and the complainant were developing countries (DS 205: Thailand – Egyptian import restrictions on canned tuna); and in the fourth case, a developing country was complaining about an SPS measure of a developed country (DS 134: India – EU import duties on rice). Jensen, M. F., 'Reviewing the SPS Agreement: A Developing Country Perspective', Working Paper Subseries on Globalization and Economic Restructuring in Africa. Centre for Development Research, Copenhagen, 2002.
48. The scenario is even worsening as SPS measures are not harmonized. For example, out of 154 notifications to the WTO on tropical fruits and vegetables by EU, Japan, USA and Canada during 1995–2004, 59 per cent were non-harmonized, and another 19 per cent were only partially harmonized. Pay Ellen, Overview of the Sanitary and Phytosanitary Measures in Canada, the European Union, Japan, and the United States (QUAD Countries) on Tropical Fruits and Vegetables Imported from Developing Countries, South Centre Trade-Related Agenda Development and Equity (TRADE), November 2005.
49. One of the principal requirements necessary to export poultry products to the US is for a country to be declared Newcastle-free. In order to enjoy this

status, countries must undergo a considerably lengthy process. Gitli, E., Arce, R. and Villalobos, E., 2002, 'Central America and the International Trade of Poultry Products', Workshop on Standards and Trade UNCTAD, Geneva.

50. Josling, T., Roberts, D. and Orden, D., 2005, 'Food Regulation and Trade, Institute for International Economics', *Journal of International Economic Law*, 8, pp.793–802.

51. Shafaeddin, M., 2007, *Cost of Compliance?*, op. cit.

52. Velez, J., 2007, *Síntesis de los estudios de evaluación de capacidades y estudios de caso relacionados con las normas sanitarias y fitosanitarias realizadas para Centroamérica y Panamá*, op. cit.

53. WTO Committee on Sanitary and Phytosanitary Measures, Summary of the Meeting of 27-28 June 2007, 12 September 2007, G/SPS/R/45.

54. Dong, F. and Jensen, H.H., 2004, 'The Challenge of Conforming to Sanitary and Phytosanitary Measures for China's Agricultural Exports', Matric Working Paper 04-MWP 8, Agricultural Trade Research and Information Centre, IOWA State University, Midwest.

55. Chia-Hui Lee, G., 2006, *Private Food Standards and their Impacts on Developing Countries*, Brussels. Seen at http://trade.ec.europa.eu/doclib/docs/2006/november/tradoc_127969. pdf (6 May 2008).

56. Accordingly, before the WTO SPS Committee, developing countries have raised specific trade concerns as regards the adoption of private standards by developed countries. WTO Committee on Sanitary and Phytosanitary Measures, Summary of the Meeting of 27–28 June 2007, 12 September 2007, G/SPS/R/45.

57. Chia-Hui Lee, G., 2006, *Private Food Standards and their Impacts on Developing Countries* op. cit. According to this author, there is an ever-increasing number of NGOs demanding new requirements, such as, those related with environment, social, worker protection, animal welfare.

58. For instance, Carrefour has adopted EurepGAP certification. From 2006, the German market only accepts EurepGAP certified products.

59. For instance, in the UK, Tesco has developed 'Tesco's Nature's Choice' and Marks & Spencer, 'Farm to Folk'.

60. Idem.

61. Mainville, D., Zylbersztajn, D. and Reardon, T., 2005, 'Determinants of Retailers' Decisions to Use Public or Private Grades and Standards: Evidence from the Fresh Produce Market of São Paulo Brazil', *Food Policy*, 30(3). For instance, small producers in Ecuador who have always produced without the use of any agrochemicals now must pay around US$3,000 per year to be certified as organic producers, which is a very high cost for small growers. cf. WTO Committee on SPS Measures, Note by the Secretariat, G/SPS/R/45/Corr.1, 31 October 2007.

62. Henson *et al.*, *Impact of Sanitary and Phytosanitary Measures* op. cit. As of 31 December 2006, 7,345 notifications were circulated, including corrigenda, addenda and revisions. The number of notifications in 2006 (1,146) was greater than the number submitted in 2005 (850). cf. WTO, *Annual Report 2007*, op. cit.

63. Finger and Schuler, 'Implementation of Uruguay Round Commitments', op. cit.

64. Bernardo, *et al.*, 'Benchmarking of SPS Management Capacity', op. cit.
65. Henson, S. and Loader, R., 2001, 'Barriers to Agricultural Exports from Developing Countries: The Role of Sanitary and Phytosanitary Requirements', *World Development*, 29 (1), pp. 85–102.
66. The EC-Israel Agreement is contained in *Official Journal of the European Union*, O.J. (2000,) L/147, p. 3.
67. *Official Journal of the European Union*, OJ (2005) L/265, p. 2.
68. Ibid., OJ (2004), L/304, p. 39.
69. Ibid., OJ (2002), L/129, p. 3.
70. Ibid., OJ (2006), L/143, p. 2.
71. Ibid., OJ (2000), L/70, p. 4.
72. Ibid., OJ (1997), L/187, p. 3.
73. Ibid., OJ (1998), L/97, p. 2.
74. The requirement for phytosanitary certification applies as follows: in respect of cut flowers, only to the genera dendranthema, dianthus and pelargonium for introduction into the Community, and only to rosa, dendranthema, dianthus, pelargonium, gypsophila and anemone for introduction into Israel. In respect of fruits, the requirement applies only to citrus, fortunella, poncirus and their hybrids annona, cydonia, diospyros, malus, mangifera, passiflore, prunus, psidium, pyrus, ribes, syzygium and vaccinum for introduction into the Community, and to all the genera for introduction into Israel. Protocol 3 (a) of the EU-Israel Agreement.
75. *Official Journal of the European Union*, OJ (1999), L/311, p. 3.
76. Ibid., OJ (2005), L/26, p. 3.
77. Ibid., OJ (2004), L/84, p. 13.
78. Ibid., OJ (2000), L/157, p. 10.
79. Article 20 (3)–(4) of the EU-Mexico Agreement.
80. *Official Journal of the European Union*, OJ (2002), L/352, p. 3.
81. On serious public, animal or plant health grounds, a safeguard provision is provided for the implementation of transitional SPS measures necessary for the protection of public, animal or plant health. *Official Journal of the European Union*, OJ (2002), L/352, Annex IV, Article 14 (2). The Party taking the measures must notify the other Party of the decision to implement such measures. Upon request, the Parties must enter into consultations. Ibid. Article 14 (3).
82. Ibid. Article 7 (7).
83. Ibid., Appendixes V and VI.
84. Ibid., Article 8 (2) (a)–(b).
85. Ibid., Article 10. Appendixes VII to IX further provide guidelines for conducting verifications, import checks and inspection fees and for certification.
86. Ibid., Article 16. The establishment of technical working groups for identifying and addressing technical and scientific issues arising from the application of this Agreement is also provided.
87. Council Regulation (EC) No 980/2005 of 27 June 2005 applying a scheme of generalized tariff preferences, *Official Journal of the European Union* (2005) L/169 p. 1.
88. Bernardo *et al.*, 'Benchmarking of SPS Management Capacity', op. cit.
89. Ibid.

90. Cf. Bernardo *et al.*, 'Benchmarking of SPS Management Capacity', op. cit., and Velez, *Síntesis de los estudios de evaluación de capacidades y estudios de caso relacionados con las normas sanitarias y fitosanitarias realizadas para Centroamérica y Panamá*, op. cit.

91. cf. Velez, *Síntesis de los estudios de evaluación de capacidades y estudios de caso relacionados con las normas sanitarias y fitosanitarias realizadas para Centroamérica y Panamá*, op. cit.. Accordingly, in a study funded by the Economic Growth and Agricultural Trade (EGAT) Bureau of the United States Agency for International Development (USAID) which aim was to review and 'benchmark' each country's SPS management capacity, considering the implications for the most important agricultural and food product imports and exports and related technical assistance requirements, it was found that the technical assistance priorities of Central American countries were training, accreditation of laboratories, funding for specific programmes, technology. Cf. Bernardo *et al.*, Benchmarking of SPS Management Capacity, op. cit.

92. Cf. Velez, *Síntesis de los estudios de evaluación de capacidades y estudios de caso relacionados con las normas sanitarias y fitosanitarias realizadas para Centroamérica y Panamá*, op. cit.

93. Idem.

94. Cf. Bernardo *et al.*, Benchmarking of SPS Management Capacity op. cit.

95. Cf. Velez, *Síntesis de los estudios de evaluación de capacidades y estudios de caso relacionados con las normas sanitarias y fitosanitarias realizadas para Centroamérica y Panamá*, op. cit.

96. The following recommendations are based on practice, that is, the SPS provisions included in the bilateral and plurilateral agreements followed by the Latin American countries, and largely refer to and agree with the analysis carried out in ECLAC, Convergence and Asymmetry in sanitary and phytosanitary measures in the region's trade agreements. Bulletin Facilitation of Trade and Transport in Latin America and the Caribbean, Issue Number 245, January 2007.

97. Indeed, cooperation of the Central American countries in SPS matters would also fortify their ongoing regional integration, where scientific and technical resources could be for instance, pooling or the establishment of regional laboratories.

98. Furthermore, a side effect of such a provision may be an increased flow of foreign investment in the region, which may introduce technological improvements that the region needs in successfully facing certain SPS measures.

99. Harmonization exists only when the rules being compared are identical. Equivalency indicates a similar level of sanitary protection, which may be obtained by means of sanitary measures that vary from one country to another. This is because of the difficulty of enforcing identical rules in countries that have different sanitary situations and different ecosystems (which may or may not be conducive to the spread of a particular disease).

100. Cf. Bernardo, *et al.*, 'Benchmarking of SPS Management Capacity', op. cit.

13
The European Court of Justice's Jurisprudence on the Right of Review of Customs Authorities' Decisions

Lorenza Mola

Consideration of the rights of businesses *vis-à-vis* customs authorities' decisions and practices, as regards both the international fora for cooperation and regulation of the customs field and the European Union (EU) legal system, has very important implications for international business indeed, although it is apparently far from the core issues of substantial customs law,[1] such as tariff classification, customs valuation, rules of origin, customs procedures. It is part of the trade facilitation efforts, which are an increasingly relevant item in the international agenda and internally.

In a globalized economic arena, reliable management of customs administration is an asset for both the business actors and the states.[2] As production takes place at different stages in different countries, which are different customs territories, customs procedures are by-side operations of all outsourcing or foreign investment activities. In such a context, firms' competitiveness also depends upon 'timely and efficient business transactions' and supported 'by modern manufacturing, information and international trade supply chain management systems'.[3] This also applies to national competitiveness, particularly for those developing countries, as well as, developed countries which aim to be the best in attracting international investments and participating in international trade. Conversely, businesses' rights of review of administrative customs decisions are increasingly relevant in order to counterbalance accrued control and enforcement powers for which customs authorities have recently been entrusted, and which are necessary to face international terrorism, counterfeiting and other threats to security or illegal practices. Judicial review of administrative decisions, along with, the rule of law, accountability, transparency and effective management of public institutions and resources against corruption, operate as a vehicle of national competitiveness and good governance. Hence, customs efficiency has increasingly become a factor of the investment/trade climate for doing business in a country and administrative/judicial review of customs administration enactable by business is an important element of an efficient and modern system of border procedures.

As for the EU, several actors at several levels play different but interrelated roles. Among these, the European Court of Justice (ECJ) has always played a major role in shaping the EU customs environment. Its rulings have far reaching implications for business in the EU, considering that they are automatically binding on all EU Member States and that European Community (EC) customs law is directly administered by twenty-seven national customs administrations.

However, developments within the EU are not isolated and de-coupled from broader evolutions occurring in many supranational arena. Multilateral organizations established by sovereign states constitute multiple settings for the development of requirements on national customs administrations, where they shape rules and procedures for the review of national customs decisions. The World Customs Organization (WCO) and the World Trade Organization (WTO), of which the European Communities is a member, are the main international bodies tackling the issue of trade facilitation and review of customs authorities' decisions. They interestingly present different patterns of *modus operandi*, legal force of their instruments, and dispute settlement provisions.

The World Customs Organization and the development of international customs standards

The WCO, or its official title, the Customs Co-operation Council,[4] provides a global setting for cooperation in customs matters among its 173 members.[5] According to the establishing Convention,[6] the Customs Co-operation Council's overall objective is 'to secure the highest degree of harmony and uniformity in [signatories'] Customs systems and especially to study the problems inherent in the development and improvement of Customs technique and Customs legislation'.[7] Within the limits of this work, it is worth analysing only the main relevant features which characterize the WCO as a forum for information-sharing, discussion, technical expertise, and development of international standards, promotion of best practices and capacity building. Under the terms of the establishing Convention, the Council carries an examination of technical aspects and related economic factors; it may also prepare draft Conventions and recommend their adoption by interested governments,[8] as well as, make recommendations to ensure the uniform interpretation and application of the Conventions and other legal instruments on the matter.[9] It ensures circulation of information and may provide for information and advice to the signatory governments.[10] The Permanent Technical Committee assists the Council in these activities and also drafts International Customs Norms, Guidelines and Model legislation, after having undertaken a systematic and comparative study of the Customs procedures in force in the various Member countries.

The WCO does not provide for an institutionalized and independent dispute settlement mechanism to enforce its decisions or to settle divergences between its members. This is due to the nature of the WCO which relies upon a network of sponsored or administered international treaties and non-binding acts with the support of an institutional structure. The establishing Convention enables the Council to make recommendations, in a conciliatory capacity, for the settlement of disputes concerning the interpretation and application of the Conventions concluded as a result of its work, in accordance with the provisions of these Conventions. The parties may agree in advance to accept the recommendations of the Council as binding.[11]

The rights of businesses *vis-à-vis* customs administrations are considered by the WCO in broader terms, primarily in the domain of trade facilitation, which is one of the main objectives of the WCO,[12] and by promoting the emergence of an 'honest, transparent and predictable'[13] customs environment. Both of these aims are pursued within the general mission of enhancing the effectiveness and efficiency of Customs administrations.

As for Conventions promoted by the WCO,[14] the International Convention on the Simplification and Harmonization of Customs procedures (the Kyoto Convention), entered into force in 1974, was revised, updated and adopted in 1999 (the Revised Kyoto Convention)[15] and finally entered into force in February 2006. Such text is not immediately binding upon WCO members, but has to be ratified on a voluntary basis by each government. The Convention is also open to non-WCO members who are members of the United Nations (UN) or its specialized agencies, as well as Customs or Economic Unions.[16]

Its structure provides for great flexibility, coupling core obligations, that is, the Body of the Convention and its General Annex, binding each party and applicable to all the Customs procedures and practices covered by the Convention, with further optional sets of norms, as in the Specific Annexes and chapters thereof. The Convention establishes that each contracting party commits to promote the simplification and harmonization of Customs procedures and, to that end, to conform to the Standards and Recommended Practices in the Annexes to the Convention.[17] Each Annex and chapter thereof sets Standards, that is, parties recognize that the implementation of those provisions is necessary for the achievement of the Conventions' objectives. The Specific Annexes also provide for Recommended Practices, recognized as constituting progress towards the objectives, and their widest possible application is desirable. Guidelines are provided for each chapter of the General and Specific Annexes, consisting of a set of explanations which indicate some of the possible courses of action to be followed in applying the Standards and Recommended Practices, and in particular recommending and illustrating best practice. The Management Committee established by the Convention and composed of all parties recommends Amendments to the Body, the General Annex and the Specific Annexes while it is competent for directly amending the Recommended Practices for the Specific Annexes, as well as for reviewing and updating the Guidelines.[18] The Body provides for some rules to be followed by parties involved in a dispute and on the application and interpretation of the Convention. These parties shall settle the dispute by negotiations between them, otherwise they shall refer the dispute to the Management Committee, which shall make recommendations. Parties may agree in advance to accept such recommendations as binding.[19]

The 'provision to affected [business] of easily accessible processes of administrative and judicial review' forms part of the governing principles of the Convention,[20] and is specified by Chapter 10 of the General Annex.[21] There are three sets of Standards and they express the most advanced and detailed international requirements currently in force on the issue, although binding on the Parties to the Convention only.

A first set of Standards (A) deals with the right of appeal. National legislation is required to provide any person who is directly affected by a decision or omission of the customs authorities with a right to make a request to them. The scope of the request is limited to the motivations of such decision or omission; and it must be satisfied within a specified period. The right of appeal must be featured in such a way that it consists of at least two degrees, the initial one before the customs authorities, the further one(s) before an authority independent of the customs administration; either way, the final instance must be of judicial nature.

Another set of Standards (B) relates to form and grounds of appeal. Their application results in national legislation requiring that an appeal is lodged in writing and that its grounds are specified. The time limit fixed for the exercise of such appeal must allow the appellant sufficient time to study the contested decision and to prepare an appeal. Customs authorities should not require any specific evidence but should allow, in certain circumstances, a reasonable time for evidence being lodged.

Finally, a third set of Standards (C) recognizes that the following provisions must be implemented upon consideration of appeal. The customs authority shall give its ruling upon an appeal and written notice thereof to the appellant as soon as possible. When this is refused the information to the appellant about the right to lodge any further appeal with an administrative or independent authority and of any time limit for the lodgments of such appeal must be provided under national rules governing the customs' procedure. When approved the customs' or judicial authorities' decisions shall be put into effect as soon as possible by virtue of national implementation of such Standard.

Recommendations adopted by the WCO Council aim to harmonize customs procedures and practices. Although they are not legally binding, they may be accepted by members. In this event, a WCO information document sets some procedural requirements and legal effects attached to acceptance, thus conferring a certain rigidity to the system.[22] Among their objectives, Recommendations may be intended to ensure that adequate legal remedies are available to the taxpayer.[23] The Council adopted a Recommendation on the right of appeal in customs matters, as well as an International Customs Norm in 1967.[24] It expresses the desirability of a right of appeal for persons involved in disputes with the customs authorities because of their decisions, acts or omissions, and considers that such a right would contribute to the uniform application of customs laws among members. As before, this Recommendation is addressed to members of the Council as well as to members of the UN and Customs or Economic Unions.[25] Its coverage and content differ to some extent from the Kyoto Convention's General Annex, Chapter 10. The Recommendation explicitly specifies that its substantial coverage is limited to appeals in matters relating to the laws and regulations which the customs authorities are responsible for enforcing, while it does not embrace appeals in penal matters, appeals against provisions of a general character or appeals against opinions expressed by customs authorities which are not binding in effect. Furthermore, this text recommends that authorities knowing of the appeal in the last resort, including an arbitral authority, are independent from customs administration. The Recommendation sets more general requirements about the forms and conditions of appeal, and minimum delays for granting decisions and notifying them to the appellant. However, the text recommends the introduction of specific provisions into national customs law on the suspension of customs procedures during an appeal, for instance, on the release of goods, provided that certain conditions are met.[26]

The World Trade Organization and its systems of rules and dispute settlement

The WTO[27] is another relevant international forum in the field of customs issues. It presents at the same time significant differences and complementarities with respect to the WCO. Complementarities are found, both statutorily and practically, in the fields of customs valuation, tariff classification, rules of origin and trade facilitation. Differences from the WCO are in the nature and force of WTO legal provisions, in the outcome of negotiations occurring in that institutional context, and in the existence of an independent mechanism of dispute settlement. This last element however must be assessed in the light of the fact that the reports by the Dispute Settlement Body, which are almost automatically adopted, are binding only upon the parties to the dispute. Another relevant element of such mechanism to be reminded here concerns its availability only to WTO Member States. Private parties are not entitled to lodge a complaint, but have to rely upon national procedures to put pressure on their government to initiate the procedure. Individuals may not invoke the report's findings before national courts.

GATT rules, together with the General Agreement on Trade in Services (GATS), Trade Related Aspects of Intellectual Property Rights (TRIPS), and the Dispute Settlement Understanding (DSU), form the core law of the WTO, binding all 152 members.[28] In particular, GATT rules have regulated international trade in goods, including some aspects of customs matters, on a multilateral basis, since 1947. The relevant provisions on customs authorities' duties *vis-à-vis* business are to be found in GATT Article X on Publication and Administration of Trade Regulations. Due process themes with respect to private parties underline this Article, which deals with the principle of transparency by requiring member states to officially publish a vast range of measures in Article X.1 and it also imposes the obligation to administer such measures 'in a uniform, impartial and reasonable manner' on member states in Article X.3(a) and to provide 'judicial, arbitral or administrative tribunals or procedures for the purpose, *inter alia*, of the prompt review and correction of administrative action relating to customs matters' in Article X.3(b).

GATT Article X.3(b) requires that members maintain or provide remedies for the prompt review and correction of administrative action relating to customs matters. There is no specific pronunciation of WTO adjudicating bodies on the meaning of 'administrative action relating to customs matters', which determine the scope of businesses' right to review.

The terms, *prima facie,* suggest that the decisions expressing such action address specific transactors and procedures, as opposed to 'measures of general application' referred to previously in the same Article. Similarly, customs administrations whose action is subject to review are defined as 'agencies entrusted with administrative enforcement'.

WTO dispute settlement practice has intended that a measure 'of general application' does not exclude administrative orders or country-specific measures.[29] However, the line is clearly drawn between measures that affect 'an unidentified number of economic operators, including domestic and foreign producers' and measures 'addressed to a specific company or applied to a specific shipment',[30] or 'the particular treatment accorded to each individual shipment'.[31] The specificity criterion has been applied in order to identify measures which are either within or outside Article X.1 or Article X.3(a), although any measure of general application must be applied in specific instances.[32] But within the concept of administration itself, there is more than one meaning. It has been expressed in terms of application[33] and 'customs officers' enforcement actions'[34] and conversely, administration of trade regulations under Article X.3(a) also applies to measures which 'provide for a certain manner of applying those substantive rules',[35] that is, rules which are administrative in nature,[36] such as, rules which 'provide for a certain manner of applying ... substantive rules'.[37] It may be deduced that the 'action' covered by the right to review under GATT Article X.3(b) is more limited then 'administrative measures' covered by other GATT provisions.

Review and correction of administrative action must be provided by judicial, arbitral, or administrative tribunals, or procedures. The possibility of an appeal is acknowledged, both on the side of the importers and by the central administration of the customs agencies. For importers, the appeal is to be lodged with a court or tribunal of superior jurisdiction within the nationally prescribed time. For customs agencies the central administration may commence to obtain a review of the matter in another proceeding if there is good cause to believe that the decision is inconsistent with established principles of law or the actual facts.

However, Article X.3(b) obligations relate exclusively to first instance review.[38] The tribunals and procedures where the first instance review of the administrative action takes place must be independent from the agencies entrusted with administrative enforcement subject to review. Such requirement has been understood, on the basis of the ordinary meaning of the term 'independent', in the sense that such tribunals and procedures must be free in institutional and practical terms of control or influence from the administrative agencies in question.[39]

In total, and apart from these requirements, Article X.3(b) leaves the specific structure of the review mechanism to the discretion of the WTO member concerned.[40] In particular, such a provision does not oblige a member to set up a single tribunal or procedure for the review of all administrative action but even expressly contemplates the possibility that there may be multiple tribunals or procedures in place in a single WTO member for the review of administrative action.[41]

According to the Panel's and the Appellate Body's textual reading of GATT Article X.3(b), the covered review decisions must not necessarily govern the practice of all the agencies entrusted with administrative enforcement throughout the territory of a WTO member. This is not clearly provided by the legal context for the interpretation of Article X.3(b). These tribunals' decisions shall be implemented by, and shall govern the practice of, only those agencies whose action has been subject to review and that are bound by the decisions of a tribunal or procedure 'with respect to identical factual situations that may arise in the future concerning identical legal issues', without always or necessarily be extended to all agencies of a member.[42] And due process objective is not undermined by such a limited implementation, so long as there is a possibility of an independent review and correction of the administrative action of every agency.[43]

Within the WTO, work on trade facilitation has been carried out firstly on an exploratory basis and then in the framework of the Doha Round of trade negotiations,[44] according to the modalities for negotiations agreed in July 2004.[45] Trade facilitation has been kept in the domain of the Single Understanding rule,[46] thus assuring that the outcome of negotiations on this issue is binding on any present and future WTO member. Of course, special and differential treatment in favour of developing countries, as well as, capacity building and technical assistance will allow for some flexibility.

In October 2004, the Trade Negotiations Committee established the Negotiating Group on Trade Facilitation. Several other intergovernmental organizations have been contributing to the negotiations, providing for data, background documents and analyses. These negotiations have so far resulted in a Compilation of Members' Textual Proposals, last revised in June 2009.[47]

Among other transparency matters, the following proposals are particularly relevant to the review issue. It has been proposed that internet publication in one of the official languages of the WTO on a national website also comprises appeal procedures entered into force through official means and relating to or affecting trade in goods in such a manner provided for in GATT Article X as to enable governments and traders to become acquainted with these. Prior publication and consultation via the national website should allow interested parties to express their comments and adopt the necessary adaptation.[48]

Conversely, were such proposals to be finally agreed, the most relevant outcome would be the obligation upon any WTO member to provide for a double degree of review. According to one proposal, any person to whom customs or another relevant border agency issues a decision should be given the right, within a member's territory, without penalty, to administrative appeal independent of the employee or office of the agency which issued the decision; and to judicial appeal of the decision. Once again, the proposed international provision does not impose any compulsory requirement on the nature of judicial appeals. It limits itself to refer the possibility that the legislation of each member requires administrative appeal to be initiated prior to judicial appeal.[49]

Challenges to the European Union system of customs law and administration

The EU is fully integrated in the international network of institutional frameworks, standards and obligations on customs matters. EC customs law and its administration are also influenced by two seminal aspects of European integration. These are EC external competence on customs issues and direct administrative and judicial implementation of EU law by Member States. Such a complex architecture has to meet the requirements established at the international level on uniformity of administration of customs measures.

As the EC is a customs union it also has exclusive competence with third countries on Common Commercial Policy, including customs matters.[50] Because of such authority and of its international legal personality, the EC is a signatory party to international treaties dealing with customs issues, such as the Convention on the Harmonized System of Tariff Classification and, most relevantly, the Revised Kyoto Convention since 2003.[51] Moreover, the EC has member status in some international organizations including the WTO. Quite recently, on 1 July 2007, the EC became a member of the WCO on an *interim* basis, pending all WCO members' ratification of an amendment to the establishing Convention which allows customs or economic unions, including the EC, to acquire membership.[52] The outcome of this is that several sets of binding international standards and rules are sources of EU law.[53] Furthermore, the EU, not having a common administration and enforcement structure, relies on national administrations' for the implementation of its common policies according to national law.

In particular, the EU must comply with GATT Article X provisions and with Chapter 10 of the Kyoto Convention's General Annex. According to the respective spheres of competence, EC and national legislations have incorporated such international provisions for the purposes of their specification, application or implementation.[54] Besides, the general principles of EU law,[55] among which is the right to an effective remedy before a court, are also relevant for EU Institutions and Member States when they apply EU law. These aspects are important internal drivers for the evolution of both customs legislation and case law on the review of customs decisions. International and external pressures point in the same direction.

EC law reflects and regulates these principles and requirements on review of customs decisions in the Regulation establishing the Community Customs Code (CCC).[56] Its Title VIII on Appeal, Articles 243–246, confers any person the right to appeal against decisions taken by the customs authorities, or their omission, 'which relate to the application of customs legislation, and which concern him directly and individually'.[57]

As for the substantive scope of this right, appeals lodged with a view to the annulment or revision of a decision taken by the customs authorities on the basis of criminal law are excluded by the CCC coverage.[58] Apart from this exclusion, decisions subject to review are uniformly defined at the EU level as any 'official act by the customs authorities pertaining to customs rules giving a ruling on a particular case' and 'having legal effects on one or more specific or identifiable persons'.[59] Customs authorities must motivate a refusal or a decision affecting the addressee, and must refer to the right of appeal provided for in Article 243.[60]

But other procedural and substantive matters relating to the right of appeal are not regulated in such details. Consistent with the administrative and judiciary autonomy of Member States,[61] appeal must be lodged in the Member State where the decision has been taken or applied for,[62] and the provisions for the implementation of the appeals procedure shall be determined by the Member States.[63] The Code does not expressly require that Member States provide for two degrees of appeal. The first instance may take place before the customs authorities designated for that purpose by the Member States.[64] However, where existing, a sub-sequent appeal must take place before an independent body, either a judicial authority or an equivalent specialized body.[65] The Code further specifies circumstances in which the disputed decision may not or must be suspended,[66] as an exception to the general rule of immediate effect of the decisions taken by the customs authorities.[67]

This set of provisions conforms to a high degree with the requirements laid down by the Kyoto Convention and GATT Article X.3(b), while it may *prima facie* be challenged under the perspective of uniformity because of national implementation. According to some authors, there is no justification for allowing such discrepancies to persist, particularly since decisions taken by national authorities, whether administrative or judicial, may be without transnational effect.[68] However, it should also be considered that primacy of EC customs law over the national law of the Member States has a double practical application: on the one hand, national provisions for appeal of customs authorities' decisions must follow the patterns set by the general principles of EU law and CCCs Title VIII on Appeal; and on the other hand, customs specific acts and circulars, or concrete customs decisions in individual instances, must abide to all applying EU principles and rules.

There are several resolutions that may be exerted in order to claim protection of rights to review and appeal against customs decisions and are related to the way review is structured in the EU legal system. Judicial protection of rights flowing from EC customs law, in particular, from Articles 243–246 of the CCC is shared among the national judges, the ECJ and the Court of First Instance (CFI). National judges have general competence to apply EU law into Member States, provided that such law has direct effects, like Regulations, or has been implemented by the Member State. Accordingly, they are competent in disapplying national legislative and customs authorities' administrative acts and circulars when they are incompatible with EU law. Proceedings, in this instance, therefore, are governed by national procedural law.[69]

The ECJ may or must be referred by a national judge on the interpretation and validity of EU law, through preliminary rulings, in order for the national judge to assess national acts' conformity with EU law.[70] This is expressly meant to ensure uniform application of EU law by national courts and other authorities throughout all the Member States, Article 234 ECT.

Moreover, the ECJ rules on actions against a Member State for not fulfilling an obligation under EU law, Article 228 ECT. Although the power to initiate such infringement procedure, Article 226 ECT, lays in the hands of the Commission, at its full discretion, it may be triggered by individuals. Business may lodge a complaint with the Commission against a Member State for any measure (law, regulation or administrative action) or practice attributable to a Member State (thus excluding complaints on private disputes) which they consider incompatible with a provision or a principle of EU law.[71] Peculiarly, anyone may exercise such possibility, without having to prove that he is interested in or directly affected by the infringment.[72] Furthermore, the CFI is competent on appeals of the European Commission's decisions in customs matters which directly and individually affect a transactor's rights.

In addition, business may have recourse to non-judicial remedies. They may ask the Commission for an administrative intervention. The European Commission may contact the national administration and inform the transactor whether it considers national action correct or not;[73] it may invite the transactor to pursue national available remedies; and/or may also decide to introduce an infringement procedure[74] against the Member State. The Commission must reply within specific time frames and its behaviour is subject to the code of good administrative conduct.[75] Finally, individuals may send petitions to the European Parliament (EP),[76] and, as far as EU institutions, bodies and agencies are concerned, file complaints before the European Ombudsman.[77]

Business may seek relief via a combination of these channels, that they appropriately determine according to whether the contested customs practice is widespread, or it has transnational effects, or it derives by legislative requirements among other relevant circumstances.

Conversely, the only formal mechanism available within the EU system that allows business to signal to the European Commission non-EU States' customs administrative action is the Trade Barriers Regulation.[78] It may result in the European Commission formally raising such issues within the WTO framework from a trade perspective. There is not a similar mechanism specifically targeted to the WCO,[79] maybe due to the fact that this international setting only provides for political dispute settlement means.

In 2004, the US challenged the EU system of customs administration before a WTO panel and, successively, the Appellate Body.[80] First, the US alleged that the system as a whole is inconsistent with the requirement of uniform administration contained in GATT Article X.3(a). Second, the US claimed that it does not provide for the prompt review and correction of administrative action relating to customs matters as required by GATT Article X.3(b). The US noted that review tribunals or procedures of the defendant consist of the courts of various Member States, thus differing from most legal systems, where there is only one central agency entrusted with enforcement of customs law. Conversely, the contested system combines review tribunals with geographically limited jurisdiction with customs authorities whose practice is limited to particular geographical regions, and this results in a geographically fragmented administration of the customs law in the EU.

The EC argued that it has not violated GATT Article X.3(b), because this provision does not require that review of administrative action relating to customs matters must have effect throughout the territory of the EU. According to the defendant, proper and uniform interpretation and application of EC law throughout all the Member States is guaranteed by the preliminary reference procedure.

The Panel found that the fact that decisions regarding review of administrative action relating to customs matters do not apply to all agencies in the EU and do not have effect throughout its territory does not result in the EC violating the obligation to provide prompt review and correction of administrative action relating to customs matters. The Appellate Body upheld the conclusion of the Panel. Therefore, the system has been found not incompatible with GATT Article X.3(b).

Although the US relied only upon the provisions of GATT Article X.3(a) and X.3(b), the whole EC's system of customs administration was challenged. This challenge could have significant and far reaching consequences on the entire EU legal system insofar as customs matters are concerned, because the balance of power between the EU institutions as well as the relationship between the EU and its Member States, including their courts, were put into discussion.[81] Indeed, the core issue of the US challenge related to 'the absence of any procedure or institution or mechanism to ensure that divergences do not occur or are reconciled promptly, and are reconciled as a matter of right when they occur'.[82] That is, the creation of a central customs court of first instance was alluded to but, as the EC argued, this would imply constitutional changes to the system and require their ratification by Member States, something which would have had too far reaching consequences if originating from WTO membership.

However, it is undeniable that the EU legal system does provide for some discrepancies in the outcome of reviews of administrative customs decisions, unless the disputed practice or act is brought before the ECJ or the CFI. Indeed, the CCC and its implementing Regulations were the result of a compromise between the different national customs procedures in force in the 1980s among the then Member States. In 2005 the European Commission adopted a Proposal of a Regulation for a modernized Customs Code.[83] This Proposal was finalized while the dispute with the US was continuing in the WTO. The proposed Regulation underwent the co-decision process, and lastly, in April 2008, the final version was adopted.[84]

Several factors inspired the Proposal for a modernized Code, among which, externally were the EC's accession to the Revised Kyoto Convention,[85] and the EC's intention to lead the trade facilitation objectives of the Doha round of WTO negotiations.[86] Internally, the modernization effort was motivated also by the better regulation initiative[87] aimed to simplify European regulation so as to reduce business costs in Europe and increase transparency and public confidence, as well as the need to bring the Code into conformity with the Charter of Fundamental Rights of the European Union, particularly with regard to the exercise of the right of defence before a decision with a negative impact on an applicant or debtor is taken.[88]

As far as the right to appeal customs authorities' decisions is concerned, the proposal builds upon the existing Code provisions, introducing some amendments. It makes a two-stage appeal compulsory, and expressly clarifies the possibility that the first stage be either administrative or judicial, adding also equivalent specialized bodies designated for that purposes by Member States.[89] Most interestingly, reservations in favour of national law are limited. The modernized Code eliminates the provision according to which implementation of the appeals procedure is regulated by Member States. Nor is reference made to decisions taken by the customs authorities on the basis of criminal law,[90] which are expressly excluded from the coverage of the Code currently in force. Therefore, as long as the decision concerned relates to the application of customs law, EC rules apply for the implementation of the appeals. Residually, national law will continue to be empowered only with regard to decisions relating to the application of customs legislation taken by a judicial authority,[91] thus excluding appeal decisions taken by customs authorities from Member States' regulating sphere, unless such customs authorities are acting as judicial authorities.[92] Finally, the adopted version does not maintain the original Proposal's provision which re-phrased the Member States' and the EC's international obligations under GATT Article X.3(b) on prompt correction of customs authorities' decisions.[93]

The European Court of Justice and the Community Customs Code-originating right to review customs decisions

As for business' right to have a customs decision reviewed by an administrative or judicial authority, the ECJ may be referred to through several channels. In particular, in the last years Member States' courts have referred to the ECJ for preliminary rulings about the right of review, along with substantive customs matters, such as tariff classification, customs value, origin of goods, customs debt, recovery of duties, transit of goods, anti-dumping procedures, as well as, preferential and association agreements.[94]

As a general matter of EU law, account may be taken of the ECJ's case law on the obligation of making a reference by national judges to the ECJ for preliminary ruling, in the customs field. First of all, it emanates from the EU legal notion of judicial authority that such reference may not be made by the customs administrative authorities which are aware of the review of customs decisions.[95] Another issue at stake is whether a court or tribunal against whose decisions there is no judicial remedy under national law is automatically under an obligation to refer to the Court questions on interpretation of EC law on tariff classification if it finds discrepancies in another Member State's administrative decisions.[96] According to the ECJ, obligation of referral for a preliminary ruling falls within the framework of cooperation between jurisdictions with a view to ensuring the proper application and uniform interpretation of EC law. It does not therefore extend to discrepancies which a national court may find in an interpretation by an administrative authority of another Member State. In such instances, of course the matter may be referred to the ECJ, but this is optional. In particular, the existence of a Binding Tariff Information on tariff classification of goods issued by the authorities of another Member State must cause a court or tribunal to take particular care in its assessment of whether there is no reasonable doubt as to the correct application of the EC relevant customs law. Were there any reasonable doubt, the national judge must refer the issue to the ECJ.[97] It follows that, in the field of customs, and in particular with regard to binding tariff classification by another Member States' authorities, there are no specific rules that oblige national courts to make a reference for a preliminary ruling before the ECJ, other than those applying throughout all EU law.

A recent decision[98] on an old dispute has raised the question of the legal effects of decisions taken by organs of the national criminal justice system on EC customs law. In particular, the question is to determine whether the need for uniform application of customs law may overcome an implicit reference to Member States' law on criminal procedures, which falls outside EC competence in the customs field. The issue at stake is, essentially, to know which national authority is competent to classify an act as 'an act that could give rise to criminal court proceedings' for the purposes of applying EC customs legislation. In particular, the question is firstly whether it is for the tax authorities or the criminal courts to make such a classification, and secondly, whether that classification is precluded by a decision to file the complaint and not take any action or by a decision to acquit taken by a judicial body.

The Advocate General[99] interpreted the separation, in principle, between customs administration and the criminal justice system as an indication that customs authorities' considerations cannot substitute for judicial determination on the criminal nature of an act. As a result, only final conviction by a criminal court of a Member State is capable of delivering an interpretation with effects for EC customs law.

The ECJ does not follow the Advocate General's reasoning. The ECJ relies upon literal terms of the relevant provisions of EC customs law to find that the authorities who are competent to classify an act as capable of giving rise to criminal court proceedings are the same authorities which were unable to administer EC customs procedures, that is, the customs authorities of the Member States. Moreover, the relevant provisions did not set requirements on parallel criminal court proceedings. The ECJ concludes that in the absence of common rules governing the matter, it is for the domestic legal system of each Member State to lay down the conditions enabling persons to contest the application of the EC relevant customs law and to request, in that respect, that consequences may be drawn from rulings in court proceedings.

As it has been seen above, the dividing line between EU law and national law applying respectively to non-criminal and criminal proceedings dealing with customs matters was respected by the CCC of 1992, but it is smoothed in the finalized Modernized Code. This provides for further uniformity being put into the customs administration system as regards review and appeal of customs authorities' decisions.

Furthermore, the ECJ has denied the mandatory nature of the two-stage review and appeal mechanism under Article 243 of the CCC.[100] In an appeal brought directly before a judicial authority against a decision taken by the customs offices, the national court was uncertain as to whether the appellant was entitled to initiate proceedings directly before it without having initially lodged an appeal with the customs authorities. The ECJ rules that there is nothing in the wording of Article 243 to indicate that the appeal before the customs authority is a mandatory stage prior to lodging an appeal before the independent body.[101] Conversely, the ECJ finds that there is anything in the EU legislation to support the conclusion that it authorizes a trader to bypass an appeal before the customs authority and appeal directly to the independent body, where under the applicable national law an appeal to the customs authority is mandatory.

Quite interestingly, the ECJ also recalls the reasons which might have led the EU legislator not to detail rules governing the appeals procedure but merely to regulate certain general aspects of the right of appeal, when adopting the CCC in 1992. In particular, the ECJ relies upon this stating: 'What makes harmonization of rights of appeal special however is not only the differences between national procedures, which are in some instances considerable, but also the fact that they often apply uniformly to the whole field of national administrative and tax law so that the harmonization of rights of appeal for the purposes of customs law only will fragment hitherto uniform national appeals procedures'.[102] This cautious approach has in turn been overcome via the legislative power, as the final version of the Modernized Code clarifies the mandatory requirement of two-stage national procedures for review and appeal of customs authorities' decisions.

As for further aspects of review right as interpreted by the ECJ, EU judges have ruled on the power to suspend the implementation of a contested decision, Article 244 of the CCC, on several occasions. Whereas Article 243 expressly lays down the procedure for bringing appeals before both the customs authorities and an independent authority, such as, a judicial authority or equivalent specialized body, it is clear that Article 244 limits the power to suspend implementation of a contested decision exclusively to the customs authorities.

However, it was decided that, in light of the system of review and appeal set by Article 243 of the Code, the provision of Article 244 does not deny the power of the judicial authorities seized of a dispute pursuant to Article 243 to order such suspension, either pursuant to rules of procedure in force under national law or in order to comply with the obligation to secure the full and effective legal protection afforded to individuals under EU law.[103] It follows from this case law that the power to suspend the implementation of a contested decision derives upon national judicial authorities from the EC customs law itself, were these authorities not entrusted with such a power by national legislation.

Finally, the ECJ has also specified some criteria to be applied when several procedures are available to individuals against customs administrative decisions.[104] First, the ECJ recalls that the national customs authorities are competent for applying substantive EU customs law and their decisions may be challenged before the national courts under Article 243 of the CCC; those courts may make a reference to the Court of Justice for a preliminary ruling. In contrast, the special procedure before the Commission provided for the remission of customs duties by the EC customs law is confined to an examination of whether the conditions for remission have been met. Consequently, in order to request annulment of the Commission's decision, a person liable for customs duties may only prove that such conditions are met, while he cannot rely on the argument that the decisions of the competent national authorities subjecting it to payment of the duties at issue were unlawful. The ECJ holds that such a situation does not adversely affect the judicial protection afforded to EU importers. Because of the division of powers between the national and EU authorities, the Commission is not competent to decide on the matter of the withdrawal of the disputed certificates. Moreover, where appropriate, there is nothing to prevent the applicant from raising such arguments in proceedings before the competent national court seeking review of the legality of the decision of the national customs authorities.

The European Court of Justice, fundamental principles of the European Union's legal order and customs law

In the ZF Zefeser opinion,[105] the Advocate General expressed a far-reaching opinion, based on the premises that 'uniform application of customs law is not only necessary in the light of the customs union's ... importance to the EU, but also of importance in ensuring that the rule of law applies as between authorities and individuals' and by pleading in favour of the need of interpreting the relevant EC customs law in the light of EU fundamental rights. The reasoning is that the Advocate interprets previous ECJ case law in the sense that Member States, because they have competence for the administrative implementation of customs law, are bound in the same way as EU institutions directly by fundamental rights under EU law when applying EC customs law. In particular, from those fundamental rights, the Court has expressly developed a general principle of EU law according to which everyone has a right to fair legal process which applies also in the area of criminal law.[106] It follows, in the Advocate General's view, that the interpretation of the EC customs law must ensure the procedural guarantees provided for by EU law based on Article 6(1) of the ECHR and Article 47 of the Charter of Fundamental Rights of the European Union, and that these guarantees could be circumvented if, for instance, a Member State were entitled to create an additional and competing jurisdiction on criminal matters, especially by allocating power to the customs authorities, which are part of the executive branch of the State.

The ECJ's judges do not discuss such issues, because they satisfied themselves with holding that when the customs authorities consider the criminal nature of an act they do not substitute for the judicial authorities, that is, customs do not find that an infringement of criminal law has actually been committed. The right to a judge is not overcome when customs authorities decide upon the criminal nature of an act only in the context and for the purposes of an administrative procedure and solely to enable themselves to apply EC customs law. Moreover, according to the ECJ, such classification is without prejudice to the review which the courts of the Member States may carry out in respect of the decisions of the customs authorities, and cannot impose any restriction on all the consequences which, pursuant to national law, may flow from the decisions of those courts.

However, in another recent preliminary ruling,[107] the Gerlach case, the ECJ adds important findings on the right of business to be heard in administrative customs procedures. The European Commission pleaded that if an administrative procedure provides for the right of the party concerned to be heard, the legal measure at the conclusion of that procedure can be taken only after the party concerned has been heard.[108] According to the ECJ, a belated communication of the time-limit available to the party infringes the right of the interested individual or firm which flows from the relevant provisions of EC customs law, that is, the right to effectively set out its views on the regularity of the customs operation, before the taking of a decision by customs authorities which is addressed to it and which materially affects its interests.[109] On the other hand, the ECJ adds that '[r]espect for this right is a fundamental principle of the community legal order which must be maintained in all proceedings ... which are commenced against a person and which are likely to lead to a measure adversely affecting that person'.[110]

As it has been correctly outlined, 'the present provisions of the Community Customs Code since Gerlach will have to be interpreted in the light of the afore-mentioned fundamental principle of the Community legal order while the EU legislator will have to fully and unconditionally take account of that principle when enacting the Modernized Customs Code'.[111] Indeed, the Commission had already proposed a new provision in this sense, in its Proposal for a Modernized Customs Code. Following the adoption of the Gerlach ruling by the ECJ, Member States in the Council have accepted such burdensome an obligation, now laid down in Article 16(4) of the finalized Regulation for a Modernized Customs Code.

Conclusion

This analysis pleads in favour of the argument that recent EU case law and legislative developments stem not only from the EU legal system itself, but also from the international system of global economic governance brought about by international organizations and networks. States' interactions with and participation in multilateral organizations establishing rules, standards, practices and procedures determine the opportunities, rights and limits business encounter in every national space where they trade or invest. This also contributes to transparency and convergence of national customs laws and practices as well as feeds business' expectations. In such a context, the issue concerning protection of these rights as expressed by global standards and good practices raises at the top of governments' agenda in the customs field.

As for the broader framework of trade facilitation, linkages occur among many international organizations and bodies, thus providing for fertilized humus to, but also challenging efficiency and consistency of, multilateral efforts. The WCO and the WTO, as well as, the World Bank, the United Nations Conference on Trade and Development (UNCTAD), the International Chamber of Commerce (ICC), and the Organization for Economic Co-operation and Development (OECD) all deal with trade facilitation. At the same time, it is difficult to imagine any benefit being limited to parties to bilateral preferential relationship in this field, as the whole national institutional and judicial structure is the core issue.

Business is naturally interested in the domain of trade facilitation, and they are involved in exchange of information, discussion and making of proposals, in all relevant institutional settings. This occurs, for instance, within the WCO, the WTO and the EU. However, modalities and degrees of business' consultation and participation vary from one setting to the other. The WCO has developed strategic partnerships with business in order to elaborate standards and implement operative programmes.[112] The WTO consults business when preparing negotiations among Member governments, but business may also address themselves to their government which may then decide to bring their case within the WTO.[113] The EU provides for direct access to its judicial system by individuals, and has adopted transparent methods of consultation as to legislative initiatives and complaining procedures.[114]

Therefore, business has great opportunities but also potentially high investment costs to get involved in the facilities and remedies available. Continuous monitoring of these different channels may enable them to choose the best strategy in order to pursue both their overall goals and their daily problems.

Notes

1. Among the English literature on customs law, refer in particular to Lyons, T., 2008, *EC Customs Law*, Oxford University Press, Oxford, 2nd edition and Feaver, D. and Wilson, K., 2007, 'Preferential Trade Agreements and their Implications for Customs Services', *Journal of World Trade*, 41(1), pp. 53–74.
2. In this sense refer to Mikuriya, K., 2006, 'The Customs Response to the 21st Century', *Global Trade and Customs Journal*, 1(1), pp. 21–28.
3. Ibid., p. 21.
4. In 1994 the Council adopted the informal operating appellation of World Customs Organization, to more accurately describe its almost universal membership.
5. Currently all the EU Member States, as well as, the EU are signatory parties to the establishing Convention, or they are WCO Members.
6. The Convention establishing a Customs Co-operation Council, signed in Brussels on 15 December 1950, entered into force on 4 November 1952 among seventeen states. The Customs Cooperation Council is rooted in the European response to the Marshall Plan in the aftermaths of the Second World War for the recovery of European economies. Sixteen European states met in Paris in 1947 charged with the preparation of a proposal about the reconstruction plan. Thirteen of these states set up a Study Group on the establishment of one or more inter-European customs unions in compliance with the General Agreement on Trade and Tariffs, which was applied in the meantime. In 1948, the Study Group established an Economic Committee and a Customs Committee. The Economic Committee led to the Organisation for Economic Co-operation and Development (OECD), formerly the Organization for European Economic Cooperation (OEEC). The Customs Committee became the Customs Co-operation Council. The text of this Convention is available at www.wcoomd.org.
7. Preamble to the Convention establishing a Customs Co-operation Council.
8. Among the most successful international treaties promoted by the WCO, there is the Convention on the Harmonized Commodity Description and Coding System, entered into force on 1 January 1988 and ratified by 131 Contracting Parties. For a Synopsis of Position on the Conventions that are sponsored or administered by the Council as of June 2009 refer to http://www.wcoomd.org/files/1. Public files/PDFandDocuments/Conventions/SG0169E1b.pdf.
9. Convention establishing a Customs Co-operation Council, Article III.
10. Ibid., Article III (f).
11. Ibid., Article III (e).
12. In the WCO context, trade facilitation means the avoidance of unnecessary trade restrictiveness. The Procedures and Facilitation Sub-Directorate of the WCO primarily deals with the simplification and harmonization of Customs procedures.

13. Cf. www.wcoomd.org.
14. These Conventions are international treaties, the negotiations phase of which takes place within the WCO. The drafted text is then signed by the Council and ratified by those Contracting Parties and, if so provided, other states that want to do so. These instruments are managed according to the international law of treaties. However, this does not mean that their provisions are binding or are self-executing obligations for signatory parties. They may also have a flexible content which nevertheless may result in harmonization of parties' norms and practices.
15. There are 56 Contracting Parties as of April 2008.
16. Revised Kyoto Convention, Article 8. All EU Member States, except Malta and Romania, as well as, the EU are Contracting Parties.
17. Ibid., Article 2.
18. Ibid., Article 6.
19. Ibid., Article 14.
20. Ibid., Preamble.
21. Significantly, such a right has been upgraded since the original Kyoto Convention, where it appeared in the optional Annex H.1. cf. http://www.unece.org/trade/kyoto/ky-h1-e0.htm.
22. Acceptance of a Recommendation means acceptance of a condition for application that implicitly commits administrations, insofar as possible, to implementing its provisions. Acceptance is manifested by customs administration through notification to the WCO in writing, specifying the date and conditions of application. Before deciding whether to accept a Recommendation, Members must compare principles and conditions of the Recommendation with those of national legislation and administrative implementing circulars, in order to assess whether they conform fully, partially or at all. Where national provisions are not applicable or are incompatible with principles and conditions set by the recommendation, national law must be amended or, where incompatible, commentaries must be made to the WCO on the conditions of application at the time of acceptance regarding the corresponding provisions of the Recommendation. As it may be seen, such indications, which have no legal value, resemble or seem to invoke the procedure of treaty reservations, transferring the mechanism in the sphere of non-binding intergovernmental cooperation with appropriate means. If this were a sustainable interpretation, it could be argued that it strengthens the argument for a modality of international cooperation which aims for harmonization but pursues it in soft ways. For further information on WCO Recommendations and the Procedures for their acceptance refer to www.wcoomd.org.
23. Ibid.
24. Texts available at www.wcoomd.org.
25. As for acceptance by these addressees, the Recommendation only provides for a duty of notification to the Secretary General of the Council of the date from which they will apply the Recommendation and of the conditions of its application.
26. Note that where a national legal order provides for penal jurisdiction for illegal goods this may not be the object of the appeal covered by this Recommendation.

27. For a broad outline and analysis of the WTO the literature on the WTO is vast and highly specialized. Among many other important contributions and handbooks, see Carreau, D., and Juillard, P., 2007, *Droit International Economique*, Dalloz, Paris; Jackson, J., Davey, W. and Sykes, A., 2002, *Legal Problems of International Economic Relations. Cases, Materials and Text on the National and International Regulation of Transnational Economic Relations*, 4th Edition, West Group, Minnesota and Picone, P. and Ligustro, A., 2002, *Diritto Dell'Organizzazione Mondiale del Commercio*, CEDAM, Padova. Suffice to state that GATT 47, an international agreement applied on a provisional basis with a certain institutional support, was absorbed into the WTO, established at the end of the 1986–94 Uruguay Round of negotiations, through the signature of the Final Act at the Marrakesh Ministerial meeting in April 1994. Attached to this Act is the Agreement establishing the WTO, which deals with the institutional provisions of the new Organization, as well as, several Agreements providing for both substantive trade rules, such as, GATT 94 to be read in combination with the previous GATT 47 on trade in goods, and the GATS and the TRIPS Agreements pertaining to trade issues relating to services and intellectual property rights respectively, and procedural rules about the system of dispute settlement (the Dispute Settlement Understanding) and the Trade Policy Review Mechanism, along with several other agreements, protocols and declarations.
28. As of April 2008. The European Communities is an original Member to the WTO together with its Member States.
29. United States – Restrictions on Imports of Cotton and Man-made Fibre Underwear, Report of the Appellate Body, 10/02/1997, WT/DS24/AB/R, Paragraph 7.65.
30. Idem.
31. European Communities – Measures Affecting Importation of Certain Poultry Products, Report of the Appellate Body, 13/07/1998, WT/DS69/AB/R, Paragraph 269.
32. Idem.
33. Argentina – Measures Affecting the Export of Bovine Hides and the Import of Finished Leather, Report of the Panel, 19/12/2000, WT/DS155/R, Paragraphs 11.71–11.72.
34. Idem.
35. Idem. Indeed, there is no requirement in Article X.3(a) that it apply only to 'unwritten' rules.
36. Idem.
37. Idem.
38. European Communities – Selected Customs Matters, Report of the Appellate Body, 13 November 2006, WT/DS315/AB/R, Paragraph 294.
39. European Communities – Selected Customs Matters, Report of the Panel, 16 June 2006, WT/DS315/R, Paragraph 7.520.
40. Idem.
41. Ibid., Paragraph 7.524.
42. European Communities – Selected Customs Matters, Report of the Appellate Body, op. cit., Paragraph 298.
43. Ibid., Paragraphs 301–302.

44. World Trade Organization, Doha Ministerial Conference, Ministerial declaration, adopted on 14 November 2001, WT/MIN(01)/DEC/1, item 27. Members agreed that the negotiations 'shall aim to clarify and improve relevant aspects of Articles V, VIII and X of the GATT 1994 with a view to further expediting the movement, release and clearance of goods, including goods in transit'. Negotiations also aim at 'enhancing technical assistance and support for capacity building in this area' and at developing 'provisions for effective cooperation between customs or any other appropriate authorities on trade facilitation and customs compliance issues'.

45. Modalities are set in Annex D of the so-called 'July Package', Doha Work Programme, Decision Adopted by the General Council on 1 August 2004, WT/L/579.

46. Idem.

47. World Trade Organization, Negotiating Group on Trade Facilitation, TN/TF/W/43/Rev.19, 30 June 2009. Further information is available at www.wto.org.

48. Ibid., p. 8.

49. Ibid., p. 12.

50. ECJ, Opinion 1/75, Local Cost Standard, [1975] ECR 1355. The Treaty establishing the European Community (ECT) provisions on the custom union and the common commercial policy constitute the primary sources of EC customs law. They establish a customs union through the abolition of trade barriers among Member States and a Common Customs Tariff, Articles 26 and 133 ECT. For these purposes, the EC is entitled to take measures strengthening "customs cooperation between Member States and between the latter and the Commission". However, the application of national criminal law or the national administration of justice is excluded from customs cooperation's scope, Article 135 ECT. In combination with such provisions, Article 131 ECT, the EC has exclusive competence to regulate all matters covered by the Common Commercial Policy through regulations or international agreements based on uniform principles, Article 133 ECT.

51. Council of the European Union, Decision 2003/231/EC, OJ L 86, 3 April 2003, pp. 21–45.

52. Council Decision 2007/668/EC, OJ L 274, 18 October 2007, pp. 11–14.

53. By virtue of Article 300(7) ECT agreements concluded by the EC are binding on the institutions of the EU and on Member States.

54. These provisions establish general standards or requirements and allow a large margin of choice to the Parties. Refer to Lux, M., 2006, 'EU Customs Law and International Law', *World Customs Journal* 1(1), pp. 19–29, for a review of this.

55. According to Article 6(2) of the Treaty on the European Union, 1992, the EU must respect fundamental rights, as guaranteed by the European Court of Human Rights (ECHR) and as they result from the constitutional traditions common to the Member States, as general principles of Community law.

56. Council Regulation (EEC) Number 2913/92 establishing the Community Customs Code, OJ L 302, 19 October 1992, pp. 1–50. The CCC is among the main instruments constituting the legislative framework for customs administration in the EU, together with its Implementing Regulation, Commission

Regulation (EEC) Number 2454/93, OJ L 253, 11 November 1993, pp. 1–766 and the Customs Tariff, Council Regulation (EEC) No 2658/87 on the tariff and statistical nomenclature and on the Common Customs Tariff, OJ L 256, 7 September 1987, pp. 1–675.

57. Council Regulation (EEC) No 2913/92, Article 243(1).
58. Ibid., Article 246.
59. Ibid., Article 4(5).
60. Ibid., Article 6(3).
61. According to Article 10 ECT Member States are responsible for taking all measures necessary for the proper implementation and application of EU law.
62. Council Regulation (EEC) No 2913/92, Article 243(1).
63. Ibid., Article 245.
64. Ibid., Article 243(2).
65. Idem.
66. Ibid., Article 244.
67. Ibid., Article 7.
68. Lux, M., and Larrieu P.-J., 2006, 'Proposal for a Modernized Community Customs Code: Reconciling Technical Progress with Simpler Law in the Interest of Increasing Competitiveness in the EU', *Global Trade and Customs Journal*, 1(2), pp. 53–71.
69. The courts of the Member States are competent to determine any dispute in instances where jurisdiction is not expressly conferred on the ECJ or on the CFI.
70. With certain expections, Member States' courts against whose decision there is no judicial remedy under national law are obliged to refer such quesitons to the ECJ, refer to ECJ, Case C-290/01, *Derudder et Cie* (2004) ECR I-02041 for an understanding of how the preliminary ruling system operates.
71. This interaction is governed by European Commission's Communication to the European Parliament and the European Ombudsman on relations with the complainant in respect of infrigements of community law, Com(2002)141def., OJ C 244, 10 October 2002, pp. 5–8.
72. Ibid., Paragraph 2 of the Annex.
73. However, only the ECJ has competence to interpret EC law.
74. Article 226 ECT ff.
75. Refer to http://ec.europa.eu/civil_society/code/dealing_en.htm.
76. Article 194 ECT.
77. European Parliament Decision 94/262/ECSC, EC, Euratom, OJ L 113 , 4 April 1994, pp. 15–18.
78. Council Regulation (EC) No 3286/94, OJ L 349, 31 December 1994, pp. 71–78.
79. Refer to Rovetta, D., The European Community Joins the World Customs Organization: Time to Create a WCO Dispute Settlement Mechanism?, 2008, *Global Trade and Customs Journal*, 3(1), pp. 51–52.
80. Cited above footnotes 38 and 39.
81. Rovetta, D., and Lux, M., 2007, 'The US Challenge to the EC Customs Union', *Global Trade and Customs Journal*, 2(5), pp. 195–207.
82. Ibid., p. 199.

83. European Commission, Implementing the Community Lisbon Programme – Proposal for a Regulation of the European Parliament and of the Council laying down the Community Customs Code (Modernized Customs Code), COM(2005) 608 final, 30 November 2005.
84. Regulation (EC) No. 450/2008 of the European Parliament and of the Council of 23 April 2008, OJL 145, 4 April 2008, p. 1.
85. COM(2005) 608 final, p. 18.
86. Ibid., p. 2.
87. Idem.
88. Idem., p. 19.
89. Article 23(2) of the Modernized Customs Code.
90. Article 246 of the Code.
91. Article 22 of the previous Modernized Customs Code.
92. Added by the Council Common Position, (EC) No. 17/2007, OJC E/2007/298, 11 December 2007 p. 1.
93. Article 26(2) of the proposed Modernized Customs Code states that Member States shall ensure that the appeals procedure enables the prompt correction of decisions taken by the customs authorities.
94. The Commission provides for a compilation of ECJ's case law in customs and customs-related matters initiated from 1995 to 2006, for which refer to http://ec.europa.eu/taxation_customs/resources/documents/common/infringements/case_law/court_cases_customs_1995-2006_en.pdf.
95. Although there is not specific case law on the issue in the field of customs, in a case involving fiscal authorities the ECJ recalled a consolidated case law according to which, in order to determine whether a body making a reference is a court or tribunal for the purposes of Article 234 ECT, which is a question governed by Community law alone, the Court takes account of a number of factors, such as whether the body is established by law, whether it is permanent, whether its jurisdiction is compulsory, whether its procedure is *inter partes*, whether it applies rules of law and whether it is independent. But relevantly, the expression 'court or tribunal' within the meaning of Article 234 ECT can mean only an authority acting as a third party in relation to the authority which adopted the contested decision. ECJ, Case C-516/99, Schmid, [2002] ECR I-04573.
96. ECJ, Case C-495/03, Intermodal Transports BV, [2005] ECR I-08151.
97. Ibid., Paragraphs 38–41, and 45.
98. ECJ, Case C-62/06, ZF Zefeser, [2007] ECR I.
99. Opinion of Advocate General Trstenjak delivered on 3 May 2007, Case C-62/06, ZF Zefeser, [2007] ECR I. The Advocates General assist the Court. They are responsible for presenting, with complete impartiality and independence, an opinion in the cases assigned to them, which is not binding upon judges.
100. ECJ, Case C-1/99, Kofisa Italia Srl, [2001] ECR I-00207.
101. Ibid., Paragraph 36.
102. Ibid., Paragraph 41.
103. ECJ, Case C-334/95, Krüger, [1997] ECR I-04517; Case C-130/95, Bernd Giloy, [1997] ECR I-04291; Case C-226/99, Siples, [2001] ECR I-00277; Case C-1/99, Kofisa, op. cit.

104. Articles 235 to 239 of the CCC and Articles 878 to 909 of the Implementing Regulation.

105. Opinion of Advocate General, Case C-62/06, ZF Zefeser, op. cit.

106. See above, Section 4.

107. ECJ, Case C-44/06, Gerlach, [2007] ECR I. The same customs issue is dealt with in Case C-526/06, Road Air Logistics Customs BV, [2007] ECR I, Case C-230/06, Militzer and Münch, [2007] ECR I.

108. Ibid., Paragraph 29.

109. Ibid., Paragraph 37.

110. ibid., Paragraph 38, emphasis added.

111. Rovetta, D., 'Good News from Luxembourg: General Principles of Community Law and the European Convention on Human Rights are Relevant for the Application of EC Customs Law', 2007, *Global Trade and Customs Journal*, 2(10), p. 365.

112. Such as the major initiative on the SAFE Framework of Standards, adopted in 2005.

113. cf. Bronckers, M., Private Appeals to WTO Law: An Update, 2008, *Journal of World Trade*, 42(2), pp. 245–260 for a detailed analysis of channels available to economic operators for appeals to the WTO.

114. The Trade Contact Group (TCG) provides a platform for regular consultation with trade representatives from the logistic field. cf. http://ec.europa.eu/taxation_customs/customs/policy_issues/customs_trade_cons ultations/index_en.htm.

Part III
Competitive and Managerial Issues in International Business

14
Intellectual Property Rights as a Means of Competitiveness

Laurent Manderieux

Many firms acknowledge the importance of Intellectual Property Rights (IPR) as an important source of competitiveness. Public authorities are progressively sharing their approach and, indeed, it is the aim of the European Union, as well as, that of the US and most OECD countries, to focus on the creation of a knowledge-based economy. In a knowledge-based economy wealth is created by transforming knowledge into value, that is, mostly into IPRs. As a result, the European Union, as its strategy for the future of the region, as well as, most OECD countries has developed political, legislative and operational IPR strategies to assist firms and economies.

Contrary to property rights on tangible goods, IPRs represent intangible rights and the concept of property on intangible goods, although rooted in Roman law, finds its modern origins in the philosophy of John Locke.[1] Intellectual property rights have rapidly developed since the nineteenth century, and this concept is now generally accepted as being the main source of promoting innovation, as well as, a source of wealth creation, although some academics and several non-Governmental Organizations (NGO) regularly challenge its merits, legitimacy or functioning.

The importance of intellectual property rights for business and best intellectual property practices

Intellectual property rights transform knowledge into value. For firms, as well as, investors IPRs allow the transformation of a knowledge driven process into a value that can be traded in the marketplace.

Being based on knowledge creation, the territory of intellectual property is, in itself, a territory open to unlimited growth and potential wealth.

There are many different IPRs that allow much opportunity for firms due to the fact that each of them protects a specific aspect of knowledge creation. For instance copyright protects expressions of ideas; patents protect inventive concepts that are industrially applicable; industrial design protects the ornamental element of products; geographical indications protect know-how linked to a determined territory; and trademarks protect consumers and honest trade. The economic value of these IPRs derives from the legal mechanisms that permit their granting, either through registration or automatically, and their enforcement.

Should control be very strong the granting of an IPR has strong value. Conversely, should it be weak, or should granting be automatic, such as, copyright, the strength of the IPR is weakened. This value is also influenced by the efficiency of enforcement mechanisms of IPRs that largely differ from one country to another, and from an intellectual property right to another. In particular, the effectiveness of court procedures at national level, as well as, the efficacy of police and customs authorities has a direct effect on strength of an IPR.

IPRs facilitate firm defensive strategies and offensive strategies. For instance, patents serve firms in both defensively and offensively. Defensively, IPRs ensure that firms' inventions are protected by creating a prohibition on the imitation by competitors of these inventions that are similar to those patented and these also ensure that internal cohesion, by constituting an economic reward for the inventing team, and also by limiting the movement of personnel to another firm and developing products similar to those already invented in their firm of origin. As an offensive strategy, IPRs may be used by firms to force competitors to obtain licences on the patented invention, or to buy the patent. In addition, these IPRs and patents offer to their owners access to markets where they may be traded, assigned or licensed, and also used to raise capital.

The evolution of intellectual property rights

The concept of IPRs was first developed in Europe, to offer protection to firms, innovators and consumers. The first trademark system was created by ancient Rome, whereas the first patent law was enacted by the Senate of the Republic of Venice in 1474. Modern author rights and copyright derive from French and English eighteenth-century legislation. With colonization and European expansion, the concept of IPRs was exported from Europe to the world. The World Trade Organization (WTO) agreement of 1994 on trade-related aspects of intellectual property rights (TRIPS), includes for the first time intellectual property protection in a comprehensive international agreement and represents a worldwide acceptance of the importance of IPRs for trade and firms. This also represents a global acceptance of a European instigated concept on how innovation and knowledge can be traded.

The territorial nature of intellectual property rights

IPRs were developed in European countries as a concept for dynamizing their economies: IPRs were developed as privileges granted by the state, normally on a temporary basis, such as, up to 20 years for patents, to reward creative work by an individual or a firm. The privilege, or monopoly, applies within the borders of the state granting the IPR. Intellectual property was therefore not developed as a concept of international law. It developed as a branch of law in national legislation and, as a result of these origins IPRs are always granted on a territorial basis, that is, country per country. This considerable burden for firms is alleviated by numerous international treaties that permit minimum standards and mutual recognition of rights, such as, patents, trademarks, industrial designs and other IPRs, in particular, the Paris Convention for the Protection of Industrial Property, 1883 and regularly updated since, the Berne Convention for the Protection of Literary and Artistic Works 1886 also regularly updated since then, the Patent Cooperation Treaty (PCT) 1970, the European Patent Convention, and the World Trade Organization Agreement on Trade Related Aspects of Intellectual Property Rights (WTO TRIPS), to which any state joining the WTO automatically subscribes.[2]

In particular, the TRIPS agreement, Articles 9 to 39, establishes a detailed list of IPRs that are protected and relates them with already existing IP Conventions administered by the World Intellectual Property Organization (WIPO), the Organization of the United Nations System competent for intellectual property, and the depository of most intellectual property treaties. The TRIPS agreement also defines minimum standards for each category of IPR, as well as, compulsory principles for their enforcement, including civil, administrative and criminal measures. As a result, although IPR protection is in theory fully territorially based and left to national laws, the TRIPS agreement ensures that national laws are harmonized and become similar from one country to another.

The new borders for patents and intellectual property rights

In an open trade environment, the promotion of any firm's business basis is guaranteed by IPR protection abroad. Patenting and licensing abroad form part of the classical strategy of any innovative firm. The most effica-cious firms use all categories of IPRs to ensure protection of their know-ledge creation. They also apply them to knowledge cross-fertilization due to interdisciplinary cooperation and inter-organizational coopera-tion, such as, between universities and firms, resulting in the virtuous circle of creation of even more knowledge and, therefore, more IPRs to manage. As a result, these new borders offer new business models for firms.

Patents and trademarks: the major intellectual property rights of international business

The most valuable IPRs, patents and trademarks, are considered as being the most important, due to the strength of the protection that they offer to their owners. Indeed, patents and trademarks are granted by a state, with its seal affixed to them, further to an examination mechanism, of a formal nature and also often of substantive character. The registration mechanism applicable to patents and trademarks differs considerably from procedures applicable to copyright, for which protection is easy to obtain, as it is granted without formalities on an automatic basis, but is hard to enforce. The legal mechanisms applicable to patents and trademarks that should be considered by international firms are mostly harmonized from one country to another.

A patent may be characterized as a property title granted by the state, in compliance with national laws, to protect an invention. However, this property right has some limitations based on the public interest. A patent is the main mechanism used for the promotion of inventions and innovations and as such patents transform creative knowledge into value. In order to be patented, an invention must be: patentable, that is, national laws establish the patentable subject matters; industrially applicable; new or novel; and non-obvious, that is, with an inventive step; sufficiently disclosed in the patent application.

The economic value of patents results from legal mechanisms for their granting/registration, their enforcement opportunities, that is, whether opposition by third parties are available or not or whether streamlined patent litigation procedures are available or not, and, as indicated, whether business strategies related to patents can be defensive and offensive.

There are many registration mechanisms that are applicable, that present various advantages and disadvantages, such as, national patents, regional patent systems, in particular the European Patent Organization

(EPO) system and the worldwide granting system, under the Patent Cooperation Treaty (PCT).

National laws establish the patentable subject matter, as well as the criteria for industrial applicability, novelty, inventive steps and disclosure and these must comply broadly with international principles, such as, the Paris Convention for the Protection of Industrial Property, and the WTO TRIPS. National laws establish the examination system applicable, such as, either formal and substantive examination or formal examination only. A system that includes substantive examination takes more granting time, is more costly for the patentee, but also provides a stronger patent title as the merits of the invention are verified by the state.

Two main regional and international systems exist that assist firms in overcoming the burden of being forced to file national patent applications in many countries and languages. These are the EPO granting system in Europe and on a worldwide basis, the PCT. These are international granting routes that permit firms obtain patents in two or more countries on the basis of a single application. They allow time and cost savings. However, the patent life, licensing and litigation, continue to be subject to national law.[3] Patents have a life on the marketplace: and may be assigned or licensed. Licences may be on a voluntary basis through licensing contracts, which may include technology transfer; or alternatively, licences may perform the function of striking a balance between public and private interests, such as, compulsory licences that state authorities may grant.

Patents may also be challenged during their life through litigation. The granting of a patent can be challenged for not respecting the national criteria for patentability, or the patent owner may have to defend it against its infringement and, as for any type of IPR, the patent owner also polices. As a result of this principle, drafting of patents and of licensing contracts is most important. As in most branches of commercial law, litigants have the option between resorting to national courts or to arbitration mechanisms.

In the context of globalization and digitalization, patenting abroad has had a double digit increase of yearly patent registrations and this phenomenon is also extending to developing economies, as, either these countries' markets are growth markets, or counterfeiting risks from these countries could threaten other markets and therefore it justifies the costs of local patent protection. Also, as patents are very convenient for their owners, firms have managed to obtain regular extensions in many countries of the patentable subject matters. In particular, patents on software are now accepted in the US and in many non EU countries.

Trademarks permit fair business for innovating firms as they offer a secure product identification system for consumers at national and international levels. They allow competition between products in the market in a fair manner. More specifically, a trademark can be any sign, such as a word, number, picture, design, or advertising slogan, used by a firm to identify its own products or services that distinguish them from other goods or services made or assigned by competitors. There are seven main categories of marks. These are denominative marks or names, figurative marks, such as, logos, complex marks, a combination of the previous, sound marks, coloured marks, three-dimensional marks and marks containing fragrances.

Although some rights may exist due to trademark use, registration is the main tool for the protection of a mark. The registration of a mark confers to the holder in the state concerned the absolute right to use the mark, normally for 10 years, and may be renewed an unlimited number of times. In order to be registered a mark must be distinctive. It is, therefore, not possible to register signs made up exclusively of general denominations of products or services or descriptive indications which refer to the products or services. Words, figures or signs contrary to law, public order or morale, coats-of-arms, flags, official emblems and other signs considered in International Conventions, signs which would infringe the copyright, industrial property right or any other exclusive right of a third person, or signs likely to deceive the public, on the geographic origin, the nature or quality of the product may not be the subject of a mark.

Well-known names may be registered as a trademark only by those who have the right to do so, or otherwise by third parties who have the agreement of the former. A mark must be new and this is why a prior search is strongly advisable before filing a trademark. The novelty of a trademark is evaluated in every country by national authorities with reference to 'classes', that is, for the goods or services for which the mark is applied.[4] Trademarks can be removed from the Registry if a registered mark is not used for several years, normally five consecutive years, after the date of registration or if its distinctive character is lost, or if it is, or becomes, deceptive.

Depending on systems used, marks may have various strengths and weaknesses, with economic and legal consequences. The national trademark system represents the historical system. A mark is registered by the applicant on a country-by-country basis. In the European Union, it is possible to obtain a Community Trademark at the Office for the Harmonization of the Internal Market (OHIM), located in Alicante: the EU registration system or 'Alicante System'[5] permits a single registration for the whole of the 27 countries. On a worldwide basis, the international registration system, commonly referred to as the 'Madrid System', is administered by WIPO.[6] All regional or international systems alleviate the burden of international business firms of filing series of national procedures.

Intellectual property right licensing and access to the marketplace

The main interest in obtaining patents and trademarks resides in the fact that they may easily be voluntarily licensed under contract between private parties. The basic contractual requirements for such type of contracts are correct identification of the parties and of the objective of the parties, that is, the scope of the licence and clear subject matter, that is, identification of product or process, identification of invention or mark, description of know-how, confidentiality clauses, provisions on access to technical advances or cross licensing, respect of the limitations of the licence and anti-competitive practices, such as, tie-in clauses on exports or patents, a correct definition of the licensee's territory, the exact definition of the permitted field of use, provisions on exploitation in terms of quality, volume, guarantees of knowledge and third parties and on settlement of disputes, duration of the contract. Other contractual requirements include remuneration mechanisms including possibly direct remuneration, lump sums, royalties percentage, fees for consultants and services and indirect remuneration, including income from related operations, dividends, subject to national legislation, cost-sharing between the parties, market information and savings, as well as currency issues well covered. For trademarks, in order to guarantee consumer protection, the contract should also include provisions ensuring a control by the owner over quality standards of the licensee and over conditions of marketing. Control by the owner over the *use* by the licensee (to avoid non-use) should also be established.

Abuse of intellectual property rights

Firms may attempt to abuse their IPRs. This is why, in most OECD countries and other countries, the validity and extension of IPRs can be challenged by competition authorities. The control made by competition authorities may also extend to IP protection and standards, for example, the numerous cases against Microsoft in the US and the EU. Negative practices can consist of firms attempting to conceal their patents while involved in defining standards, or firms attempting to block the adoption of standards involving use of patents owned by a competitor. Good firm practices on IP and standards may consist in firms granting licences to make and sell a standard compliant product and a separate licence for the use of the product. Those who are trying to make use of their IPRs in an unfair way are exposed to the risk of being forced by public authorities to grant a compulsory licence.

The central role of intellectual property for competitiveness

For firms, the European IP landscape is a 'work in progress' area, yet offering many Europe-wide protection tools. Europe's IP protection mechanisms are relatively recent: Thirty years ago, several economic sectors were already integrated in Europe. However, IP laws and practices were left to national authorities. Each country had its own laws and practices for each IPR and this represented a major problem for firms seeking IP protection, and as a result was slowing down innovation potential and competitiveness of firms in Europe, in particular if compared to the US.

Pressure from business circles forced governments to embark in the European harmonization of IP law. The European states did not follow a single path. For patent granting, a specific organization was created: the European Patent Office (EPO), whereas for other IPR harmonization, the European Union is handling European IP integration.

This lack of consistency of 'European IP' is linked to the weakness of the EU Treaties on the subject of intellectual property. This subject matter was not indicated in the EU founding Treaties, and still is not. As a result, any legislation on intellectual property is the product of a legal construction still in progress: the EU legislator uses the general, non IP-specific, provisions of the European Community (EC) Treaty, primarily Articles 308 and 95, as a basis for IP Regulations and Directives.[7]

As only limited legal harmonization seemed possible, the European states opted for a multidirectional/multiple speed method of work. They did so in creating more IPRs, useful for firms, and rendering the existing rights stronger acting in all IP fields, such as, trademarks, copyright, patents, but acting only as and when possible.

Three levels of integration

Three levels of integration exist: fully integrated rights, for trademarks and designs, partly integrated rights under the EU aegis, and partly integrated rights for patents under the EPO aegis. The main European successes relate to trademarks and designs. New EU-wide integrated IPRs were created, respectively by EU Regulation creating the Community Trade Mark (Regulation 40/94) and EU Regulation creating the Community Industrial Design (Regulation 6/2002). Both enable firms to obtain a single EU trademark or a single industrial design right valid and enforceable easily in the 27 EU countries, and have met real success, as they established IP rights that are key to firms. National marks and designs do survive in parallel but in case of conflict, the EU wide right prevails upon the national right. The procedure to obtain and defend the right is a single one for all countries, simple and inexpensive.

Being under the aegis of the EU, the IPR is a single one, is granted for the whole EU, the 27 member states in one right, and is also applicable and enforceable EU-wide; if the right is judged void or invalid, it is cancelled by an EU jurisdiction for the whole EU.[8]

Whenever full integration was not yet mature, European national laws were partly streamlined: EU Directives bring closer the IPRs governed by national laws. In this case, harmonized IPRs are still governed at national level, but the related national laws are supposed to be only marginally diverging from one country to another. However, these directives are often hampered by slowness in their transposition into national laws by each of the EU countries, and often they contain too many options/exceptions that, for some of them, limit their effectiveness.

The most important Directives in the field of IP relate to copyright-related legislation; and these are: the Database Directive,1996/9, establishing *sui generis* rights for protection of new databases that cannot be protected by copyright, the Directive on the legal protection of computer programs 1991/250, establishing the principle of software protection in the EU by copyright law, the Directive on the harmonization of certain aspects of copyright and related rights in the information society, 2001/29, also referred to as the EU Copyright Directive or EUCD, that is, extending copyright protection to the digital environment.

Several other Directives were however less successful, in particular in the field of patents. With reference to biotechnology, the EU enacted a Directive on biotechnological inventions (1998/44) in order to promote the take-off of the biotech industry in Europe. However, the Directive became a source of friction between the EU and its Member States for diverging implementing laws. On software patents there is no consensus on the draft Directive on computer-implemented inventions, whereas in the US there has been a clear system for many years. On patents in general, the EU law-making process is totally blocked despite a 30 year-long negotiation: a Community patent would be extremely convenient for business as it would reduce granting and litigation costs, and streamline patent procedures in general, just as the Community Trademark (CTM) does for trademarks. Current issues under discussion relate to translation of patents into national languages. Several countries are insisting that their language be an official one for patents but, if too many translations are compulsory, firms would have no cost advantage compared to the present system and no interest in the new system. Also several states have constitutional reservations on the establishment of an EU-wide jurisdiction on an EU-wide patent right.

For patent granting a Europe-wide mechanism outside of the EU structure, the EPO system, was created in 1973 to meet the needs of innovating firms, for a simple Europe-wide patent system. Most countries of the continent are party to it, including Switzerland and Turkey. Therefore, the EPO system is not in the European Union, although all EU countries are party to it. Patents may still be granted by each country through a national procedure but in accordance with the EPO rules firms may alternatively follow a convenient route to obtain national patent protection in numerous European countries through a single centrally EPO administered procedure. The centralized procedure may cover up to all EPO countries, has more limited costs than a multiple use of national routes for the protection of an invention, is efficient, takes place in only one of the three EPO working languages, English, French and German, and allows the granting of high-quality patents. The EPO system is still incomplete: once a 'European patent' has been granted by the EPO, its 'European' character disappears as its unitary form ends. At this stage the patentee is required to file expensive translations of the full patent at the national patent offices of most countries in which protection is to be enjoyed, and to renew annually patent rights in each state according to the various national applicable fees and is subject to national courts for patent disputes, including licensing disputes, and to decisions from courts that may be different from one country to the other. In particular, each country has its own jurisprudence and its own legal system, whether civil law or common law.

As a result of pressure from business, an impressive but incomplete IPR harmonization is taking place in Europe, for better competitiveness of business operators. Trademarks and industrial designs are now widely integrated in the EU, and a partly integrated system exists for patents under the EPO. While business operators are still awaiting an EU deadlock on patents, the EPO is successfully working on further refining its system and reducing its current weaknesses, in particular, on translation requirements for granted patents, and on nationally judged litigation.[9] Thus the next challenges that Europe is facing in order to improve its competitiveness thanks to IP are relating to patents[10] and copyright. In the latter field, current directives contain good basic principles, but allow too many exceptions. This is impairing the creation of an EU copyright industries market. Any harmonization in this respect is in any case expected to remain limited, due to differences between continental Europe's author's right system and British influenced copyright system. Whatever the current limits of 'European IP' may be, statistics are in any case clearly showing that firms massively prefer European IPRs (EPO system, EU Trademarks and Designs) whenever they exist, and that business has therefore anticipated politicians in opting for a European IPR protection.[11]

Intellectual property as a challenge for emerging economies: China

IPR protection for improving firm competitiveness is not the privilege of Europe and OECD economies. Whereas economies from industrialised countries are trying to reinforce IPR protection and to avoid counterfeiting from developing countries, the pressure for a change in innovative firm approaches is now also reaching firms in emerging markets. In countries such as China, an impressing transformation is taking place, from an economy of imitation to an economy of innovation. In China, government leaders are encouraging this change, stimulated by the globalization effect; they clearly consider this change with an imperial ambition: if China, as Permanent Member of the Security Council of the United Nations, could combine quantity, quality and novelty, its population's well-being could be increased, although the process would take place slowly it is important politically, and its weight in global affairs could be enormous. Patent statistics show a change of strategy from Chinese firms: they now massively patent in China, but also in the rest of the world.[12] Many other developing economies are following a similar path that contradicts the simplistic and somehow Euro-centric approaches that counterfeiting is the only threat for the economy of industrialized countries, and that their competitiveness on innovative capacity and abilities is not threatened. Still, the rapid development of counterfeiting and piracy is impairing a clear vision in OECD countries of the fundamental change in the business models of firms from developing emerging economies.

Counterfeiting as a threat to firms in developed economies

Counterfeiting and piracy is remaining a current issue for two reasons, the combination of digital revolution and globalization which permits and facilitates production and sale of goods anywhere in the world. With the acceleration of international trade, counterfeited and pirated goods can circulate and hide easily among enormous quantities of legitimate goods. Although it is often a domestic issue, such as, sufficient monitoring and controlling, it has become an international trade issue and a worldwide issue handled in many fora, such as, the WTO, WCO, WIPO, and the Group of Eight.

Both the EU and the US have developed a dynamic reaction against counterfeiting and piracy. The EU has built a sophisticated anti-counterfeiting system, although this system only developed recently, as a result of diverging national interests. The US reaction is based on trade retaliation against countries allowing counterfeiting. The EU passed numerous legislation and adopted a strategy: not less than four key texts were adopted: Regulation 3295/94/CE: border measures: marks, industrial designs, copyright; Regulation 241/99 CE: border measures: extension to patents; Regulation 1383/03/CE: consolidation, reinforcement of border measures and extension to plant varieties and geographical indications plus single application form; Directive 2004/48/CE: harmonization and facilitation of legal proceedings, and seizure and destruction of goods.

In addition, the EU strategy for enforcement of IPRs in third countries introduced in 2004 establishes mechanisms for identifying priority countries, that is, the most problematic countries in terms of IPR violations; awareness raising, such as, promoting initiatives to raise public awareness about the impact of counterfeiting, including a guidebook on the enforcement of Intellectual Property Rights; and political dialogue, incentives and technical co-operation, ensuring that technical assistance provided to third countries focuses on IPR enforcement, especially in priority countries, including exchanging ideas and information with WIPO, the US or Japan. Other procedures include IPR mechanisms in multilateral, regional and bilateral agreements: raising enforcement concerns in the framework of these agreements more systematically; dispute settlement/sanctions: in case of non-compliance with the required standards of IPR protection; and the establishment of public–private partnerships: supporting, or participating in, local IP networks in relevant third countries.

The US, beyond its approach based on trade retaliation against countries allowing counterfeiting, developed the STOP initiative, or the 'Strategy of Targeting Organized Piracy' initiative, a government plan to combat piracy and counterfeiting in the US and around the world.

The STOP initiative is a comprehensive programme designed to confront intellectual property theft and to dismantle criminal networks that traffic in counterfeit and pirated goods. It seeks to empower US firms to protect their IPRs, to stop trade in counterfeit products at US borders, to keep such products out of the global supply chain, and to ensure that American firms receive the benefits of the trade agreements signed by the US. Although formatted differently, the US STOP initiative is relatively similar to the EU initiative.

Conclusion

As briefly described, IPRs are major sources of competitiveness for firms. This is why business circles are lobbying energetically, and to date mostly successfully, for better harmonized IPR granting procedures, and stronger granting mechanisms that would be more efficient and effective in the international environment. Recent developments in Europe perfectly illustrate this issue.

The acceleration of globalization and digitalization renders the economic value of intangible goods more and more important. Emerging economies are now also starting to value their importance for their growth. However, in a globalized trade environment, the national nature of IPRs becomes a drawback to their effectiveness. This is why there are wide business interests for a further international harmonization of IPR granting and life in Europe and the world.

The emergence of intellectual property as a better system for management of knowledge in order to promote firms' competitiveness is also raising the issue of new borders and limits for IPRs. The expansion of patents that, in the US and in many countries, may now cover software, as well as the emergence of 'business method patents', may result in an excess of patents that may become business tolls instead of business tools. The extension of the Digital Rights Management systems (DRMs) in the field of copyright may limit the traditional flexibilities for public interest offered by copyright law, and has provoked the emergence of a counter-business model, based on open approaches.

Excess protection may bring adverse reactions to classical IPR protection. Intellectual property protection, although massively favoured by firms, is therefore remaining a fast evolving subject, at the crossroads between issues of competitiveness, consumers' rights, development, public access to knowledge and individual freedom.

Notes

1. Locke, J., *Two Treatises of Government*, 1689, and *An Essay Concerning Human Understanding*, 1690.
2. The list of WIPO administered Treaties is accessible from the WIPO website http://www.wipo.int/treaties/en/ that also contains summaries of these Treaties.
3. The PCT section of the WIPO website: http://www.wipo.int/pct/en/index. html contains complete information on PCT procedures. The EPO website, under http://www.epo.org/patents/Grant-procedure.html contains regularly updated information on EPO procedures.
4. The Nice Agreement, 2001, administered by WIPO, http://www.wipo.int/ treaties/en/classification/nice/summary_nice.html, and regularly updated, establishes a classification for all products and services, allowing an easy search of existing trademarks in databases.
5. An exhaustive presentation of the Alicante System can be found on the OHIM website, http://oami.europa.eu/en/mark/role/brochure/br1en.htm.
6. The Madrid Agreement pages of the WIPO website, http://www.wipo. int/treaties/en/registration/madrid/summary_madrid.html, contain a full description of the system.
7. As this situation is imperfect, political EU government declarations intend to reinforce the EU's IP mandate. For instance, the EU Charter of Fundamental Rights of 2000 that declares IP as a protected freedom , Article 17.2, or the EU Lisbon Declaration of 2000 and Barcelona Declaration of 2002 that establish target objectives for boosting Europe's research activities and competitiveness. In addition, the European Court of Justice established that on most IP issues, the EU is empowered to unify and harmonise as it may decide, cf. C-350-92: *Spain* v. *EU Council [1996]* I- ECR 1985 on the term of patents.
8. Apart from marks and designs, some integration took place in the following IP, or IP related, fields. Anti-cyber squatting of the domain name '.eu' (Regulation 733/ 2002); fighting counterfeiting and piracy (Regulation 1383/ 2003), focusing on the enforcement of intellectual property rights, mostly during customs operations; protection of geographical indications; EU Programmes: within the framework of EU financed Programmes, efficient intellectual property guidelines and policies are embedded, which beneficiaries of these programmes must respect, such as, in the Seventh Framework Programme for EU Research, the multi-billion Euro plan financing research projects.
9. Separate Agreements are to cover each of the two issues. The London Agreement of 2000 will soon create in the EPO member states a system of waivers for translations requirements into their national language of European patents, whenever they are subsequently nationally registered. Under the European Patent Litigation Agreement (EPLA), still under negotiation, a central European Patent Court would be established for EPO states, working mostly in English, French and German, and enabling to handle patent infringement and revocation actions at European level.
10. Despite the existence of the EPO system, protection for the same invention in, for instance, the eight largest EU markets currently costs on average five times more than in the US, mostly due to translation costs.

11. EPO complete statistics are accessible through http://www.epo.org/about-us/office/statistics.html. OHIM complete statistics are accessible through http://oami.europa.eu/en/office/stats.htm.
12. Statistics from the Chinese Patent Office (SIPO), http://www.sipo.gov.cn/sipo_English/statistics/ and from WIPO, respectively demonstrate this major change), in China and in emerging economies in general. Cf. http://www.wipo.int/pressroom/en/articles/2007/article_0008.html.

15
Considerations for Trade of Terms of Sales, Documentary Collections and Documentary Credits

Antonio Di Meo

Grand strategies, great works of art and historic scientific discoveries are all accomplished by people with complete mastery of the technical aspects of their field. Similarly, a full understanding of the various aspects of commercial transactions is essential for successful business relations. It is important to recognize from the outset that whatever the business transaction, the buyer and seller both seek to ensure that the counterparty is under the first obligation to honour the main contractual provisions, before having to comply with his part of the agreement.

Unless there is a compromise solution, one of the parties to an agreement will always bear the risk of breach of contract by the other party. To minimize that risk the reliability, creditworthiness and country of residence of the counterparty, the financial sustainability of the business transaction envisaged and the impact on the firm's liquid assets, and the payment instruments best suited to safeguard firm profitability and financial stability must be carefully assessed. Careful assessment of the commercial and financial risks of a business deal means close examination of the terms and conditions of the contractual undertaking in question and a clear understanding of its various phases.

A crucial issue is the delivery of goods by a seller to a buyer. An agreement must be reached as to which party is to bear transport and insurance costs and any customs duties. Most importantly, this is the delicate moment when ownership, or the risk and liability for the goods, passes from seller to buyer.

All these factors were defined with terms and/or abbreviations that are recognized throughout the world. But the very fact of being universally employed led to many divergent interpretations. As a result, the same term and/or abbreviation came to mean different things in different countries, leading to different understandings of aspects such as cost allocation or the rights, duties and liabilities of the parties.

International commercial terms[1]

In an attempt to regulate the apportioning of costs and risks when a seller dispatches goods to a buyer, an international series of 'delivery terms' were established. They are known as the International Commercial Terms, or Incoterms, and define the transportation and delivery of goods. With the enormous growth of international business transactions over the years, they are now universally recognized and adopted. Set down for the first time in 1936 in Paris by the International Chamber of Commerce (ICC), Incoterms have been periodically revised. The latest update was released in 1999 and came into force in 2000 under the title Incoterms 2000.[2]

Aims and object of Incoterms

Incoterms aim to provide a universally accepted interpretation of the main terms covering the transportation and consignment of goods in international trade in order to eliminate misunderstandings generated by different interpretations.

Incoterms deal especially with four key issues. These relate to who pays the main transportation, or carriage, costs; where the goods are to be delivered; where and when title and risks pass from seller to buyer; who pays for all the other costs connected with transportation, such as, issuing of documents, charges, unloading of goods, customs clearance, where necessary, and insurance of goods in transit.

The object of Incoterms is limited to the rights and obligations of the parties, that is, the seller and buyer, under a contract of sale involving a consignment of goods. It is important to understand that Incoterms refer to the sales contract and not to the transport contract. It is equally important to recognize that Incoterms are not statutory laws. They are optional rules and their legal effectiveness resides in the willingness of the parties to adopt them as part of their contractual agreement by specifying as much in the contract with wording such as, 'The parties hereby undertake to regulate their mutual rights and obligations regarding the delivery of the goods on the basis of Incoterms 2000 of the ICC'. Another, simpler option would be to indicate, for instance, a Free on Board (FOB) price followed by the name of the port and referenced 'as per Incoterms 2000 ICC'.

How Incoterms are structured

Incoterms 2000 comprise 13 terms listed in ascending order of obligation for the seller. Each of these is three-letter term and begins with the letter of one of four groups depending on the group to which it belongs. The letters E, F, C and D denotes the four different groups, and these represent respectively, Ex works, Free, Cost and/or Carriage and Delivery. Thus Group E contains a single term -EXW. This is not a group proper though as there is only one term: EXW signifies that all costs and risks pass to the buyer when the merchandise is made available for loading on to some means of transport at the seller's door. Another group, Group F, contains three terms, FCA, FAS, FOB. The terms in this group signify that the seller undertakes to 'free', or make available, the goods to the buyer at an agreed place of departure, delivering them to a carrier named by the buyer, that is, FCA. The seller incurs all costs up to that named place. The place in question may be either the warehouses of the carrier, or the actual means of transport sent by the carrier on which the goods are to be loaded at a place named by the seller, or the quay or wharf of the port alongside the ship, that is, FAS, or on board the ship at the port of departure, that is, FOB. Whichever is relevant, the main cost of transportation, or carriage, is borne by the buyer since the merchandise is 'freed' or delivered in an agreed location at the place of departure. Title and risk pass from seller to buyer at the moment the merchandise is delivered to the carrier indicated by the buyer. Group C contains four terms, CFR, CIF, CPT and CIP. Two terms in this group, CFR and CIF, relate exclusively to transport by sea or inland waterway, from one port to another. The other two terms, CPT and CIP, relate to any type of transport including multi-modal transport. Whereas the main transportation costs are borne by seller, title and risk pass from seller to buyer at departure, that is, at the moment the goods are delivered to a named place of departure, which may be on board ship or at the carrier's premises. It should be noted that the moment at which risks and liability for the goods pass to the buyer is the same for Groups C and F. In particular, the critical moment is the same under terms CPT, CIP and FCA while the critical moment is the same under CFR, CIF and FOB. The other group, Group D contains five terms, DAF, DES, DEQ, DDU and DDP. Group D terms are delivery terms and are the most onerous for the seller who has to bear all costs and risks right up to the arrival of the merchandise at destination. These are outlined in Table 15.1

The following considerations, outlined in Table 15.2, are intended as a practical checklist to assist in ensuring the correct use of Incoterms.

Table 15.1 International Chamber of Commerce Incoterms 2000

Group	Incoterm	Mode of transport
Group E Departure	EXW (Ex works)	Any mode of transport
Group F Major transport cost not paid	FCA (Free Carrier) FAS (Free Alongside Ship) FOB (Free On Board)	Any mode of transport Only maritime transport Only maritime transport
Group C Major transport cost paid	CFR (Cost and Freight) CIF (Cost, Insurance and Freight) CPT (Carriage Paid To) CIP (Carriage and Insurance Paid To)	Only maritime transport Only maritime transport Any mode of transport Any mode of transport
Group D Arrival	DAF (Delivered At Frontier) DES (Delivered Ex Ship) DEQ (Delivered Ex Quay) DDU (Delivered Duty Unpaid) DDP (Delivered Duty Paid)	Any mode of transport Only maritime transport Only maritime transport Any mode of transport Any mode of transport

Source: Adapted from Publication Number 560, Incoterms 2000, ICC-Italy, 1999

Table 15.2 Checklist for the correct use of Incoterms

1 Define the terms and conditions of delivery of goods using Incoterms. Make specific reference to the Incoterm chosen in the contract of sale concluded with the other party.
2 Make sure to use the ICC Incoterms 2000 appropriately, applying them only to the mode of transport for which they are intended, cf. Table 15.1.
3 Be careful not to use former terms now replaced by more recent versions. FOR/FOT – Free on Rail/Free on Truck and FOB AIRPORT, for example, have been replaced by the more general FCA. Similarly, C&F is now CFR. Adopting the updated term will avoid possible misunderstandings caused by the use of non-standard variants.
4 Bear in mind that Incoterms are designed only for use in sales contracts. In other words, Incoterms refer to agreements between seller and buyer, not the arrangement between seller and carrier, for which there is a separate transport agreement. Business operators must give **detailed instructions to their forwarders** based on the Incoterm they have adopted in the sales agreement. This will ensure consistency between the transport and sales contracts.
5 Do not forget that Incoterms regulate only the transfer of risk and the sharing out of costs between seller and buyer, as well as certain customs obligations (if the case), and insurance of the merchandise.
6 Remember the terms CFR, CIF, CPT, CIP signify that the main transport cost is to borne by seller. In other words, they are not 'arrival' but 'departure' terms. This means that title and risks pass to buyer at the country of departure as under Group F terms (FCA, FAS, FOB).

One of the main issues facing business operators selling their goods abroad is to identify the safest way of ensuring they are paid for their deliveries, and to reduce the risk of late or non payment. The seller therefore proposes provisions to ensure payment of the amount owed. The buyer, on the other hand, is anxious to have sufficient liquidity to meet debts, and so attempts to defer payment as long as possible after the delivery of the goods or service. The contrasting interests of the two parties are accommodated in an agreement on the terms and condition of payment. In international trade, the choice of payment terms depends on a series of considerations. These are: the business risk in terms of insolvency of the counterparty, the political and economic condition of the counterparty's or buyer's country, that is, country risk, the feasibility of obtaining insurance coverage on the commercial and/or country risk, the possibility of obtaining information on the creditworthiness and solvency of the counterparty, the rapport between and mutual knowledge of the parties, the negotiating position and particular condition of the market and industry involved, the type of business agreement, that is, contract of sale, distribution, know-how or joint venture, among others, and the supply volumes involved, import practices, customs and regulations in the individual countries, distances, warehousing and mode of transport, the currency regime in the buyer's country, the possibility of credit recovery in the event of non-payment, the possibility of being replaced by other suppliers, and the banking system in the counterparty's country.

Aims of parties to a business transaction

Whereas the buyer will try and ensure the purchase order is honoured, the seller is primarily concerned that the goods and/or services supplied are paid for in compliance with the provisions of the contract.

The main aims for a buyer as party to a business transaction are to receive the specified quality and quantity of goods and/or services at the time(s) and place(s), and in the manner indicated in the contract, to avoid paying the seller the amount due until the latter has honoured his obligations; to plan cash flow to his best advantage, including obtaining funds from a bank; and to defer payment as long as possible after receipt of goods and/or services. Conversely, for a seller the main aims are to deliver the goods and/or services ordered by the delivery dates agreed; to identify the means of ensuring payment for supplies delivered; to receive payment in full from the buyer in the currency stipulated in the agreement; and to ensure that the firm has sufficient liquidity to develop its business.

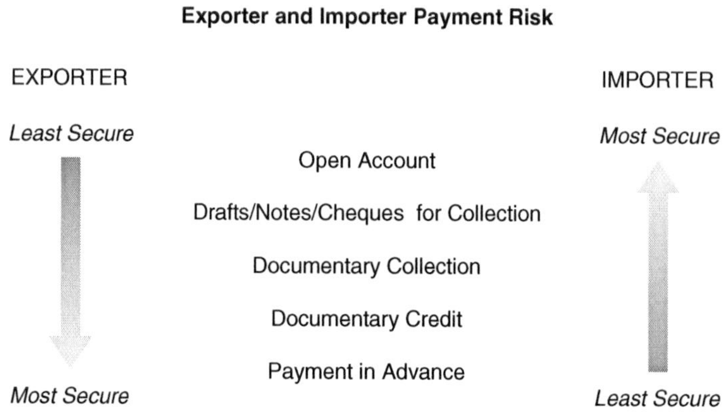

Exporter and Importer Payment Risk

EXPORTER   IMPORTER

Least Secure   *Most Secure*

Open Account

Drafts/Notes/Cheques for Collection

Documentary Collection

Documentary Credit

Payment in Advance

Most Secure   *Least Secure*

Figure 15.1   Payment risk for importers and exporters

The difficulty of finding a compromise between the contrasting requirements and interests of seller and buyer led the international business community to seek alternative payment solutions to bank transfers executed before or after the delivery of goods. These include documentary transactions. Compared to other instruments, such as, an open account or drafts, notes or cheques sent for collection, documentary operations are a form of payment that meet both the seller's payment reassurance requirement and the buyer's requirement to pay only when in receipt of the goods ordered. Two types of documentary payment are widely used in international trade. These are the documentary collection and the documentary credit. The risks associated with payment for both exporters and importers are outlined in Figure 15.1.

Documentary collections

A documentary collection is a form of payment whereby the seller instructs the bank to collect the amount owed for goods delivered to a buyer, or to accept a draft or any other financial document used for obtaining the payment on a specified date, against the presentation of commercial documents such as invoices, transport documents, title documents, packing lists, certificates or other documents referring to the merchandise supplied. Documentary collections have three different forms. These are, documents against payment (D/P), documents against acceptance (D/A) and documents against bank guarantee (D/G).

Documents against payment means that the buyer, in order to take possession of the commercial documents giving title to the goods, is obliged to pay the stated document's amount. This type of payment is also known as cash against documents or CAD. Documents against acceptance means that the buyer may take possession of the title documents on accepting a draft, on signing a promissory note or by a written commitment to pay at a future date. Documents against bank guarantee refers to when a buyer can take possession of the title documents to the merchandise on accepting a draft or signing a promissory note, both payable at a future date, if at the same time a bank issues a bank guarantee in favour of the seller, or guarantees the above mentioned instruments, thereby guaranteeing payment of the amount at maturity should the buyer default or refuse to pay.

Uniform rules for collections

In an attempt to uniform the different interpretations used in international trade and set down a common set of obligations and liabilities for the parties to an agreement, the ICC developed the regulations on 'Uniform Rules for Collections', and more commonly referred to with the abbreviation URC.[3] These rules came into force in January 1996.[4] The parties to a collection are the principal, who is, usually, the seller, and who instructs a bank to collect payment while presenting the bank with the requisite documents and a formal request to collect payment. The remitting bank is the bank to which the principal has entrusted to collect the money owed. On receipt of the documents, the bank complies with the instructions received, transmitting them to the collecting bank. The collecting bank is a bank that, in compliance with the instructions received from the remitting bank, is involved in processing the collection. The presenting bank is the bank that presents the documents to the drawee in compliance with instructions received. This may also be the collecting bank. The drawee, usually the buyer, is presented with the documents in compliance with the collection instructions. The flows in this process are illustrated in Figure 15.2

Contrary to common belief, this form of payment is by no means risk-proof for the creditor. The banks involved are obligated merely to execute the order to collect the amount due according to instructions received from the principal. In other words, banks accept no liability regarding the payment itself or the undertaking to pay on the part of the debtor. They merely follow the collection instructions given, acting in compliance with the URC governing such operations. Nor does a bank assume any liability if instructions issued by them are not performed, even when the collecting bank is specified by the bank in question. Documentary collection is therefore not a failsafe means of securing payment. This

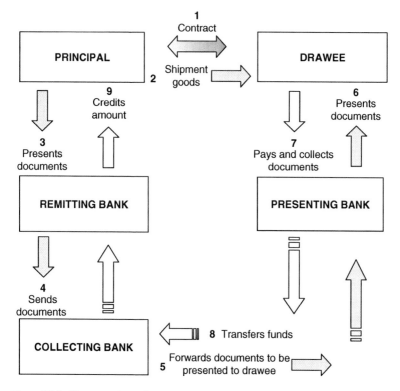

Figure 15.2   Documents against payment

form of settlement is advisable only when there is no country risk in the
form of political or economic instability in the buyer's country; when
there is no issue of customer reliability, that is, buyer's character and
solvency is beyond reproach, as the documentary collection does not
fully safeguard the seller; when there is fungibility of the goods, that is,
a documentary collection is best used only where merchandise can be
sold elsewhere in the event of original buyer non-payment; and, finally,
in terms of transport management, it is advisable not to use either delivery terms in the 'F' group or, especially, the 'Ex Works' group. Group 'C'
Incoterms are preferable since they permit the seller to choose how to
ship the goods.

Documentary credits

A documentary credit[5] is an irrevocable undertaking issued by a bank,
on written instructions from the buyer, the applicant, to honour the

Table 15.3   Aims of parties in a documentary credit

The Seller	Buyer
Does not intend to run the risk of goods ordered and shipped not being collected by the buyer.	Does not want to pay before the goods are shipped.
Wants assurance collection on his credit.	Wants to be sure of receipt the goods ordered at the time and under the terms and conditions agreed.
Wants to ensure that the buyer cannot hold up payment.	Wants to improve liquidity position by obtaining bank financing.
Wants to make goods available only once the above conditions have been realized.	

operation requested in favour of a seller, the beneficiary, against pre-sentation within an expiry date of the requisite documents, provided these are in compliance with the terms and conditions indicated in the documentary credit. The bank's irrevocable undertaking in favour of the beneficiary may be to pay a sum at sight if the credit is available by sight payment or at maturity, in the event of deferred payment, to accept a draft drawn by the beneficiary, payable at sight or at maturity, or negotiate draft(s) and/or documents received by the beneficiary.[6]

A documentary credit is by far the safest means of payment for seller and buyer alike, striking the right balance between the contrasting inter-ests of both parties. It is without doubt the form of payment that offers greatest guarantees to exporting companies since, unlike the other means of payment used by firms throughout the world, remittance to the seller or beneficiary is guaranteed by a bank.

If the seller presents the requisite credit documents in due form, in accordance with the terms and conditions of the credit, the applicable international rules and international standard banking practice, and also within the expiry date specified, payment of the amount due is assured. The undertaking to pay is given directly by the bank and can in no way be revoked or challenged by the buyer. The buyer, however, has the guar-antee that the bank will pay only after ascertaining that the documents are in order. The aims of the parties involved in a documentary credit are outlined in Table 15.3.

It is important to remember that a documentary credit concerns only the documents and not the merchandise, services or performance to which the documents may relate and may be the reason for the original commercial transaction.

Uniform customs and practice for documentary credits

Due to the use and importance of documentary credit for international trade the Paris headquarters of the ICC in 1933 first adopted a uniform set of rules governing the use of documentary credit. Entitled the 'Uniform Customs and Practice for Documentary Credits', or UCP, these rules were adopted by most countries. Subsequently, these were updated and adapted to keep abreast of developments in transport techniques and to offer greater guarantees to all parties involved. The latest version was approved in 2006. It came into force on 1st July 2007.[7]

To facilitate the checking of documents presented in documentary credit transactions, the ICC also decided to compile the most common banking practices into a single document. The resultant document, entitled the 'International Standard Banking Practice for the Examination of Documents under Documentary Credit', or ISBP, was approved in 2002. This was the first time a worldwide survey had been made of the criteria adopted by banks to check documentary credit documents. This document was subsequently updated in July 2007.[8]

Main features of and parties to a documentary credit

Autonomous by its very nature, a documentary credit is a separate, distinct transaction from the contract of sale or any other type of contractual agreement that may have given rise to the credit in the first place. A documentary credit is abstract and not connected to the cause that generated it, that is, the underlying contractual agreement. It is formal and banks are obliged to examine the documents presented to them to ascertain whether they conform to the terms and conditions of the credit. The bank performs its obligation if the documents requested and submitted are compliant. Furthermore, the undertaking of the issuing and/or confirming bank is irrevocable, provided, however, the requisite documents presented to the confirming and/or issuing banks comply with the terms and conditions of the credit, the applicable provisions of the UCP 600 and ISBP 681.

The applicant is the buyer who, on closing a deal with the seller, instructs his bank to issue a documentary credit. The issuing bank is the bank that, on instructions from the applicant, the buyer, issues the documentary credit in favor of the seller, the beneficiary, with the undertaking to meet its obligation, that is, either by payment, acceptance or negotiation. The advising bank is the bank to which the documentary credit is sent by the issuing bank with instructions to advise the beneficiary/seller that credit has been issued. Advice of credit is sent to the seller with a copy of the documentary credit and the nominated bank is the bank authorized by the credit, or any bank in the case of a credit available with any bank, to ensure performance as indicated by the issuing bank. Usually the nominated bank is the same as the advising bank. The confirming bank is the bank that, at the request of the issuing bank, adds its own definite undertaking to honour or to negotiate a complying presentation and the beneficiary is the seller in whose favour the credit is issued. The beneficiary is paid only on the presentation of documents to the nominated and/or confirming bank or issuing bank, whichever is the relevant bank, that meet the prescribed credit terms and conditions and complying with presentation requirements. The reimbursing bank is the bank that, on instructions from the issuing bank, reimburses the bank that actually performs the undertaking, whereas, the transferring bank is the bank that, on instructions from the first beneficiary of a transferable documentary credit, transfers the original credit to one or more secondary beneficiaries.

Types of documentary credit

A documentary credit is irrevocable, even if there is no indication to that effect and may be issued under two forms, that is, without confirm and with confirm. A documentary credit without confirm or unconfirmed is a credit issued by an issuing bank without the express request for confirmation to a correspondent nominated bank. As a result, the irrevocable undertaking in order to honour the credit belongs, by right, exclusively with the issuing bank which, on presentation of documents complying with the terms and conditions of the credit, proceeds to honour its undertaking. If the issuing bank has made the credit available at another nominated bank, this latter does not impose any obligation to honour or negotiate, except where the nominated bank, in compliance with the authorization received, accepts to honour or negotiate and so informs to the beneficiary. Unconfirmed documentary credits should be used only when the issuing bank is a highly rated bank and where the buyer's country is politically stable with an economic and banking system that offers sufficient guarantees to the beneficiary. An unconfirmed documentary credit only covers customer risk, that is, the commercial risk. A documentary credit with confirm or confirmed is used when the issuing bank requests another bank, the confirming bank, to confirm the credit issued, thereby adding another undertaking to honour or negotiate a complying presentation. A confirmed documentary credit means an irrevocable undertaking of the confirming bank, in addition to the original undertaking by the issuing bank, to honour or negotiate a complying presentation.

The form of documentary credit chosen by the exporter depends on the type of commercial agreement entered into and the safety margins. If there were a country risk on account of an unstable political scene with heavy indebtedness and an unreliable banking system, the exporter would be wise to opt for a confirmed documentary credit, especially when the goods in question would be difficult to place on other markets. A confirmed documentary credit covers both issuing bank risk and country risk.

Phases of a documentary credit

A documentary credit involves several successive operational phases following the initial commercial agreement between the seller and buyer. There is a chronological order to each phase and these are: the contract; instructions to issue a documentary credit, issuance; advice of credit; confirmation; amendments; utilization; checking of documents; and settlement.

It is essential to define every aspect of the documentary credit to be employed with the counterparty. Of particular importance are the various items to be complied with before documentary credit will be accepted and the time limit within which the beneficiary must be notified to be able to execute the buyer's purchase order in compliance with the time frames agreed in the contract of sale.

In compliance with the terms and conditions of the sales agreement, the buyer, the applicant, will instruct his bank to issue the relative documentary credit in favour of the seller, the beneficiary. The buyer knows that his bank will make the documentary credit available only when in possession of the requisite guarantees.

On instructions from the buyer, the applicant, the buyer's bank, the issuing bank, issues the documentary credit in favour of the seller, the beneficiary, and transmits this to another bank, the advising bank, usually operating in the same geographical location as the seller, following the steps outlined in Figure 15.3. Transfer is by the Society for Worldwide Interbank Financial Telecommunication system (SWIFT) using the 'MT 700' format.

On receiving the advice-of-credit message, the advising bank advises, or notifies, the beneficiary/seller. The bank only advises its client after checking the authenticity of the credit by checking signature and/or keys.

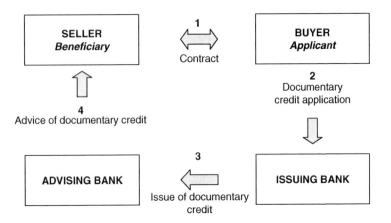

Figure 15.3   Issuing of a documentary credit

Should the type of documentary credit require, and if the bank receiving the credit agrees, the bank may confirm the credit, thereby adding a further irrevocable undertaking to honour, that is, to pay at sight or deferred payment, accept the draft and pay at maturity or negotiate in favour of the beneficiary. The definite undertaking will, however, be subject to presentation of documents, in accordance with the terms and conditions of the credit as establish under UCP and ISBP. The confirming bank agrees to confirm the credit only if the country risk and issuing bank risk are deemed satisfactory.

On receiving the text of the documentary credit, the seller must check that this has been issued in compliance with the terms agreed with the buyer in the contract of sale. The seller/beneficiary should also check his ability to meet all the terms and conditions set down in the documentary credit. If the beneficiary thinks he will be unable to comply with even just one of the conditions indicated, he must contact the buyer and ask for an amendment to be made. Amendments will be considered valid only when accepted by all parties, including the banks, and notified in writing to the beneficiary.

Once the merchandise has been manufactured and shipped to the buyer, the seller prepares the documents in compliance with the terms of documentary credit and with UCP 600 and ISBP 681. These documents are then delivered by the expiry date to the bank charged with credit performance. Performance may be payment at sight or at a maturity date in the future, acceptance of a draft drawn by the beneficiary and paid at sight or at maturity at a future date or negotiation of drafts and or documents.

On receiving the documents from the beneficiary, the nominated and/or confirming bank, or the issuing bank when it is an unconfirmed credit made operable at the counters of the issuing bank, has five working days from the day subsequent to document receipt, to examine them, ascertain whether they comply with the terms and conditions of the documentary credit, and if so, honour the credit by paying the beneficiary the amount due less bank charges and commissions, or promising to pay at a fixed date in the future. Should the documents be refused because they do not comply with the credit, the bank must notify the beneficiary. The documents held by the bank are made available to the beneficiary and the credit is not performed.

Once the documents have been found compliant with the credit and accepted, the nominated and/or confirming bank proceeds to credit the beneficiary at the due dates indicated by the documentary credit. At the same time, the nominated or confirming bank requests reimbursement of the amount from the reimbursing bank indicated by the issuing bank for this purpose. Once payment has been made, the operation is concluded with delivery of the documents to the buyer/applicant, debiting of the amount, followed by the collection of the goods shipped by the seller.

Documentary credit variants

A transferable documentary credit is a particular form of documentary credit that allows the seller or beneficiary, the first beneficiary, to transfer the whole or part of the amount contemplated in the documentary credit opened in his favour to another beneficiary, the second beneficiary, under specific conditions. A transferable credit is generally used when the agent who negotiates the sales agreement for a good or service is not the actual manufacturer but an intermediary, such as, an agent or an import-export firm, who consequently has to buy the goods from the producer, the second beneficiary, guarantees their payment and retains ownership of the goods. It should be noted that the documentary credit must be transferred exactly as issued, with the only exception of a few terms that are at the discretion of the first beneficiary and specifically indicated under UCP 600.

A revolving documentary credit is a credit that is renewed by the bank each time it is performed for a specified amount, number of times and time frame. A revolving documentary credit is typically used in the case of an exporter with an agreement to supply goods to an importer on, say, a monthly basis over a given period of time. The exporter can obtain revolving credit for the amount of a single consignment that will automatically be renewed for the number of deliveries agreed between seller and buyer. All this information must be duly indicated on the revolving documentary credit.

Also known as credit and counter-credit, a back-to-back documentary credit is when the beneficiary of a documentary credit requests, and obtains, a *new* documentary credit, back-to-back, in favour of a second beneficiary. Whereas the first documentary credit and the back-to-back documentary credit are linked and interdependent from the financial point of view, they are two completely distinct credit arrangements from the legal standpoint.

Now infrequent, a red clause documentary credit is still sometimes employed when the seller, usually in less a developed economies, requests a buyer to issue a credit permitting the nominated and/or confirming bank to honour the credit before the relevant documents are submitted. It is called red clause credit because it was printed in red ink. Another form of advance credit is known as a green clause credit. A green clause credit is extended only against trust receipt of the goods in public storage facilities.

Standby letter of credit

A standby letter of credit is a particular form of documentary credit. Unlike the other forms of documentary credit, a standby letter of credit does not imply a direct undertaking on the part of the issuing and/or confirming bank to pay, accept or negotiate; rather it provides the beneficiary with an irrevocable guarantee that the bank will pay the amount due in the event of buyer payment default.

A standby letter of credit is a useful instrument in all circumstances in which the seller agrees to be paid by bankers' draft after delivery of the goods but wants to have assurance that all credits due of whatever nature will be settled. A standby letter of credit is not an original payment mechanism. Rather it guarantees the beneficiary that payment will be forthcoming even in the event of counterparty default.

A standby letter of credit does not constitute a direct undertaking by the bank in the transaction. It is an independent guarantee of payment issued in favour of the beneficiary. Whereas bank guarantees are governed by the laws of the country concerned, the standby letter of credit is subject to ICC Uniform Customs and Practice for Documentary Credits where specific mention is made of the standby letter of credit when summing up the fundamental characteristics of documentary credit. To be valid, a standby may require the presentation, together with copies of the documents, of a declaration by the beneficiary that the debtor/applicant has failed to meet his obligation. A standby letter of credit is advantageous especially in the case of repeated, albeit irregular, consignments for the same amounts since at any one time it will cover maximum buyer exposure.

A standby letter of credit could be used in the following circumstances of an order for a total of USD 1,000,000 to be delivered in 10 monthly consignments of USD 100,000 each, payable by bank draft at 60 days from day of shipment. The buyer, who has requested his bank to issue a standby letter of credit, commits to a credit line with the issuing bank for an amount of approximately 30–40 per cent of this and this is the maximum exposure to the seller. Had the buyer opened a documentary letter of credit under this multiple consignment sales contract, there would have been a commitment to a credit line for the total amount involved. As well as, credit line charges, the buyer would also have incurred the cost of opening documentary credit for the entire amount compared to the USD 300,000–400,000 of the standby credit.

Issues requiring attention by seller and buyer

For the abstract notion of documentary credit security to become certainty of payment for the seller, the beneficiary, and certainty of collection of compliant goods for the buyer, the applicant, the parties must pay special attention to certain fundamental aspects of the operation. To ensure against the bank's refusal to pay, the seller must specify expressly that payment should be carried out on the basis of documentary credit issued by the first bank, indicate that the credit should be issued via SWIFT message, include a specific provision that the credit is subject to UCP 600 ICC rules; specify whether the documentary credit is issued with or without confirmation; specify that goods consignment is conditional to receipt of the credit, and indicate the time, that is, the day and month allowed after receipt of documentary credit to deliver the goods to destination. The seller must also agree all items to be indicated on the documentary credit, the documents, terms and conditions and on receiving the text of the documentary credit, check who the issuer is and whether issuance complies with the contract of sale. The seller should also assess whether he is able to honour all the terms and conditions. The buyer, on the other hand, has different issues. The buyer must safeguard against the risk that any exposure with the bank is not for goods that do not meet the specifications on the purchase order.

Since documentary credit operations are fairly complex and entail several steps, it is essential that firms availing themselves of this sort of credit in their foreign dealings have an in-depth knowledge of how they work. The same applies to banks, whose credit, financing, and document checking services are instrumental in furthering international trade, and transporters, the carriers and forwarders who have the responsibility of producing the transport and other documents for goods shipped required to complete a documentary credit submitted to the bank. An issuing and/or confirming bank has to honour its obligation to pay the beneficiary at sight or at a future date, accept or negotiate drafts and/or documents only if the documents received conform to the credit.

Unlike a documentary collection where the bank's obligation is fulfilled when it honours the principal's collection instructions, assuming no liability or responsibility for the outcome of the commercial operation, a documentary credit obliges the issuing bank and/or confirming bank, if involved, to honour or negotiate when the documents are compliant.

Conclusion

As detailed previously it is evident from a payment by documentary credit that the bank is debtor towards the seller and, consequently, the last resort if the bank does not honour the credit or does not negotiate it due to non-compliance of documents. Moreover, the bank may refuse the seller/beneficiary only in the exception that the documents are not in acordance with the terms and conditions of the documentary credit and with what the ICC UCP 600 and ISBP 681 prescribe.

A documentary credit is characterized by distinct contractual relationships. For instance, the relationship between buyer and seller that stipulate the sales contract, buyer and the issuing bank which opens a documentary credit at the request of the buyer, the issuing bank and seller after the issue of a documentary credit, whereby the issuing bank must honour to pay the beneficiary the amount against presentation of complying documents, and the confirming bank and the seller when following the issuing bank's authorization or request the confirming bank adds its obligation towards the beneficiary, that is, the seller, to honour or negotiate the amount against presentation of complying documents. Therefore a sale contract between a buyer and seller is separated unlike a documentary credit operation, as UCP 600 authorizes.

Examining the seller's obligations towards the buyer in an international sale compared with the undertaking taken up in a documentary credit, we notice the seller has certain obligations. In an international sale, the seller has to deliver the merchandise ordered from the buyer in accordance with the purchase order, within and/or on the exact date agreed in the contract, in the place established according to the ICC Incoterms, and by the transport method defined in the sales contract. Merchandise has to be in accordance with the characteristics and technical specifications defined in the sales contract.

For a documentary credit, instead, the seller has to deliver the required complying documents, within the expiry date established and in the place defined in the documentary credit, with the issuing bank or with the nominated/confirming bank, in accordance with availability modality established in the documentary credit.

The object of the sales contract is merchandise to be delivered to the buyer without fault compared with the purchase order, whereas in a documentary credit the object is the documents to be delivered to the bank, complying with the terms and conditions of the documentary credit and to the provisions of UCP 600 and ISBP 681.

It is important, as illustrated, that the buyer and the seller carefully evaluate the main critical aspects of this transaction in order to agree the operational nature and obligations in the sales contract; have a knowledge of the logistic aspects resulting from the term of the sale with respect of the terms of Incoterms, and the other aspects of the transport documents presentation; to be in a position to presents all the documents required; and respect the terms and conditions prescribed in the documentary credit.

An understanding of these aspects could make it easier to ascertain the legal right and effective management of a documentary credit operation, reducing or eliminating the commercial credit risk and, where necessary, also the country risk, because the payment is assured by the bank, while the buyer goods comply with the purchase order. However, it is important that the buyer is informed about the financial and business reputation of the seller.

Notes

1. For a more detailed analysis of the practice of international trade from a legal perspective refer to Di Meo A., 2007, *Manuale Pratico del Commercio Internazionale*, Maggioli Editore, Rimini.
2. International Chamber of Commerce, 1999, 'Incoterms 2000', Publication Number 560, Paris.
3. International Chamber of Commerce, 1995, 'Uniform Rules for Collections, URC 522', Publication Number 522, Paris.

4. For more information on collection operations refer to Wickremeratne, L., 1996, 'Guide to Collection Operations', Publication Number 561, International Chamber of Commerce, Paris.
5. For a detailed legal analysis of documentary credits refer to Di Meo A., 2007, *Il Credito Documentario*, Ipsoa Editore, Milano.
6. For a more information on documentary credit operations refer to del Busto, C., 1994, 'Guide to Documentary Credit Operations', Publication Number 515, International Chamber of Commerce, Paris.
7. International Chamber of Commerce, 2007, 'Uniform Customs and Practice for Documentary Credits, UCP 600', Publication Number 600, Paris.
8. International Chamber of Commerce, 2002, 'International Standard Banking Practice, ISBP', Publication Number 645, Paris; International Chamber of Commerce, 2007, 'International Standard Banking Practice, ISBP 681', Publication Number 681, Paris.

16
Knowledge as a Guiding Principle in the Organization of International Marketing Departments in Service Firms

Eric Stevens

The internationalization of markets offers enormous development potential for most companies including service firms. Global opportunities are created only when marketing teams are in a position to understand international contexts and to adapt and position specific offers for customers. However, it is well understood that the organization of marketing departments in firms is challenging, specifically when international issues have to be considered. Marketing structures are usually designed by taking into account five dimensions, which are organization, division of functions, geography, product range, and client specificities. The marketing function, however, has recently developed a new framework by placing the emphasis on major perspectives, such as marketing orientation, brand orientation, e-marketing and CRM. These dimensions have led to a redefinition of the way international marketing organizations are structured.

Design of a marketing department organization

There is no doubt that the constant increase in the volume of international trade, resulting from trade liberalization, opens considerable opportunities for most firms, whatever their sectors, activities and size may be. By reducing trade barriers through reciprocity, liberalization and non-discrimination, the WTO agreements have facilitated access to new and and potentially attractive markets. In this globalized context, firms have had to develop operations abroad and adapt their organization, their internal and external processes and extend their range of activities and products.[1]

More specifically, marketing functions are directly concerned by such change to the point that it is difficult to dissociate the decision to operate abroad and the decisions related to the organization of marketing activities. Entry mode options emphasize, among others, the consequences of such choices on risks, costs and control. Furthermore, access to local information, such as the identification of major opportunities and threats, the identification of competitors' strategies, the management of major distribution channels and the understanding of customers' expectations and preferences are due to the efficacy of the marketing function. Thus, it should be considered that, when expanding operations abroad, the organization of marketing operations in the respective countries influences the information processing, dissemination and flows within a firm that are, eventually, transformed into a flow of decisions leading to products that incorporate the clients' expectations.

Managing the marketing function usually includes acquiring, gathering, processing and using information to be transformed into knowledge related to competitors and environments, products and clients' expectations in the purpose of generating profitable flows of demand. To do so, the international marketing department has to design and implement structures capable of understanding the environments of every foreign market in which it operates, to adjust action plans to a firm's strategies and to manage the outcome of the implemented marketing strategy. Five global principles are usually adopted for guiding organizational design. These are geography, the span of centralization and decentralization, the range of product offered, the division of functions and competencies and the client specificities.

Understanding the local economic and political contexts, as well as local competitors' strategies entails being geographically focused. In multicultural and complex contexts, the access to relevant information relies on insiders who, due to their personal experience, are capable of providing the right interpretation of situations and facts. Similarly, the implementation of marketing and sales decisions requires a strong local presence, made of people capable of acting by using both professional and cultural competencies. There is no doubt that the efficiency of action plans addressing local customers is supported by the organization's marketing department designed specifically to address these local contexts. According to this principle, organizations define homogeneous geographical areas where managers have the responsibilities to define and reach objectives. Due to local involvement, the adoption of geographic areas of responsibilities generates 'close fit' with the local environment. This is particularly important during negotiation stages where closeness to clients is required for success. However, this principle generates limits as the coordination of multiple areas is difficult. It is expected in such an organization to see brand and product lines proliferate, as well as poor level of standardization resulting in low levels of economies of scale. Further limits will be encountered when a broad portfolio of sophisticated products/services requires high levels of technical skill. Then, organization charts designed for the product range may be beneficial.

The design of value products requires an in-depth knowledge related to the design, production and distribution of these products and/or services. A careful definition of all the attributes and their adaptation to clients' and retailers' expectations, the prospective management of specific technologies and the optimization of the production costs require specialization of marketers on specific products range, brands and/or portfolio. According to this principle, managers in charge of a specific product have to commercialize it whatever the geographical area may be. For instance, Procter & Gamble in the late 1990s decided to adopt this principle by structuring the marketing department per major brand.[2] As result, it was possible to launch new products in more than 14 different countries at a higher pace resulting in an improved performance. When this organization performs well each time the different countries present similarities in distribution systems, it may lead to a lack of synergies and may experience transfer from one specific offer to the other, and an increasing of the costs as the sales, management and functional staff may be duplicated. This last point may be particularly sensitive when a greater level of functional specialization is required to perform on the market. In this case the third principle may be relevant.

As marketing is becoming more and more complex, a greater functional specialization may lead to higher efficiency. Specific export departments, with experienced managers, may be created. But as operations require managing, sophisticated market research, clients' databases, distribution through websites and e-technologies, call centres and flows of negotiations with complex clients, competencies appear to be more and more differentiated and lead to a strong degree of specialization. In such contexts, the adoption of organizational charts defining highly differentiated expertise and sharing this expertise among different countries for costs reduction is expected to lead to better results.

Marketing performance relies on the fit of the offerings with clients' expectations. Under the pressure of increased competition, firms achiev this goal by adopting a one-to-one policy where a unique offer is designed in order to fit with the specific needs and requirements of each client. To achieve this purpose marketing, and more specifically sales departments, redesigned their organization by specializing people on specific clients or group of clients. This resulted in specific functions such as Account Managers in charge of negotiations with one specific and usually strategic client or Category Managers, in charge of supporting the retailers in their assortment policy. This kind of organization leads to customer intimacy during negotiation stages and is frequently adopted for strategic clients. This, however, increases the costs per client. Moreover, and especially for clients operating in multiple countries, a strong coordination in price and assortment policy is required to avoid incoherence. In this case, as for the geographic and functional organization principles, centralization appears as a mean to overcome risks of dispersion.

The management of international marketing operations requires, among other strategic priorities, planning resources allocations, adapting local marketing plans to the overall corporate strategy, and controling the operations in every local market. Those tasks raised the debate on centralization/decentralization very early.[3] Centralization is required to support the fit between global and strategic decisions and to control that current operation fit with initial plans. Centralization rates is especially, beneficial in businesses with rapid technological change rate or when economies of scale may be achieved by centralized production. Moreover, centralization is useful each time multiplication of local environment and cultures may result in fragmented, duplicated marketing efforts leading to diseconomies of scale. Conversely, centralized systems are very often perceived by local managers as slowing the reactions to changes in the local environment and competition and sometimes slowing the decision by having to integrate too much data in the decision-making process.

As the five guiding principles lead to their own limits and sometimes to diseconomies of scale, they are frequently combined in matrix forms, made up of two or more competencies. For instance, international product/services departments in charge of worldwide development of new offerings are crossed with geographic organizations made up of local sales forces. Thus the design of new offerings entails getting information from local environment, summarizing overall expectations, if any, and designing the offerings at the international level, and then assigning objectives to local sales force for selling the new product. This however presents a number of disadvantages, usually associated with matrix forms. By apportioning equal importance to the different parts of the organization, it is not clear how decisions are made, especially when conflicts about specific issues occur. Moreover, as multiple centres are involved in every decision, it is expected that this kind of organization will slow down decision speed.

Multiple research, gathered under the umbrella of contingency theory, demonstrated that effectiveness of a marketing structure depends on the extent to which it is aligned with the uncertainties in the market place.[4] Thus, managerial choices should not address the optimal structure but should aim at identifying which principle fits with the firm's environment. Structural centralization, formalization and connectedness of departments have to fit with local context as demonstrated by Burns and Stalker[5] that the same choices lead to opposite results in stable or turbulent environments. Given the problems and limits of every organizational form, and the overall turbulence of markets, it is not surprising to note that firms very often change their design.[6]

The five guiding principles, their main benefits and limits, constitute the corpus developed when the organization of an international team becomes the focus. It is developed by Albaum *et al.* (2005),[7] which included development on contingent factors influencing the centralization/decentralization decisions, as well as in Cateora and Graham (2005),[8] in Mühlbacher *et al.* (2006)[9] and in Cravens and Piercy (2003),[10] who opened discussions on new forms of organizational design.

However, the marketing discipline is facing major changes in its environment, which lead to reconsideration of the principles adopted for organizing a firm's activities. Over recent years, three major trends emerged from marketing literature and practices: market orientation, brand management and customer relationship management. Even though the initial developments were sometimes conceptual, their adoption by firms entailed changing the organizational design so that it could fit with the new way of defining objectives, leading operations and controlling results.

Marketing orientation

Marketing orientation is based on the underlying assumption that how an organization is structured influences how employees may think, decide and act. In this perspective, the efficiency of any organization lies in its ability to link the market situation to an organizational structure able to produce, due to its own design processes and competencies, appropriate actions for customers. Linked to the development of an international organization, it has been demonstrated that market orientation, as well as marketing competencies, is a significant antecedent of international performance.[11]

Three main literature streams discuss extensively market orientation. The behavioural perspective assumes that market orientation is achieved when organization-wide market intelligence results in the generation of, dissemination of and responsiveness to information.[12] The cultural perspective emphasizes the values and attitudes of the whole organization, paying attention to current and emerging needs of the customers, so that superior value offerings may be proposed.[13] Third, the competitive perspective focuses on the understanding of current and potential competitors and uses this knowledge for producing superior customer value through improved coordination of organizational resources.[14] As the different perspectives partially overlap, market orientation is synthesized as comprising the following elements:

Customer orientation: consists of the regular measurement of customer satisfaction levels, careful attention to complaints and comments, and to after-sales service, and also in how customer value is generated.

Competitor orientation: consists of how and by whom information from competitors is gathered, analysed and used during the elaboration of marketing plans.

Interfunctional coordination: consists of the involvement of all departments in the preparation of the business plans, in information sharing across departments, in joint assessment of customer needs, and in the interaction of marketing personnel with other departments.

Profit emphasis: based on how profitability of major customers, retailers, product lines, sales territory is reported, processed and included in the preparation of business plans and strategies.

As the link between marketing orientation and international efficiency was found to be relevant,[15] there is no doubt that firms willing to foster marketing orientation have to include the different items in their organizational design. Based on Avlonitis and Gounaris[16], it may be recommended that market-orientated organizations should adopt at the same time 'flat' and decentralized organizations as well as formalized procedures and communication systems aiming at supporting the vertical and horizontal dissemination of information.

This first recommendation appears initially contradictory. Centralization is often adopted for gathering the whole information for the purpose of designing global strategies when decisions taken at the local level only lead to incoherence and diseconomies of scale. However, as it is known that centralization results in longer decision processes, the sharing and integration of local information has to be achieved by other means. Thus, specific organizational designs and procedures have to be implemented for this purpose. Implementation of international information systems, aimed at supporting information exchanges, multinational teams in charge of the projects, power given to multifunctional teams to decide locally on communication, prices, distribution and promotion strategy, lead to higher efficiency of organizations.

Furthermore, the management has to develop beliefs, values and norms that will lead the entire organization to consider the client's expectations as well as competitors' positions before making any decision. As the market-oriented firms have to learn continuously from the market, managers must adopt and apply market sensing and sense-making principles.[17] This entails adopting an open-minded analysis of situations, a willingness to systematically collect and distribute information related to customers and competitors, the capacity to renew the interpretations of situations in order to avoid routines, and a willingness to convert information into action and reasoning based on outcomes assessments. This also entails increasing competencies at the middle management level as the sensing and sense-making processes are usually complex operations, including market intelligence techniques, collective interpretation of information and changes in action plans.

As such, market orientation has to be considered as a guiding principle for implementing efficient international marketing teams. It leads to a greater importance for local decisions so that they may fit with local environments. The resulting organizational chart will display 'flat' organizations, decision centres implemented at a local level and a greater responsibility for middle management. More important than organizational features are the beliefs, values and norms adopted for the purpose of transforming local access to relevant information into shared strategic and action plans.

Brand management

There is no doubt that the way brands are managed has a major impact on the overall results of a firm. The concept of brand equity emerged in the 1990s to address the goodwill realized during mergers and acquisitions. Strong brands facilitate the access to offers, provide differentiation and affect positively customers' purchasing decisions. As such they are considered as a major intangible asset, resulting from many years of heavy investment and strategic planning. Branding strategies impact both product offerings and corporate image. By creating a brand associated with specific offerings, the organization delivers a statement on what consumers may expect. However, particularly in service activities where internal marketing plays an important role, branding is more than the outward manifestation of marketing activities. Due to the simultaneous production and consumption, branding provides a link between the positioning of the offers and staff working behaviour. More than name, logo and visual presentation, the brand incorporates corporate core values. As such, corporate identity is holistic, incorporating the aims and values of the organization in a unique aggregate differentiated from existing competitors. According to this, brand coherence, aligning multiple sub-components in a unique direction, is vital to nurture and reinforce overall efficiency of corporate strategies. Consistent internal and external images among stakeholders transforms the brand into a valuable corporate asset.

Organizing this strong coherence encompasses managing the multiple dimensions of brands. The concept of brand identity means the brand must have both a permanent nature whatever the circumstances may be and a difference from other brands. To do so, unique traits of the brand are incorporated into the logo, names, product features, communication documents, as well as in the choice of specific symbolic components and values associated to the messages. Consistency is then obtained by repeating similar features over time, media, promotional actions and interactions with customers.

The objective of achieving consistency will constitute a guiding principle all through the brand life cycle. During the launching of new brands, managers have to carefully define the mission and values as well as language and territory of communication on which it is to be positioned so that there is clear identity from repeated promotional campaigns. Similarly, during brand extension, the brand capital is used for the purpose of introducing new offerings at lower costs. Managing identity requires identifying the features that may be common between existing and new offerings.

Achieving the coherence requires adopting a brand orientation defined as: 'an approach in which the processes of the organization revolve around the creation, development and protection of the brand identity in an ongoing interaction with target customers with the aim of achieving lasting competitive advantages in the form of brands'.[18] From the existing research and managerial perspective, six main elements are considered as brand orientation leverages.[19] In a context where everything sends a message, the management of shared brand vision, shared brand functionality, shared brand positioning, brand return on investment, brand symbolism and brand value adding capability align firms' action plans to stakeholders representations and expectations.

Given the investment required for settling brand awareness, international expansion of existing brands may appear as promising. Global brands are particularly attractive when the products or service are similar whatever the country may be as in the computer sector. They are equally opportune when the clients themselves operate worldwide. However, due to the constraint of producing idiosyncratic features, it may be difficult to benefit from brand capital each time cultural dimensions are variable. As the brand icon expresses to the customer which attribute may be expected, a global brand may lead to a proposition that is of no interest to foreign clients. Thus, as for brand extension, common features have to be identified to be able to extent cohesive brand internationally.

Considering the reasons which lead to differentiated international brand policies, Kapferer[20] noticed that legal differences, competition, consumption habits and distribution structure are the main reasons assumed by managers for adapting brands locally. However, adaptation policies may include diverse leverages, such as logotype and brand names, product features, communication policies including advertising and packaging, pricing and sales efforts. Even though globalization is decided, it remains possible to standardize only some of those elements. A great difference is observed by Kapferer in the extension of brands abroad. When brand names, logotypes, product features and packaging are globalized, pricing policies, and advertising – both positioning and execution – and direct marketing are adapted at the local level in more than half of these. To the statement that some core elements of the brand strategy are centralized, Theuerkauf *et al.* (1996)[21] made comparisons between internationalized firms and underlined that successful firms adopted central coordination for brand positioning.

Achieving brand consistency in international contexts has direct consequences on organizational design, which has to incorporate coordination mechanisms supporting decision making processes. Multiple options are listed by research, sorting multiple means such as formally centralized to fully decentralized coordination mechanisms. The brand champion, brand equity manager and the global brand manager provide consistency by centralizing on one position decision for the main brand attributes. Similar coordination mechanisms may be achieved by a global brand council, brand expertise centres and network based hubs which combine expertise from local context and centralized decision. According to Theuerkauf et al.,[22] when very few firms adopt fully centralized coordination means, coordination mechanisms are more likely to succeed over the fully decentralized decision processes.

Linking organizational design adopted for brand management to success in international operation underlined that the brand orientation has to be considered as a guiding principle at the international level. More specifically, the way coordination is achieved should aim both at effective coordination while integrating local constraints and events. To do so, guiding principles such as geography, product, clients or functions are revealed to be insufficient. In itself, the necessity to manage brands may be considered as a guiding principle for designing international marketing organizations.

Relationship marketing perspective

There is no doubt that the relationship established between sellers and clients is at the centre of any purchasing decision process. Aiming at facilitating information exchanges as well as establishing trust, a close relationship helps to avoid opportunistic behaviour. This function was performed by sales persons and the development of information technologies offers new possibilities to replace the one-to-one, and therefore cost intensive, relation with electronic systems designed to address one-to-one relationship for a much larger number of clients. Websites, emailing, call centres and data warehouses are among some of the multiple means used to implement, nurture and increase the relationship established with clients. Distinct but convergent concepts were associated to the recent increase in customer relationship management (CRM) practices and publications.

Central to the overall development is the concept of relationship. Coined by Berry[23], relationship marketing was the object of progressive refinement during the 1990s, notably due to the efforts of the Nordic School of Services[24] as well as the IMP group.[25] At the opposite of the transactional approaches of sales, Grönroos defined relational marketing as: 'the process of identifying and establishing maintaining and enhancing and when it is necessary terminating relationship with customers and other stakeholders, at a profit, so that the objectives of all the parties involved are met. And this is done by mutual exchange and fulfilment of promises'.[26] Underlying this assumption is the assertion that the firm cannot succeed based on prefabricated product but due to the way available resources of the firm – people, technology, governing departments and sometimes customers themselves – interact in a way which results in satisfactory offerings. In this perspective, interaction is defined as a process made of acts, episodes and sequences, those different events being the relationship itself.

The processual nature of interactions is necessary for understanding the concepts of customer life time value (CLTV) and of loyalty. A time perspective on customer interaction leads to the conclusion that not only one purchase matters. Analysing long term contribution of every customer to firm profitability may lead to focus action plans on loyalty. By designing multiple opportunities to interact using multiple tools such as loyalty cards, rewards and other promotional actions and by implementing cross and up selling actions to the existing clients' portfolio, relationship marketing may improve overall profit.

Managing multiple interactions on a large scale may lead to significant increases in costs. When it is possible to maintain individual relationships in business-to-business activities, where the amount of every purchase generates important flows of cash, the cost intensive interaction process may appear to be unprofitable in sectors such as FMCG or retail banking. This leads to the design and adoption of tools capable of improving productivity. Internet interactive websites, call centres, emailing, interactions through mobile phones, access to online databases and more generally speaking information systems all transformed how marketing departments organized their activities. Managing multiple interaction channels with the aim of reducing costs while keeping customers loyal became a major focus of sales and marketing departments.

Guiding principles for organizing international marketing

The guiding principles for organizing international marketing departments are outlined in Table 16.1. These provide broad orientations during the development of the organizational design of international marketing.

Conclusion

The reorganization of the interaction process has led to the creation of different functional areas. Database managers, webmasters, managers of

Table 16.1   Guiding principles, purpose and the type of organizational feature usually associated with international development

Guiding principle	Main purpose	Type of organizational feature usually associated with international development
Geographic	Define sales responsibility in a given territory. Establish customer intimacy	Responsibility on territory including on countries or geographic areas abroad
Products	Optimize product features. Support development processes	Product manager for international markets
Functions	Enhance expertise for improved marketing performance	Export manager responsible for developing sales abroad
Clients	Adapt marketing policies for specific clients	Key account manager for international clients
Market orientation	Organize the process of transforming local information into collective action plans.	Flat, decentralized organizational chart. Empowerment of middle management. Specific beliefs, values and norms.
Brand management	Maintain and develop brand cohesiveness	International brand managers. International brand committee
Relationship perspective	Adapt marketing plans to customer acquisition and retention objectives	Specific functions created. Information systems for delivering knowledge at the point of action

call centre activities, among others, illustrate this development with, in most instances, an international dimension associated with them. For instance, it is known that call centres are frequently outsourced abroad in order to reduce costs and extend the schedule. Similarly, as they may be accessible worldwide, the offerings delivered by websites have to be coherent and must fit with brand identity wherever their location. Organizing cohesiveness is achieved by organizational design through the standardization of website visual identity, by gathering information related to clients into a central database, by making this central database accessible from every location in the world, and by standardizing the interaction processes with the clients during the calls. Central to the different tools is the concept of 'knowledge at the point of action'. This means that whatever the process, the time, or the people involved in the interaction, there must be complete information available, including the history of the relationship, in order to take appropriate decisions. Knowledge at the point of action leads to the consideration that the management of the information flows has to be part of the international marketing design.

Thus, the introduction of the relationship perspective in marketing leads to new functional expertise, new tools associated with them and leads to new organizational design at the international level to be capable of achieving brand cohesiveness and market efficiency. Due to this, the relationship perspective has to be considered as one of the guiding principles for organizing marketing at an international level.

Notes

1. Refer to extensive development on contingency approaches of the marketing function in Olson, E., Slater, S., and Hult, G. 2005, 'The Performance Implication of Fit Among Business Strategy, Marketing Organisation Structure and Strategic Behaviour', *Journal of Marketing*, 69, (3), July, p. 49
2. Albaum, G., Duerr, E. and Strandskov, J., 2005, *International Marketing and Export Management*, London, Pearson, 5th edition, p. 628.
3. Centralization being defined as the delegation of decision making authority throughout an organization and the extent of participation by organizational members in decision making. Deshpandé R. and Zaltman, G., 1982, 'Factors affecting the use of market research information: a path analysis', *Journal of Marketing Research*, 19, February, pp. 14–31, have outlined that the greater the degree of centralization, the lower a firm's ability to utilize information from the market.
4. Olson, E., Slater, S. and Hult, G., 2005, 'The Performance Implication of Fit Among Business Strategy, Marketing Organisation Structure and Strategic Behaviour', *Journal of Marketing*, July, 69, (3), p. 49 and Lysonski, S., Levas, M. and Lavenka, N., 1995, 'Environment Uncertainty and Organizational Structures: a Product Management Perspective', *Journal of Product and Brand Management*, 4, (3), pp. 7–19.
5. Burns, T. and Stalker, R., 1961, *The Management of Innovation*, London, Tavistock.
6. Bremmer, B., 2003, in Cateora, P. and Graham, J., *International Marketing*, McGraw Hill, 12th edition, p. 337.
7. Albaum, G., Duerr, E. and Strandskov, J., 2005, *International Marketing and Export Management*, London, Pearson, 5th edition.
8. Cateora, P. and Graham, J, *International Marketing*, McGraw Hill, 12th edition, p. 340.

9. Mühlbacher, H., Leihs, H. and Dahringer, L., 2006, *International Marketing, a Global Perspective*, Thomson, 3rd edition, p. 394.

10. Cravens, D., and Piercy, N., 2003, *Strategic Marketing*, McGraw Hill, 7th edition, p. 487.

11. Knight, G. and Dalgic, T., 2000, 'Market Orientation, Marketing Performance and International Firm Performance, American Marketing Association', Conference Proceedings, 11, Winter; Cadogan, J., Diamantopoulos, A. and Pahud de Mortanges, C., 1999, 'A Measure of Export Market Orientation: Scale Development and Cross-cultural Validation', *Journal of International Business Studies*, 30, (4), p. 689.

12. Kohli, A. and Jaworski, B., 1990, 'Market Orientation: the Construct, Research, Propositions and Managerial Implications', *Journal of Marketing*, 54, pp. 1–18 and Jaworski, B. and Kohli, A., 1993, 'Market Orientation: Antecedents and Consequences', *Journal of Marketing*, 57, July, pp. 53–70.

13. Deshpandé, R. and Farley, J., 1989, 'Organizational Culture and Marketing: Defining the Research Agenda', *Journal of Marketing*, 53, January, pp. 3–15 and Day, G., 1994, 'The Capabilities of Market-driven Organisations', *Journal of Marketing*, 58, October, pp. 37–52.

14. Narver, J. and Slater, S., 1990, 'The Effect of a Market Orientation on Business Profitability', *Journal of Marketing*, 54, October, pp. 20–35.

15. Harris, L., 2000, 'The Organisational Barriers to Developing Marketing Orientation', *European Journal of Marketing*, 34, (5–6), pp. 598–624.

16. Avlonitis G. and Gounaris, S., 1999, 'Marketing Orientation and its Determinants: an Empirical Analysis', *European Journal of Marketing*, 33, (11–12), p. 1003.

17. Day, G., 2002, 'Managing the Market Learning Process', *Journal of Business and Industrial Marketing*, 17, (4), pp. 240–52.

18. Urde, M., 1999, 'Brand Orientation: a Mindset for Building Brands into Strategic Resources', *Journal of Marketing Management*, 15, (1–3), pp. 117–33.

19. Reid, M., Luxton, S. and Mavondo, F., 2005, 'The Relationship between Integrated Marketing Communication, Market Orientation and Brand Orientation', *Journal of Advertising*, 34, (4), Winter, pp. 11–23.

20. Kapferer, J., 1997, *Strategic Brand Management: Creating and Sustaining Brand Equity Long Term*, Kogan, 2nd edition, p. 364.

21. Theuerkauf, I., Ernst, D. and Mahini, A., 1996, 'Think local, organize...?', *International Marketing Review*, 13, (3), pp. 7–12.

22. Ibid.

23. Berry, L., 1983, 'Relationship Marketing in Emerging Perspectives of Services Marketing', in Berry, L., Shostack, L. and Upah, G., (eds), *American Marketing Association*, Chicago, pp. 25–28.

24. Grönroos, C. and Gummesson, E., 1985, 'The Nordic School of Service Marketing', in Grönroos, C. and Gummesson, E., (eds), *Service Marketing – Nordic School Perspectives*, Stockholm University, Stockholm, Sweden, pp. 6–11 and Grönroos, C., 1990, 'Relationship Approach to the Marketing Function in Service Context: the Marketing and Organisational Behaviour Interface', *Journal of Business Research*, 20, pp. 3–12 and Grönroos, C., 1994, 'Quo Vadis, Marketing? Toward a Relationship Marketing Paradigm', *Journal of Marketing*

Management, 10, pp. 347–60 and Grönroos, C., 1997, 'Value Driven Relational Marketing: from Product to Resources and Competencies', *Journal of Marketing Management*, 13, pp. 407–19.
25. Hakansson, H. and Snehota, I., 1995, *Developing Relationship in Business Networks*, Routledge, London.
26. Grönroos, C., 1997, '*Value Driven Relational Marketing*', op. cit.

17
Managing International Projects through Virtual Communications

Andreas Knaden and Stefan Schlangen

In the course of globalization and increasing competition it is not only firms that must face new challenges. There are also challenges for not-for-profit organizations, such as non-Governmental Organizations (NGO) and especially, universities with internationalization of curricula and international collaboration being recent phenomena. The new technical infrastructure of information technologies offer the possibility to communicate efficaciously and cost efficiently.[1] However, there is an intercultural aspect to all international communications and this is exacerbated by the communicating through information technology. Furthermore, the cooperation of participants in virtual meetings is the centre of attention in location-spreading working groups. The virtual meeting may only run optimally if suitable tools are used and the meetings are turned off to the virtual surrounding field. Of particular interest, is how to generate success factors for intercultural cooperation. A goal is the development of an action step catalogue to accomplish successful virtual participation in teams at an international and intercultural level.

Teams

Working groups in the classical sense are defined as a group of collaborators who accomplish a mutual task in a functional and a working part.[2] Bullinger and Warnecke and also Antoni use the terms 'working group' and 'teams' as synonyms. However, not all working groups are also teams. A team is rather a special form of a working group and is also a social group.[3] The fundamental processes within a team can be described through the terms teamwork and team leadership. Throughout the close collaboration within teams, the quality of communication is an important factor for the success of the collaboration. This communication is characterized by frequency, openness and timeliness of disclosure of information. A target oriented success is not possible without an efficient information flow.[4]

Another crucial element is the term 'team leadership' as a team requires members as well as leadership. Of course, leadership does not necessarily have to be concentrated in one person within the group. It is still necessary to concentrate on team leadership in order to create efficient task scheduling. Projects and tasks must be planned and progress stages may already be defined at the commencement of the project. This requires selecting the appropriate communication media and establishing control mechanisms to monitor the progress of the project, the team and teamwork. However, it is important to allow creative ways of collaborating, as well as; providing feedback to the team and team members.[5]

Virtual teams

A virtual team is a specialization of a classical team. The difference to the term of a classical team is that it owns the feature 'virtual'. The term 'virtual' infers 'being something in effect even if not in reality or not conforming to the generally accepted definition of the term'.[6] A virtual team operates similarly to a classical team in order to reach a certain target. This is achieved in spatially different and temporally different conditions. Within a geographic zone it is possible for virtual teams to meet physically in the same location and it could be, other than in their common firm location, at regional or national level with other participants. Where actual physical presence supports meeting virtually the communication between the team members is complemented. Since pure virtual team members are separated, spatially the communication between the purely virtual team members themselves and then with other team members who also meet physically requires specific management.

Intercultural factors

There is initially a certain reticence on the part of participants to communicate using an audio-visual medium and there may at first be some difficulties in motivating participants to collaborate and many participants are not capable of expressing themselves appropriately on camera.[7] On occasions, group-dynamic aspects sometimes certainly play a role in this. Nevertheless, after a certain time period the inhibitions of participants diminish creating an adequate discussion climate. However, it is especially burdensome when the leader or animator in the respective locations of the virtual meeting is also responsible for the technical control of the meeting and this should be avoided.[8] Of course, where there has been some previous personal contact and previous real meetings among participants it is more conducive to virtual communication and meetings.

While no intercultural issues may manifest themselves, they may exist nonetheless. To minimize these issues it is important to specify the precise goals and mission of the team early on in its formation.[9] As described before, the high degree of diversity can have a positive as well as a negative effect on the team performance. Where it is possible to decide on the configuration of the virtual team it is, therefore, possible to avoid differences in terms of competence, knowledge and behaviour. Conversely, some teams self select and others have no choice in team members.

Furthermore, the cultural behaviour of some team members is influenced by the behaviour of other team members. This could occur when one team member dominates or controls the entire group discussion and other team members, despite being capable of contributing positively and imparting knowledge, are prevented from contributing. As a result of this, the team and communication process is limited in efficacy. It is suggested that the meeting leader invites participants to consider how their cultural behaviour could affect, both positively and negatively, the behaviour of other team members.[10] The awareness and the constant consideration of these cultural effects on virtual teams and meetings assists in improving team performance.

An intercultural virtual team consists of team members of at least a few different linguistic and cultural origins and these further complicate the organizational and spatial factors, as well as possibly temporal factors.[11] Culture may be defined as specific, collectively anchored expectations in relation to manners, values, world pictures and social thought patterns.[12] When cooperation between team members from different cultures is required intercultural factors increase in importance. Mauritz defines interculture as 'a culture of relations between persons or organizations across culture boundaries'.[13]

This intercultural factor generates a new specific culture including its own action and orientation norms that develop during process. By then, collective judgement and interpretation norms do not exist and this could be a potential for conflicts and misunderstandings within the intercultural virtual team.[14]

This form of intercultural communication may manifest itself differently, such as, in a national culture or a firm culture, as well as in various functional cultures. Hofstede's 40-country study established, for example, the empirical foundations for the dimension of national culture formally specified as power distance. The different values of Hofstede's power distance have consequences for the team, because they have to work together. Team members within cultures with a high power distance expect that the leader will give clear orders what they have to do as opposed to team members who grow up within cultures with a low power distance. They will expect a democratic leader, who calls in the different opinions of the team members.[15]

Furthermore, when team members are from different firms they bring in different firm cultures. If you get an heterogeneous group the communication and the collaboration will be more complex.[16] The issue is that the members of the team do not have the opportunity to have a 'face to face' meeting to study and experience the different firm cultures. In addition team members might have a special education, have worked in other areas and have had different job experiences. As a result they have developed a functional culture so called a special job culture. Consequently we also can find the dimension of Hofstede's study in the different types of jobs. This study shows that the degree of power distance in one country can vary between similar occupation groups.[17]

Heterogeneity of team members may be a positive factor in intercultural virtual teams, such as during creative and complex interaction in comparison to a classic single culture team. In addition, it is easier in a virtual team to unite specialists.[18] With this, innovative solutions of high quality may be forthcoming more rapidly and simultaneously the costs of a physical single location meeting may be reduced. Intercultural teams though are confronted with a high potential of challenges. With increased linguistic and cultural heterogeneity trust between the team members is developed more slowly. When conflict occurs in a group it is complicated and costly before there is consensus and this, along with the management of the group and managerial behavior, may reduce the efficient and performance of the group.

Technical specifications for virtual communications

Modern hardware-based video conference technology allows communication on the internet with rather good quality. Video conference systems with a compatible standard, currently at least to the standard H323, are required for this. The video conference could be bilateral and by application of a multiple connection unit (MCU) more locations could be included.[19] Connection may be by IP addresses of the participating console or by telephone. Different transference rates are possible. With 128 Kbit a notification is possible, and also a connection with ISDN and is often sufficient. If there is interference the image is affected first followed by distorted sound or both, so that the conference is disrupted. Using motor-driven and swivel-mounted cameras the installed software for the control of the camera systems may be controlled through a website and also via Wireless Local Area Network (W-LAN) transfer enabling remote control by any participant. Incoming acoustic signals are amplified through connected loudspeakers and outgoing acoustic signals are supported by microphone which is constantly powered. A video conference system should be capable of digitizing analogue image and sound signals and connects with other conference systems and correspond with valid open standards and supports participants using software.

Technical specifications of virtual meetings

The technical aspects of virtual meetings also pose challenges. A transmitter encodes information and sends this through a channel to a receiver. The receiver decodes and interprets the information. Already with this conventional communication process, misunderstandings and interruptions within the process may occur.[20] In intercultural teams it is possible that there is no common language for encoding and decoding, between the receiver and sender of information. In virtual teams the communication by written communication, such as, email, chat and spoken communication through video conference is added. Additionally instruments like application sharing software programmes may be used for the information exchange. Therefore, the team members have to be capable of operating these instruments.

Partner locations may reach each other through information of the IP addresses of the involved console or choosing a suitable phone number. Different transference rates are possible from 128 Kbit a notification is possible, and also a connection with International Standard Dialling Number (ISDN) is sufficient. If disturbances occur, the picture quality transference diminishes. Later on the tone is distorted and the communication might be completely impossible. The installation of three motor-driven and swivel-mounted cameras is also required. The reproduction of acoustic signals occurs through an amplifier with connected loudspeakers. For better intelligibility speakers have a radio microphone in addition which is constantly powered. The centerpiece of the console is a video conference system which digitizes the analogous camera and sound signals and connects with other conference systems. The system corresponds to valid open standards to the video-communication and supports in this way the cooperation by conference members who use merely software-supported clients. As a Codec (Encoder – Decoder) a communication terminal video conference system that communicates with a H.323 standard for ISDN or IP to video conferences IP is required.[21] With the creation of an efficient automated solution form, light and equipment of the room and in particular the spatial arrangement of the conference participants must also be considered.

The behaviour of the participants during a virtual meeting differs in some essential aspects from their usual behaviour. Thus, it requires training in virtual communications for those participating. The same is true of conference leaders: technical staff are required for the installation, preparation and instruction. Playing in pre-recorded audio sequences and video sequences using different media is also possible. It is not possible to have a virtual teamwork without the use of communication media. The more complex the technical management is, the more does the advantage of efficiency get less.

There is a dual purpose and effect of virtual meetings. The purpose is to impart knowledge, share information, discuss issues, suggest solutions and finally to complete its task and purpose. In addition, members of virtual teams also acquire the competency to interact at a distance using communication technology. The increasing globalization of firms and the pressure to reduce costs is therefore a catalyst for the increasing use of communication technology and virtual teams and meetings.[22] Those who are competent in the use of this technology and in interacting effectively have an advantage in a personal competency. However, not every individual is capable of interacting in an intercultural virtual team. When integrating a new team member, one has to consider the individual's sense of community, interdependency, as well as the autonomous behaviour of the other existing team members. While these factors are also important for conventional teams, for virtual cooperation they are more important and essential. An optimal virtual team is composed of members who interact with each other with ease and are competent with the communication and computer technology.

The team members must be capable of operating the various technical communication media to select the correct medium required and to know how to behave with the selected medium of communication. They must also be sensitive to the more difficult work dynamic than usual with those technical communication media. Therefore, those team members that are spatially located such that they communicate only virtually must acquire additional communication media competencies.

Issues with virtual communications

There are many issues in videoconferencing, such as, specific intercultural conditioned, personality, insecurity in dealing with the technology, understanding when participants may be operating in a foreign language or inability for participants express themselves naturally in front of a camera, and groups-dynamics certainly plays a role.[23] While it is possible through personal contact to have impressions, such as through non-verbal communication and reaction, on other participants, this is limited during a video conference. To minimize these issues it is important, before commencing on a project to be managed virtually, to communicate clearly the exact goals and intentions of the project and to introduce the individual participants.[24] As outlined earlier, the high degree of diversity may have a positive, as well as, a negative effect on team performance.

Participants are also conditioned by the behaviour of others. One or a few participants could dominate or, indeed, control the whole group discussion and it may not be possible for others who have valid and worthwhile contributions to the meeting to participate fully. This must be overcome by the leader outlining the consequences of this behaviour for the team.[25]

Due to spatial, capital and temporal pressures firms operating at an international level multilocational, and perhaps multicultural, virtual meetings and project management are an efficacious solution. Even though the current technical infrastructure is very user friendly there are challenges using videoconferencing. The selection of the right communication media depends on the specific goal, task, situation and competence of participants.

However, one has to consider that team forming and team development processes are more time consuming. It is a central task of the seminar leader or the team leader to actively support the team formation. Members, who join a multicultural team for the first time, do usually mistakenly assume that they will not see the other team members very often, because of the technical infrastructure and the regional distance. For this reason, it is the task of the leader to take care that the team members do meet and get to know each other at the beginning of the teamwork. Only through this, is it possible to support a quick team formation, a distribution of roles and to specify the rules for the teamwork. This is consequently the basis for working fluently.

Furthermore, the managing and controlling processes are limited as is dialogue between team members. Furthermore, the intercultural differences lead to different kinds of senses as well as to different kinds of behaviour. This leads to the possibility of misunderstandings, communication problems and conflicts within a team. Considering these obstacles, the team members and managers have to be aware of this in order to assure the efficiency of the team. Certainly, though, multicultural teams tend to be more creative and innovative, though it is significantly longer for agreement considering rules for communication and teamwork. It is useful to hold a workshop at the beginning of the project in order to agree about team rules and project schedules. A cultural analysis may assist in overcoming the difficulty of cultural differences in multicultural virtual teams. The five components of culture to be aware of are: symbols, heroes, rites, values and norms, and basic acceptations. To improve communication it is suggested that there is delineation of the different cultures on the basis of the cultural theories defined by Hall.[26] Communication is the centre of Hall's theory and supports the understanding of communication in the team. Depending on the specific goal, it might be useful to integrate a country expert. Despite the cost of investment in communications technology and the recurrent costs of communication using this technology it is outweighed by the reduction in other costs in terms of personnel efficiency and productivity.

Conclusion

The increasing internationalization of, and the increasing dynamic environment for firms require increased agility. More firms develop, produce and sell through partnerships with other enterprises than before and managing these complex challenges may be achieved through a multicultural virtual team.

The described video conference supports the communication of the virtual teams in combination with application sharing and through this technology and software it is possible to overcome the spatial aspects of international collaboration within teams. Although the technology is so advanced and the technical infrastructure easy to use there are other barriers and interdisciplinary challenges for virtual collaboration. The selection of the appropriate communication media depends on the specific goal, task, situation and competence of the team members. Conversely, intercultural teams tend to be more creative and innovative.

However, team forming and team development process must be considered and, additionally, the control process is limited. Furthermore, the intercultural differences lead to different kind of senses, as well as, to different kinds of behaviour, and there is a possibility of communication problems and conflict within the team. Considering these obstacles, the team members and managers have to be aware of this in order to assure the efficiency of the team.

It is a central task of the team leader to support team formation actively and it is the task of the leader to ensure that team members do meet physically as soon as possible. Only through this, is it possible to support a smooth team formation, a distribution of roles and the specification of the rules for the team. Multicultural teams require significantly more implementation resources for agreement on rules for communication and division of tasks. To overcome the difficulties associated with multicultural virtual teams the five components of culture, symbols, heroes, rites, values and norms, could assist in improving performance. It is suggestive that the different cultures, based on the cultural theories defined by Hall, be delineated. Communication is the core of Hall's theory. Depending on the specific goal, it might be useful to integrate a country expert.

Forming a multicultural virtual team is cost intensive and prohibitive for many firms. However, the return on investment as opposed to to the expense of a physical meeting is high. This investment also facilitates a more efficient organization and productivity is increased among the participants.

Notes

1. Brauweiler, J., Knaden, A. and Sommer, A., 2004, 'Nachhaltigkeit an Hochschulen durch blended learning' in *Umweltmanagement und Nachhaltigkeit an Hochschulen*, pp. 5–17.
2. Bullinger, H.-J. and Warnecke, H.-J., 1996, *Neue Organisationsformen in Unternehmen. Ein Handbuch für das Moderne Management*, Springer, Berlin, p. 493; Antoni, C., 1997, *International Dimensions of Organizational Behaviour*, Cincinnati, South Western College Publishing, p. 9.
3. Katzenbach, J. and Smith, D., 1993, *The Wisdom of Teams: Creating the High Performance Organization*, McGraw Hill, Maidenhead, p. 164ff.
4. Weinkauf, K. and Woywode, M., 2004, 'Erfolgfaktoren von virtuellen Teams – Ergebnisse einer aktuellen Studie', in *Zeitung für betriebswirtschaftliche Forschung*, Düsseldorf, No. 56, p. 393–412.
5. Ibid., p. 396.
6. Betteridge, H., 1978, *Cassell's German – English, English – German Dictionary*, Macmillan, New York, p. 1546

7. For further information on media competence training refer to Döring, N., 'Online Lernen', in Issing. L and Klimsa, P., (eds), 2002, *Information und Lernen mit Multimedia und Internet*, Winheim, pp. 247–64 and Kerres, M., 2001, *Multimediale und telemediale Lernumgebungen*, München, p. 263.

8. Schremmer, C. and Effelsberg, W., 1999, *Multimediales Teleseminar in Lehren und Lernen mit neuen Medien*, Hildesheim, pp. 35–42 and Gieseking, M. and Knaden, A., 'Organisatorische Umsetzung eines eLearning-Konzepts einer Hochschule am Beispiel des Zentrums virtUOS der Universität Osnabrück', in Kerres, M., and Voß, B. (eds), 2003, Conference Proceedings at Universität Münster, pp. 63–73.

9. Duarte, D. and Snyder, N., 2006, *Mastering Virtual Teams: Strategies, Tools and Techniques that Succeed*, Jossey-Bass, San Francisco, p. 97.

10. Ibid., p. 134–5.

11. Boll, K. and Schenk, B., 2001, 'Unterstützung verteilter interkultureller Zusammenarbeit durch Teamentwicklungsmaßnahmen', in Reinike, R. and Fussinger, C. (eds), *Interkulturelles Management*, Gabler, Wiesbaden, p. 193.

12. Hofstede, G., 1997, *Cultures and Organizations: Software of the Mind*, McGraw-Hill, New York, p. 5.

13. Mauritz, H., 1996, *Interkulturelle Geschäftsbeziehungen – Eine interkulturelle Perspektive für das Marketing*, Deutscher Universitätsverlag, Wiesbaden, p. 96.

14. Bolten, J., 2003, 'Interkulturelles Coaching, Mediation, Training und Consulting als Aufgaben des Personalmanagements internationaler Unternehmen', in Bolten, J. and Ehrhardt, C. (eds), *Interkulturelle Kommunikation*, Wissenschaft und Praxis, Sternenfels, pp. 369–391.

15. Hofstede, G. and Hofstede, G.J., 2005, *Cultures and Organizations: Software of the Mind*, McGraw-Hill, New York, p. 59.

16. Duarte and Snyder, 2006, op. cit., *Mastering Virtual Teams*, p. 59.

17. Hofstede and Hofstede, op. cit., *Cultures and Organizations*, p. 48.

18. Gignac, F., *Building Successful Virtual Teams*, 2005, Artec House, Boston and London, p. 23.

19. Kerres, M., 2001, *Multimediale und telemediale Lernumgebungen*, München, p. 262.

20. Robbins, S.P. and Langton, N., 1998, *Organizational Behaviour – Concepts, Controversies, Applications*, Prentice-Hall Canada, Scarborough, Ontario, p. 320ff.

21. Knaden, A. and Rolf, R., 2003, 'Automatisierte Kamerasteuerung zur Übertragung von Seminaren und Vorlesungen', in Dötsch, V., Schade G. and Hering K., (eds), *e-Learning and Beyond, Proceedings of the Workshop on e-Learning*, HTWK, Leipzig, pp. 87–97.

22. Picot, A., Reichwald, R., Wiegand, R., 1998, *Die grenzenlose Unternehmung*, Wiesbaden, p. 152.

23. Kerres, *Multimediale und telemediale Lernumgebungen*, op. cit., p. 263.

24. Duarte and Snyder, *Mastering Virtual Teams* op. cit., p. 97.

25. Duarte and Snyder, *Mastering Virtual Teams* op. cit., p. 134.

26. Hall, E., 1989, *Beyond Culture*, Anchor Books, Doubleday, New York, p. 91.

18
Futurescope 2020: Global Management Support Systems in the Knowledge Age

Kathryn A. Szabat and Madjid Tavana

The rapid evolution of information technology (IT) has drastically changed organizational problem-solving and decision-making. Innovation and the free flow of information are considered the primary drivers of the accelerating pace of change in the global business environment, an environment characterized by great uncertainties ignited by opportunities and threats. The environmental forces of change have altered the rules of management to utilize information and knowledge in lieu of data in problem-solving and decision-making.[1] Managers face challenges as they strive to add value to their organizations' bottom lines. The gut instinct management style is history. Today's business leaders must acquire real-time information across many time zones, adopt algorithmic decision-making techniques and use highly sophisticated technology to run their organizations effectively and efficiently.

The industrial age paradigm of replacing human labour with machinery gave way to the information age that shifted the focus away from the production of physical goods and toward the manipulation of information. The information age has emerged into a knowledge age. To be successful in the knowledge age, organizations must recognize this on-going transition and prepare their processes to leverage knowledge. Global management support systems (GMSS), based in concept on the closely related fields of information systems (IS) and operations management (OM), may provide comprehensive and integrated support for problem-solving and decision-making in the knowledge age.

Data, information and knowledge in the knowledge age

Over the last several decades, a philosophy and a body of intuitive and analytical decision models have been developed to help decision makers

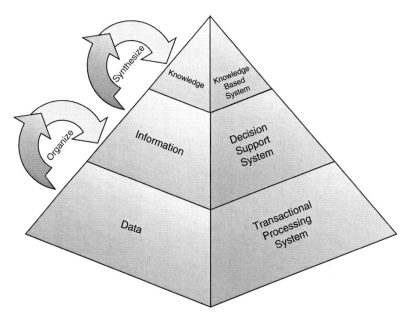

Figure 18.1   Information system pyramid

decompose, synthesize, and solve problems. Pivotal to problem-solving and decision-making in the knowledge age is the processing of data, information, and knowledge. Data are a collection of bits, bytes, and characters; information is derived from organizing data; knowledge is extracted from synthesizing information. Raw data by itself have few or no applications. No decision may be made without first organizing and synthesizing data. Figure 18.1 presents the evolution of data and its relationship with information and knowledge, visualized as a pyramid of interdependent layers on the top of each other with data at the bottom, information in the middle, and knowledge on the top.

Computers, more specifically computer-based information systems (CBIS), are used to collect, store, and process (organize and synthesize) data, information, and knowledge. Data are collected by a transactional processing system (TPS) and stored in a database management system (DBMS). Data are organized into information by a management information system (MIS) and used in a decision support system (DSS) for decision-making. Information is synthesized into knowledge by a knowledge based system (KBS) and used in an expert system (ES) for problem-solving.

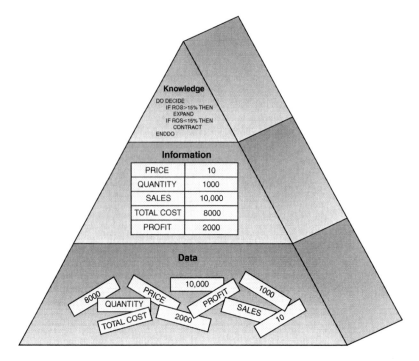

Figure 18.2   Data pyramid

Consider the pyramid in Figure 18.2 where a retailer collects data on revenues and expenses for every purchase expense. Those data are then stored in the retailer's DBMS. The accounting department may retrieve and organize these data into meaningful information by way of a report such as an income statement. The operations department may use this information in a DSS to assess profitability. The finance department may synthesize this information in a KBS and make expansion or contraction decisions.

GMSS have emerged as a force in global managerial decision-making. GMSS are integrated DSS that use data in conjunction with analytical and mathematical models as well as a user interface to solve complex problems and provide calculated solutions to human decision makers.

Decision support systems in the knowledge age

There is a significant amount of evidence that intuitive decision-making is far from optimal and it deteriorates exponentially with problem complexity. GMSS, as an integrated DSS, support decision-making activities by utilizing analytical tools and databases to formulate, visualize, and interactively analyse semi-structured and unstructured problems that require human reasoning. Models and algorithms from disciplines such as decision sciences, mathematical programming, operations research, statistics, simulation, and logic modelling, support scenario planning and choice among alternative courses of actions. GMSS are proven to be especially valuable where the amount of available data is too much, the problem is too complex, or precision is highly important.

Building a GMSS requires expertise in decision analysis, programming, and user interface design. A GMSS also requires connectivity to other enterprise applications in real time as well as the internet. Using the mode of assistance, the DSS component of a GMSS may be classified into three different categories: data-driven, model-driven, and knowledge-driven DSS. Data-driven DSS emphasizes accessing and manipulating internal firm data or external and real-time databases with historical data. Model-driven DSS focuses on design and development of financial, operational, statistical, optimization, or simulation models. These systems typically use data and models provided by users to analyse problems that are not data intensive. Knowledge-driven DSS provides specialized problem solving expertise by using facts, rules, or procedures stored in a knowledge base.

DSS generator software embedded in GMSS provides facilities for evaluating alternatives and trade-offs in uncertain, dynamic, and multi-criteria problems. DSS generators are either data-driven or decision-driven. Interactive database query user interface is the most commonly used data-driven DSS. Traditional spreadsheets, natural language programming, and influence diagramming, are among the well-known and commonly used model-driven DSS generators offering textual and/or visual language. Expert system shells that allow construction of a knowledge base and interaction with this knowledge base through use of an inference engine are the most common form of knowledge-driven DSS. Using DSS generators, managers and end-users that are familiar with the problem domain and the relevant modeling paradigm may develop a DSS application quickly and without technical help.

The global organization in the knowledge age

A global organization is defined as any firm that is driven to design, engineer, manufacture, purchase, assemble market, distribute, and/or service its products or services internationally to achieve competitive marketplace performance.[2] Furthermore, a global organization is viewed as having significant operations and market interests beyond the geographical boundaries of their home countries.[3] Global organizations operate within the manufacturing sector as well as the service sector; the service sector now constituting the largest economic sector in post-industrial societies.

Manufacturing firms operating in global markets today purchase raw materials in one location, ship them elsewhere for production, then, sell their finished products worldwide. Most strive to build local presence, while at the same time, achieve economies of scale. Service organizations operating in global markets today have central customer information depositories in one location and coordinate flow of customer information to/from business units worldwide. Most strive to maintain diverse information requirements at the business level, the management level closest to the customer, while at the same time, create policy and future strategic business plans at the corporate level, the level responsible for the strategy of the entire firm.

Decision-making in these settings is challenging, often crossing boundaries between global and local management levels, therefore, striking the right balance between global and local authority is crucial. Decision-making within these global firms occurs both at the business unit level, as well as the centre; therefore, involving the right people at the right level of the organization is critical for good decision-making. Decisions within these global firms cut across functions, therefore, cross-functional collaboration, that is, fluid decision-making across function teams, is essential for identifying the most attractive and viable business plans. In addition, these global firms are frequently involved in strategic arrangements, namely, outsourcing, joint ventures, alliances, and franchising. Decision-making between separate organizations on different continents requires clear authority and ownership of decision-making among the internal management and their external partners.

As challenging as this decision-making environment is, global organizations that are decision-driven organizations reap benefits; making good decisions and making them happen quickly are the hallmarks of high-performing organizations. According to a study of global firms, the most effective organizations outscore competitors on major strategic decisions – which markets to enter or exit, which businesses to buy or sell, where to allocate capital and talent, how to drive product innovation, how to position brands and how to manage channel partners.[4]

Decision-making in the global organization

Decision-making is the process of selecting one course of action from among several alternatives. While most decisions are connected with problem-solving, many are not. That said, however, most managerial activities involve components of the decision-making process. The decision-making activity involves gathering and evaluating information about a situation, identifying a need for a decision, defining alternative courses of action, choosing the best, the most appropriate or the optimum action, and then applying the choice in the situation.

Decision models are used in the decision-making process to help decision makers decompose and structure problems. Choice of decision model is dependent on the nature and complexity of the decision and often reflects the management activities within the hierarchy of an organization. Managers at different levels of the organization perform different kinds of activities but one activity typically dominates within each: top managers involve themselves in strategic planning; middle managers exercise management control, and first line managers are involved in operational control. The organizational decisions at different levels are depicted in Figure 18.3.

Global organizations depend on the continuous and seamless flow of information in order to make decisions and perform activities in the new global economy. Global firms use the virtual enterprise strategy to manage suppliers, business partners, employees and contract workers.[5] In order to help meet their organizations' business objectives, global managers rely on information systems and tools. Generally speaking, management support systems are used to support decision-making processes at the mid-level and/or senior level of management; operations support systems are used by managers to support their operations and business processes.

Marginal differences in speed, accuracy, and comprehensive nature of information delivered for decision-making may make the difference in gaining and sustaining competitive advantage. An organization's competence in timely decision support capability has been given recognition by the total quality movement such that 'the ability to access and act on timely, reliable business data is requisite to the achievement of quantitative continual improvement in the delivery of products and service'.[6]

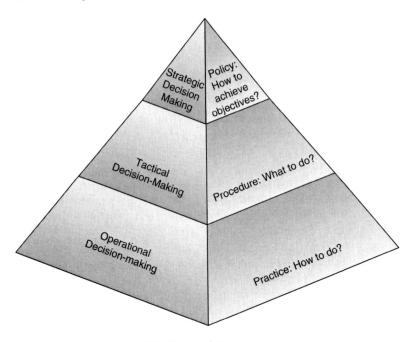

Figure 18.3   Organizational decision-making

An integrated global management support system for the future

As organizations enter the age of the global village where spatial and temporal boundaries are shrinking rapidly, GMSS continue to emerge as a key element in global managerial decision-making and as an essential weapon against global competitors.[7] Stand-alone DSS are no longer effective in coping with problems that involve multinational issues such as multiple currency management, multinational tax management, and global consolidated reporting. It is essential that GMSS integrate DSS with TPS, and KBS.

GMSS must support an integrated global decision-making framework. The framework for integrated global decision-making should link and align daily tactical activities to global organization-wide strategic outcomes. The framework for integrated global decision-making should allow for fact-based and risk adjusted decisions, mindful of geospatial impacts. The framework for integrated global decision-making should enable measurement of horizontal as well as vertical performance across the entire global enterprise. By aligning this process with the value chain, performance metrics may be developed and monitored for compliance; gaps in performance may be identified; and alternative solutions may be analysed for their impact on the entire global organization.[8]

GMSS must support system internalities and externalities. Integrated global decision-making is driven not just by customer demand but also by laws, executive orders, regulations, directives and mandates that govern organizational operations and logistics.[9] Custom specific issues must be taken into account, including the technological, social/cultural, political/legal and economic environments.

GMSS must support emerging technologies. GMSS need to support the needs of the mobile manager operating in the borderless 24/7 economy; the rapid increase in the application of emerging technologies, such as, internet, intranet, e-commerce, m-commerce, voice over internet protocol, and wireless, has influenced manager's decision-making methodologies.[10]

And GMSS must support an IT-savvy mindset. Research is increasingly demonstrating that IT materially improves business performance.[11] High IT savvy is linked to performance measures such as costs, profits, innovation and market capitalization. Characteristics of IT savvy include IT for communication, that is, high use of electronic channels such as email, intranets and wireless devices for internal and external communications and work practices; digital transactions, more specifically, a high degree of digitalization of the firm's repetitive transactions, particularly sales, customer interaction and purchasing; use of internet architectures for key processes such as sales force management, employee performance measurement training and post-sales customer support; firm-wide IT skills with high capability of all employees to use IT effectively; and business management involvement, that is, strong senior management commitment and championing of IT initiatives.[12] Characteristics of firm-wide IT skills and business management involvement point to a need for IT to be fused with the business; seemingly, this would enhance overall decision-making within the organization. Within the global enterprise, the information system organization must understand the impact organizational strategy has in the IT infrastructure. Furthermore, IT architecture must be created to best support a horizontal business strategy.[13]

Supporting global business activities is a most important and extremely complex task. It is essential to develop a systems oriented, value aligned, integrated GMSS. GMSS must integrate not only TPS, DSS, and KBS, it must also integrate emerging technologies. A new business-focused

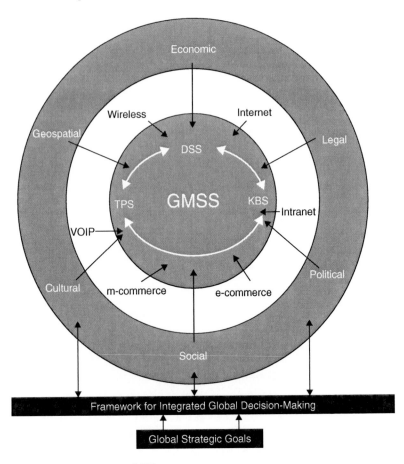

Figure 18.4   Futurescope 2020

global organizational model is necessary in which global business/IT-savvy managers assume responsibility to design, build and support the development of GMSS that support a framework for integrated global decision-making. Figure 18.4 presents a schematic of the Integrated Global Management Support System for the future.

Implications for management

The global managers of the world must be prepared to efficiently and effectively manage processes in a global business environment.[14] They are required to make business decisions, global and cross-functional in nature, using sophisticated integrated computer-based information support systems. Global managers are more mobile; they require telecommunications and technology solutions to allow them to conduct business while on the move.

Management development that blends the quantitative business operations and decision-making techniques learned in OM, with the application of IS technology for solving business problems would benefit managers. An integrated OM/IS approach would enhance their understanding of problem-solving and decision-making in the integrated global environment as they prepare to enter the future of business.

Conclusion

Competitive advantage may be won or lost by marginal differences in the speed, accuracy, and comprehensive nature of information being delivered to decision makers. An organization's competence in timely decision support capability is pivotal in the knowledge age. The fact that IT materially improves business performance is not in dispute. Seamless IT infusion with business would enhance overall decision-making within the organization. The organization within the global enterprise must understand the impact organizational strategy has on the IT infrastructure. Furthermore, it must determine and create IT architecture to best support its needs for the future. DSS clearly enhance a manager's ability to make decisions, but lack optimal benefit as stand-alone systems. As the global environment within which organizations operate becomes more complex, leaders will most certainly recognize the need for an infrastructure to support integrated global decision-making. GMSS, as integrated information/emerging technology systems, designed by IT-savvy managers, can satisfy the infrastructure needs of the global organization in the knowledge age.

Notes

1. Cuffe, S., 2005, 'Emerging Management Support System Models for Global Managers in the New Economy', *Journal of Knowledge Management Practice*, Volume 6.
2. Passino, J. H. and Severance, D. C., 1991, 'Harnassing the Potential of Information Technology for Support of the New Global Organization', *Human Resource Management*, 29, (1), pp. 69–76.
3. Hout *et al.*, 1982; Anthony *et al.*, 1984; Vernon and Wells, 1986; Neo, 1991, Cited in Bryd, T.A., Sankar, C. and McCreary, J. D., 1997, 'The Risks Associated With Planning and Implementing Global Information Technology

Systems', in Deans P.C and Karwan K.R., *Global Information Systems and Technology: Focus on the Organization and Its Functional Areas*, Harrisburg, PA: Idea Group Publishing.

4. Rogers, P. and Blenko, M., 2006, 'Who Has the D? How Clear Decision Roles Enhance Organizational Performance', *Harvard Business Review*, 84 (1), pp. 52–61.

5. Cuffe, 2005, Management Support System Models, op. cit.

6. Sloan, R. and Green, H., 1993, 'An Information Architecture for the Global Manufacturing Enterprise', *Information Management: Strategies, Systems and Technologies*, 5, (5).

7. Eom, S. B., 2001, 'Decision Support Systems', in Warner, M., *International Encyclopedia of Business and Management*, 2nd edition, London, England: International Thomson Business Publishing Co.

8. Hammond, D., 2006, 'The Framework for Integrated Decision-Making', Publication of the Government/Industry Forum, National Academies' Federal Facilities Council, Washington, DC: National Academy of Sciences.

9. Idem.

10. Cuffe, 2005, Management Support System Models, op. cit.

11. Sloan and Green, 1993, Information Architecture, op. cit.

12. Weill, P. and Aral, S., 2006, 'Generating Premium Returns On Your IT Investments', *MIT Sloan Management Review*, 47, (2), pp. 39–48.

13. Sloan and Green, 1993, *Information Architecture*, op. cit.

14. Silva, D. and McFadden, K., 2005, 'Combining Operations Management and IS Curricula: Assessing Alumni Perspectives for the Workplace', *Decision Sciences Journal of Innovative Education*, 3, (2), pp. 307–21.

Index

Key: **bold** = extended discussion or concept highlighted in the text; f = figure; n = endnote/footnote; t = table; a page number in brackets denotes an oblique reference.